D1524145

ROFILES OF REVOLUTIONARIES IN ATLANTIC HISTORY 1700-1850

EDITED BY

R. WILLIAM WEISBERGER
DENNIS P. HUPCHICK
DAVID L. ANDERSON

Social Science Monographs, Boulder
Distributed by Columbia University Press, New York
2007

Dedication

This book is gratefully and enthusiastically dedicated
to the contributors of this volume.

Preface

This book could not have been written without the efforts of numerous people. I am indebted to these individuals for their help. I first wish to thank Dr. Stephen Fischer-Galati, the editor of both the Social Science Monographs and the East European Monograph Series of Columbia University Press. Because of his support, this book has been published. I next would like to thank the internationally renowned scholars who contributed essays to this work. Special gratitude is expressed to Dr. Seymour Drescher and Dr. Steven Béla Várdy for advice proffered. I also am indebted to my associate, Dr. Dennis P. Hupchick, for assisting in the editing and for typesetting this book, as well as to my colleague, Dr. David Anderson, for reading all of the fine essays in this volume and for spending many hours in doing the computer work required for the publication of this study. Finally, I wish to express my deepest gratitude to my beloved wife, Patricia B. Weisberger, for her assiduous efforts in serving as an assistant copy editor of this book.

R. William Weisberger
Butler County Community College

Contents

Introduction:
Eminent Revolutionaries and Atlantic History

This book, which is intended for scholars, college students, and general readers, concerns biographies of significant revolutionaries on both sides of the Atlantic. There are incisive and stimulating essays about prominent individuals associated with various revolutionary movements, namely: The revolutions in science and in technology, the political revolutions in the Americas between 1776 and 1812, and those in Europe between 1789 and 1848. Topically and chronologically arranged, this work also examines and assesses the accomplishments and failures of these revolutionaries in relation to the vibrant field of Atlantic history.

Salient themes concerning various revolutions in Atlantic history are developed in this book. Newtonian principles of mechanism postulated in the *Principia* and those of materialism advanced in the *Opticks* constituted the core of the Scientific and Industrial revolutions. The importance of major Newtonian concepts for prominent individuals who contributed to the advancement of scientific culture in the eighteenth-century British Atlantic world is examined and assessed.[1] Newtonian principles of motion were also applied to the machine technology of the Industrial Revolution: Such concepts were associated with machinery used in the first textile and iron factories that appeared in towns and cities in the British Atlantic world between approximately 1750 and 1830.[2] These significant changes in science and in industrial technology were associated with two other pertinent revolutionary themes suggested in this book. Emphasizing the profit motive, merchant capitalism and consumerism greatly intensified in Britain and in her American colonies during the eighteenth century.[3]

This biographical work likewise treats tumultuous political and social revolutions that undermined the authority of the empires in the Atlantic world between 1776 and 1848. During this time, revolutionary nationalistic ideologies surfaced to shape new institutions and civic societies in the North and South Atlantic littorals; these ideologies became intertwined with republican and liberal aspirations in the 1776 American Revolutionary War and with those in the

1

1789 French Revolution.[4] Between 1810 and 1848, nationalism became contextualized on both sides of the Atlantic: It was directed against the Spanish Empire in Mexico and in South America and was especially involved with revolutionary programs to uplift the status of whites, blacks, and reds.[5] Reflecting cultural tenets, which in some cases accentuated romantic beliefs, nationalism as well was intimately associated with state-building activities during the 1830-31 Revolution in the Polish lands of Russia and with those during the 1848 Revolutions in Ireland, France, and Hungary.[6]

Other ancillary and predominant themes are accentuated in the book and reveal much about Atlantic history. Republican doctrines and liberal tenets, which emphasize the significance of natural liberties, emerged in the revolutions both in the Americas and in those of 1848 in Eastern Europe that were directed against the Habsburg Empire.[7] Furthermore, a few revolutionaries on both sides of the Atlantic advocated in their programs egalitarian, radical, and socialist concepts, but ultimately experienced failure and repression.[8] Two other themes also emerge and illustrate how revolutionary ideologies were diffused in the Atlantic world. The role of printers, to some extent, contributed to trans-Atlantic revolutionary movements.[9] Lastly, the vehicle of freemasonry directly helped to foster revolutionary movements in the United States, Argentina, Russia, and Poland.[10]

This book illustrates that John Theophilus Desaguliers, who was a prime organizer of speculative freemasonry, served as a Newtonian demonstrator and helped to advance both the Scientific and Industrial revolutions. His career between 1710 and 1717 was quite distinguished: He was elected to the Royal Society of London, served as its curator, earned a doctorate from Oxford University, and held the position of chair of experimental philosophy in Oxford's Hart College. A pragmatist, this apostle of the Newtonian creed gave lectures and presented demonstrations in many London taverns or "penny universities."[11] Lectures regarding weights, levers, fired cannon balls, and various steam engines explained Newtonian mechanical laws. Likewise, demonstrations concerning electrical charges passed through wires, iron tubes, and brass balls described Newtonian materialistic theories.[12] The versatile and realistic Desaguliers can well be perceived as an Atlanticist, for he helped to contribute to major transformations in science and in industry, supported representative government and Whiggish ideologies, and exerted an impact on the thinking of Benjamin Franklin.[13]

The suggestive essay of William Pencak reveals in numerous ways the thinking and major activities of Benjamin Franklin and his ties to the eighteenth-century revolutionary Atlantic world. Pencak demonstrates that Franklin, who was a trickster in some respects, had many faces and that he often effectively masked himself. By unmasking Franklin, Pencak persuasively evaluates the salient accomplishments of this multi-dimensional man first to British colonial civic society and then to the American republican revolutionary world. Pencak shows that the talented Franklin established himself in the eighteenth-century world of print culture, masking himself in the "Silence Dogood" and the "Busy-Body" essays.[14] Fame, fortune, and immense profits marked the career of Franklin as a Philadelphia printer: *Poor Richard's Almanack* and *The Pennsylvania Gazette* became paragons of excellence in the eighteenth-century Atlantic world of print culture.[15] Pencak as well shows that Franklin emerged as the prime symbol of Philadelphia boosterism: He, among other things, provided direction to the Junto or Library Company, to the American Philosophical Society, and to the Pennsylvania Hospital.[16] Franklin, moreover, became a deist and a Newtonian, recognizing the "Supreme Creator" as the source of the universe and nature and postulating the tenets and applications of electrical science.[17]

An advocate of expansionism and western settlements and an avid supporter of colonial consumption of British merchandise, Franklin denounced the British for the unconstitutional imposition of the Stamp Act in 1765 and thereafter became an American republican revolutionary.[18] He was involved with sterling trans-Atlantic achievements as a late eighteenth-century revolutionary diplomat in France. Skilled, intimidating, and patient, he succeeded in negotiating the Treaty of Amity and Commerce with Vergennes, in securing loans from the French foreign minister, and in utilizing his position as master of the Parisian Masonic Lodge of the Nine Sisters to recruit financial and military support for the revolutionary republic. Having played a major role in negotiating the 1783 Paris Treaty, which recognized American independence, the elderly and sickly Franklin returned to Philadelphia and served in the 1787 Constitutional Convention. Like George Washington, Franklin, who headed the Pennsylvania Society for Promoting the Abolition of Slavery, took a stance on the divisive slavery issue three years prior to his death on April 17, 1790.[19]

In his probing and pensive account of the career of George Washington, Richard Rutyna develops a cogent case in assessing the role of this prominent eighteenth-century Virginian in the British Atlantic world. Rutyna's essay contains comprehensive and suggestive accounts regarding major works about Washington and regarding his involvement in eighteenth-century military and political activities. The son of Mary and Augustine Washington, George was born on Wakefield plantation on February 22, 1732 (New Style), was reared in a Colonial Virginia gentry family, and obtained a rudimentary education prior to the death of his father eleven years later.[20] Thereafter, a teenaged Washington, who seemed not to be closely attached to his mother, spent considerable time at Mount Vernon with his half brother, Lawrence Washington, a man who served as George's surrogate father until his passing in 1752 from tuberculosis. Portrayed as being honorable, dignified, genteel, poised, and shrewd, the young Washing-

3

ton acquired knowledge about tobacco planting, developed skills as a surveyor, and, in light of his connections with the aristocratic Fairfax family, was appointed surveyor for Culpeper County in 1749.[21] Moreover, the ambitious Washington became an expansionist, purchasing numerous properties in the wilds of the Shenandoah Valley.[22]

He emerged in several ways during the 1750s as a significant figure in eighteenth-century Atlantic history.[23] Rutyna's detailed account reveals how Washington continued to ascend in the ranks of the Virginian aristocracy during this decade. He became a master mason in the Fredericksburg Masonic Lodge #4 on August 4, 1753, evidently exhibiting interest in the Craft for its Enlightenment doctrines and for its genteel practices. Moreover, he became at this time a member of the Ohio Company, purchasing lands in western Pennsylvania. Appointed by Robert Dinwiddie in 1752 as an adjutant general of Virginia's militia forces, the ambitious Washington began his military career and two years later became involved in the Anglo-French imperial struggle for the control of North America.[24] Two years later, he went to the western country where, on May 27, 1754 Washington defeated French troops at Great Meadows and was accused of being responsible for the death of De Jumonville, an alleged French diplomat. On July 4 of that year, Washington failed to complete the building of Fort Necessity, was forced to surrender to the French, and retreated to Virginia.[25] As Rutyna well explains, there were trans-Atlantic implications concerning Washington's expedition during this war for imperial domination of North America: He was denounced in Paris for the death of De Jumonville, criticized in London about this incident, but was hailed as an effective military officer by numerous leaders in Williamsburg. Rutyna also shows that, after 1754, Washington played a central role in the western country during this war. Despite the admonitions of Washington that conventional European tactics could not be deployed against the French and their Indian Allies, General Edward Braddock refused to listen to his sagacious advice and was ambushed on July 8, 1755 along the banks of the Monongahela River. Having escaped from this military disaster, Washington, along with his men from the Virginia Regiment, worked three years later with Brigadier General John Forbes and his British troops to extirpate the French from Fort Duquesne on November 24, 1758 and then to establish Fort Pitt.[26]

Rutyna describes the accomplishments of Washington during the American Revolutionary War. Rutyna ascribes convincing motives for Washington's disenchantment with the British after England's victory during the trans-Atlantic war for control of North America: Namely, the British refusal to promote him militarily during the war and the imposition of the 1763 proclamation to restrict expansion into the western country. Moreover, this Virginia planter blamed the London firm of Cary & Company for minimal profits secured for the sale of his tobacco to it during the early 1760s.[27] Honest but obstinate, Washington, who served in the House of Burgesses during the 1760s, vociferously denounced both the 1765 Stamp Act and the 1767 Townshend Act as abridgements of American constitutional liberties.[28] Perceiving himself as being an American and an advocate of republicanism during the early years of the 1770s, Washington on June 16, 1775 accepted the appointment to serve as commander-in-chief of the American revolutionary army by the Second Continental Congress.[29] As the "Revolutionary Republican General," he considered this appointment the defining moment of his career and began to develop plans for a Fabian strategy of hit and run tactics against the world's strongest army.[30] Rutyna believes that his Fabian strategy proved to be fairly effectual: In 1776 commander Washington succeeded in dodging General William Howe's troops during the New York campaign, and in late 1776 and early 1777 won victories at the battles of Trenton and Princeton. Washington displayed effective leadership skills at Valley Forge from late 1777 to early 1778, offering personal aid to sick and starving Continental soldiers and securing European leadership from the Marquis de Lafayette and the Baron von Steuben.[31] Three years later, having abandoned with some reluctance his Fabian strategy and having consented to accept French support, Washington, supported by the army of General de Rochambeau and by the ships of Admiral de Grasse in the Chesapeake Bay, besieged Yorktown, forced the surrender of British General Cornwallis on October 17, 1781, and thus brought an end to the American War of Independence.[32]

Rutyna lucidly explains the role of Washington in the federal republic and assesses his importance to the Atlantic revolutionary era. Realizing that the Articles of Confederation government lacked national powers and was incapable of resolving the vexing economic and financial problems prevalent in America during the 1780s, Washington in 1787, as in 1775, consented to go to Philadelphia to provide leadership for the formation of the federal republic. Serving as head of the Philadelphia Convention in 1787, he remained rather reticent during its deliberations but seemed to be an advocate of the doctrines of republicanism: Washington, among other things, supported a viable national government endowed with the power of taxation, the functioning of a presidency rather than that of a monarchy, and the veto privilege of the chief executive. Furthermore, he endorsed the concept of the separation of powers and provisions regarding checks and balances among the three national branches of government. He also backed major trans-Atlantic Enlightenment concepts, believing that the federal republic should assure orderly operations within civil society, should uphold the natural liberties of its citizens, and should promote the doctrine of virtuosity in the newly formed nation.[33] During his two terms as president of the republic, Washington incessantly called for harmony. After the strident debate about the creation of the first Bank of the United States in 1791, he encountered constant dissension, the rise of a two party system, and the politicizing of the federal constitution.[34] In other respects, the place of Washington in the Atlantic revolutionary world proved to be of preponderant significance. He did much to foster the cause of Jewish civic emancipation in the federal republic, and included in his will a provision that emancipated his Afro-American slaves after his death as well.[35] In a greater context, Washington became a radiant symbol of Enlightenment and republican ideologies to revolutionaries in Latin America and in Europe.[36]

Ellen E. Dodge investigates the activities of Molly Pitcher during the American War of Independence. Molly Pitcher, which was a legendary name, was, in fact, Mary Ludwig Hays. She well might have been born in 1754 and came to marry William Hays. She participated with her husband in the Battle of Monmouth and carried pitchers of water to quench the thirst of Continental artillerymen. After her husband was wounded on June 28, 1778, she allegedly dropped her pitcher, cleaned his gun, and continued to fire it against British soldiers. As a result of these feats during the battle, she acquired the nickname of Molly Pitcher. Moreover, she became a virtuous heroine of the American Revolution and has been identified with the concept of feminine republican activism in the revolutionary Atlantic world.[37]

David Geggus offers a pensive and a persuasive account of the career of Toussaint Louverture, revealing the revolutionary dynamics in the Caribbean Atlantic world during the last decade of the eighteenth century. Geggus discusses major scholarly perceptions of Toussaint: This black revolutionary was considered by Erwin Rüsch to be an opportunist, by C.L.R. James as being a humane and shrewd black Jacobin, and by Pierre Pluchon as a conservative black racist. Although controversial, Toussaint became the predominant figure in the Haitian Revolution between 1791 and 1804. Geggus accentuates the theses that this black leader played a major role in the abolition of slavery in the Caribbean's most opulent colony and in establishing the second independent state in the Americas. In many respects, the career of Toussaint reveals the cross-fertilization currents that wrought potent transformations in Haiti and in France and, for that matter, in the European, Caribbean, and South American revolutionary worlds.[38]

Geggus vividly depicts the early career of Toussaint. Born probably in 1746 in the French colony of Saint-Domingue, Toussaint was the eldest son of Hyppolite, a slave who worked on a Bréda sugar plantation at Haut-du-Cap, which was located in the northern region of the colony. Hyppolite, who was respected by his fellow slaves, received favorable treatment from his master and attempted to render assistance to his eldest son as he was being reared. The efforts of his father succeeded, for the young Toussaint worked as a stable-lad and later as a coachman. As a coachman, which was a prestigious position in the slave community, he embraced the tenets of Catholicism and developed fluency

6

in French. Emancipated between 1769 and 1772, Toussaint became a free man
and a landowner. He was clever, deceptive, and fairly mobile, moving in the
social worlds of Africans, Frenchmen, and creoles.[39]
    Toussaint played an active part during the complex revolutionary decade of
the 1790s in Saint-Domingue. With the eruption of the 1791 slave revolt on
Saint-Domingue, he became an advisor to General Georges Biassou, unsuccessfully tried to effectuate negotiations between planters and African rebels, and, in
1792, did not embrace the abolition of slavery. Moreover, even after the Saint-
Domingue Slavery Emancipation Decree on August 29, 1793, Toussaint seemed
to be manipulative, supporting until the following year the pro-royalist Spanish
forces on the island. A short time after the French Convention on February 4,
1794 proclaimed the abolition of slavery in all of its colonies, the ambitious and
cunning Toussaint shifted his allegiance from royalty to republicanism, supporting France and declaring himself open to doctrines of equality and liberty for
former slaves. Thus, Toussaint succeeded in melding black militancy with radical French revolutionary ideologies and in becoming the major leader on the
island to vindicate the cause of slave emancipation.[40]
    Between 1796 and 1802 Toussaint was involved with other pertinent devel-
opments associated with the Haitian Revolution. He thwarted British efforts in
1796 to take Port-au-Prince and other places in the southern part of the island.
He suppressed a rebellion led by Villatte to overthrow Governor Laveaux. In
recognition of these accomplishments, the French government named the former
slave Toussaint deputy-governor of Saint-Domingue in April of 1796, and the
next year he was made the colony's commander-in-chief. In 1798 he once again
came to the aid of his friend, Governor Laveaux, crushing enemies of both France
and of the Haitian Revolution. By 1798 Toussaint, who controlled lands in the
northern and western districts of the island, entered into conflict with Rigaud
and his armies, who occupied lands in the southern peninsula. During this power
struggle, the poised and confident Toussaint brutally defeated his opponent, forcing Rigaud and his leaders to flee to France.
    By 1800 Toussaint had established supreme control over Saint-Domingue.
Two years later, he lost it. During the intervening period he attempted to rebuild
the island's decimated economy, even allowing the return of former white plantation owners. Moreover, he set up schools and tried to reduce racial prejudice.
He also boldly acted, promulgating a constitution in 1801 that moved Saint-
Domingue toward statehood, which also contained a provision that made him
governor for life. Fearful of the ambitious Toussaint, in 1802 Napoleon sent an
army of 10,000 troops under General Leclerc to Saint-Domingue. The terrible
conflict between the armies of Toussaint and Leclerc culminated in the surrender of the black leader in early May 1802. This autocratic black radical revolutionary, who died from pneumonia and apoplexy in a French dungeon on April

8, 1803, was identified with several significant legacies in the Atlantic revolutionary world. Toussaint emerged as an advocate of slave emancipation, of black nationalism and self-determination, and of citizenship rights for newly emancipated African men. Moreover, his ideologies and activities ultimately contributed to the independence of Haiti in 1804 and inspired other early nineteenth-century revolutionary leaders in Latin America.[41]

Edward T. Brett vividly profiles the significant career of the early nineteenth-century Mexican revolutionary, Padre Miguel Hidalgo. Brett's splendid essay embodies several salient theses. First, a *criollo*, or a Spaniard born in Mexico, Hidalgo the parish priest predominantly embraced secular nationalistic doctrines while also using an important Catholic symbol to foster his revolutionary movement. Second, like Toussaint, Hidalgo became an advocate of radical revolutionary ideologies. He moved with ease in the circles of both *criollos* and lower Mexican classes, and he supported measures to abolish the inequities inflicted on Mexican Indians and *mestizos*. His egalitarian program also was based on instituting political and economic reforms to ameliorate conditions for these two oppressed groups. Last, despite his call for independence from Spain during the 1810 Mexican Revolution, Hidalgo failed as an insurrectionary leader. He encountered military defeat, was captured, and was put to death on July 31, 1811.[42]

Brett presents a lucid and stimulating account regarding germane events and ideas that shaped Hidalgo's career. Born on May 8, 1753 to Ana Maria and Cristóbal Hidalgo Costilla, Miguel was one of six children in a fairly wealthy *criollo* family. He spent his childhood years on the hacienda San Diego Corralejo, an estate located southwest of Guanajuato. At age eight, his mother died and Miguel was sent to live for a brief time with his uncle, José Manuel Villaseñor, a priest who provided him with the basics of education.[43] Thereafter, young Miguel returned to live at the Corralejo family estate until about age twelve, came into contact with Mexican Indians, and apparently developed a sympathy for this persecuted indigenous group. Along with his older brother, José, Miguel at age twelve was sent by his father to study at the College of San Francisco Javier, a Jesuit school. Miguel became well versed in the liberal arts and the natural sciences, which evidently helped to shape his thinking about entering the priesthood and well might have produced significant influences on his later career as a revolutionary. During the 1770s he studied at the University of Mexico City, receiving a bachelor's degree in theology in 1773. On September 8, 1778, at age twenty-six, he was ordained a priest. Soon thereafter, he entered a doctoral program, which he never completed. For approximately sixteen years, Hidalgo taught theology and philosophy at the College of San Nicolás Obispo and was recognized as a fine teacher. He failed to reform the school's curriculum and left the college in 1792.[44]

8

A decade later, this aggressive and compassionate man, who in 1803 was named pastor of Nuestra Señora parish in Dolores, expressed sympathy for his impoverished congregants and advocated radical doctrines of social equality. Hidalgo taught the oppressed Indians of his parish to read and helped them with their modest business projects. By 1809 he was actively involved with conspiratorial activities, participating in literary clubs that advocated revolution in the Valladolid region against the *peninsulares*, Spanish-born leaders who administered Mexico for their own personal gain. After leaders of this class succeeded in having the *Junta Suprema*, the ruling government in Spain, appoint Francisco Xavier Venegas as Mexican viceroy in September 1810, Padre Hidalgo favored launching a Mexican revolution that would aim to create an independent state, with rights granted to Indians and other oppressed lower classes.[45]

Brett astutely investigates the leadership role of Hidalgo during the 1810 Mexican Revolution. Hidalgo took measures to recruit a large Indian and peasant army and established friendships with Ignacio de Allende and other Valladolid *criollo* conspirators in an effort to depose the *peninsulares*. On September 16, 1810, Padre Hidalgo helped to launch the Querétaro Conspiracy. He gave an inspiring speech, which is known as the *Grito de Dolores*, calling for Mexican Indians and peasants to take up arms against the *peninsulares* and to work for an independent nation based on justice and social equality. His small and poorly equipped army moved from Dolores to San Miguel, recruiting other poverty-stricken supporters along the way. Leaders of Hidalgo's army displayed the banner of Our Lady of Guadalupe, thus using the Catholic symbol of the Mother of God to generate nationalism, especially among the oppressed Mexican Indians.[46] After his army captured and plundered San Miguel, Hidalgo, who perceived revolution as a mass movement, began to lose the support of some *criollo* leaders, whose property had been destroyed by Hidalgo's soldiers. The revolutionary priest ordered his troops to Guanajuato, a city that he wished to liberate from three-hundred years of Spanish occupation and oppression. On September 28, 1810, the troops of Hidalgo attacked the city, won the battle against the army of Juan Antonio Riaño, but lost over two thousand men. His forces next took Valladolid in October of that year. As a result of his revolutionary army causing much damage, Hidalgo was excommunicated by the Catholic church and he lost additional support from *criollo* leaders as well.[47]

The revolutionary priest was to suffer defeat but became identified with legacies significant to the Atlantic revolutionary world. Although lacking trained troops and *criollo* backing, Hidalgo and his army moved against Mexico City, but on October 30, 1810 withdrew from the nation's capital. In early 1811 Hidalgo and his seditious army quickly retreated. On January 17 of that year, his forces were defeated at the Battle of Puente de Calderón, twenty-nine miles north of Guadalajara. Thereafter, Hidalgo, who was blamed by Allende and other *criollo*

9

officers for the failures of the Mexican Revolution, was captured in March by a royalist force. Four months later was put to death. Despite his failures, this priest was of special importance to the red Atlantic, for he espoused and gave direction to a nationalist and radical revolutionary movement that was intended to bring equity and social justice to Mexican Indians and peasants.[48]

Likewise, Joan Supplee meticulously assesses the place of José Francisco de San Martín in the Atlantic revolutionary world. She shows that, similar to those of Padre Hidalgo, the nationalist and radical ideologies of San Martín were intended to foster the cause of state formation in South America during the early nineteenth century. Supplee also demonstrates that, unlike Hidalgo, San Martín was a trans-Atlantic military leader who had first distinguished himself in European wars prior to his involvement in South American independence movements. Furthermore, she convincingly makes a case for his involvement in the trans-Atlantic and international worlds of freemasonry and other secret societies in trying to achieve Argentine, Chilean, and Peruvian independence from the Spanish Empire.

Supplee vividly depicts the early and complex career of this prominent man of two worlds. Born probably on February 25, 1778 as the youngest son of Lieutenant Juan de San Martín and of his wife, Gregoria, the young José Francisco first studied as a child in Buenos Aires. He then crossed the Atlantic in 1786 to pursue military studies in the Madrid Seminary for Nobles. As a young cadet in 1789, San Martín participated in the Battle of Melilla against the Ottomans in North Africa. During the next nineteen years, he advanced his military career. San Martín fought against Napoleon at the Battle of Bailén in July 1808, helping the Spanish army to retake Madrid. For his efforts, he was promoted to the rank of lieutenant colonel. In 1811, at age thirty-three, he was made adjutant-general but resigned his commission from the Spanish army that same year.[49]

In 1811 San Martín also went to Argentina and began to work for the cause of independence for this nation. San Martín, who had been admitted into the Masonic Lodge of the Rational Knights in 1808, worked with other members of this body to effect the aim of Argentine liberation from Spain. After the Triumvirate had defeated the ruling *junta* in 1812, San Martín assisted the Triumvirate in suppressing a royalist coup and was authorized by its leadership to train forces to fight against the Spanish in Peru as well. Meanwhile, in 1812, he worked with Carlos María de Alvear in organizing the Lautaro Masonic Lodge, whose leadership and members secretly operated as a radical revolutionary underground and attempted to secure control of major Argentine institutions. Forcing the formation of a new Triumvirate in 1812, members of this lodge demanded that an assembly be convoked to draft a new constitution for the United Provinces.[50]

During the Argentine struggle for independence, San Martín displayed skills as a capable military leader. Having trained revolutionary soldiers of his grena-

garians lauded him, Habsburg authorities took firm measures against Kossuth. He was arrested in May 1837, tried and found guilty of treason, and received a four year jail sentence. Having been granted an amnesty after serving three years of this sentence, he left prison and, between 1841 and 1844, edited the daily *Pesti Hirlap,* in which he featured his ardently nationalist and radical ideologies. These views led to a sharp split with Count István Széchenyi and other Hungarian moderate leaders prior to the outbreak of the 1848 March Revolution.[92]

Kossuth became the primary impetus of the revolutionary movement in Hungary in the spring of 1848. In a petition on March 3 to Austrian Emperor Ferdinand I, he proposed an envisaging program for Hungary: The introduction of a uniform taxation system; the abolition of feudal legislation and practices; and the appointment of a Hungarian government responsible to an elected legislature. By the middle of March the contents of this petition became known and well circulated, helping to stimulate revolutions in Vienna, Buda, Pest, Prague, and other major Habsburg cities. Moreover, after Emperor Ferdinand consented to the formation of a Hungarian government responsible to an elected Hungarian parliament, a new government was established in Hungary. Count Louis Batthyány was named as its prime minister, and Louis Kossuth was appointed as the minister for finances. Furthermore, Kossuth played a central role in formulating major provisions of the April Laws. Its egalitarian contents reflected his views about parliamentary democracy, universal courtroom rights, Jewish civic privileges, and peasant reforms.[93]

Yet Kossuth was to encounter major problems that would lead to the discrediting of his revolutionary movement. Kossuth and his revolutionary supporters failed to resolve vexatious issues in Hungary with such minority groups as the Slovaks, Romanians, Ruthenians, Croats, and Serbs. As the revolutionary movement began to encounter challenges, the moderate Batthyány and his supporters resigned in September 1848. Kossuth then assumed power in Hungary. As a consequence of pressure from the Habsburg army, he moved his revolutionary government to Debrecen. Allowing himself to be elected as governing president and making ineffective decisions about Hungarian military leadership and strategy, Kossuth entrusted his powers to General Arthur Görgey on August 11, 1849. After the failure of the Hungarian War for Independence, this frustrated man in 1849 began his lengthy career in exile.[94]

Kossuth, who arrived in the United States on December 4, 1851, became a trans-Atlantic revolutionary. He came to America in search of diplomatic and financial backing for his revolutionary cause. An impeccable dresser and a gifted speaker, Kossuth, who made an indelible imprint on Abraham Lincoln, looked for backing to Senator Lewis Cass and other leaders of the expansionist Young America movement. Cass and the movement's leaders unfortunately gave him more rhetorical support than financial and diplomatic assistance.[95]

Kossuth looked as well for aid from another major group in America during the early 1850s. Lauding his egalitarian ideologies, American abolitionists encouraged Kossuth to affirm their cause regarding the slavery issue. However, after this Hungarian champion of liberty, equality, and freedom refused to vindicate the emancipation of American black slaves, William Lloyd Garrison and his supporters expressed indignation and disgust with this Hungarian revolutionary. Despite being inundated with letters from major abolitionists, Kossuth circumvented the slavery issue. Thus, his concern was not with slavery but was rather with the Hungarian revolutionary movement.[96]

The dejected Kossuth, who failed to secure American assistance for his cause, can be viewed in several different ways as a trans-Atlantic revolutionary. Similar to other revolutionaries discussed in this book, Kossuth was an adamant supporter of nationalist and egalitarian ideologies. However, he lacked a sense of realism and pragmatism and failed to conduct a revolution that would enable Hungary to achieve independence from the Habsburg Empire. Federalist ideol!gBes, which were espoused by both American and European revolutionaries, well might have contributed to enhancing the status of Hungary within the Habsburg Empire during the middle years of the nineteenth century.[97]

R. William Weisberger
Butler County Community College, 2006

Notes

1. I. Bernard Cohen, *Franklin and Newton: An Inquiry into Speculative Newtonian Science* (Cambridge: Harvard University Press, 1966), 113-18, 153-58; Robert E. Schofield, *Mechanism and Materialism: British Natural Philosophy in an Age of Reason* (Princeton: Princeton University Press, 1970), 3-4, 19-39, 64-72.

2. David S. Landes, *The Unbound Prometheus: Technological Change and Industrial Development in Western Europe from 1750 to the Present* (Cambridge: Cambridge University Press, 1976), 100-16; Margaret C. Jacob, *The Cultural Meaning of the Scientific Revolution* (New York: Alfred A. Knopf, 1988), 120-31.

3. T.H. Breen, *The Marketplace of Revolution: How Consumer Politics Shaped American Independence* (Oxford: Oxford University Press, 2004), 10-29; David Hancock, *Citizens of the World: London Merchants and the Integration of the British Atlantic Community, 1735-1785* (Cambridge: Cambridge University Press, 1995), 1-36.

4. Lloyd Kramer, *Nationalism: Political Cultures in Europe and America, 1775-1865* (New York:Twayne Publishers, 1998), 1-4, 16-17; David C. Hendrickson, "The First Union: Nationalism and Internationalism in the American Revolution," in Eliga H. Gould and Peter S. Onuf, eds., *Empire and Nation: The American Revolution in the Atlantic World* (Baltimore: The Johns Hopkins University Press, 2005), 35-44 .

5. Bernard Bailyn, *Atlantic History: Concept and Contours* (Cambridge, MA: Harvard University Press, 2005), 110-11; Alison Games, "Atlantic History: Definitions, Challenges, and Opportunities," *The American Historical Review* 111 (June, 2006): 741-57.

6. Piotr S. Wandycz, *The Lands of Partitioned Poland, 1795-1918* (Seattle: University of Washington Press, 1974), 105-9; Peter F. Sugar and Ivo J. Lederer, eds., *Nationalism in Eastern Europe* (Seattle: University of Washington Press, 1971), 318-24; Peter N. Stearns, *1848: The Revolutionary Tide in Europe* (New York: Norton, 1974), 147-48); J.L. Talmon, *Romanticism and Revolt: Europe,1815-1848* (New York: Harcourt, 1967), 110-49.

7. Lester D. Langley, *The Americas in the Age of Revolution, 1750-1850* (New Haven: Yale University Press, 1996), 262-65; R.J.W. Evans, ed., *The Revolutions in Europe 1848-1849: From Reform to Reaction* (New York: Oxford University Press, 2000), 183-86.

8. Stearns, 236-37.

9. Michael Warner, *The Letters of the Republic: Publication and the Public Sphere in Eighteenth-Century America* (Cambridge, MA: Harvard University Press, 1990), 73-96; Jeffrey L. Pasley, *The Tyranny of Printers: Newspaper Politics in the Early American Republic* (Charlottesville: The University Press of Virginia, 2001), 33-40.

10. R. William Weisberger, Wallace McLeod, and S. Brent Morris, eds., *Freemasonry on Both Sides of the Atlantic: Essays Concerning the Craft in the British Isles, Europe, the United States, and Mexico* (New York: East European Monographs of Columbia University Press, 2002), 279-346, 489-524; Donna Gabaccia, "A Long Atlantic in a Wider World," *Atlantic Studies* 1, no. 1, (2004): 8.

11. R. William Weisberger, *Speculative Freemasonry and the Enlightenment: A Study of the Craft in London, Paris, Prague, and Vienna* (New York: East European Monograph Series of Columbia University Press, 1993), 25-27; Aytoun Ellis, *The Penny Universities* (London: Secker and Warburg, 1956), 159-64; David S. Shields, *Civil Tongues and Polite Letters in British America* (Chapel Hill: University of North Carolina Press, 1997), 55-98.

12. Margaret C. Jacob, *The Radical Enlightenment: Pantheists, Freemasons, and Republicans* (London: Allen and Unwin, 1981), 122-26; Cohen, *Franklin and Newton*, 255-57; Weisberger, *Ibid.*, 38-46.

13. Margaret C. Jacob, *The Cultural Meaning of the Scientific Revolution*, 141-51; I. Bernard Cohen, *Science and the Founding Fathers: Science in the Political Thought of Jefferson, Franklin, Adams, and Madison* (New York: W.W. Norton, 1995), 285-87; Alan Taylor, *American Colonies* (New York: Viking, 2001), 272-85.

14. Warner, 76; Walter Isaacson, *Benjamin Franklin: An American Life* (New York: Simon & Schuster, 2003), 60-64.

15. Warner, 76-79; Isaacson, 64-71, 94-101.

16. Esmond Wright, *Franklin of Philadelphia* (Cambridge, MA.: Harvard University Press, 1986), 38-39.

17. Alfred Owen Aldridge, *Benjamin Franklin and Nature's God* (Durham: Duke University Press, 34-46; Cohen, *Franklin and Newton*, 285-333, 481-488.

18. For Franklin's support of eighteenth-century American consumerism and his opposition to the Stamp Act, see T.H. Breen, 195-99; Gordon S. Wood, *The Americanization of Benjamin Franklin* (New York: The Penguin Press, 2004), 105-38.

19. On Franklin's role as a trans-Atlantic revolutionary diplomat, see Jonathan R. Dull, *A Diplomatic History of the American Revolution* (New Haven: Yale University Press, 1985), 75-93; Stacy Schiff, *A Great Improvisation: Franklin, France, and the Birth of America* (New York: Henry Holt and Company, 2005), 105-44; R. William Weisberger, "Benjamin Franklin: A Masonic Enlightener in Paris," *Pennsylvania History* 53 (July,1986): 165-80.

20. Marcus Cunliffe, *George Washington: Man and Monument* (New York: Mentor Books, 1982), 22-24.

21. Joseph J. Ellis, *His Excellency George Washington* (New York: Alfred A. Knopf, 2004), 9-11; Edward G. Lengel, *George Washington: A Military Life* (New York: Random House, 2005), 15.

22. Ellis, 9-10.

23. For explanations about the significance of the French and Indian War to Atlantic history, see especially Fred Anderson, *Crucible of War* (New York: Alfred A. Knopf, 2000), xv-xxiii.

24. Ellis, 11-12.

25. *Ibid.*, 12-16; Anderson, 62-65.

26. Ellis, 31-35; Anderson, 233-36, 267-69; Thomas Bender, *A Nation Among Nations: America's Place in World History* (New York: Hill and Wang, 2006), 79-80.

27. Ellis, 48-50.

28. *Ibid.*, 59.

29. *Ibid.*, 68-69.

30. Don Higginbotham, ed., *George Washington Reconsidered* (Charlottesville: University Press of Virginia, 2001), 8-9.

31. Ellis, 112-16.

32. *Ibid.*, 130-36.

33. *Ibid.*, 177-79.

34. Jack N. Rakove, "Thinking Like A Constitution," *Journal of the Early Republic* 24 (Spring, 2004): 22. For the economic and financial problems in America during the 1780s, see Woody Holton, "Did Democracy Cause the Recession that Led to the Constitution," *The Journal of American History* 92 (September, 2005): 442-69.

35. R. William Weisberger, "Freemasonry as a Source of Jewish Civic Rights in Late Eighteenth-Century Vienna and Philadelphia: A Study in Atlantic History," *East European Quarterly* 34 (January, 2001): 419-45; Ellis, 166-67, 257-64.

36. Garry Wills, *Cincinnatus: George Washington and the Enlightenment* (New York: Doubleday & Company, 1984), 99-148, 217-41.

37. Edward Countryman, *The American Revolution* (New York: Hill and Wang, 1985), 236-38; Mary Beth Norton, *Liberty's Daughters: The Revolutionary Experience of American Women, 1750-1800* (Boston: Little, Brown and Company, 1980), 298-99.

38. Lauren Dubois, *Avengers of the New World: The Story of the Haitian Revolution* (Cambridge, MA: Harvard University Press, 2004), 2-3.

39. David Geggus, "Toussaint Louverture and the Slaves of the Bréda Plantations," *Journal of Caribbean History* 20: 30-48.

40. David Barry Gaspar and David Patrick Geggus, *A Turbulent Time: The French Revolution and the Greater Caribbean* (Bloomington: Indiana University Press, 1997), ix; Dubois, 3.

41. Langley, 135-39; Dubois, 4-7, 296-97, 305-6; Seymour Drescher, *The Mighty Experiment: Free Labor versus Slavery in British Emancipation* (Oxford: Oxford University Press, 2002), 100-5.

42. Langley, 179-81.

43. Hubert J. Miller, *Padre Miguel Hidalgo: Father of Mexican Independence* (Edinburg: Pan American University Press, 1986), 1-7.

44. *Ibid.*, 17-18, 64.

45. Langley, 180.

46. Brian R. Hamnett, *Roots of Insurgency: Mexican Regions, 1750-1824* (Cambridge: Cambridge University Press, 1986), 16.

47. Langley, 181-82.

48. *Ibid.*, 182-83; Hamnett, 16.

49. J.C.J. Medford, *San Martin: The Liberator* (Oxford: Blackwell, 1950), 16-17; Robert Harvey, *Liberators* (Woodstock: The Overlook Press, 2000), 318-19.

50. John Crane, *San Martín: Liberator of Argentina, Chile, and Peru* (Washington: Pan American Union, 1948), 12; Harvey, *Ibid.*, 322-27.

51. Medford, 50; Langley, 200-1.

52. Langley, 202-5.

53. *Ibid.*, 207-10; Harvey, 414-15, 423-25. For the connections of race to the Spanish American Wars of Independence movements, see the conclusions of Marixa Lasso, "Race War and Nation in Caribbean Gran Columbia, Cartagena, 1810-1832," *The American Historical Review* 111 (April, 2006): 359-61.

25

54. For comments about the importance of print culture in the Atlantic world, consult Adrian Johns, "How to Acknowledge a Revolution," *The American Historical Review* 107 (February, 2002): 106-25.

55. About these arguments, consult Bender, 98-100.

56. Daniel Roche, *France in the Enlightenment*, Arthur Goldhammer, trans. (Cambridge: Harvard University Press, 1998), 315, 316.

57. Durand Echeverria, *Mirage in the West: A History of the French Image of American Society to 1815* (Princeton: Princeton University Press, 1957), 114-15, 129-30, 157-61.

58. For Brissot's involvement in the Lodge of the Nine Sisters and the ancillary cultural institutions of this body, see Weisberger, *Speculative Freemasonry and the Enlightenment*, 89-90.

59. Daniel P. Resnick, "The *Société des Amis des Noirs* and the Abolition of Slavery," *French Historical Studies* (Autumn, 1972): 563.

60. J.-P. Brissot, *Discours sur les causes des troubles de Saint-Dominigue* (Paris: Imprimerie Nationale, 1791), 40.

61. François Furet, *Revolutionary France: 1770-1880*, Antonia Nevill, trans. (Oxford: Blackwell Publishing, 1988), 110-15.

62. Susan Dunn, *Sister Revolutions: French Lightening, American Light* (New York: Faber and Faber, 1999), 89-96; and Furet, *Ibid.*, 122-50.

63. Talmon, 157, 161.

64. Weisberger, McCleod, and Morris, xix.

65. A fine discussion about the connections of masonry to Russian liberalism during the 1820s appears in: Anatole G. Mazour, *The First Russian Revolution, 1825: The Decembrist Movement* (Stanford: Stanford University Press, 1937), 46-58; Avrahm Yarmolinsky, *Road to Revolution: A Century of Russian Radicalism* (New York: Collier Books, 1962), 25-63.

66. Lauren Leighton, *The Esoteric Tradition in Russian Romantic Literature: Decembrism and Freemasonry* (University Park: The Pennsylvania State University Press, 1994), 131-94.

67. Weisberger, McCleod, and Morris, xx-xxi.

68. W.H. Zawadzki, *A Man of Honour: Adam Czartoryski as a Statesman of Russia and Poland, 1795-1831* (Oxford: Clarendon Press, 1993), 1-20, 30-32, 52-55, 82-83, 90, 270-72, 289, 290-91. See also Marian Kukiel, *Czartoryski and European Unity: 1770-1861* (Princeton: Princeton University Press, 1955), 11, 25, 30-31.

69. Zawadzki, *Ibid.*, 35-37, 45-50.

70. Frank W. Thackeray, *Antecedents of Revolution: Alexander I and the Polish Kingdom, 1815-1825* (New York: East European Monograph Series of Columbia University Press, 1980), 139-44; Wandycz, 74-78.

71. David Saunders, *Russia in the Age of Reaction and Reform, 1801-1881* (London: Longman, 1992), 177; Joan S. Skurnowicz, *Romantic Nationalism and Liberalism: Joachim Lelewel and the Polish National Idea* (New York: East European Monograph Series of Columbia University Press, 1981), 58-59.

72. Skurnowicz, *Ibid.*, 59.

73. R.F. Leslie, *Polish Politics and the Revolution of November 1830* (London: Athlone Press, 1956), 212-13; Wandycz, 109-10, 114-15; Zawadzki, 307, 314-15, 318.

74. Wandycz, 132-37; Kukiel, 251-55.

75. Wandycz, 137-50.

76. Zawadzki, 334.

77. Sugar and Lederer, 314.

78. William Dillon, *Life of John Mitchel* 1 (London: Kegan, Paul, Trench & Company), x-xi, 1-16.

79. T.F. O'Sullivan, *The Young Irelanders* (Tralee: Kerryman Limited, 1945), 134.

80. Dillon, 180 and 192-195; and Cecil Woodham-Smith, *The Great Hunger* (New York: Harper & Row, 1962), 335-57.

81. Stearns, 171-72.

82. Patrice Higonnet, *Sister Republics: The Origins of French and American Republicanism* (Cambridge: Harvard University Press, 1988), 1-10; Bender, 74.

83. George W. Pierson, *Tocqueville and Beaumont in America* (New York: Oxford University Press, l938).

84. Drescher, *The Mighty Experiment*, 145.

85. Seymour Drescher, ed. and trans., *Tocqueville and Beaumont on Social Reform* (New York: Harper & Row, 1968), 123, 184.

86. Higonnet, 5-10, 273-80.

87. Bender, 127-29.

88. Steven Béla Várdy, *The Life of Governor Louis Kossuth With His Public Speeches in the United States, And a Brief History of the Hungarian War of Independence*, 2nd ed. (Budapest: Osiris Kiadó, 2001), 9.

89. *Ibid.*, 9-10.

90. István Deák, *The Lawful Revolution: Louis Kossuth and the Hungarians, 1848-1849* (New York: Columbia University Press, 1979), 91-99; and Steven Béla Várdy, *Historical Dictionary of Hungary* (Lanham: The Scarecrow Press, 1997), 106.

91. Deák, *Ibid.*, 321-29.

92. Donald S. Spencer, *Louis Kossuth and Young America: A Study in Sectionalism and Foreign Policy, 1848-1852* (Columbia: University of Missouri Press, 1977), 60-63, 83-120; Willard Carl Klunder, *Lewis Cass and the Politics of Moderation* (Kent: The Kent State University Press, 1996), 257-58.

93. Spencer, *Ibid.*, 65.

94. For a discussion of the failure of salient "isms" during the 1848 revolutions, see Stearns, 225, 234-37, 248-49.

27

John Theophilus Desaguliers and the Newtonian Revolution

R. William Weisberger
Butler County Community College, PA

> *Desaguliers taught two gracious kings to view*
> *all Boyle ennobled and all Bacon knew.*

Sir Isaac Newton, the master of experimental science, found within the Royal Society of London such disciples as Edmund Halley, James Keill, and Stephen Hales to promote his natural philosophy. Trained in the tradition of Baconian experimental science, John Theophilus Desaguliers, from 1712 until his death in 1744, also became a faithful disciple of Newtonian science. With an interest in fusing craft teachings with Newtonian mechanistic and materialistic concepts, Desaguliers concentrated his efforts on the popularization and implementation of Newtonian doctrines and, perhaps more importantly, on the application of basic Newtonian discoveries to technology.

The thesis of this essay centers on the belief that, through the institutions of the Royal Society and speculative freemasonry, Desaguliers successfully transmitted to two British kings, and to his many friends from the English nobility and middle class, the scientific, technological, and philosophical teachings of Isaac Newton. Attention is now directed to the career of John T. Desaguliers as a Newtonian experimental scientist.

The terse statement above from Hawthorn's poem about Desaguliers assists in placing Desaguliers into the perspective of eighteenth-century Newtonian experimental science—the methods and objectives of the Newtonian school being based on those of Bacon and Boyle. In this essay, our attention is directed first to his educational career during his early life and then to a treatment of his views and demonstrations about motion, technology, light, and electricity.

This man who achieved prominence as a member of the Royal Society and as a Newtonian demonstrator was born in La Rochelle on March 1, 1683 and spent the first two and a half years of his life in France. Since in 1685 Louis XIV proclaimed an act revoking the Edict of Nantes, Desaguliers's father, a Huguenot minister, sold his possessions and prepared to leave France. Concealed in a

29

barrel on a ship departing from La Rochelle, the infant John and his parents successfully escaped from the jurisdiction of the Sun King. The family first went to the Island of Guernsey and then to England.[1] After the arrival of this Huguenot family in London, the Reverend Mr. Desaguliers entered the Church of England, was ordained a deacon, and then was appointed minister of the French chapel in Swallow Street. For uncertain reasons, the Reverend Desaguliers left the ministry to direct a school in Islington until his death in February 1699 (new calendar).[2]

From 1700 to 1705, the young John Theophilus Desaguliers received his education in a society characterized by tolerance and optimism. After Newton formulated his law of gravity, nature appeared benevolent and orderly. By advocating the supremacy of Parliament and the social contract theory, Locke attempted to justify the Whigs' actions during the 1688 Glorious Revolution and to infuse a spirit of liberalism and toleration into Augustan society. Thus, for the governing English aristocracy and the enterprising English middle class, it was imperative to acquire an understanding of Newtonian experimental science and the liberal and tolerant Lockean political philosophy. Dominated by these two classes, English society attempted to emulate the cultural models of the ancients—especially those of Augustan Rome.

The study of the ancient classics and the recent Newtonian experimental science constituted the major part of the education of the young Desaguliers. Before the death of his father, Desaguliers learned the fundamentals of Latin, Greek, English, and history while attending the Islington school. Rather than attending a grammar school, between 1700 and 1705 Desaguliers studied with a Mr. Sanders of Sutton Coldfield.[3] Serving as the tutor of Desaguliers, Sanders made his aggressive student read Cicero's *Letters*, Caesar's *Commentaries*, and the works of Virgil, Horace, and Livy. While continuing his study of the classics and history, Desaguliers demonstrated competence in mathematics, astronomy, and mechanics.[4]

With this foundation, in 1705 Desaguliers entered Christ Church College, Oxford. He spent five fruitful years at Oxford, earning excellent grades in classical studies, theology, geometry, astronomy, and mechanics. For his academic efforts, Desaguliers received his bachelors degree and was ordained a deacon in June 1710. Acquiring a reputation as a scientist, Desaguliers was invited that same year to occupy the chair of experimental philosophy in Hart Hall College, Oxford. The elated young scholar accepted this offer, replacing the distinguished Dr. Keill, and then proceeded to earn his Masters of Arts from Oxford in May 1712 and his Doctor of Laws in March 1718.[5]

With his marriage to Joanna Pudsey in 1712, the following year Desaguliers moved from Oxford to London. There he became a close friend of Sir Isaac Newton and delivered lectures on natural philosophy and experimental science in his attractive home on Channel Row, Westminster, located near the Thames. The intimate friendship between Newton and Desaguliers culminated in the election of Desaguliers as a Fellow of the Royal Society of London on July 29, 1714.[6]

With her many uneven cobblestone streets, her stately aristocratic mansions designed in the Palladian style, her capacious middle class homes, and her exquisitely maintained gardens, London served as the political, social, and cultural hub of Augustan society.[7] Early eighteenth-century London was associated with the spirit of political toleration. The Whig Revolutionary Settlement, with its emphasis on the Lockean notion of civil liberties, embodied the spirit of toleration and favored the ascending middle class and the dissenting groups primarily located in London. From 1714 to 1721, the Whigs, guided by the ambitious Stanhope, were exceedingly active, suppressing the attempts of the Jacobite supporters to place the Stuart pretender, James III, on the English throne and consequently discrediting such eminent Tories as Bolingbroke and Oxford. Since the major Tory leaders were repudiated because of their support for the Stuart cause, the Whigs rose to promote the consolidation of the Hanoverian dynasty. From approximately 1717 to 1745, the Whigs, under Robert Walpole, came to master English politics. During the era of Whig supremacy, characterized by an atmosphere of tolerance, English culture and the London middle class flourished.[8]

A district typifying the commercial and exciting cultural life of Augustan London was Covent Garden. Living above the Bedford Coffeehouse in Covent Garden, Desaguliers observed the busy world of this district. In looking toward the great piazza of the Garden, he saw farmers pushing their carts with produce to the Garden's enormous marketplace. Desaguliers also saw the products and items displayed in the Covent Garden shops. He knew that customers were forced to bargain with the shrewd merchants and shop-owners to purchase such items and articles as shoes, socks, gloves, silks, pants, engravings, china, and furniture for a reasonable price.[9]

John Desaguliers often spent his late afternoons and early evenings in Hanoverian London's major social and cultural institution—the male-dominated coffeehouse. The Bedford Coffeehouse, under Covent Garden Plaza, served as a convivial meeting place for London authors, actors, artists, wits, merchants, politicians, and scientists. Drinking tea, chocolate, or coffee and conversing about the most recent articles appearing in Addison's *Spectator*, Steele's *Tatler*, the *Gentlemen's Magazine*, and the *London Courant*, Londoners from these occupations and professions seemed to form a "Republic of Letters."[10] By appealing to the London nobility and middle class, which constituted the "Republic of Letters," and by enabling the dissemination of the most recent ideas emerging in English culture, such coffeehouses as the Rainbow, the Crown and Anchor, Dick's,

Pontack's Head, and the Grecian came to fulfill a vital function in Augustan England.[11]

Desaguliers knew that the English middle class and aristocracy patronizing the London coffeehouses eagerly sought simplified and lucid explanations and demonstrations of the Newtonian system of the world. On his election to the Royal Society in 1714, Desaguliers was appointed curator of the society and began working actively with Hans Sloane, Edmond Halley, and Henry Pemberton for the popularization of Newtonian natural philosophy. As curator, Desaguliers assisted in contriving Newtonian experiments. Meeting either in the Grecian or in Slaughter's, Newton and Desaguliers spent long nights perfecting their experiments and demonstrations.[12]

Desaguliers quickly earned a reputation as an accomplished Newtonian demonstrator. Assembling in the Bedford Coffeehouse and in others, his English middle class and aristocratic friends from London applauded him for using clever techniques to reveal masterfully Newtonian principles.[13] Watching Desaguliers perform his experiments in Hampton Court, George I and Frederick, Prince of Wales, were impressed with his competent lecturing style and with the originality of his convincing demonstrations.[14] Before beginning his presentations, Desaguliers asked his assistants, William Vreen and Richard Bridges, to tell the audience that "only common sense and undivided attention were required" for an understanding of the Newtonian experiments expounding the concepts of motion, light, and electricity.[15]

Motion and Gravity

Dedicated to Frederick, Prince of Wales, *A Course of Experimental Philosophy*, published in 1734 by this respected demonstrator and Fellow of the Royal Society, described and summarized the pertinent characteristics and concepts of Newtonian science. In the dedication to the Prince of Wales, Desaguliers defined the objectives of Newtonian experimental science:

> To contemplate the Works of God, to discover Causes from their Effects and to make Art and Nature subservient to the necessities of life, by a skill in joining proper Causes to produce the most useful Effects, is the business of science.[16]

Having stated this objective, seemingly shared by the major figures of the Enlightenment and by the Baconian and Newtonian experimental scientists, Desaguliers then expressed his acknowledgment and gratitude to his many patrons. From the English nobility and middle class, these patrons subsidized him, many attending faithfully his demonstrations. These patrons included prominent figures from all realms of English society: Dr. James Anderson, the Scot with whom Desaguliers collaborated to write *The Constitution of the Free Masons*; Sir William Billers, the Lord Mayor of London; the Earl of Burlington, a prominent architect responsible for popularizing the Palladian style in England; the Duke of Chandos, the patron of the arts for whom Desaguliers faithfully served as chaplain at his Cannons estate; Colley Cibber, the clever Irish poet and actor named poet laureate in 1730; Martin Folkes, a leading member of the Royal Society and a grand master of the Grand Lodge of England; Sir Stephen Hales, a friend of Desaguliers and the inventor of ventilators and of methods for distilling water.[17] A leading contributor to the Georgia colony, Hales convinced his friend and sponsor of Georgia, James Oglethorpe, to subscribe to this important work of Desaguliers.[18]

In the preface, Desaguliers described the ingredients and methods of Newtonian experimental science. He offered the contention that scientists should rely on empirical and observational methods for the exploration of nature, since: "all the Knowledge we have of Nature depends upon facts. Without Observations and Experiments, our natural Philosophy would only be unintelligible jargon."[19] To give order and understanding to the facts within nature, and to determine "the Causes of Nature from Her effects, the experimental scientist should constantly work with precise mathematical instruments."[20] An adamant advocate of inductive and observational techniques for the investigation of nature, Desaguliers launched a bitter attack on Descartes and his followers. He maintained that the Cartesians, without mathematical evidence, took "a few Principles for granted, without examining their reality or consistence with each other."[21]

The discoveries of Newton relating to light and gravity led to the victory of inductive experimental science over the Cartesian rationalists. Since the supporters of the Cartesian school, whom Desaguliers associated with the armies of the Goths and Vandals, were defeated, "wild guesses at the motion of the planets and comets" and about the constituent ingredients of light and colors were no longer to be offered."[22] Newton's laws pertaining to gravity, to attraction and repulsion, to the ebbing and flowing of the tides, and to the properties of light and color should replace unwarranted and non-mathematical speculations in the examination of motion and light.[23]

Desaguliers emphasized the empirical, inductive, and observational techniques and features of experimental science to explain the reason for the success and acceptance of the Newtonian system of the world. Other prominent Augustan Englishmen came to acknowledge the Newtonian models and methods in their examination of nature. "The great Mr. Locke," Desaguliers explained, "was the first who became a Newtonian Philosopher without the help of geometry."[24] After reading *The Principia*, Locke gained new insights for his classic work in political thought, *The Second Treatise on Civil Government*. The first to teach publicly the principles and methods of Newtonian natural philosophy was John Keill, who applied Newtonian laws of motion to advance the study of hydrostatics.[25] While Keill gave his demonstrations at Oxford about 1705, Mr. Hauksbee performed his hydrostatic and pneumatic experiments in London.[26]

In *Lectures of Experimental Philosophy*, an intriguing work dedicated to his friend, Sir Richard Steele, and published in 1719, Desaguliers explained his reasons for being attracted to Newtonian natural philosophy. Expressing admiration for Dr. Keill and Mr. Hauksbee, Desaguliers asserted that he began to deliver Keill's lectures at Oxford. He also added to these lectures several recent Newtonian mechanical and optical propositions.[27] Desaguliers stated that the Newtonian principles of motion could be easily understood by the use of machines in experiments and required no knowledge of mathematics.[28]

In his many non-mathematical experiments, Desaguliers exhaustively treated the Newtonian principles of motion. If the principles of motion were demonstrated accurately, Desaguliers believed that experimental scientists could fulfill the major objective of natural philosophy—the determination of "the Reasons and Causes of the Effects and Changes which naturally happen in bodies."[29]

Relying on their senses, natural philosophers were able to determine the constituent elements found in "simple bodies."[30] Influenced by Aristotelian models, eighteenth-century natural philosophers worked with four elements in their examination of simple bodies: Earth being cold and dry; water being cold and moist; air being hot and moist; and fire being hot and dry.[31] Attempting to prove the validity of the doctrine of "acids and alcalis" and experimenting with sulfur, mercury, diamonds, and sand, experimental scientists found the ancients' classification of the four elements faulty.[32] New criteria were established to determine the constituent ingredients in all bodies of matter:

1. The matter of natural bodies was the same; namely, a substance extended and impenetrable.
2. All natural bodies must have motion, in some or in all of their parts.
3. Local motion is the chief principle among second causes, and the chief agent of all that happens in nature.[33]

Having surveyed the views of the ancients and the moderns about the elements, Desaguliers proceeded to demonstrate the principles of matter and motion. Matter, according to Desaguliers, possessed the attributes of extension and resistance.[34] Acknowledging the view of the ancient Greek philosopher and scientist Democritus, Desaguliers claimed that matter could be split into small particles, the smallest ones being known as "atomes."[35] These atoms formed "the constituent or component Part of natural Bodies, being created by the Wise and Almighty Author of Nature as the original Particles of Matter."[36] Atoms "are solid, firm, impenetrable, and moveable."[37]

Constantly in motion, atoms were governed by the principle of attraction. If particles from bodies were drawn near to each other, the force of attraction would be strong; if these particles moved away from each other, the force of attraction would decrease.[38] That force enabling particles to attract and to repel each other and causing nature to be in a state of perpetual motion was gravity. To Desaguliers, God was the first and final cause of the world, while the mysterious force of gravity was the second cause of nature, giving order and harmony to all bodies and matter within the universe.[39]

His second lecture in *A Course of Experimental Philosophy* was devoted to demonstrations associated with motion and with the law of gravity. To determine the quantity of motion, the experimental scientist had to multiply the mass—or the quantity of matter in each body—by the velocity.[40] The concept of velocity was defined as "the swiftness with which a moving Body changes its Place" and was determined by the space it occupied in time.[41] Desaguliers explained that if either or both the mass and the velocity of a body were increased, the motion of the whole would be equal to the sum of the motion of all the parts.[42]

Related to the concepts of mass and velocity were those of weight and power. Any body sustained, raised, or depressed was defined as a weight; any object applied to raise a weight was considered a power. The intensity of power was an absolute force, able to move or act according to its velocity.[43] A power was capable of moving in any direction, a weight in only one direction. Applying these concepts to the movement of terrestrial bodies, Desaguliers asserted that the "Line of Direction of a Weight is a Line drawn from its Center of Gravity to the Center of the Earth. As the Middle of the Weight of a Body, the Center of Gravity is a Point about which all the Parts of a Body are in *Aequilibrio.*"[44] Giving examples to demonstrate the concept of the center of gravity, Desaguliers discussed the relation of the planets to the sun. In the solar system, the sun served as the common center of gravity, being located in the center of the system. The center of gravity of the planets and their moons was to be found within this immovable body, larger than all the planets combined.[45]

The annotation of the second lecture also contained an explanation for the determination of the center of gravity of the earth and the moon. In this demonstration, Desaguliers illustrated the lever principle of Archimedes. If the fulcrum, or the fixed point, of the lever represented the common center of gravity between the earth and the moon, Desaguliers contended that "the distance of the Center of Gravity of the earth from the lever's fulcrum amounts to 6,000 miles; that of the Center of Gravity of the moon is 40 times as far."[46] Using simple techniques to explain the features of motion, velocity, power, and the center of gravity, Desaguliers brought to a conclusion his second lecture.

35

Before distinguished royal and noble guests, he demonstrated the significance of Newtonian mechanistic laws. In 1717 at Hampton Court, George I praised Desaguliers for his demonstrations of Newton's laws of motion. In 1734 Desaguliers received a cordial invitation from his friend, George II, to perform his experiments pertaining to Newton's gravitational laws for Queen Caroline and the court. Among the visitors invited to observe were the earls of Dalkeith and Darnley, Lord Chesterfield, Sir Robert Walpole, the Duke of Chandos, Martin Clare, and Martin Folkes.

Members of this audience were interested in the lucid explanations of Desaguliers regarding the first Newtonian law of motion: "Every body perseveres in a state of rest, or of uniform motion in a right line, unless it be compelled to change that state by forces impressed thereon."[47] Desaguliers proceeded to provide interpretations and examples to demonstrate the validity of this law. Since all matter contained a force of inactivity, known as the *Vis Inertiae*, Desaguliers maintained that a force must be impressed upon an object to give motion to and to change the shape of that body.[48] A corollary supporting this law followed: "If bodies with similar masses and velocities move from the same point or height, these objects will reach simultaneously a common point."[49] To confirm this corollary, Desaguliers offered the example of similar cannonballs fired from cannons located in the same place and simultaneously reaching a common point.[50]

Desaguliers defined in a corollary the essential features of centrifugal and centripetal forces. Contending that a centrifugal force made a body move from the center of motion and a centripetal force made a body move toward the center of motion, Desaguliers referred to these forces to disprove the Cartesian theory of motion in the solar system.[51] Descartes advanced the vortex theory, believing that a "Whirlpool of celestial matter (known as a Vortex) produced the motion of the planets around the Sun."[52] These whirlpools, or vortices, in turn forced the sun to rotate on its axis and gave motion to celestial bodies. Descartes believed that, since the vortices were denser and heavier than the planets, the orbits of the planets seemed to move away from the sun. Desaguliers argued that, if the vortices were heavier than the planets, the centripetal forces of the planets "would make them go continually towards the Sun in a spiral line, until they fall into it."[53] Descartes also thought that, since all the planets were of equal bulk and possessed similar gravities, their revolutions about the sun were equal in time. "That all planets have equal periodical times is contrary to observation;" Desaguliers maintained. He stated that "the periodical times of the planets' revolutions are different, since Mercury performs its revolution approximately 120 times faster than Saturn."[54] He concluded that the Cartesian hypothesis amounted to an invalid deductive statement, since gravity was the force "keeping the planets and moon in their orbits about the Sun."[55]

In exhaustive detail, Desaguliers examined the second Newtonian law of motion: "The Change of Motion is always proportionable to the moving force impressed; and is made in the right Line in which that Force is impressed."[56] Desaguliers interpreted this law to mean that, "if any force generates a motion, a double force will generate double the motion, a triple force triple the motion."[57] If the new force acted at right angles, the velocity would increase; if the new force acted at acute angles, its effects would be determined by the degree of acuteness of the angle. If the new force was greater than the impressed force, it was apparent that the body would increase its velocity. The distance of a falling body could be determined if the velocity was multiplied by the time or if the velocity was squared.[58] As a result of falling through space, a body acquired velocity, the latter enabling it to pass through a double space in the same time.[59] By knowing the height and the weight of bodies, one could determine the momentum of such descending projectiles as cannonballs and bombs, since the momentum of these falling objects was determined by the squaring of the spaces and by the multiplication of the velocity by the mass and the weight.[60]

Desaguliers cited numerous examples to illustrate and confirm Newton's second law. In an organ circulating around the center of an axis, the fly operated according to Newton's second law, being capable of accumulating powers impressed upon it. Such a mechanical organ, attached to a screw, could be transformed into a machine for impressing stamps upon coins.[61] Similar to a fly, a circular pendulum could accumulate motion, thus becoming capable of exerting its impressed force to move objects of great weight.[62] The last instrument demonstrating Newton's second and third laws was the sling. That instrument, free from friction, easily accumulated power and thus had been used by ancient and modern engineers for operating such machines as the rammer.[63]

Desaguliers also discussed the elliptical motions of the planets in light of Newton's second law. Desaguliers charted the elliptical revolutions of the moons circling around the planets and the planets revolving around the sun. In charting the movements of the celestial bodies, Desaguliers determined the aphelion— the greatest distance between the planets and the sun—and the perihelion— the least difference between the planets and the sun.[64] In their eccentric elliptical orbits, revolving celestial bodies moved faster at the perihelion than at the aphelion, accelerating their movements from the aphelion to the perihelion, and consequently retarding their movements from the perihelion to the aphelion. The ellipse of the bodies at the perihelion and the aphelion determined the increase and the decrease of the velocities of objects. If a planet was more strongly attracted at its perihelion than at its aphelion, the sun would not be able to attract that planet into its sphere. By acquiring a great centrifugal force and increasing its velocity, a planet consequently balanced the attraction of the sun and thus maintained its orbit. Those planets nearest to the sun performed their revolutions in shorter times than more distant planets; the nearer planets possessing a centrifugal force to balance their centripetal force toward the sun.[65] That centripetal force responsible for maintaining the orbits of the planets and for driving bodies toward each other, Desaguliers remarked, was gravity.[66] Moreover, Desaguliers maintained that, since a comet's centrifugal force was less than its centripetal force, such a body was destined to fall into the sun.[67]

In the last section of lecture five, Desaguliers directed his attention to Newton's third law: "To every action there is always opposed an equal reaction; or the mutual actions of two bodies upon each other, are always equal, and directed to contrary parts."[68] In interpreting this law, Desaguliers explained that, if a body struck another and the motion of the other body was altered by its force, the former body would experience an equal change in its motion. The changes resulting from such an inter-reaction were equal, not in the velocities, but in the motions, or "momenta," of the bodies.[69]

Desaguliers alluded to numerous examples demonstrating Newton's law of action and reaction. If a cannon was fired, the explosion of the powder would push the cannon backward as much as the ball would be pushed forward. Swimmers, in pushing water backward, were equally pushed forward. In flight, birds were pushed forward by the reaction of the air against their expanded wings; if a bird struck the air downward with its wings, the reaction of the air would push it upward with the same force.[70]

Newton's third law also explained the movement of tides. The gravitational thrust of the moon forced the waters in the seas to swell.[71] Referring to *The Principia*, Desaguliers explained that the "ocean ebbed and flowed, twice each day, the tides being greatest about the equinoxes, when the luminaries are nearest the earth."[72]

From the tides rising and falling in the sea, it was possible to determine the gravitational forces of the moon and the sun.[73] Rising and falling twice per day, during the times of both a new and a full moon the tides were greater than during the time of a half moon—the latter known as quadratures. During the quadratures, the tides caused by the action of the sun and the moon on the waters were known as neap tides. If the gravitational forces of the sun and moon were acting jointly, the gravity of the moon was capable of raising ocean waters ten feet, while that of the sun was capable of elevating ocean waters two feet, resulting in a tide rising to twelve feet.[74]

Desaguliers correctly asserted that, since the depths and the shores of the seas were very irregular, waters running from bays, gulfs, and straits into the seas would cause the irregularity of the tides; only in the free ocean would regular tidal movements be found.[75]

These precise inductive demonstrations—especially those concerning the movements of the tides—seemed to confirm the three major Newtonian laws so lucidly and gracefully expressed in *The Principia.* These experiments also conformed to the Newtonian system of the world. The Newtonian world was based on the belief that the planets moved in elliptical orbits, having their common focus in the sun's center.[76] Since the time of such ancients as Aristarchus, Democritus, and the Pythagoreans, it had been taught that the planets revolved in circular motion and in free space around the fixed sun. The moderns discovered that the earth and other planets were circling the sun in elliptical orbits, since centripetal forces were directed to the centers of the planets and since each planet shared a common center of gravity—the sun.[77] Functioning like the parts of a machine, the Newtonian world—placed in motion by the Supreme Architect—found celestial and terrestrial bodies moving in absolute time and space.

"The Congress of Bodies," the sixth lecture in *A Course of Experimental Philosophy*, provided demonstrations of those principles relating to the action and elasticity of bodies. Desaguliers first discussed the quantity of motion. The sum of motions directed toward the same parts and the difference of those directed toward contrary parts comprised the quantity of motion. Further, the quantity of motion did not change from the action of bodies among themselves. If one body struck another, the sum of the motions of the parts of the two bodies would be the same after as before the collision of the two bodies.[78] If two bodies moving in contrary directions struck one another, the sum of the motions of the parts of the two bodies would be the same before and after the meeting of these bodies. With the collision of two or more bodies, the common center of gravity of each body was not altered, either remaining at rest or moving uniformly in a straight line.[79]

Desaguliers then enumerated several principles governing the movements of bodies without elasticity. Two bodies without elasticity, after striking one another, would be fused.[80] If two non-elastic bodies met one another, the magnitude of the blow would be proportionate to the velocity of the striking, or "percutient," body. If two non-elastic bodies with contrary or opposite motions struck against each other, the magnitude of the blow would be the same as if one of the bodies remained at rest.[81] Demonstrating these principles of non-elastic bodies through experiments with clay balls, Desaguliers emphasized that the magnitude of the blow of two striking non-elastic bodies would always be proportional to their respective velocities.[82]

The movements of elastic bodies briefly occupied the attention of Desaguliers. If two elastic bodies collided against each other, their velocity would remain the same before and after they struck. Perfectly elastic bodies would recede from each other with the same velocity that forced them to hit each other. After collision, two elastic bodies would restore themselves to their former shapes, with a force equivalent to that by which both bodies were compressed.[83]

As curator of the Royal Society of London, Desaguliers performed experiments and gave demonstrations before the members of that distinguished scientific academy to illustrate the Newtonian laws of matter in motion. Desaguliers offered thoughts and conjectures about the cause of elasticity. His contended that elasticity was intimately related to the principles of attraction and repulsion. In *Vegetable Statistics*, Dr. Hales, an intimate friend of Desaguliers, demonstrated that the elasticity of air seemed to be dependent on the repulsive powers of the air's particles. Agreeing with Hales's findings, Desaguliers asserted that, if air was in an elastic state, particles would be brought nearer together and thus would cohere to one another. The principle of air's elasticity was proportional to its density and its compression served as an explanation for particles being able to cohere to each other. If a fluid, whose parts repelled each other but attracted particles in the air, was mixed with that air, the repulsion of any two particles of air would be proportionally diminished. If two elastic fluids were attracted to each other in elastic air, Desaguliers contended that the result would be the formation of solid substances and that further fermentation would result, demonstrating that a solid could be formed from elastic fluids. Citing an example of fermentation, Desaguliers placed burning brimstone matches in a tall glass receiver standing in a dish containing water. Since the brimstone matches slowly burned out and, since the water began to rise from the dish into the receiver, Desaguliers explained that the effluvia—or small sulfur particles—attracted particles from the air to form an inelastic compound. From this experiment with brimstone matches, and from a demonstration with steel springs heated to the point of fluidity, Desaguliers concluded that the principles of attraction and repulsion were dependent on elasticity while, in turn, they also explained the reason for objects absorbing and generating air.[84]

Other intriguing experiments performed before the Royal Society concerned the velocity and weight of bodies. To demonstrate that the force of moving bodies was proportional to their velocities, Desaguliers performed experiments with lead balls of varying size and weight.[85] In an experiment with weights hanging from each end of a scale, Desaguliers explained a mechanical paradox: Two bodies of equal weight, being removed from a balance, did not destroy the equilibrium of the scale. Desaguliers manipulated the weights to show that the equilibrium could be maintained. He contended that, since "there are many cases in which the velocities are not proportionable to the distances from the center of motion of a machine, we can only state as a corollary of the general rule, that weights act in proportion to their true velocities."[86]

In an experiment with six solid leaden balls and six hollow balls, Desaguliers attempted to determine how much the resistance of the air retarded descending bodies. Dropping the balls from the upper gallery on the dome of St. Paul's Church, Desaguliers used a wheel chronometer to determine the fall of each ball. He found that the leaden balls fell in four and one-half seconds, the hollow glass balls in five seconds, and the pasteboard balls in six and one-half seconds. Thus, the resistance of the air for retarding the fall of the hollow balls was greater than that for retarding the descent of the leaden balls.[87]

In contrast to such demonstrations with air, Desaguliers gave experiments requiring the use of vacuums to determine the properties and motions of various objects in circumstances where air was not prevalent. To exemplify Newton's principle of the resistance of matter, Desaguliers dropped a guinea, a piece of fine paper, and a feather simultaneously into a glass receiver exhausted of air. He found that all three objects descended simultaneously to the bottom of the receiver since the interspersed vacuum provided no medium of resistance for the falling objects.[88] Pouring three pounds of mercury into an interspersed vacuum and three pounds of water into another, Desaguliers added hot and then cold water to the liquids in the vacuums. After the temperature of each liquid was taken, Desaguliers then determined the quantity of each liquid remaining in the vacuums. He concluded that, since the mercury received more heat than the water, the amount of mercury remaining from the original three pounds was greater than that of water from the three-pound quantity. His conclusion was that bodies of similar bulk subjected to activities in an interspersed vacuum do not always contain equal quantities of matter.[89]

The question of the properties and motions of water particles in clouds occupied Desaguliers. He challenged Dr. Niewentyt's contention about the rise of vapors in the formation of clouds and in the descent of rain. Dr. Niewentyt argued that, upon their separation from sunbeams, particles of water rise, forming vapor clouds. Once their former gravity was restored, maintained Niewentyt, these water particles can no longer be sustained by the air and consequently fall to the earth in the form of rain. Rejecting this view as the valid cause of rain, Desaguliers explained rain in terms of repellent forces acting on particles of fluids. Since water particles in clouds were changed from an inelastic to an elastic state, the repellent forces of these water particles increased, causing the heated, steamy particles to rise. As the air and the earth cool, Desaguliers explained, the water particles condense and descend to earth as raindrops.[90]

Desaguliers performed an experiment to determine the role of the force of gravity in influencing the rise and fall of water in the seas and rivers. Placing a box to float in a vessel of water, Desaguliers adjusted the level of the water in the vessel by manipulating a plug. This manipulation adjusted the water levels in the vessel to resemble the influence of the moon's gravitational force in causing the rise and fall of water in the seas and rivers.[91]

A central experiment given by Desaguliers centered on the shape and motion of the earth. In his rejection of the view of Mr. Cassini that the earth was an oblong spheroid higher at the poles than at the equator, Desaguliers confirmed

Newton's contention about the earth's shape: That it is higher at the equator than at the poles, and that it is flat at the poles. Through experiments with pendulums and with a plumb, Desaguliers demonstrated the principle of gravity and the diurnal rotation of the earth. Those principles, in turn, served as supporting evidence for the proof of the earth's flattened poles and elevated equator. If the earth were an oblong spheroid, its heaviest parts would move toward the center and its lightest parts toward the surface. Concluding this refutation of Cassini, Desaguliers maintained that the possibilities of the earth being an oblong sphere remained remote, since the action of gravity did not force the waters of the sea to rise and to overflow in the equatorial regions.[92]

A discussion of tidal movements, gravity, velocity, and weight appeared in *Vegetable Statistics*, by Stephen Hales. Desaguliers reviewed before the Royal Society this detailed work of his friend, asserting that *Vegetable Statistics* exemplified the inductive and empirical tradition of Newtonian science. This work advanced the study of "Nature's Knowledge," since experiments were conducted to demonstrate the application of Newtonian laws to biology, chemistry, and technology.[93]

The Application of Newtonian Laws to Technology

The technological advancements resulting from the application of Newtonian laws to machinery led to the Industrial Revolution in England. Consisting of the business-oriented middle class and aristocracy, English merchant capitalists, well equipped with liquid capital, sponsored the funds for building such major British canals as the Trent, the Mersey, and the Worsley.[94] Once transportation facilities were improved, the English merchant capitalists concentrated their attention on the production of iron and textiles.

Technical improvements in textile machinery were required for the accelerated production of cloth. With the development of the silk throwing machine by Thomas Lombe in 1717, John Kay, a Lancashire weaver and cloth maker, contrived a machine in 1733 to increase the output of cloth. The flying shuttle served as a significant improvement of the loom, since this machine, resting on mounted wheels and propelled by hammers, was able to produce cloth that formerly had required the work of two persons. By passing cotton or wool through rollers that revolved at different speeds, Lewis Paul of Birmingham induced the expansion of the cotton industry.[95] Influenced by Paul's idea of the roller spinning of cloth, in 1765 James Hargreaves devised the spinning jenny, and in 1768 Richard Arkwright invented the water frame.[96]

The invention and improvement of the steam or fire engine gave impetus to the British iron and coal industries. To increase the output of iron, in 1709 Abraham Darby of Coalbrookdale, in Shropshire, produced a quality grade pig iron, smelted with coke. By producing the coke-smelting pig in his tall blast furnace, Darby encouraged the building of iron foundries and the use of coke.[97] From the production of guns in Birmingham, cutlery and tools in Sheffield, and anchors and nails in Newcastle-upon-Tyne, Britain emerged as the leading industrial nation in Europe. To maintain this status and to stimulate growth in the factory system, Britain placed great reliance on the perfection of the steam engine.[98] In 1698 Thomas Savery constructed a steam-operated pumping engine that consisted of a boiler and a condenser. In pipes connected to the condenser, steam forced the water into the shaft; then fresh steam injected from the boiler was used to raise the water from the shaft to the ground level. Since Savery's engine proved to be inefficient, in 1708 Thomas Newcomen, an ironmonger from Dartmouth, invented an atmospheric engine. Newcomen's engine produced steam from a rotating piston attached to a vertical beam. As the piston rotated, steam appeared, being directed to and then condensed in the cylinder. Finally, pump rods were propelled by the steam, which raised the water from the shaft to the surface of the earth. With modifications, Newcomen's piston and cylindrically powered steam engine was in use throughout Europe by 1711.[99]

This engine, acclaimed as the invention most responsible for England's transformation into a mass industrialized nation, received comprehensive treatment in Desaguliers's lectures and experiments. Examining the characteristics and categories of machinery and engines, Desaguliers explained that simple machines were those instruments that operated in accordance with the principles of mechanical power. Mechanical power referred to the ability of weights from machinery to be manipulated to accelerate or to impede resistance. Asserting that engines contained simple machines, Desaguliers listed the categories of simple machines: The pulley, the axis in Peritrochio, the inclined plane, the wedge, and the screw.[100]

Desaguliers formulated propositions governing the operation of machinery. Once placed in motion, a pulley did not increase the force of its power. However, the pulley operated successfully because, as a simple machine, it minimized friction.[101] When a rope rotated about the roller of a pulley, it was possible to determine the pressure exerted on the pulley's axis since such pressure was equivalent to the quadruple of the product of the weights multiplied into one another and divided by the sum of the same weights.[102] By discussing the movements of wheels, Desaguliers demonstrated the motion and functioning of the pulley. A wheel encountered difficulty in passing over a rub, and a wheel could not be drawn over a rub whose top was as high as the axis.[103] High wheels, Desaguliers maintained, passed over rubs more easily than low ones.[104]

In elaborate detail, Desaguliers described the friction of wheels produced in carriages and on engines. If the friction of weights was to be reduced, Desaguliers maintained that either oil or grease should be applied to wood surrounding the wheels. If water permeated the pores of wood, twice as much force would be required to move the wheel. Grease and oil, correctly applied, would lead to the smooth functioning of metal parts in small engines. Desaguliers contended that grease served as an excellent lubricant for wagon wheels, maximizing the spinning of the wheel and reducing its friction. For the operation of a carriage, Desaguliers maintained, force and motion should be appropriately generated; further, the wheels should be round, the hind wheels being high and the forewheels being low.[105] In driving carts and chariots, the ancients discovered that motion was more quickly generated from high back wheels than from low back wheels. With high back wheels, carriages were able to maintain their equilibrium.[106] By installing large rather than small wheels on the rear axles of a carriage, owners of vehicles would find that the friction of the hind wheels was minimized. Friction was reduced, Desaguliers asserted, since a large wheel turned less than a small one and thus created less friction.[107]

Desaguliers mentioned the advantages of vehicles with four wheels over those with two. Carriages, wagons, and coaches with four wheels moved more simply than did carts with two wheels. With the weight equally distributed on its four wheels, a carriage was easily moved by either oxen or horses. This equal distribution of weight enabled animals to pull a wagon without easily tiring.[108] On the other hand, a cart climbing a hill would force the horse to lift upward, while in descending a hill, the cart would force the horse to assume the weight of the vehicle. From experiments with wheels on clay and sand, Desaguliers found that wagon wheels with large diameters and of similar height could be more easily moved from ruts than those wheels with small diameters and of similar height.[109] On a smooth surface or a pavement, wagon wheels generated less friction and seemed to enable more precise steering than those of the cart.[110] In dry weather, wagons and carts were more simply driven on dirt pavement than on sand roads. During rainy weather, such vehicles generated more force and were maneuvered with more precision on sand than on earth roads. In ending his demonstration about carriages and carts, the practical and utilitarian Desaguliers stated that, if England encouraged the building and maintenance of "paved streets and solid roads," wagons and carriages would replace awkward carts and would thus promote a significant change in transportation.[111]

By explaining in detail the principles governing the operation of hydrostatic and hydraulic engines, Desaguliers demonstrated the British advancements in technology and engineering. Desaguliers first surveyed the development of the engine, contending that "the fewest mechanical blunders came from civil and military architecture, since architects and engineers were skilled in the use of mechanical organs."[112] Appreciating the mechanical instruments of the ancients, British engineers and architects, familiar with hydrostatics and pneumatics, developed the engine for industrial projects.[113] Eighteenth-century English engineers were indebted to Hadley and Sorocold for the advancement of the engine. To improve the efficiency of the engine, engineers acquired the knowledge and operative skills of the mason, the bricklayer, the carpenter, and the millwright. "Probing these crafts for the mystery of their art," engineers combined the practical knowledge of these professions with the Newtonian laws of motion and gravity to design and perfect the steam engine.[114]

Desaguliers described Mr. Vauloué's engine for driving piles. In operation at the new Westminster Bridge, this engine was propelled by a great wheel, the cogs of which turned a trundle-head with a fly, forcing a great rope to pass over the pulley. As horses circled around the shaft, the rope continued to wind about the drum, moving objects from one place to another.[115]

After describing the operation of the corn mill, Desaguliers directed his attention to the steam engine. Preponderantly influenced by *A Century of Invention*, a work published by the Marquis of Worcester in 1663, Captain Savery described in *Harris's Lexicon* an engine designed to drain mines.[116] This fire engine converted water into steam and then forced the steam to raise or lift the water from the mines. Desaguliers, having observed Savery's demonstrations at York, discussed the problems of this steam engine. Unregulated steam either melted or damaged parts of the engine.[117] Used to drain marshes, to pump water from mines, and to supply water to such mansions as Lord Chandos's Sion House, the Savery steam engine was improved on by John Cawley and Thomas Newcomen—the atmospheric engine of the latter being operated by a piston moving in a great cylinder, thus forcing water to be generated from a pump. Exhibited in 1740 by Desaguliers for King's College, London, the Newcomen engine was adopted in the northern coalfields surrounding Tyne and Wear and served as a symbol of the first stages of the Industrial Revolution emerging in Hanoverian England.[118]

Another mechanical device frequently used for lifting and moving bulky objects during the inceptive stages of the Industrial Revolution was the crane. Desaguliers elaborated on the capabilities of a crane, maintaining that a "fixed crane with its moveable gibbet could raise stones from a great depth."[119] On the gibbet, an iron wheel was attached, being propelled by an engine. Capable of turning a complete circle, a "rat's tail crane" operated in accordance with the principles of the lever and the pulley, applying appropriate force to raise weights from the ground and to lower them into the carriages for shipment.[120]

Monsieur Perault contrived a device known as the axis in Peritrochio to improve the performance of the crane. Desaguliers discussed the functioning of this machine, since Perault claimed that his invention eliminated wasteful friction produced by the engine of a crane. Confirming Aristotle's view that rollers reduced engine friction, Perault maintained that the axis in Peritrochio, with rollers in its engines, enabled the axle to wind smoothly the rope lifting weights from the ground. Desaguliers offered comments about Perault's imaginative invention, claiming that the axis in Peritrochio produced an enormous amount of friction from bending rope and that the equilibrium of the machine's engine was difficult to maintain. Desaguliers terminated his experiment of Perault's machine by emphasizing that, despite its inadequacies, the axis would contribute to the improved operation of the crane.[121]

In a lecture about a machine with perpetual motion, Desaguliers suggested that a science of mechanics, based on the Newtonian laws of motion, was emerging to produce an industrialized and mechanized society in England. His lecture demonstrated that the purported self-moving engine of Orsireus of Hesse Cassel was not governed by the principle of perpetual motion, since a spurious view was offered to explain the operation of the engine: ". . . the velocity of any weight is not the line which it describes in general, but the height that it rises up to, or falls from, with respect to its distance from the center of the earth."[122] In correcting this fallacy about the operation of the self-perpetual engine, Desaguliers stated that "a weight in rising near the engine's center may not only lose its velocity, but rather be made to gain velocity, in proportion to the velocity of counter-poising weights descending in the circumference on the opposite side of the engine."[123]

An account was given by Desaguliers to explain the operation of Joshua Haskins's water engine. Since hydraulic engines tended to lose water, Haskins attempted to rectify this problem. By leathering the pistons, Haskins reduced water loss and concomitantly increased the machine's lifting power. Since mercury was used to prevent air from eluding the pistons, Haskins's hydraulic engine was capable of raising water and pumping it through pipes and into barrels.[124] In another experiment concerning the distribution of water throughout pipes, Desaguliers exhibited a machine able to eliminate impurities in water pipes. Known as a jack in the box, this machine pumped water through its cast-iron pipes from a reservoir near Cavendish Square to mansions in the vicinity. As the water was being pumped, glass tubes, attached to the iron pipes, carried away noxious air circulating the pipes.[125]

A humanitarian and a utilitarian man, Desaguliers contrived engines to correct the problem of air in mines and hospitals. To draw damp air from mines, an engine consisting of a triple crank and three working pumps would be employed. Operating with three regulators, the engine would pump the impure air from the mines into square wooden trunks. Describing the circumstances under which the engine operated, Desaguliers asserted that if the damp air were lighter than the common air, the engine would pump fresh air into the mines, driving the foul air to the ceiling, where pipes would carry it from the mines. If the damp air were heavier than the common air, the engine would suck out the foul air from the mines.[126] A similar ventilating system was developed for use in hospital

46

rooms. Two pipes were attached to an engine: The first sucking foul air from the room, and the second pumping and blowing fresh air into it.[127] In 1721, after the engine was installed in London hospitals and prisons, Desaguliers offered proposals to Edinburgh officials for the use of ventilators in the homes and hospitals of that Scottish city. Before his trip to Edinburgh, in 1720 Desaguliers directed the erection of a ventilating system for the House of Commons.[128] Installed with the London and Edinburgh ventilating systems were air barometers measuring the air's weight and temperature.[129] During the early 1720s Desaguliers invented a machine used by British breweries for drying malt with blowing warm air.[130]

The dissemination of the Newtonian laws of motion corresponded to the development of British technology during the first half of the eighteenth century. The Savery and Newcomen engines, pumping engines for reservoirs and mines, and the rat's tail crane suggested and attested to the success of the science of mechanics during the important formative years of the Industrial Revolution. Like technology, optics was profoundly influenced by Newtonian models and concepts.

The Newtonian Concepts of Light

From his experiments with and observations of light rays, Newton attempted to define the properties of light. His desire to discover the primary and occult properties of light, and his determination to prove that the force governing the movements of light rays resembled the universal force governing the motion of nature's matter, prompted his investigation of light and colors.[131] Newton's efforts in his experiments with light resulted in the discovery of the colors of the rainbow, the formulation of the principles of reflection and refraction, and his acceptance of the corpuscular theory as an explanation for the movement of minute light particles.

These important discoveries appeared in the *Opticks*, the first edition of which was published in 1704 and the second edition in 1717. First defining the principles and properties of light, Newton asserted that "the refrangibility of light rays is their disposition to be refracted or turned out of their way in passing out of one transparent body into another. Reflexibility of light rays is their disposition to be reflected or turned back into the same medium from any other medium upon whose surface they fall."[132] The sun emitted light rays, varying in color and differing in degrees of refrangibility and reflexibility.[133] Newton maintained that all colors in the universe possessed light and consisted either of the colors of homogeneal lights or of a compound of these.[134]

Before the members of the Royal Society, Desaguliers gave a lucid account of the major characteristics of light and colors discussed in Newton's *Opticks*.

To illustrate Newton's major findings on light and colors, Desaguliers performed numerous experiments with prisms. By passing light rays through a prism, Desaguliers projected the various colors of the rainbow on a spectrum: From violet emerged the colors of red and blue; from orange appeared red and yellow. If the door to a dark room were slightly opened, Desaguliers demonstrated that the colors of the spectrum would appear clearly: Red, orange, yellow, green, blue, purple, and violet (the last color being so faint as to be scarcely perceptible).[135] Directing light rays from a candle to a prism, Desaguliers illustrated convincingly that "rays of light pass with more facility through glass than through air."[136] In performing experiments with rays emitted from a candle, Desaguliers discussed the activities of refrangible rays, maintaining that "refrangible rays are easily inflected and make the least curves when beamed upon a prism. The most refrangible rays consist of smaller particles than the least refrangible and therefore move with the least momentum."[137] To confirm Newton's views about refrangible rays, Desaguliers projected light rays from a candle onto a surface covered with mercury, on which surface the colors of red and green were observed. He then demonstrated that "the least and most refrangible rays will appear as a double spectrum."[138] Desaguliers went on to explain how refrangible as well as refractable rays would enter the eyes, contending that the nerve fibers of an eye's retina communicate with one another and transmit color and light images to the brain.[139]

Desaguliers urged his patrons to consult the queries in the *Opticks*, since this section contained Newton's imaginative speculations about the properties and activities of light rays. From his experiments with mercury and fire, Newton suggested that the emission of light and heat from bodies could be attributed to the vibrating motions of their parts.[140] Large bodies seem to conserve their heat the longest and to emit light copiously. Light rays produced by large and small bodies tended to excite the retina through their vibrations. These vibrations, in turn, were sent by the solid fibers of the optic nerve to the brain, thus producing the sense of sight. The harmony and incongruence of colors were determined by the vibrations sent to the brain.[141] Vision was also governed by the aethereal medium, the latter being responsible for the reflecting and refracting of light rays. Newton was convinced that gravity and the aether shared similar qualities, since the former explained the motion of celestial and terrestrial bodies, and the latter explained the movements of light rays. The movements of light particles, like those of bodies, were governed by the forces of attraction and repulsion.[142] In the concluding sections of the queries, Newton implored his students and readers to explore nature and to determine the reasons for its operation, uniformities, and design.

Electrical Studies

In late life, Desaguliers was intrigued by the study of electricity. In studying the properties of this occult force, Desaguliers believed that the validity of the corpuscular theory could be tested and that an explanation for the cause (or perhaps, the Cause) motivating the most minute particles found in all matter in nature could be observed. Other reasons were offered by Desaguliers for conducting his experiments with electricity. Desaguliers praised the *Opticks*, since this work suggested that the activities of electrical particles seemed to resemble those of light rays and of liquid and solid substances.[143] During his journey to Holland in 1731, Desaguliers found the Dutch Newtonians performing electrical experiments, attempting to confirm and advance Newton's contentions about atomism and electricity found in the *Opticks*.[144] Like the eminent eighteenth-century Dutch physician Hermann Boerhaave, the Dutch natural philosopher Gravesande, and the Englishman Stephen Hales (known for his *Statical Essays*), Desaguliers diligently pursued his electrical studies. His experiments centered on an attempt to demonstrate that the principles of attraction and repulsion seemed to govern the activities of electrical effluvia and those of the atomistic particles found in matter.[145]

In his first experiments about electricity before the Royal Society, Desaguliers reviewed the findings of Stephen Gray and discussed objects rejecting and receiving an electrical charge. The aim of this first series of electrical experiments was to determine "the property of electrical bodies, and to discover what useful influence electricity has in Nature."[146]

Desaguliers made some significant observations about electricity. Producing friction from a tube, he found that the following objects received electrical charges: Gold, silver, and copper metals; brass and steel balls; sulfur; bee's wax and sealing wax; resin; ivory, human bones, and flesh; wax and tallow candles; and pipe tobacco.[147] Tying a heavy thread to a man suspended in air, Desaguliers passed electrical charges through the thread and the man to the following objects: Parchment, woolen cloth; cadis, or worsted tape; a sword belt; a white hat; mercury; and wax and tallow candles. These substances became exceedingly electricized, forcing the thread to move. Desaguliers discovered that such materials as hemp ropes, packthreads, dry sponges, wire tubes, swords, and iron tubes would serve as supporters, being saturated with and transmitting the electrical virtue of other bodies.[148] He found that electrical charges did not excite and pass through either dampened wax, dried ox-guts, or a moistened silk string.[149]

Often conducting numerous experiments with glass, brass, and iron tubes, Desaguliers defined the qualities and properties of electricity. Electrical bodies were those capable of exciting electricity by either rubbing, patting, hammering, melting, or warming. A non-electrical body could not be transformed into an electrical object by any action imposed on it. However, non-electrics were endowed with the quality of receiving an electrical charge from an electrical per se.[150]

Desaguliers impressed the point upon observers that circumstances should be considered in the production of electricity. If the air was saturated with moist vapors, electrics per se would encounter great difficulty in exciting electricity. In dry weather, electrics per se experienced minimal difficulty in communicating their virtue. By being kept near to or enclosed within other electrical bodies, electrics per se were able to retain their virtue for a long period of time. On contact with non-electrics, electrics per se communicated their charges. On contact, non-electrics received the powers of attraction and repulsion. Once exposed to a non-electric, an electric per se relinquished the power of communicating its excited virtue. On exposure to moisture, electrics per se were transformed into non-electrical bodies.[151]

Desaguliers presented to the society further observations about the characteristics of electrics and non-electrics. Electrics per se inherently possessed the powers of attraction and repulsion. A body, excited by an electric charge, whether an electric or a non-electric, would attract all non-electrics and repel other bodies in a state of electricity. If reduced to a non-electric state, an electric per se might be excessively electric in one part and remain a non-electric in another part. An electric per se gradually relinquished its electric charge, whereas a non-electric, on receiving the electric virtue, lost its charge immediately.[152]

Desaguliers conducted several experiments to demonstrate the principles of attraction and repulsion as related to electricity. Using dry cat gut, an electric per se, he rubbed wax against the gut, thus "electricizing" the former substance. The wax possessed the power as an electric per se of attracting a feather. By touching the feather with his finger, Desaguliers forced the feather to lose its electric virtue. Transformed into a non-electric, the feather was attracted to the wax. Like others, these experiments with the feather and the wax exhibited the characteristics of electrics and non-electrics in relation to the principles of attraction and repulsion.[153] To determine those substances with the capability of conducting electricity, Desaguliers did experiments with rubbed tubes, concluding from his observations that non-electrics received and transmitted as electrical conductors the electricity generated from the tubes.[154]

A splendid review of Desaguliers's electrical observations appeared in "A Dissertation Concerning Electricity," which won the Prize of the Bordeaux Academy in 1742. In this dissertation, Desaguliers first defined succinctly the qualities of electricity: Those bodies endowed with electricity "alternately attract and repel small bodies" on exposure to each other.[155] Desaguliers then distinguished two kinds of electrical bodies: Electrics per se, capable of generating

50

electrical effluvia; and non-electrics, unable to excite electricity but able to receive electrical charges.[156] As in his experiments before the Royal Society, Desaguliers discussed the properties of electrics, non-electrics, and conductors, using rubbed tubes, bee's wax, feathers, brass balls, packthreads, and even a human suspended in air to emphasize the principles of electricity for his readers. Exemplifying his training in the inductive and empirical Baconian and Newtonian tradition, Desaguliers ended the dissertation with experiments about the effects of the mysterious effluvia on sulfur, glass, vapor, and air.[157] His study of the occult effluvia well suggested his earnest attempt and interest to discover in nature the ultimate cause of electrical motion. While failing to formulate a principle governing the cause of effluvia, Desaguliers, from his electrical experiments, exerted immense influence on prominent men of the Enlightenment—the most famous being the young Benjamin Franklin, a man diligently reading the electrical works of Desaguliers.[158]

Conclusion

Desaguliers's work received acclaim from such eminent figures as Voltaire, Franklin, Priestly, Jefferson, and Boerhaave, since his experiments lucidly explained the principles governing the Newtonian system of the world. Adhering to the inductive and empirical methods characteristic of experimental science during the early eighteenth century, Desaguliers demonstrated the validity and applicability of Newton's three laws of motion. This benevolent man, always distinguished by his full face and amiable mannerisms, defined the notions of mass, velocity, attraction, and repulsion to exhibit that matter in nature was constantly in motion. By charting the tides and plotting the movements of the planets and comets, Desaguliers in his experiments skillfully confirmed the law of gravity in relation to the motion of celestial bodies in the solar system. His treatment of the Savery and Newcomen engines, ventilating systems for hospitals and mines, and the "rat's tail crane" reflected the fact that Newtonian laws were being applied to technology in early Hanoverian England to foster industrial expansion and capitalism. Using prisms to experiment with the diffusive rays of the colors of the rainbow, Desaguliers exemplified the laws of refractibility and refrangibility. From his electrical studies, he determined the properties of electrical and non-electrical substances. Desaguliers later offered speculations about the mysterious electrical effluvia, attempting to establish the foundations of the modern science of electricity.

From his experiments with light rays and electricity, Desaguliers, who effectively used London taverns and coffeehouses to promote gentility and sociability, showed that the Newtonian system of the world was encompassing and was related to other realms. His poem, "The Newtonian System of the World, the Best Model of Government," displayed the unlimited possibilities of the application of Newtonian models to the physical and social sciences emerging in Augustan England, in Europe, and across the Atlantic in Colonial America:

> When Majesty diffusive rays imparts
> And kindles Zeal in all the British Hearts
> When all the powers of the Throne we see
> Exerted to maintain our Liberty:
> When Ministers within their Orbits Move,
> Honour their King, and show each other Love:
> When all Distinctions cease, except it be
> Who shall the most excel in loyalty:
> Comets from far, now gladly would return,
> And Pardon'd with more faithful Ardour burn,
> Attraction now in all the Realm is seem,
> To bless the reign of George and Caroline.[159]

Notes

1. Versions of this author's essay have appeared in volume 7 of *Heredom* (1998): 207-49; and in R. William Weisberger. ed., *Freemasonry on Both Sides of the Atlantic: Essays Concerning the Craft in the British Isles, Europe, the United States, and Mexico* (New York: East European Monographs, 2002), 243-75. See also: R. William Weisberger, "John Theophilus Desaguliers: Huguenot, Freemason, and Newtonian Scientist," *Transactions of the Huguenot Society of South Carolina* 90 (1985): 63-67. Recent sketches of Desaguliers appear in Margaret C. Jacob, *The Radical Enlightenment: Pantheists, Freemasons, and Republicans* (London: Allen & Unwin, 1981), 122-25; and in *id.*, *The Cultural Meaning of the Scientific Revolution* (New York: Knopf, 1988), 126-31. Another useful sketch has been written by John Stokes, "Life of John Theophilus Desaguliers," *Ars Quatuor Coronatorum* 38 (Quatuor Coronati Lodge No. 2076, 1925): 285-306.

2. Stokes, 285.

3. *Ibid.*, 286.

4. A.S. Tuberville, *Johnson's England* 1 (Oxford: Clarendon Press, 1933), 208-14.

5. Bernard Faÿ, *Revolution and Freemasonry* (Boston: Little Brown, 1935), 89-92.

6. Stokes, 286.

7. Paul Lang, George *Frederic Handel* (New York: Norton, 1966), 127.

8. Basil Williams, *The Whig Supremacy*, 2nd rev. ed. (Oxford: Clarendon Press, 1962), 150-69.

9. R.J. Mitchell and M.D.R. Leys, *A History of London Life* (Baltimore: Penguin Books, 1963), 210-21; David S. Shields, *Civil Tongues & Polite Letters in British America* (Chapel Hill: University of North Carolina Press, 1997), 52-60.

10. Louis Kronenberger, *Kings and Desperate Men* (New York: Vintage Books, 1942), 83-88.

11. Tuberville 1, 179-82.

12. Frank E. Manuel, *A Portrait of Isaac Newton* (Cambridge: Belknap Press, 1968), 270-76.

13. Faÿ, 94-96.

14. I. Bernard Cohen, *Franklin and Newton: An Inquiry into Speculative Newtonian Experimental Science* (Cambridge: Harvard University Press, 1966), 245.

15. R.T. Gunther, *Early Science in Oxford* 9 (Oxford: Oxford University Press, 1937), 296-97.

16. J.T. Desaguliers, *A Course of Experimental Philosophy* 1 (London: Senex, 1735), i.

17. Williams, 384-86.

18. *Ibid.*

19. Desaguliers, *A Course of Experimental Philosophy* 1, xi.

20. *Ibid.*, i.

21. *Ibid.*, xi.

22. *Ibid.*, xii.

23. *Ibid.*, xii, xiii.
24. *Ibid.*, xiv.
25. *Ibid.*, xv.
26. *Ibid.*, xiv.
27. J.T. Desaguliers, *Lectures of Experimental Philosophy* 1, 2nd ed. (London: Mears, 1719), iv.
28. Desaguliers, *A Course of Experimental Philosophy* 1, xvi-xviii.
29. Desaguliers, *Lectures of Experimental Philosophy* 1, 1.
30. *Ibid.*, 4.
31. *Ibid.*, 5.
32. *Ibid.*, 6.
33. *Ibid.*, 7-12.
34. Desaguliers, *A Course of Experimental Philosophy* 1, 2.
35. *Ibid.*, 4.
36. *Ibid.*, 2.
37. *Ibid.*, 4.
38. *Ibid.*, 10.
39. *Ibid.*, 42.
40. *Ibid.*, 43.
41. *Ibid.*, 42
42. *Ibid.*, 43.
43. *Ibid.*, 48.
44. *Ibid.*, 49.
45. *Ibid.*, 54.
46. *Ibid.*, 65.
47. *Ibid.*, 284.
48. *Ibid.*, 65.
49. *Ibid.*, 300.
50. *Ibid.*, 65.
51. *Ibid.*, 306.
52. *Ibid.*, 305-6.
53. *Ibid.*, 307.
54. *Ibid.*, 308.
55. *Ibid.*, 307.
56. *Ibid.*, 317.
57. *Ibid.*, 307.
58. *Ibid.*, 323.
59. *Ibid.*, 324.
60. *Ibid.*, 327.
61. *Ibid.*, 334.
62. *Ibid.*, 335.-37.
64. *Ibid.*, 348.
65. *Ibid.*, 348-49.
66. *Ibid.*, 349.
67. *Ibid.*, 353.
68. *Ibid.*, 356.

69. *Ibid.*, 353.

70. *Ibid.*, 359.

71. *Ibid.*, 360.

72. Sir Isaac Newton, *Principia* 2, Motte's Translation, Revised by Florian Cajori (Los Angeles: California University Press, 1966), 574-82.

73. *Ibid.*, 594.

74. Desaguliers, *A Course of Experimental Philosophy* 1, 365.

75. *Ibid.*, 366.

76. *Principia* 2, 419-20.

77. *Ibid.*, 549-51, 554-75.

78. J.T. Desaguliers, *A Course of Experimental Philosophy* 2 (London: Senex, 1735), 9.

79. *Ibid.*, 9-10.

80. *Ibid.*, 11.

81. *Ibid.*, 14, 16.

82. *Ibid.*, 16-18.

83. *Ibid.*, 20-21.

84. J.T. Desaguliers, "Some Thoughts Concerning the Cause of Elasticity," *The Abridged Transactions of the Royal Society of London* 41 (1739): 340-46.

85. J.T. Desaguliers, "Experiments to Prove That the Force of Moving Bodies Is Proportionable to Their Velocities," *Transactions Abridged* 32 (1723): 632-37.

86. J.T. Desaguliers, "An Experiment Explaining a Mechanical Paradox," *Transactions Abridged* 37 (1731): 482-84.

87. J.T. Desaguliers, "An Account of Some Experiments to Find How Much the Resistance of the Air Retards Falling Bodies," *Transactions Abridged* 30 (1719): 428-29.

88. J.T. Desaguliers, "An Account of an Experiment to Prove an Interspersed Vacuum," *Transactions Abridged* 30 (1717): 321-22.

89. J.T. Desaguliers, "An Experiment Before the Royal Society to Show That Bodies of the Same Bulk Do Not Contain Equal Quantities of Matter in an Interspersed Vacuum," *Transactions Abridged* 31 (1720): 480-81.

90. J.T. Desaguliers, "The Rise of Vapours, the Formation of Clouds, and the Descent of Rain," *Transactions Abridged* 36 (1729): 323-31.

91. J.T. Desaguliers, "An Attempt to Account for the Rising and Falling of the Water of Some Ponds Near the Sea," *Transactions Abridged* 33 (1724): 39-41.

92. J.T. Desaguliers, "A Dissertation Concerning the Figure of the Earth," *Transactions Abridged* 33 (1724): 61-69.

93. J.T. Desaguliers, "An Account of a Book Entitled Vegetable Statistics,: *Transactions Abridged* 34 (1727): 188-91.

94. Paul Mantoux, *The Industrial Revolution in the Eighteenth Century* (New York: Harper Torch, 1965), 122-26.

95. T.S. Ashton, *The Industrial Revolution, 1760-1830* (London: Oxford University Press, 1968), 25.

96. Mantoux, 216-22.

97. Ashton, 29-30.

98. *Ibid.*, 31.

99. *Ibid.*, 27-28.
100. Desaguliers, *A Course of Experimental Philosophy* 1, 88.
101. *Ibid.*, 163.
102. *Ibid.*, 164.
103. *Ibid.*, 172-173.
104. *Ibid.*, 173.
105. *Ibid.*, 202-5.
106. *Ibid.*, 206-7.
107. *Ibid.*, 208.
108. *Ibid.*, 209-10.
109. *Ibid.*, 210-12.
110. *Ibid.*, 217-20.
111. *Ibid.*, 221-27.
112. Desaguliers, *A Course of Experimental Philosophy* 2, 414.
113. Desaguliers, *A Course of Experimental Philosophy* 1, 221-27.
114. Desaguliers, *A Course of Experimental Philosophy* 2, 414, 415-17.
115. *Ibid.*, 417-18.
116. *Ibid.*, 465.
117. *Ibid.*, 466-67.
118. J.T. Desaguliers, *A Course of Experimental Philosophy* 2, 367-68; Arnold Toynbee, *The Industrial Revolution* (Boston: Beacon Press, 1956), 28.
119. J.T. Desaguliers, "Observations on the Crane with Improvements," *Transactions Abridged* 36 (1729): 369-70.
120. *Ibid.*, 370-74.
121. J.T. Desaguliers, "An Examination of Perault's Axis in Peritrochio," *Transactions Abridged* 36 (1729): 377-79.
122. J.T. Desaguliers, "Remarks on Perpetual Motion," *Transactions Abridged* 31 (1721): 544.
123. Desaguliers, "Perault's Axis:" 377-79.
124. J.T. Desaguliers, "A Description of an Engine to Raise Water by the Help of Quicksilver," *Transactions Abridged* 32 (1722: 550-55.
125. J.T. Desaguliers, "An Account of Experiments Concerning the Running of Water in Pipes," *Transactions Abridged* 34 (1726): 137-40.
126. J.T. Desaguliers, "How Damp or Foul Air May Be Drawn from Mines," *Transactions Abridged* 35 (1727): 208-10.
127. J.T. Desaguliers, "An Account of a Machine for Changing the Air of Sick People," *Transactions Abridged* 39 (1735): 12-13.
128. Stokes, 286-87.
129. J.T. Desaguliers, "A Contrivance for Taking Levels," *Transactions Abridged* 33 (1724): 49-53.
130. Stokes, 287.
131. Stephen Mason, *A History of the Sciences* (New York: Collier Books, 1962), 212.
132. Duane Roller, ed., *Opticks* (New York: Dover Publications, 1952), 2-3.
133. *Ibid.*, 20, 63.
134. *Ibid.*, 132-34, 158, 277.

135. J.T. Desaguliers, "An Account of Some Experiments on Lights and Colors," *Transactions Abridged* 29 (1716): 229-37.

136. J.T. Desaguliers, "Optical Experiments," *Transactions Abridged* 35 (1728): 295.

137. *Ibid.*, 296, 300.

138. J.T. Desaguliers, "Sir Isaac Newton's Doctrine of the Refrangibility of the Rays of Light," *Transactions Abridged* 29 (1716): 229.

139. *Ibid.*, 240-41.

140. Roller, *Opticks*, 340.

141. *Ibid.*, 343, 345-46.

142. *Ibid.*, 350, 352, 376.

143. Cohen, 122-27.

144. *Ibid.*, 213-38, 261-80.

145. *Ibid.*, 249-53.

146. J.T. Desaguliers, "Some Thoughts and Experiments Concerning Electricity," *Transactions Abridged* 41 (1739): 346.

147. Desaguliers,"Refrangibility of Light:" 229.

148. Desaguliers, "Thoughts Concerning Electricity:" 349.

149. *Ibid.*, 350-51.

150. *Ibid.*, 350.

151. *Ibid.*, 355-56.

152. J.T. Desaguliers, "Some Remarks and Experiments Concerning Electricity," *Transactions Abridged* 41 (1740): 470-72.

153. J.T. Desaguliers, "Some Electrical Experiments," *Transactions Abridged* 41 (1740): 472-74.

154. J.T. Desaguliers, "Some Electrical Experiments," *Transactions Abridged* 41 (1741): 479-80.

155. J.T. Desaguliers, *A Course of Experimental Philosophy* 2, 316.

156. *Ibid.*, 317.

157. *Ibid.*, 332-33.

158. Cohen, 345-46.

159. Stokes, 306. On sociability and gentility, see Shields, 31-39.

57

Benjamin Franklin:
The Many Faces of an American Revolutionary

William Pencak
Professor of History,
The Pennsylvania State University

At the age of sixteen, he made his entry on the public stage as an elderly woman, criticizing the pretensions and hypocrisy of Massachusetts' lapsed puritanical elite. At eighty-four, he took his final bow as a North African Muslim, fallaciously arguing for the enslavement of Christians using the arguments offered by pro-slavery advocates in the United States to keep Africans in bondage. In between, he appeared as a "poor" writer of almanacs, a pregnant unmarried woman, a "plain man," the King of Prussia, and in many more guises, including an enigmatic character in his autobiography known as "I." He was the only person in history simultaneously ranked among the finest authors, serious scientists, practical inventors, and political figures of his age. He so effectively hid whatever true self he possessed that, over two centuries after his death, scholars have built careers arguing whether he was a capitalist or a communitarian, a shameless self-promoter or a selfless public servant, a deist or a child of the Puritans, a patriot or (as one serious scholar makes a plausible case) an enemy spy.[1]

Of course "he" is Benjamin Franklin. As preparations are under way to celebrate the three hundredth anniversary of his birth, what more can be said about one of the most "biographied" characters in history? Franklin's fictional personae are the clue to understanding him as the embodiment of the classic figure of Trickster. C. W. Spinks, Professor of English at Trinity University in San Antonio, founder of the on-line journal *Trickster's Way*, author and editor of numerous books on the subject, variously defines Trickster as: ". . . the hero who . . . is used to satirize the conventions of culture." But he grows "from being a buffoon and joker to being a culture hero who will forward the goals of culture or slay the monsters that threaten the culture." Despite his humorous exterior, he "risks all and brings whatever sacred gifts a people use." He accomplishes his task not through the heavy-handed indoctrination of the ideologue, but through the "generation of marginal signs, either as personifying cultural change, or dissolution and growth"; he is "the border creature who plays at the margins of self, symbol, and culture."[2]

The signs Franklin created to play at the margins of society were marginal people (aged women or unwed mothers; "poor" and "plain" men) behaving or arguing sensibly, or authority figures (the King of Prussia or a Muslim aristocrat) acting or ranting tyrannically. He also perpetuated hoaxes that made fun of social prejudices, but whose authenticity continued to be argued after his death. Like the jester-figures from Native American, Australian Aboriginal, Hawaiian, and South American mythology who are more frequently investigated by scholars of Trickster, Franklin is best known not as the great Dr. Franklin, an exalted personage like Washington, Adams, or Jefferson. Instead, we see him as "Ben" (imagine Georgie, Johnnie, or Tommy!), the amorphous embodiment of whatever one wishes to believe (for good or bad) represents America: "The first downright American" for D. H. Lawrence; the "father of all the Yankees" for Thomas Carlyle.[3] Franklin was the man who consciously, in a lifetime of writing and playing the trickster, undertook to represent nearly the entire world of the eighteenth century: Men, women, blacks, whites, and people from different classes and continents. His writings under assumed names offer us rich insights and delightful anecdotes of contemporary life.

It is easy enough to locate the roots of Franklin's populism. Although his father was a reasonably prosperous candle maker in Boston, Ben was his seventeenth child, his mother's seventh. Apprenticed to his brother James, a printer and publisher of the *New England Courant*, America's first anti-establishment newspaper, young Ben became Silence Dogood, an elderly woman, wise but unlearned. He described Harvard College as a temple where wealth, rather than merit, guaranteed admittance to "dunces and blockheads" who graduated "as great blockheads as ever, only more proud and self-conceited ."[4] Franklin chose the name Dogood in honor of Cotton Mather, the Boston minister who had allowed him to borrow books from his large personal library and author of a collection of writings popularly known as *Essays to Do Good.* Yet Franklin was playing the double trickster. Mather wrote and preached incessantly, identifying his pronouncements with those of the Deity. The name "Silence" suggests implicitly that, without his pretentious and argumentative personality, Mather's ideas would have been taken more seriously.

In 1723, writing again in the *Courant* under the pseudonym Timothy Wagstaff, Franklin took on the New England clergy collectively. He condemned preachers who "serve our God . . . with all the dismal solemnities of a gloomy Soul, and a dejected Countenance . . . who upon all Occasions are so apt to condemn their Brethren." Rather, they "should study to know the State of their Flocks in General, and acquit themselves in their office accordingly."[5]

Subsequently, in 1729 in Philadelphia, as the "Busy-Body" in the *American Mercury*, published by his soon-to-be competitor Andrew Bradford, Franklin remarked: "Thou sowre Philosopher! Thou cunning Statesman! Thou art crafty, but far from being Wise." He suggested government officials imitate Cato, the virtuous, simple-living Roman, who was treated with "unfeign'd Respect and warm Good-Will" rather than the "cringing, mean, submissive" deportment of those who flattered the high and mighty. Even in his twenties, Franklin exemplified the optimistic and generous spirit of the American Enlightenment he would ultimately embody.[6]

Franklin did more than criticize Harvard and the dreary clergy. He founded his own educational institutions, the first in America (if not the world) that—as their historian George Boudreau has pointed out—made available to aspiring middle-class men the learning obtainable only in the colonies' three colleges. After he settled permanently in Philadelphia in the 1720s, Franklin founded the Junto, a club where members would discuss philosophical and practical issues, and the Library Company of Philadelphia. Those who purchased a membership in the latter—the money was used to buy the books—would have the borrowing privileges Mather gave the young Franklin. Franklin replaced the traditional classroom setting and juvenile discipline of the colonial colleges with a vigorous symposium attended only by those who craved learning and intelligent conversation. The Library Company persists to this day at Thirteenth and Locust Streets, a statue of Franklin (minus a nose) enclosed within its façade. It contains Franklin's own library and one of the most extensive collections of early American printed matter in the nation: Serious researchers are no longer charged.[7]

In Philadelphia, other women followed in Silence Dogood's footsteps. Martha Careful and Celia Shortface wrote letters protesting that Samuel Keimer—with Franklin and Andrew Bradford one of three printers in the city—had begun publishing a serial encyclopedia that spoke of "abortion" in the first issue. Childbirth in colonial America largely was the realm of midwives, many of whom, such as the German women discussed by historian Renate Wilson and Martha Ballard of Maine, the subject of Laurel Thatcher Ulrich's biography, enjoyed a percentage of healthy births that would still be enviable today. By pretending to know the secrets of this female art and making it available to the "vulgar" in taverns and coffee houses, Keimer left himself open for Franklin's fictional women to threaten to cut off his beard and his ear.[8]

Franklin also produced two of his most famous hoaxes—the witchcraft trial at Mt. Holly, New Jersey, and the story of Polly Baker—to protest mistreatment of women. Colonial witches were found almost exclusively in Puritan New England, the society Franklin found oppressive. In arguing that she ought to be rewarded rather than punished for increasing the population, unwed mother Polly Baker was a riposte to those who criticized Franklin's own common-law marriage and the offspring he himself sired.[9]

60

Franklin was not above taking both sides in the battle of the sexes in letters he wrote to his own *Pennsylvania Gazette* to drum up sales. Having himself sought a dowry from a wealthy father for a woman he did not marry, Franklin arranged for "Anthony Afterwit" to complain that, not only did his father-in-law renege on the promised dowry, but his wife expected to be supported in the genteel manner to which she was accustomed. Calling attention to the numerous "baubles from Britain" historian T.H. Breen has shown were becoming increasingly more desirable and available to colonists in the mid-eighteenth century, Afterwit complained that his wife sought a fancy new looking glass, table, china, silverware, a maid, a horse, and a clock—a very rare and expensive item at the time. In keeping with a nascent upper-class habit, she began to experience imaginary ailments and withdraw from the city in the summer to avoid the heat and humidity. Afterwit planned to solve these problems by getting rid of all these items and putting his wife to work spinning flax. Nevertheless, he offered to restore his wife to her "former way of living . . . if [her] *Dad* will be at the expense of it."

Two weeks later, Afterwit met his match in Celia Single, another Franklin character. She chided men who during courtship promised to treat their wives like gentlewomen only to lack the means once married. As for idleness, Mr. Billiard the pool shooter, Mr. Husselcap the dice player, Mr. Finikin the dandy, Mr. Crownhim the checker-board enthusiast, Mr. T'otherpot "the tavern-haunter, Mr. Bookish the everlasting reader" and others were "mightily diligent at anything besides their business." Their families survived thanks only to the diligence of their wives. Franklin even used Miss Single to satirize himself: She told the printer he ought not to stir up marital disputes by printing articles such as Afterwit's. In this exchange, Franklin not only offered a glimpse of colonial leisure and the contemporary version of the battle between the sexes, but also caught the ambivalence industrious inhabitants felt about the influx of luxury goods, which they both desired yet feared as a threat to a virtuous social order.[11]

Writing in his own *Gazette* again, in 1732 as Alice Addertongue, Franklin criticized the "Ideot Mock-Moralists" who blamed the "enormous" crime of gossiping on the "fair sex." Alice rebutted that judging by the way Pennsylvania's male voters gossiped about their political leaders, one would think that they "chose into all their Offices of Hour and Trust, the veriest Knaves, Fools, and Rascals in the whole Province."[12] In 1733, also in the *Gazette*, Franklin impersonated a "Blackamore, or Molatto Gentleman," who lamented that mulattoes were shunned by both blacks and whites as a prelude to denouncing snobbery of all kinds: "*The true Gentleman*, who is well-known to be such, can take a Walk, or drink a Glass, and converse freely, with honest Men of any Degree below him, without degrading or fearing to degrade himself." Franklin became a "Blackamore" to attack racism and explode the pretensions of the nouveau riche, that "monstrously ridiculous Molatto gentleman," "an unnatural compound of clay and Brass, like the Feet of Nebuchadnezzar's idol." "For my part," the Blackamore/Franklin claimed, "I am an ordinary Mechanick, and I pray I may always have the grace to know my place and Station." When he met people who put on airs, the Blackamore dubbed them "*half Gentry* . . . the Ridicule and Contempt" of both rich and poor, the real "*Molattoes* in *Religion,* in *Politicks.*"[13]

The young Franklin not only transformed himself into a variety of lower-class people, he even did not publish his almanac in his own name, but took on the sobriquet "Poor Richard" Saunders. To show identification with the common man, it was customary for American colonial writers to lower themselves a peg or two on the class hierarchy: John Adams, for instance, first appeared in print as Humphrey Ploughjogger (a derogatory term for farmer) while wealthy lawyer and estate owner John Dickinson penned the famous "Letters from a Pennsylvania Farmer." Few Americans would have known that Franklin was paying tribute to Richard Saunders, one of the finest almanac makers in England, whose work Franklin encountered on his youthful journey to the mother country. In the late 1770s, however, everyone knew that John Paul Jones's warship, "the Bonhomme (Poor) Richard" was both financed and named after Franklin, the almanac writer and minister to France; its guns trained on the coast of a nation that had failed to understand the people he represented in so many ways.[14]

Franklin transformed himself again, into Obadiah Plainman, when he defended the evangelist Rev. George Whitefield on his first visit to Philadelphia in 1740. Whitefield's supporters included Richard Bolton, the owner of the building in which the city's elite Dancing Assembly met—it still holds a formal ball each year. Bolton barred the group—which would not admit tradesmen such as Franklin, regardless of his wealth or social standing—from his premises. The assembly's anonymous apologist responded with a letter to Franklin's *Gazette* on May 8 charging that Whitefield's ministry was false. His language was condescending: The Dancing School rooms were "theirs" (the members') even though Bolton owned the space they merely had rented. The spokesman also condemned Whitefield's "low Craft" in pretending that "he had met with great Success among the better Sort of People in Pennsylvania," who in fact "had both him and his mischievous tenets in the utmost Contempt."[15]

"Obadiah Plainman" responded with a letter that appeared in the *Gazette* on May 15. The pseudonym he chose was significant: It sounded like "Obeyed I A Plain Man." He leveled his cannon at the two words—"BETTER SORT"—that his opponents used to describe themselves. Franklin made sure to capitalize these words whenever Plainman quoted them to mock his opponents' inflated self-opinion. For instance: "*We* take Notice, that you have ranked yourself under the Denomination of the BETTER SORT of People, which is an Expression always made use of in Contradistinction to the *meaner Sort,* i.e. the Mob, or the Rabble . . . Terms of outrageous Reproach, when applied to Us by our enemies . . . Your *Demonsthenes* and *Ciceroes*, your *Sidney*s and *Trenchards* never approached *Us* but with Reverence: *The High and Mighty Mob, the Majesty of the Rabble, the Honour and Dignity of the Populace, Or such like* Terms of Respect."

Franklin here appealed to the canon of English "New Whig" thought, in which ancient statesmen like Greece's Demosthenes and Rome's Cicero took their places as exemplary defenders of popular liberty beside British figures such as the Elizabethans Philip and Algernon Sidney and the contemporary writer John Trenchard. A real elite, worthy to govern, these heroes "never took upon them to make a Difference of Persons, but as they were distinguished by the Virtues and Vices."

In contrast stood those Philadelphians who "usurp'd the title of the BETTER SORT . . . without any previous application to or Consent first had of their Fellow-Citizens." By styling themselves the "better sort," the members had sinned against history, political theory, and a true civility embodied in public spirit and mutual respect rather than private affectation.

To clinch his case, Plainman accused his adversaries of entering public life and placing their case before the reading public yet refusing to play by the rules. The elite had voluntarily forsaken the walled-in spaces of churches, government buildings, and dancing societies to write for the papers, thus ironically making the very "Mob" they condemned into their own "*Judges* of this IMPORTANT Controversy." Franklin put IMPORTANT in capitals to indicate that much was being made of little. Using the same capital letters he did to denote "BETTER SORT," he suggested, literally, that they were falsely elevating themselves. In contrast, Franklin italicized *Us, Mob,* and *Rabble*, a typesetting convention indicating that something was indeed worthy of emphasis, to call attention to the derogatory words the Dancing Assembly's defenders used to describe their critics.[16]

As he won honors for his scientific experiments and praise for his colonial agency, Franklin ceased to be a creator of symbols and became one himself. Fellow almanac maker Nathaniel Ames of Dedham, Massachusetts, whose work sold some 60,000 copies per year in New England, six times the circulation of Franklin's Poor Richard, presented Franklin as proof that America could produce geniuses as well as Europe, even though it had only been settled for a little over a hundred years. In his 1755 almanac, referring to Franklin's famous kite experiment, Ames waxed poetic:

who'ere presum'd, till FRANKLIN led the Way,
To climb the amazing Highth of Heaven,
And rob the Sky of its Tremendous Thunder.[17]

Interestingly, as Tom Tucker has recently argued, Franklin's kite experiment may have been his greatest hoax. The experiment as he described it would have been nearly impossible to survive.[18] This possibility, however, went unnoticed until 2003. At the time, Ames echoed the general consensus that Franklin ranked with Newton as one of the greatest scientists of all time. He had written the last chapter in human intellectual history thus far, permitting new insight into the principles by which the Almighty had structured the cosmos.

Eight years later, Ames recalled Franklin the demographer, who in 1751 had written in his "Observations Concerning the Increase of Mankind . . . " that land in America was so plentiful that "the Farmer may have Land for nothing" in a "territory large enough for a Kingdom." In the last of the Ames, Sr. almanacs, completed in 1764, it was "the Bostonian the Hon. Benjamin Franklin" that Ames praised, claiming Franklin's hometown as the source of his public spirit and intellectual bent, although he had left in 1723 and never returned. Franklin's observations were "justly held in the greatest honor by all the polite and enlightened Nations of Europe." Ames even predicted that a musical instrument Franklin invented, the glass harmonica, a mechanical version of producing sounds on glasses filled to different levels, would "chant forth his honor for generations to come" (although its main function has been providing occasionally ghostly background music).[19]

A major change occurred in Franklin's self-presentation in the year 1748. Previously, his almanacs had praised women and rarely entered the political arena. However, shortly before he retired from the printing business—although he continued to compile Poor Richard's almanac until 1758—Franklin became involved in provincial politics in spite of himself. In his twenties and thirties, his efforts to do good were uncontroversial: Promotion of discussion groups, libraries, fire companies, and street paving. In 1747, however, when defenseless Pennsylvania was threatened by privateers during King George's War, Franklin again turned to the voluntary association. To get around the pacifist Quakers who dominated the assembly, he enrolled those willing to fight in companies of associators. Even this limited effort at defense, however, generated a huge controversy in the press: Quaker spokesmen argued the Almighty had spared Pennsylvania the ravages of war precisely because it refrained from any military activity, and tried to disband the association.[20]

Both Franklin and Poor Richard thereafter turned more and more to the public sphere. The almanac praised the "HERO" of "PUBLICK SPIRIT" (1752) as opposed to the military/dynastic "Hero" who "in horrid grandeur . . . reigns," rulers such as Louis XIV of France and Charles XII of Sweden who ruined their kingdoms through military ambition. The plebeian hero, of course, was none other than Franklin himself.

64

Pencak: BENJAMIN FRANKLIN

Franklin occasionally adopted fictional personae during his years as a diplomat, but with much less frequency. Scholars are familiar with his "Edict of the King of Prussia," where he selected Europe's most despotic monarch to impose fictive regulations on unrepresented Britons in the hope of persuading them not to treat the colonists so arbitrarily. As minister to France, he wore a fur cap rather than the elite powdered wig to suggest the French were allied to an uncorrupted people living close to nature. (Earlier in his career, he made sure his portraits depicted him with a wig and in elegant clothes.) Also, if we are to believe Cecil Currey, Franklin was Code Number 72 or Moses, a double agent for the British secret service who kept them informed of French and American plans during the war. (It is more probable that Franklin, as always, never revealed a "true" self; in a complex world of diplomatic intrigue, he stayed in touch with people from different nations, playing them against each other. If he was pro-British, he certainly fooled his fellow negotiators John Jay and John Adams, who thought he was too submissive to the French.)

Returning to America just short of his eightieth birthday, Franklin was not allowed to rest. He was elected as a Pennsylvania delegate to the Constitutional Convention. Franklin never spoke except when fellow Pennsylvania delegate James Wilson read his speeches. During the hot Philadelphia summer of 1787, the convention kept its doors and windows closed so that people outside would not mistake disagreements over particular points for fundamental divisions over the need for a constitution. Franklin probably dozed off a fair amount. When the disputes awakened him or threatened to become as hot as the room, he had Wilson remind the delegates of their need for unanimity, for if a handful of committed nationalists could not bury their differences, what hope was there for the nation as a whole? Franklin's final plea to the convention contains, as his biographer Walter Isaacson notes, "the most eloquent words Franklin ever wrote—and perhaps the best ever written about the magic of the American system and the spirit that created it."[21] Admitting that, as he grew older, he was more inclined to doubt his own infallibility, Franklin agreed "to this Constitution with all its faults, if they are such, because I think a general government necessary for us, [and] there is no form of government but what may be a blessing to the people if well administered." Predicting that the constitution would last until "the people shall become so corrupted as to need despotic government," he urged the delegates to forget their objections: "Within these walls they were born, and here they shall die."[22]

Not only was Franklin's speech an inspiration to the delegates, it was widely circulated among the American people and played an immeasurable but important role in popular ratification. At the Constitutional Convention, Franklin became the representative of an entire nation that put the common need for a strong central government ahead of their particular interests. Perhaps as many citizens

65

voted against the constitution as for it, and final approval was only obtained after considerable skullduggery by the victors. Yet following Franklin's cue, with the election of Washington as president, the people put aside their doubts and gave the republic a fair chance. Except for the southern secession, they have continued to do so to this day.

Even the convention did not end the octogenarian Franklin's service. He trained his grandson, Benjamin Franklin Bache, to follow in his footsteps as a printer and engaged participant in public life. As editor of the *Philadelphia Aurora* during the 1790s, Bache championed Americans of diverse religions and ethnic groups—such as the Jews, the French, and the Irish—whom the Federalists would have excluded as un-American. On pleasant days, Franklin sat in his front yard with a model of a bridge designed by Thomas Paine to cross the Schuylkill River. Such a bridge was built shortly after his death. The aged Franklin became a spokesman for the nation's commercial and economic development.[23]

In his last work, published less than a month before his death in 1790 and a month after he had personally petitioned congress to abolish slavery, Franklin assumed the identity of Sidi Mehemet Ibrahim, an Algerian potentate, justifying the enslavement of Christians on exactly the same grounds a southern representative had recently used to support African slavery. (To make the argument more telling, at that very moment American sailors were enslaved in North Africa.) Without Christian slaves, the Muslim argued, the economy of North Africa would collapse, since the people there were unsuited to doing heavy work in a hot climate. Furthermore, by living in an Islamic nation, the Christians could be civilized and their souls saved as they could not in the heathen and barbaric lands of Europe and America. "Let us then hear no more of this detestable proposition, the manumission of Christian slaves, the adoption of which would, by depreciating our lands and houses, and thereby depriving so many good citizens of their properties, create universal discontent, and provoke insurrections, to the endangering of government, and reducing general confusion." Franklin closed his public career as president of the Pennsylvania Abolition Society, pleading that "Mankind are all formed by the same Almighty Being, alike objects of his care, and equally destined for the enjoyment of happiness."[24]

Even after his death, Franklin hoped to represent the American people. He left the money he had earned as president of the state of Pennsylvania to the cities of Philadelphia and Boston to educate young tradesmen to duplicate his path to fame and fortune. The Franklin Institute, in Philadelphia, and the Franklin Union (now the Franklin Trade Institute), in Boston, were two fruits of the interest on his bequest after a century. Yet his gifts exposed the problems of passing on his legacy, of reproducing Franklin's success in an increasingly complex society. Just as the University of Pennsylvania became an elite institution, defeating

Franklin's hope—at least until the present age of tuition scholarships—that it would serve to advance lower and middle-class people, the trade schools that opened a century after his death in Philadelphia and Boston provided vocational training that, in the late nineteenth century, educators were urging as the only way immigrants and their children, like African Americans, could attain a limited social mobility while children of the established elite continued to receive the traditional college educations that trained them for political and business leadership.

The fate of most of Franklin's bequests to his own family showed that his rhetoric of patriotism and industry represented one sort of America, but his later life another, less savory, one. To his son, William Franklin, who through his father's efforts had been appointed royal governor of New Jersey and who remained loyal to the British crown, Franklin left some worthless land in British Canada. To his daughter Sally, on the condition that it remained intact, Franklin left a portrait of King Louis XVI framed by 417 diamonds, which the monarch had presented to Franklin. She promptly broke up the frame, sold the jewels, and used the money to travel in high style with her husband in England and reunite with her much-loved brother, William. Sally had been born in 1743, and her father had been absent in Europe from her fourteenth through thirty-second years, except for two years in the early 1760s. Sally thus symbolically and retrospectively sided with her brother and former mother country against Franklin and the French alliance that had facilitated independence. Franklin left most of his property to her husband, Richard Bache, on the condition that he free his slave Bob. Bache did so but, lacking education or opportunity, Bob took to drink, asked to be re-enslaved, and lived out his life as a dependent.[25]

Franklin's heirs, with the exception of his grandson "Benny" Bache, whose brief career—he died of smallpox aged 29 in 1798—placed him among the small minority who carried on the spirit of Franklin's revolution on behalf of the common person, followed the example of his mature life rather than his carefully cultivated image as the common man. Franklin lived twenty-five of the last thirty-three years of his life in Paris and London, enjoying the highlife, company, and praise of the very aristocrats he mocked in his earlier writings. For all his sympathy for ordinary people of whatever race or gender, Franklin remained the quintessential American in that, like the nation he founded, he never confronted the fact that the success he enjoyed was only possible in a society where some workers would always serve masters.

Perhaps this is why Franklin's final, and most puzzling persona, "I," never finished his story. In reading *The Autobiography*, which Franklin began in 1771 and left unfinished at his death, the memorable passages concern the young man who came to town with the loaves of bread under his arms, who strove to be virtuous, and who created various associations to benefit the city of Philadelphia.

Once Franklin retired from printing in 1748 and entered the morally complicated realm of high politics, his story became convoluted, the justice of his causes less clear, and he soon ceased to tell it. That he was too old and ill is one explanation for why he never finished the book.[26] However, I prefer to think that Franklin wanted to be remembered as Ben rather than the man who, in stealing thunder from the skies and the scepter from tyrants, was so effectively seduced by the very aristocratic society and political intrigue he had satirized so effectively earlier on in both word and deed. The eighteenth century brought political liberty to the white men who owned property in France, America, and elsewhere without laying the foundation for a society that enabled all people to own property. Rhetorically, and to some extent by example and financial donations, Franklin tried to expand that class. Like the America that he still personifies, however, these efforts were far too little, and now they are far too late. In theory, we continue to venerate the poor boy who makes good while making it tough for poor girls and boys to follow in Franklin's footsteps. We have put Franklin on the hundred dollar bill, and institutionalized him in mints and institutes to pat ourselves on the back. Franklin is no longer the jester and critic, but the paragon of virtue. We need to bring back Trickster Ben, as he did himself at the last minute, when he became Sidi Mehemet Ibrahim.

Notes

1. For the capitalist, see Peter Baida, *Poor Richard's Legacy: American Business Values from Benjamin Franklin to Donald Trump* (New York: William Morrow, 1990); for the communitarian and public servant, James Campbell, *Recovering Benjamin Franklin: An Exemplary Life of Science and Service* (Chicago: Open Court, 1999); for the self-promoter, D.H. Lawrence, *Studies in Classic American Literature* (New York: Viking, 1951), 19-31; for the deist, Alfred O. Aldridge, *Benjamin Franklin and Nature's God* (Durham, NC: Duke University Press, 1967); for the Puritan, David Levin, *The Puritan in the Enlightenment: Franklin and Edwards* (Chicago: Rand McNally, 1963); for the patriot, Paul W. Conner, *Poor Richard's Politicks: Benjamin Franklin and the New American Order* (London: Oxford University Press, 1965); and for the spy, Cecil B. Currey, *Code Number 72: Benjamin Franklin, Patriot or Spy?* (Englewood Cliffs, NJ: Prentice Hall, 1972).

2. For the journal, see <http://www.trinity.edu/org/tricksters/TrixWay/>; for quotations in this paragraph, see C.W. Spinks, "The Laughter of Signs: Semiosis as Trickster," <http://www.trinity.edu/cspinks/myth/trixsem.html>.

3. Lawrence, 19-31; Esmond Wright, *Franklin of Philadelphia* (Cambridge, MA: Belknap Press of Harvard University, 1986), 7.

Pencak: *Pencak:* BENJAMIN FRANKLIN

4. *New England Courant*, May 14, 1722. Numerous editions of Franklin's writings include a volume in the Library of America, a website (The History Carper), and a complete edition of his papers being edited at Yale University Press. Most writings can be consulted wherever found, but it is important, however, only to use the authoritative edition of the *Autobiography* edited by J.A. Leo Lemay and Paul Zall (New York: Norton, 1986), which shows additions and corrections Franklin made over the last two decades of his life that are a valuable guide to his changing thoughts and conception of himself.

5. *New England Courant*, April 15, 1723.

6. *American Weekly Mercury,* February 18, 1729.

7. George Boudreau, "'Done By A Tradesman': Franklin's Educational Proposals and the Culture of Eighteenth Century Pennsylvania," *Pennsylvania History* 69 (2002): 524-57; *id.*, "'Highly Valuable and Extensively Useful': Community and Readership Among the Eighteenth Century Philadelphia Middling Sort," *Pennsylvania History* 63 (1996): 302-29.

8. *American Weekly Mercury*, February 18, 1729; Renate Wilson, *Pious Traders in Medicine: A German Pharmaceutical Network in Eighteenth Century North America* (University Park: Pennsylvania State Press, 2000); Laurel Ulrich, *A Midwife's Tale: The Life of Martha Ballard, Based on Her Diary, 1785-1812* (New York: Knopf, 1990).

9. *Pennsylvania Gazette*, October 22, 1730; Max Hall, *Benjamin Franklin & Polly Baker: The History of a Literary Deception* (Pittsburgh, PA: University of Pittsburgh Press, 1997).

10. *Pennsylvania Gazette,* July 10, 1732;; T.H. Breen, *The Marketplace o f Revolution: How Consumer Politics Shaped American Independence* (New York: Oxford University Press, 2004).

11. *Pennsylvania Gazette,* July 24, 1732; J.E. Crowley, *This Sheba, Self: The Economic Life of Eighteenth Century America* (Baltimore, MD: Johns Hopkins University Press, 1974).

12. *Pennsylvania Gazette*, September 12, 1732.

13. *Ibid.,* August 20, 1733.

14. William Pencak, "Politics and Ideology in Poor Richard's Almanack," *Pennsylvania Magazine of History and Biography* 116 (1992): 183-211.

15. William Pencak, "Beginning of a Beautiful Friendship: Benjamin Franklin, George Whitefield, the 'Dancing School Blockheads,' and a Defense of the 'Meaner Sort'," *Proteus* 19 (2002): 45-50; John Williams, "The Strange Case of Dr. Franklin and Mr. Whitefield," *Pennsylvania Magazine of History and Biography* 102 (1978): 399-421.

16. *Pennsylvania Gazette,* May 15, 1740.

17. William Pencak, "Nathaniel Ames, Sr., and the Political Culture of New England," *Historical Journal of Massachusetts* 22 (1994): 141-58.

18. Tom Tucker, *Bolt of Fate: Benjamin Franklin and the Electric Kite Hoax* (New York: Public Affairs Press, 2003).

19. Pencak, "Nathaniel Ames, Sr."

69

20. Pencak, "Politics and Ideology in Poor Richard's Almanack."

21. Walter Isaacson, *A Benjamin Franklin Reader* (New York: Simon and Schuster, 2003), 363.

22. William George Carr, *The Oldest Delegate: Benjamin Franklin in the Constitutional Convention* (Newark: University of Delaware Press, 1990).

23. I owe this information to Barbara Oberg, currently editor-in-chief of the Papers of Thomas Jefferson, who presented it in a paper at the Pennsylvania Historical Association annual meeting, October, 2002.

24. *The Federal Gazette*, March 23, 1790.

25. See Isaacson, 380-93, for Franklin's will.

26. For my own attempt to interpret the *Autobiography,* see "Benjamin Franklin's *Autobiography,* Cotton Mather, and a Puritan God," *Pennsylvania History* 51 (1984): 1-25.

George Washington:
Reluctant Rebel and Ardent Nationalist

Richard A. Rutyna
Associate Professor of History, Emeritus
Old Dominion University

Introduction

Almost everyone recognizes the name George Washington, but relatively few (mostly dedicated Washington scholars) really have a very clear understanding of, and appreciation for, the real person. So who was this complex man we call "The Father of Our Country," this man we regard with an iconic reverence accorded few men in United States history? What made him tick?

These certainly are not trivial questions. To attempt an evaluation of the importance of George Washington in United States revolutionary and early national history is a daunting task, particularly at the beginning of the new millennium, more than 200 years after his death. One reason is the simple fact that so much has been written about him. A modern researcher seeking to ascertain just how much is "out there" about him might use a computer as an internet search tool to get at least an imperfect idea. One might execute a Google.com search for the number of "George Washington" pages, for example, and score about 6,210,000 "hits" (on this particular August day). The number of "hits" changes constantly as each new biographer/hagiographer or historian publishes yet another volume or essay (such as this one). Some of those "hits" may even be for some other "George Washington" (such as "Carver") rather than the "Sword of the American Revolution." Even if only half this number of "hits" is for the subject of the search, however, the sheer volume staggers the imagination. Should our inquirer search further, he or she might find that a Yahoo.com search of the web yields no fewer than 10,500,000 "George Washington" pages, with about 2,800,000 of them falling into the category of biography. This great body of writings about Washington complicates the task enormously, as strange as that might seem to some. Those who think it so need to conceive of the situation as being too much of a good thing. In other words, it is not merely a matter of finding *something* about Washington, since that is no problem at all. The problem is winnowing the proverbial wheat from the chaff.

Washington's own writings, being edited afresh at the University of Virginia, in Charlottesville, are a bonanza. One scholar familiar with the work tells us that:

> The project began with a comprehensive search for Washington documents in public and private repositories all over the world. Since then it has amassed a collection of photographic copies of some 135,000 documents, including letters written to and from Washington; his diaries, accounts, school exercises, and miscellaneous personal papers; and reports, returns, and other administrative materials relating to his careers in the military and in politics. The search continues, and the project turns up new documents almost monthly. At the time of [this] writing, the project had transcribed, annotated, and published fifty-two volumes of Washington's papers, with another forty yet to go."[1]

On the downside is the fact that Washington left no autobiography, as did some of his peers such as Thomas Jefferson. Washington thought that would be vainglorious, perhaps, because he had no compunctions about helping others who chose to write biographies about him. Perhaps he simply thought it best to leave the writing of his memorials to posterity. Moreover, while he seemed reluctant to share his "thoughts" with some people, he seems to have been more than willing to share his carefully crafted words with anyone and to allow them to draw their own conclusions as to their merit.

Washington was not formally educated. He never went to college, and he always felt uncomfortable when around often highly educated men of the American Enlightenment. He never learned a foreign language, for example, unlike many of his contemporaries, and was somewhat embarrassed when he had to deal with foreign dignitaries, delegations, and ambassadors. Washington, however, was dedicated to recording his correspondence, whether it had to do with personal matters, such as business, trade, and estate management, or public matters, such as military affairs and politics. He was less conscientious about preserving letters written to him. He knew that his own papers would be important, however, so he had them recorded, kept close at hand, and well preserved. His modern editor, W.W. Abbot, acknowledges that Washington's "appetite for paperwork [was] unrivaled by any Virginian of his generation, perhaps including even Thomas Jefferson." In the management of these matters he had the capable assistance of secretaries such as David Humphreys, Capt. Richard Varick, and Tobias Lear.[2]

Washington wrote that he viewed his papers "as a species of Public property, sacred in my hands."[3] Moreover, Washington knew that his reputation would rise or fall depending, to a very great extent, on the preservation of his recorded words. He believed that his deeds alone would not be sufficient to secure his reputation and the fame he so earnestly pursued. Thus he exhibited what Abbot has called "An Uncommon Awareness of Self."[4] There is nothing ignoble about that. Indeed, like other men of his generation, Washington sought to cover himself with fame and glory for the right reasons: Duty, honor, and country. As Douglass Adair explained some years ago: "Of course they were patriots, of course they were proud to serve their country in her need, but Washington, Adams, Jefferson, and Madison were not entirely disinterested. The pursuit of fame, they had been taught, was a way of transforming egotism and self-aggrandizing impulses into public service; they had been taught that public service nobly (and selfishly) performed was the surest way to build 'lasting monuments' and earn the perpetual remembrance of posterity."[5]

Another reason for any evaluation of George Washington being such a daunting task is that opinions about him have been shifting in recent years. He has always been a man about whom there were differing opinions, and he has had critical detractors from the beginning. The pace of Washington revisionism, however, has quickened in the last decade, and scrutiny of his life has intensified since the 1999 bicentennial of his death.

It has been popular since the end of World War II for key United States historians to rank the nation's presidents according to their own professional evaluations of those men. These rather meaningless occasional polls have traditionally ranked Washington at the top of the list until fairly recently. As the distinguished historian Gordon S. Wood informed us in 1992: "A recent poll of 900 American historians shows that Washington has dropped to third place in presidential greatness behind Lincoln and FDR. Which only goes to show how little American historians know about American history."[6] As for himself, Wood left little doubt as to how he ranked Washington, saying: "Washington was truly a great man and the greatest president we have ever had."[7]

Wood conceded that the whole business of ranking presidents by polls in this manner was "probably pretty silly"[8] but, in saying as much, he discounted the great affection Americans have for playing the polling game. Americans love participating in polls. Casting their vote in polls makes them feel that they are really doing something about something. It is part of the democratic mythology to which they subscribe. It confirms their illusion that they are actually in control of things, actually shaping decisions, policy, and history. After all, is any presidential poll less valid than the quadrennial presidential election in the United States? The United States Constitution makes clear that the Electoral College, and not the people, elect the president of the United States. The former chief justice of the U.S. Supreme Court, William H. Rehnquist, was joined by Associate Justice Antonin Scalia after the 2004 presidential election in reiterating the constitutional reality that the people, in fact, have no *right* to elect the president of the United States.

As if to certify Professor Wood's conclusion that polling people to determine how important George Washington was as president was "probably pretty silly," consider the poll conducted by the cable television Discovery Channel and broadcast on June 26, 2005, which proclaimed that the "Greatest American" *ever* was Ronald Reagan, followed in positions two through four, in order, by Abraham Lincoln, Martin Luther King, Jr., and George Washington. Such polls are, of course, instructive in themselves and may even explain the reasons for which the Founding Fathers created the Electoral College in the first place.

Another reason for Washington's declining popularity in certain quarters has to do with silly questions about the "relevance" of Washington, as well as that of other "dead white men" in the minds of some public school teachers and, as we have just seen, even some American historians. It is as if the merits of our heroes have something to do with race or ethnicity. How retro is that?

This trend suggests that pluralism (as in *E Pluribus Unum*) is no longer relevant or valuable as a cultural goal. The new school mantra is "multiculturalism" *über alles*. As a consequence of this de-emphasis of American history, we increasingly find in the academy a trend toward "balkanization" or fragmentation of society (re-segregation and ethnic tribalism); the teaching of bad history (history being used as a political weapon, the falsification of data, deliberate distortion, and invented tradition); the creation of cultural "norms" that are meaningless to immigrants many generations removed from their distant places of origin; and the dismissal of a history and culture that is the shared common denominator for all Americans of every race, creed, and national origin.[9] This conclusion is given some credence by the fact that college seniors, who might be expected to know something, know little about Washington in particular and their own national history in general, even when we allow for the ethnic, national, and racial diversity in our schools these days, and for the "political correctness" that such engenders.

In 1955 an ordinary freshman in a liberal arts college was required to complete six hours of study in United States history, as well as six hours in European history, by the time that he or she graduated. By the early 1990s such requirements were under heavy attack and alternative studies courses were being substituted as options. Western civilization and culture were downgraded as being of almost minimal significance in a multicultural world, and often portrayed as being essentially evil on top of that. Non-Western cultures were being promoted as inherently superior to those of the West despite some considerable evidence to the contrary in many cases. At the very least, the new multiculturalism proclaimed that any culture was just as good and just as important as any other.

Vice regent of the Mount Vernon Ladies' Association, Mrs. Robert E. Lee IV, in her association's Fall 2004 newsletter essay, "Restoring George Washington to an Honored Place in America," cited the results of "a recent poll of seniors at

74

50 top colleges and universities by the American Council of Trustees and Alumni [reflecting that] *only 32% could identify George Washington as the general who won our freedom at the Battle of Yorktown.* Thirty-six percent thought it was Ulysses S. Grant. Six percent said it was Douglas MacArthur."[10] Some academics refer to findings such as these as evidence of the "dumbing-down" of America. What public school teachers teach is sometimes what they learned as college students. That, in turn, filters down through the public schools, where other community dynamics come into play, engendering revisionism of the sort that relegates a figure like George Washington, a slave-holder during his lifetime, to a rank lower than that of Abraham Lincoln, who was not a slave-holder and who freed some American slaves as a wartime measure in 1863 (which actually was sixty-four years after Washington freed his slaves upon his death).[11]

In some cases, public elementary schools are even being renamed if they bear the name of our first president. "In 1998 New Orleans renamed the George Washington Elementary School because it carried the name of a slave master,"[12] as if that is all the "Father of His Country" ever was. We shall say more about Washington and slavery below.

At present, there is no requirement for any United States history course in many academic degree programs, and as little as three hours may be required in some liberal arts disciplines or degree programs. Arthur M. Schlesinger, Jr., the noted presidential historian, has analyzed this devolution in academic thinking, and the denigration of American history in modern education, in a 1992 study of both cause and effect, entitled: *The Disuniting of America: Reflections on a Multicultural Society.* He says, for example: "The impact of ethnic and racial pressures on our public schools is more troubling. The bonds of national cohesion are sufficiently fragile already. Public education should aim to strengthen those bonds, not to weaken them. If separatist tendencies go on unchecked, the result can only be the fragmentation, resegregation, and tribalization of American life."[13] But whose fault will that really be? Will it be the fault of those who have abandoned the public schools in favor of a "better" education in private academies and parochial schools, or will it be the fault of those who have inherited the abandoned public schools, so that they become demographically more and more homogenous all of the time?

Schlesinger also made another interesting point concerning the burden of public education, saying: "The ethnic upsurge (it can hardly be called a revival because it was unprecedented) began as a gesture of protest against the Anglocentric culture. It became a cult, and today it threatens to become a counter-revolution against the original theory of America as 'one people,' a common culture, a single nation."[14]

It is this last which would most disturb George Washington were he alive today, because Washington firmly believed in, and devoted himself to, achieving that goal for the newly independent nation he struggled so valiantly to establish. "George Washington was a sternly practical man. Yet he believed no less ardently in the doctrine of the 'new race.'"[15]

The Young Man

The Reverend Mr. Lawrence Washington died in England in 1653 after having been removed from his position as an Anglican minister by the Puritans during the civil wars. His sons, John and Lawrence, both immigrated to Virginia to begin new lives. John became a justice of the peace and a member of the House of Burgesses, the lower house of the Virginia General Assembly, and Lawrence likewise became a member of the House of Burgesses. Unfortunately, however, Lawrence died in 1698 at the age of thirty-nine and his widow returned to England and soon remarried. She died not long afterward. Two of Lawrence's sons, Lawrence and Augustine, then returned to Virginia. Augustine, the elder of the two, began to acquire parcels of land throughout the Northern Neck of Virginia (lying between the Potomac and the Rappahannock rivers), which by 1726 totaled about 4,250 acres, including purchases and his wife's property (1,300 acres). When Jane Washington died, he inherited her land in 1729. Two years later he married Mary Ball.[16]

Augustine and Mary Washington had a son, George, on February 22, 1732 (New Style) at what later became Wakefield plantation (also sometimes known as Pope's Creek) in Westmoreland County. Six additional children followed in "rapid succession," one of whom died in infancy (Mildred), leaving Elizabeth (also known as Betty), Samuel, John, Augustine, and Charles.[17] Thus George was born into an upper-class land-owning, gentry family with a substantial legacy of public service, a class that was growing more accustomed to important participation in its own governance, a class roughly equivalent to the yeomanry of England.

Not much is known about George Washington's early years, although it is widely believed that he received some home and outside schooling. It may probably be safely assumed, however, that he was not quite the angelic youth his first hagiographer, the Reverend Mr. Mason Locke Weems (Parson Weems), would have us believe. It was Weems who published the "immortal" cherry tree story in the fifth edition of *The Life of George Washington the Great* (1806).[18] Weems was primarily interested in providing moral role models for the youth of his time, and for giving the new nation heroes worthy of the great nations of the past. He was interested in the story and in the moral lessons to be inculcated, not so much in the facts, and he never let the facts stand in the way of a good story. Additionally, he was a bookseller. Many of George Washington's early biographers took their cues from Weems and set about to deify and mythologize

Washington.[19] That was what the public seemed to want, and that was what it got.

George moved around with his family before settling into Ferry Farm on the Rappahannock River near Fredericksburg in 1738. Over the next five to eight years his half-brother Lawrence entered George's life in a very meaningful way. After Lawrence returned from school in England, a well-educated and "worldly" young man fourteen years George's senior, the younger Washington developed a great respect for him. Lawrence had a genuine affection for his younger brother and soon came to have an enormous influence over the awe-struck youngster. They became close friends. The older brother also served as a captain in the Virginia volunteer regiment that took part in the disastrous 1741 Cartagena Expedition in Colombia led by British Admiral Edward Vernon. The deadly rout of British-American forces in that affair was blamed by Virginians on the ineptitude of the British officers leading the expedition, and most of the Americans who survived the fiasco— as did Lawrence Washington— came through it with unblemished reputations. Lawrence then retired from the navy.[20] He lived with the family at Hunting Creek, which Augustine, Sr., had "seated" in 1735 before moving on to Ferry Farm and giving the Hunting Creek estate to Lawrence. Lawrence built a respectable Georgian mansion there that he named Mount Vernon, in honor of Admiral Edward Vernon, for whom he had high personal regard. For his part, George viewed his brother as a hero, and the governor and Executive Council of Virginia, who appointed Lawrence adjutant general of Virginia in 1743,[21] also obviously looked on him with favor.

Other events of 1743 were even more momentous for the Washingtons. Augustine (Gus), in the prime of his life, got caught in a sudden rainstorm while out riding about his property, took a bad chill, and unexpectedly died on April 12, 1743. George, who was eleven years old, was thrust into a new role with new responsibilities. Augustine's holdings at the time of his death were substantial. In addition to about fifty slaves, he also owned "something over ten thousand acres, as enumerated in his will."[22] Mount Vernon went to Lawrence, Pope's Creek went to Austin (Augustine, Jr.), and Ferry Farm went to George, as had been planned, though George had not yet come of age. He therefore remained at Ferry Farm with his mother. There he developed, if he did not flourish, under the watchful supervision of his mother, whose influence over him was no doubt greater than he would have liked, though not as great as she might have hoped. George had a lot of growing-up to do very fast. His informal training progressed, though he "was not highly educated, and never became what might be called an intellectual . . ." and although "he managed to express himself on paper with a degree of clarity and force, through long practice, and his spelling likewise improved . . . he was never a brilliant writer."[23]

George did not achieve the "felicity of expression" that Jefferson did in his writings, nor did he ever achieve the eloquence in oratory of, say, Patrick Henry or even Alexander Hamilton. Indeed, he was taciturn and noted for the *gravitas* of a serious and aloof individual. He did, however, refine his gentry skills, becoming an estate manager "trainee," a capable marksman, and an excellent horseman (many contemporaries expressed the opinion that he "sat" a horse very well, and was as fine a horseman as any).[24] In short, even as a youngster, he cut a very fine figure as a "man on horseback." These skills distinguished young Washington as a future leader of men, which grew even more so as he developed into an imposing and attractive young man.

Lawrence married about two months after his father's death, taking as his bride Anne Fairfax, the daughter of the eminent and wealthy Colonel William Fairfax of "Belvoir," a property lying very near Mount Vernon. This marital connection to the Fairfax family was one that would benefit the Washingtons, and perhaps George in particular, by providing great opportunities and advantages. George spent as much time as he could with Lawrence at Mount Vernon, partly no doubt because he loved Lawrence not only as a brother but also as a surrogate father, and partly because he delighted in the company of the Fairfaxes.[25]

Washington specialists and historians generally agree that George had very little affection for his mother, Mary Ball Washington, and that life must have been "difficult" for him at Ferry Farm. His mother has been described as domineering, obstinate, narrow, possessive, and an unimaginative harridan, among other unflattering things. George "respected" her but gradually came to resent her very much, though he did build a home for her close to that of her daughter, Betty, near Fredericksburg, and saw to it that she was provided for as befit her station in life and his filial responsibility toward her. It is quite interesting to note, however, that she remained a British Loyalist throughout her life and never embraced the American Revolution that her son led. One may only guess, then, what the early relationship between mother and young son must have been like, and it should surprise no one that, as soon as he was able to, in 1746 George left Ferry Farm to go to Mount Vernon and live with Lawrence and his family.[26]

Psycho-historians have made a great deal of young George's loss of his father at such a tender age and the influence that his mother attempted to exert over him, but the most balanced appraisal of that situation probably is that offered by historian Edward G. Lengel: "George Washington's devoted and strong-willed mother played an important role in his development as a child and young man, overseeing the family estates after her husband Augustine's death and managing her children's education. George came to resent his mother's influence in his life, however, and after the French and Indian War their relationship gradually grew more distant."[27]

According to Lengel, Washington was thinking about running away from home to join the navy in 1746, apparently at the instigation of his brother Lawrence and with his active encouragement.[28] George's mother would have none of that, however, and enlisted the support of Joseph Ball, her half-brother in England, to dissuade young George from this "cockeyed" scheme. So George deferred to his mother, for what was probably not the first time, and did the next best thing. He "ran away" to be with Lawrence at Mount Vernon. George then was about fifteen years of age.

By that time, George had already begun to take his life into his own hands, at least to the extent that he could as a "minor" with a patrimony of some value. At an earlier date, perhaps when he was as young as thirteen, George had already given some thought to the kind of man he wanted to be and conscientiously began to mold and to craft that persona. It was clear that he would become a landowner and big-time "farmer," but was that all? Politics was a tradition in his family. Lawrence had been elected to the House of Burgesses in 1744, as other family members had been before him, so that was one possibility. Something else, however, appealed to George even more, and that was service in the military; if not in the navy then in the British army. "In all he did, young Washington shaped himself to the pattern prescribed by his culture."[29]

For his own self-study and improvement, George copied-out for himself a collection of 110 maxims known as the "Rules of Civility and Decent Behaviour in Company and Conversation." They were not original with George and, indeed, may have been used originally by Jesuit schoolmasters. Most were simply common sense rules of civilized behavior, but just the kind of guides that a rustic young man with little formal schooling might put to good use in his plan to develop a strong character, polish his social skills, establish an honorable name, and create a reputation worthy of praise.[30]

It cannot have taken George long to calculate what he must do to achieve his objectives. He had to identify himself with as many of the ruling elites of society as he could—the landed gentry, the religious establishment, the provincial aristocracy, the royal authorities, the political leadership, and the military—and he must win their acceptance and respect. He was born into the landed gentry and would become one of the exemplary members of that class. He was likewise born into the established Anglican church in Virginia. His friendship with the members of the Fairfax family, including Lord Fairfax, established solid aristocratic connections. At age fifteen he was well on his way.

By the time he was sixteen, George was working as a professional surveyor-in-training for the Fairfaxes. William Fairfax gave George his first employment, which was to accompany and assist his son, George William Fairfax, Washington's good friend, in surveying the Fairfax properties in the Northern Neck and Shenandoah Valley. The young Washington kept a journal of the 1748 expedition, which lasted from March 11 until April 13.[31]

Washington wrote very business-like letters to his brother Lawrence in 1749 discussing estate matters with him.[32] This was all heady stuff for a lad his age, even considering the precocity of youth in that enlightened period, but the health of his brother had not improved and everyone, no doubt, realized that George's role in family affairs might soon be increasing. Not long after his return from the expedition across the mountains, while he was still seventeen, George was given the position as surveyor of Culpeper County, thanks to the influence of the Fairfax family. The historian Edward G. Lengel has said of this particular matter that Washington's "appointment was a blatant act of patronage [in deference to the Fairfaxes]. Any other young man his age could only have hoped for an assistantship, at best."[33]

The point Lengel makes is an interesting and important one that requires some elucidation because the world George Washington lived in was not the same as today's. That world had different standards and rules. To be sure, they were in transition during the Enlightenment, but they had not yet become settled principles, and for that reason we may not judge them as though we understand them, because then we would be guilty of "presentism," that is, of projecting back on to those who could not know the future, the values of the future. Democracy, for example, certainly did not mean the same thing to the people of that world that it means to those living in the present generation. Likewise, meritocracy was an idea whose time had not yet come. Washington lived in a world in which various elites wielded influence and others usually simply deferred to them, as many eighteenth-century voting records show.[34]

Washington would have been the first to acknowledge that he had deficiencies, but virtually everyone who has ever written about him agrees that character and integrity were his hallmarks. The people who knew him best, those whose lives were encompassed by his world as well, recognized that he had those qualities.[35]

In any event, Washington went about his business as surveyor for Culpeper County. When he showed disdain for the ordinary routine of that position, William Fairfax offered to send him wherever he wanted to go, and George chose to go to the southern Shenandoah Valley. He had fallen in love with the wilderness and the frontier in 1748, and this new experience stimulated his own intense yearning to acquire land. He spent some of his earnings for land in 1750 when he purchased 1,459 acres in a plot "on Bullskin Creek in the lower Shenandoah." He was then eighteen, and that was his first purchase of land.[36] "The price of membership in the small club of Virginia's prestigious families was *land*. Mere money 'will melt like Snow before a hot Sun,' Washington would later write, explaining that 'lands [alone] are permanent, rising fast in value.'"[37]

In the autumn of 1751, Lawrence decided to go to Barbados for his health and asked that George join him.[38] George kept a journal of their sojourn in

Barbados from the time of their departure (September 28, 1751) until George returned to Virginia (March 4, 1752). Sending George home, Lawrence had gone on to Bermuda in pursuit of a better climate for his tuberculosis.[39] The diary contains few important details, save for oblique statements reflecting the state of medicine in that period. Lawrence got no better, though he was given cause by a doctor there to believe that he could be cured, so he went on to Bermuda and, after a brief stay, returned to Mount Vernon in 1752. For his part, George reported being "strongly attacked with the small Pox" (November 17 through December 12) and complained of seasickness, which suggests that his choice of the army over the navy may well have been inspired.[40]

Shortly after his return to Mount Vernon, Lawrence Washington died on July 26, 1752. His 2,500-acre plantation at Mount Vernon became "part of the estate that [George] Washington eventually inherited."[41] Lawrence's death also left vacant the position of adjutant general of Virginia's militia forces. George promptly applied for the position and was made adjutant for the Southern District, which included the counties of Princess Anne, Norfolk, Nansemond, Isle of Wight, Southampton, Surry, Brunswick, Prince George, Dinwiddie, Chesterfield, Amelia, and Cumberland.[42] Joseph J. Ellis, one of Washington's modern biographers, comments that: "He [Washington] had no military experience whatsoever, and, apart from being an impressive physical specimen, [had] no qualifications for the job." Once again, it was William Fairfax who intervened on behalf of young George; this time with Royal Governor Robert Dinwiddie, vouching that George "was up to the task." Dinwiddie agreed. Washington took the position, and rank of major, at age twenty, stating that "my best endeavors will not be wanting."[43] Historian James T. Flexner is not so sure, saying of Washington's pursuit of the office that: "He went after it in the Fairfax manner; not by becoming proficient in military matters, but by paying semi-social calls on influential members of the government. Thus following the mores of an aristocratic world, he secured, at the age of twenty, the title of major and the responsibility of training militia in skills he did not himself possess."[44] Washington was not happy with his assignment to the Southern District, however, and in February 1753 requested that he be transferred to the Northern Neck (which was his home territory) and Eastern Shore. His request was granted in November of that year.[45] Flexner concludes his commentary on this issue by saying: "Hardly anyone could have sounded more insignificant if mentioned in the chancelleries of Europe. Yet in his obscure forests Washington was soon to fire the first shots in what became a world war."[46]

On November 4 that same year (1752), Washington became a freemason in Lodge No. 4, in Fredericksburg, becoming a master mason on August 4, 1753.[47] A cynic might suggest that this was just one of Washington's ploys to forge a link with another group of elites, and one might be able to make that case. The evidence suggests, however, that he was a keen mason throughout his life, though not always a frequent lodge attendee for obvious reasons. When the Grand Lodge of Virginia was established in 1777-78, the membership wanted Washington to become the first grand master, but he declined because of his duties in the War of the Revolution. He was never grand master, but in 1788 he did become charter master of Alexandria Lodge No. 22 after the war.[48]

Someone other than a cynic might find it easier to believe that George became a freemason to become a better man and to continue his personal quest for disciplined self-improvement. The goal of freemasonry was, after all, to make good men better. In this case, his becoming a freemason was no less than a logical extension of his childhood ambition to master the "Rules of Civility and Decent Behaviour."

In 1749, both Lawrence and Austin Washington became members of the very important land development company known as the Ohio Company, as did many of their peers.[49] In late October 1753, Governor Dinwiddie, who took control of the company in 1752, dispatched Washington to the Ohio River Valley, "then one of the most sensitive boundary regions in the world," to ascertain exactly what it was the French were up to in the area, particularly with regard to the Indians and Virginia interests.[50] Washington very quickly set out for the area around present-day Pittsburgh, engaging along the way Jacob Van Braam, a Dutchman, to act as interpreter, and Christopher Gist, who also knew some French, to serve as guide or pilot.[51]

Washington spent most of his time during the next five years (1754-59) "leading a series of expeditions into the Ohio Country that served as crash courses in the art of soldiering."[52] That was to prove one of the most difficult and critical periods in the young man's life.

The Young Soldier

At this point, one might well ask: "How did he do it?" What was the secret of his success in advancing so far so fast? Influential friends is certainly one answer, as we have seen. Another lies in the fact that he had self-evident stature. That is to say, at age twenty-one Washington was a "buff" young man, much more attractive, to both women and men, than the figure we are accustomed to seeing on one-dollar bills. Virginius Dabney, the historian, speaks of his "statuesque grandeur."[53]

Joseph J. Ellis, perhaps Washington's most acclaimed modern biographer, says of him that: "He was the epitome of the man's man: physically strong, mentally enigmatic [and] emotionally restrained." He describes Washington as being very tall (he was sometimes referred to as a giant), at least 6'2" in height, with an athlete's trim body, and weighing about 175 pounds. He was well-muscled, with strong thighs and legs (which made his horsemanship easier and more elegant) and big hands and feet; but coordinated, with a natural grace of movement. Washington had widely set gray-blue eyes and hazel brown hair, usually tied in a que in back.[54] These attributes, as well as his known strength of character, his aloofness,[55] and a certain élan with which he carried himself, combined to give him the appearance of a natural leader of the strong, silent type. In a single word, he had charisma. People felt that if he was not eloquent in learning or in speech, he was like most of them, and he more than made up for any inadequacy in those regards with a most elegant appearance, especially in uniform.

Washington's charisma did not translate into diplomatic or language skills in the Ohio territory, however, and he would have been better served there if he had more skill in those, as well as the military, arts. His first major parley with the Indians took place at Logstown, where he made a speech and met the Iroquois leader whom the British called the Half-Chief.[56] James T. Flexner says of this occasion: "The greenhorn [whom he also calls a "tenderfoot"] now tried his hand at the exquisite art of Indian diplomacy: he proceeded brashly and made a fool of himself."[57] After this, Washington pushed on to Fort Le Boeuf, where he planned to deliver Dinwiddie's ultimatum to the French to vacate the premises. The French commander treated Dinwiddie's ultimatum with contempt and vowed that the French would keep and settle the Ohio River Valley.[58] Washington reported to Dinwiddie of this experience: "I can't say that ever in my Life I suffered so much Anxiety as I did in this Affair."[59] The next day he set out for Williamsburg to report to Governor Dinwiddie.

Washington reported to the governor in the capital on January 16, 1754. In March, Dinwiddie sent Washington, a lieutenant colonel, back to the Ohio as second-in-command to Colonel Joshua Fry, who led a regiment of volunteers numbering about three hundred. The governor had given up on using the militia, especially after Washington, the militia adjutant in the Northern District, had been unable to raise any troops there. With what one author calls "disingenuous modesty,"[60] George asked to be named second to Fry because he did not think himself qualified to act as principal commander due to his own inexperience in combat warfare. Washington set out ahead of Fry, who was supposed to rendezvous with him later, but Fry took longer than expected and Washington soon found his force overextended with only 186 men on the frontier. At that point, he made a clumsy mistake when, joined by some of his officers, he complained to the governor about being underpaid. Dinwiddie was not at all happy about the complaints or their timing.[61]

While awaiting some response or redress, Washington pushed on, seeking to protect a small work force that had been sent ahead by Dinwiddie to erect a fort at the forks of the Ohio. Meanwhile, the French had taken over the site and

PROFILES OF REVOLUTIONARIES

erected Fort Duquesne. When he was told by some of his Indian allies that the French were maneuvering nearby, Washington planned a surprise attack on the French encampment. No thanks to interpreter John Davidson, Washington apparently thought he was about to be attacked by the French. According to Edward G. Lengel, "Washington *wanted* a fight." The French Ensign Joseph Coulon de Villiers, Sieur de Jumonville, had been ordered by his superior to lead a small detachment to Great Meadows to chase the British away.[62]

At about seven o'clock on the morning of May 28, 1754, after watching the French encampment all night, Washington and his Indian allies fell on the French and, in a battle that lasted about fifteen minutes, killed Jumonville and nine others, wounded one, and took twenty-one prisoners. "Jumonville's men never had a chance."[63] With what must have been almost his last breath before dying, Jumonville asked Washington to take from him and examine some papers he had clutched in his hand. What Washington saw were papers that "offered evidence that he [Washington] had just massacred a diplomatic mission." Jumonville "insisted that Washington had made a terrible mistake" and died. The French fanned the international diplomatic furor that followed.[64] For his part, George insisted he had done nothing wrong.

To make matters worse, when Washington was compelled to surrender the hastily built Fort Necessity, "an exercise in pure inexperience," after losing about 100 of his men to death and wounds, it was to Coulon de Villiers, the very brother of the slain Sieur de Jumonville. Jacob van Braam, Washington's interpreter, returned from negotiating with Villiers apparently quite pleased with himself. The Virginians would all be allowed to return to their homes after Washington signed a parole document on July 4, 1754. Exactly who knew what the document said is warmly debated. Whether he knew it or not, however, Washington signed a statement that got the French off the hook, and put George on it, by acknowledging that the French had acted righteously in avenging the "assassination" of Jumonville. In effect, Washington confessed to murdering the French diplomat who was merely on his way to parley with the Virginians.[65] Washington drew a good deal of criticism abroad for his conduct at Great Meadows, but not from his fellow Virginians. At home, he was hailed as a conquering hero, and anticipated that he would be given a promotion as a regular in the British army. When he was told that no provincial officers would be integrated into the British army at a rank higher than captain, George was very disappointed and grew bitter about the distinctions being drawn between metropolitans and colonials.[66] Governor Dinwiddie wrote to the secretary of state in October 1754 urging that such a policy be implemented to resolve what he saw as a problem with provincial officers outranking regular army officers who held their commissions from the king. The problem, of course, was that regular British officers did not want to take orders from provincials of higher rank, whom the British thought of as inferiors. Feeling humiliated, Washington resigned from the army because his First Virginia Regiment was to be broken up rather than incorporated into the British army.[67]

Paul K. Longmore says that the proximate issue surrounding the event that precipitated the entire *L'affaire de Jumonville,* which culminated in Washington's resignation, was not that he had killed Jumonville, because "the Jumonville incident simply provided a justification for what would have happened anyway. George's error was that he precipitated the fighting before Virginia was ready."[68] There can be little doubt, however, that these developments crushed George's spirit. He had long striven to excel so as to "win the regard of others" and had sought to "find a means to greater glory."[69] He knew from his youth that he had an inclination for the military, and that the army (he hoped the regular British army) would be the means of his success. If that possibility was not now utterly impossible, it certainly had become much less likely. He wrote to his young brother, John Augustine, from Great Meadows on May 31, 1754: "I fortunately escaped without any wound, for the right wing, where I stood, was exposed to and received all the enemy's fire, and it was the part where the man was killed, and the rest wounded. I heard the bullets whistle, and, believe me, there is something charming in the sound."[70] Was this mere bravado, or hubris? For George it was much more—"It was an issue of honor, public recognition of his merit."[71]

The late political scientist Clinton Rossiter ascribed the following quotation to John Adams writing in 1818: "But what do we mean by the American Revolution? Do we mean the American war? The Revolution was effected before the war commenced. The Revolution was in the minds and hearts of the people . . . This radical change in the principles, opinions, sentiments, and affections of the people, was the real American Revolution."[72] What Adams was saying, simply, is that the American Revolution was a thing of the mind, first and foremost. That was certainly true for George Washington, and it was with his resignation that his opinions, sentiments, and affections began to change. He went back to Mount Vernon in December.

Over the next several years, George performed his duty to Westmoreland and the Northern Neck ("his country") to the best of his ability. There was a war coming. It had already begun at Great Meadows (as what Americans would call the French and Indian War) and would soon erupt into a world war between the British and the French in what the rest of the world would call the Seven Years' War. It would be a "Great Struggle for Empire" that would not end until the 1763 Treaty of Paris.

Renting Mount Vernon from Lawrence's widow, Anne, George resumed the life of a citizen-soldier. In March 1755, he met General Edward Braddock in Alexandria as the latter was passing through to Fort Duquesne, and agreed to serve as Braddock's aide on a volunteer basis. George knew from conversations with him that Braddock was not inclined to take his advice, even though George knew more about Indians and the Virginia frontier than any available British regular. As Braddock advanced, Washington fell back because of illness, but caught up to the main body by July 8, 1755, when Indians attacked Braddock's forces. The British, who declined Washington's advice about how to fight them, broke in panic and hysteria as the British bodies piled up. George's horse was shot out from under him twice and a number of bullets passed through his clothing. He believed that the hand of Divine Providence protected him, and others were beginning to believe it as well. A certain mystique began to develop around him. Braddock died of wounds suffered in the battle, the surviving British forces made for Philadelphia, and Washington struggled to get back to Mount Vernon.[73]

Braddock's defeat was a disaster for the British, but the Virginians hailed Washington as the hero in the debacle because the British had not taken his advice. Thus George became a continental hero, whose reputation now spread beyond the borders of Virginia. The area west of Virginia was abandoned by the British, though Washington was ordered to defend Fort Cumberland against Indian attack for two years. At age twenty-two he was "elected Colonel of the Virginia Regiment and Commander in Chief of all Virginia forces."[74]

The next few years must have been miserable for Washington. The Virginians were not very enthusiastic about the war to begin with and the militia could not do an effective job with the little they had. There was almost constant tension and quarreling between the Virginians and, first, the Maryland regulars, and, then, the Virginia governor and assembly. In the autumn, George was back at Mount Vernon; ill again with the same malady that had befallen him earlier, and it was March 1758 before he returned to the capital from Mount Vernon, where he was convalescing.[75] He next had a strong disagreement with the high command (Brigadier General John Forbes) that, according to James T. Flexner, "rose in his [George's] mind to an obsession," with Washington protesting "loudly concerning matters he did not understand." It was about a road into Pennsylvania, and George lacked perspective regarding the grand strategy of the war that had finally broken out between England and France in June 1756. Flexner again, states that "Forbes had every reason to dislike Washington" and "yet he could not deny that the Virginian was the army's greatest expert on the wilderness and its warfare." Washington was raised to the rank of temporary brigadier general,[76] but he must certainly have known that his hoped-for career in the British army was over.

Washington got a big break, however, when he encamped his men near Fort Duquesne on November 24, 1758. The French, for very good reasons of their own, had abandoned the fort under pressure from Brigadier General Forbes and moved down the Ohio River. George was astonished when the burning fort was taken without a shot being fired. He had taken part in a great victory as second-in-command. The frontier was now secured, "his duty was done," and he resigned and returned to Mount Vernon, hoping to spend the rest of his life as a civilian, plantation owner, and politician.[77]

For the American colonists, the war was over by 1760. William Pitt became the prime minister of Great Britain in 1757 and devised a new strategy to wage the war by making America the main theater, and to win it by launching an aggressive and daring series of campaigns against the main French fortifications. This was the grand strategy that Washington was not completely aware of when he challenged the planning and skill of Brigadier General John Forbes, who was to lead one of three major attacks in 1758, in his case against Fort Duquesne. Ticonderoga and Louisbourg were the other targets. Only the Ticonderoga force of almost 15,000 men, about half of whom were Americans, failed. The plan for 1759 was for three more complex campaigns, first against Fort Niagara, then from the Lake George region against Quebec, and finally against Quebec, by sea and by land, from the Saint Lawrence River. The brilliant but moody British Brigadier General James Wolfe sailed into the Gulf of Saint Lawrence in June 1759 to launch what was to be the decisive battle of the war, the battle on the Plains of Abraham, September 13, 1759. Quebec fell to Wolfe's brilliant tactics on September 18, 1759, and Montreal was surrendered, with the rest of Canada, on September 8, 1760.[78]

The Politician

George had grown to manhood around politicians and had dealt with them during his tenure in the military. He came to understand that it was in the political arena where real influence reposed, and if that was where "the action" was, then that was where he wanted to be. If one door had closed to him, another had opened. Joseph J. Ellis gives him too much credit, perhaps, when he says that: "His abiding respect for civilian authority, most especially his insistence on strict obedience to the principle of civilian control over the military, eventually became one of his greatest legacies."[79] "Eventually" may be the key word here, because Washington was never one to suffer criticism lightly, and was also not one to tolerate disagreement with his view. Indeed, as Ellis pointed out: " . . . the truth was that he [Washington] had come to feel superior to his superiors, just as he had come to regard his Virginia Regiment as perhaps the finest fighting unit in North America."[80]

Washington was not an easy man to work with. Among his many sterling character traits were some that did not endear him to superiors, or even his peers. He could be charming and gracious, and was a man of character and integrity, but he was often honest and forthright to a fault, aloof, quick to anger, slow to forgive, convinced of his own convictions, and stubborn. In this regard he was very much like his dowager mother. Whenever he did not get his way, he was inclined to quickly write to his friends and authorities in high places to use their influence to bend the will of his opponents more to his favor. Some of the letters among his writings illustrate this. In the eighteenth century, politics could be rough and tumble, and the "flaws" in Washington's personality were not necessarily disabilities.

For the most part, however, Washington did the right things to become a political leader of Virginia. While he was still on campaign with Braddock in 1755, he wrote to his younger brother, John Augustine ("Jack"), and asked him to assay George's chances of being elected to the House of Burgesses. His backers must have thought his chances at least reasonable and put his name forward. He lost that first election in 1755, but he was not about to give up.[81] He ran again (July 24,1758) and won election to a seat in the House of Burgesses, in Frederick County in the Valley, even though he was away serving at Fort Cumberland. It was an expensive campaign, with his friends expending an extravagant if not scandalous sum in "treating" the voters with food, wine, strong beer, and rum, as was the custom in that day. The bill came to £ 39.6s.[82] George was re-elected to the House of Burgesses in 1761, and elected to the House from Fairfax County, in 1765, 1768, 1769, 1771, and 1774.[83]

Washington also tended to his obligations with regard to the Anglican church of Virginia. It was the state church, the established church, both in England and in Virginia until 1786. Performing service to the church was yet another way to establish connections with the colonial elites and was expected of the gentry and rising prospective colonial leaders. George believed in God more than he believed in religion, but he did serve as a church vestryman and a churchwarden at Pohick Church, in Truro Parish,[84] and did attend services elsewhere on occasion, particularly when in transit. When he spoke or wrote about God, Washington always (certainly almost always) used euphemisms, so as to avoid using what he perhaps thought of as the name "God." His clear preference was to use such impersonal terms as Providence, Supreme Being, Architect of the Universe, Creator, and Destiny, among others. He preferred to stand rather than kneel when he prayed, for reasons that are not clear, and "he *never* took Communion," according to Ellis,[85] though precisely how the historian knows that for a certainty is not clear to this writer. Washington was clearly influenced by Enlightenment Deism in his thinking.

Bishop William Meade of Virginia quotes Chief Justice John Marshall as saying of Washington that: "He was a sincere believer in the Christian faith, and a truly devout man."[86] Yet there seems to be no mention of Jesus in his writings. At any rate, he was an Anglican-Episcopal rationalist and not an evangelical. Again, Meade states that George Washington even attended Quaker, Presbyterian, and Roman Catholic services at least once each, while attending Anglican-

Episcopal services more often.[87] He also says that George was "*pious*, just, humane, temperate, and sincere."[88] Meade "inferred" from some of his other actions that Washington was, in fact, a communicant, but offers no direct proof, and does point to the fact that, while he was a delegate in Philadelphia, he did not commune. Meade also relates the story that "in Philadelphia, General Washington was, with his family, a regular attendant at one of the churches under the care of Bishop White and his associates. On Communion-days, when the congregation was dismissed, (except the portion which communed), the General left the church, until a certain Sabbath on which Dr. Abercrombie, in his sermon spoke of the impropriety of turning our backs on the Lord's table—that is, neglecting to commune—from which time . . . Washington came no more on Communion-days."[89] Washington was notable for his toleration of all religious faiths, which meant more than simply acknowledging them from a position of presumed superiority.[90]

Governor Francis Fauquier appointed George a justice of the peace on the Fairfax County court in 1760. The justices of the peace, perhaps as many as a dozen of them, were, with the militia and the vestrymen, the key personnel in county government at that time. The county court functioned in executive, legislative, and judicial capacities, with a broad range of authority over county maintenance and criminal as well as civil matters to come before the court. They also served as overseers of the poor, which is to say that they were charged with what moderns might call social welfare responsibilities as well as tax issues.[91]

This was the way Virginia political leaders were groomed for higher office.[92] George sought to rise higher by "earning" his way up to the House of Burgesses, which most (gentry) "gentlemen" thought of as the highest civilian level to which most of them might reasonably aspire. The pinnacle, the executive council, was "reserved" for the high and the mighty, such as the Fairfaxes and their peers.[93] The House of Burgesses, like the British House of Commons, was the usual preserve of the lesser gentry.

This raises an important question to consider concerning Washington because he publicly disdained politics and disavowed any interest in it. At the same time, however, Washington had played politics all his life, and as one studies him closely one begins to see the picture of a consummate politician begin to emerge. By the time he was twenty-five, the fundamental traits of his character and personality were well established, and by that time also he had become an artful politician. He learned about *noblesse oblige* and the way the aristocracy practiced politics from the likes of Lord Thomas Fairfax, William Fairfax, and their peers, since he was about sixteen. In the military, and later in politics, he used the same skills to advance himself. In a word, he used modesty, which Ellis in at least one case recognizes as "disingenuous," or as meaning to create a false impression of complete disinterest. The pattern that emerges is one of

Washington placing himself just outside the perimeter of the arena, having prepared himself as well as he might, in his own mind, to enter the arena. Then he induced his friends to "nominate" or recommend him for the sought-after position. He wanted to be courted, asked, and invited. When an offer was made, he would then likely demur, out of modesty, on the grounds that he was not suitably qualified, when, in fact, he was probably as well qualified as any applicant. Then if he failed, he could easily be excused on the grounds that he had been pressed to accept; but if he won, he was a hero who had risen above the challenge. The same pattern can be seen in some letters to his superiors in the military,[94] and in his letter to his brother Jack in 1755 asking him to assay George's chances of election.[95] Was there anything wrong or unethical about any of this? Certainly, there was not. In the modern era it would be a foolish politician who did not "test the waters" before jumping in. The custom these days is to run numerous polls to test one's support, and to engage "focus groups" to advise a candidate as to what he should talk about. George was simply an early-modern politician honing his skills to become a typical political dissembler. George always hated to lose and, as Joseph Ellis points out, "deference did not come naturally to him, since it meant surrendering control to a purported superior, trusting his fate and future to someone else."[96] Ellis also makes the point that: "If we are looking for emergent patterns of behavior, then the combination of bottomless ambition and the near obsession with self-control leaps out."[97]

In the House of Burgesses, Washington associated with yet another elite group, the gentry who dominated the legislature. There he also mingled with some of the bright young minds of his revolutionary birth cohort, men who had been born in America rather than Britain, of an age young enough to be rambunctious, but also of an age mature enough to experience the Great Awakening and the stirrings of the Enlightenment. He joined them at a critical juncture, when they were beginning to think of themselves as Americans and no longer as British colonials.

Washington's legislative career in the House of Burgesses was important but not illustrious. His philosophy was that of a conservative evolving into a moderate. Many who shared the chamber with him were more radical, better educated, more articulate, and more vocal. Soon enough, he found himself overshadowed by men like Richard H. Lee, Patrick Henry, Thomas Jefferson, Richard Bland, George Mason, James Madison, Edmund Randolph, and even venerable older men such as George Wythe and Edmund Pendleton. It was a remarkable time and place for truly remarkable men.

January 6, 1759, George Washington married the widow Martha Dandridge Custis. She may very well have been the wealthiest woman in Virginia at the time, with both her Dandridge and Custis inheritances of 18,000 acres worth about £30,000.[98] This, along with Mount Vernon, which George inherited in

1761 subsequent to the death of his sister-in-law, Anne Washington, in addition to his other holdings, made George one of the important landowners in Virginia. Martha also brought 300 slaves with her to Mount Vernon. She was about nine months older than George; whereas, she had been younger than her late husband Daniel Parke Custis, her godfather, by about twenty-one years. The diminutive Martha, who was less than five feet tall, also brought two Custis children to the marriage, John (called Jack), and Martha (called Patsy). Martha's marriage to George was childless, although she had borne four children to Custis, two of whom had died in infancy. George seems to have thought he might have done better with a younger girl, but the fact is that he was probably sterile. That was not something, however, that he and his supporters wanted talked about.[99] Martha's dowry "immediately catapulted Washington into the top tier of Virginia's planter class and established the economic foundation for his second career as the master of Mount Vernon."[100]

Washington might have believed, and even hoped, that his retirement from the army would assure him of a life of bucolic tranquility as a plantation squire, but that did not prove true for long. A perusal of his diary during this period reveals little about his reading habits, but it does reveal something about his key interests. He devoted himself to caring for his estates, foxhunting, visiting neighbors, breeding dogs and cattle, shearing sheep, attending balls, going to church, entertaining friends at Mount Vernon (especially the Fairfaxes, who were near neighbors), playing cards, attending cock fights (he was "temperamentally a gambler"), and dining with friends at their homes.[101] Flexner states that "in the seven years between 1768 and 1775, the Washingtons entertained about two thousand guests, who ranged from relations and intimate friends to passersby put up at nightfall."[102]

Meanwhile, Washington entered into one of the more peaceful periods in his life, although, beginning in 1760-1763 with the French surrender of Canada and the Anglo-French Treaty of Paris in 1763, his world began to spin out of control. There were two dynamics at work. The first was the reality that the French were no longer a "menace" to British subjects in America after 1760. Lawrence Henry Gipson, the historian, long ago pointed to this circumstance as the beginning of the American Revolution. Specifically, he pointed to British efforts in 1763 to implement a "new colonial system," characterized by new regulations and their strict enforcement, as the critical point in relations between the mother country and her colonists. In short, the absence of the French so emboldened the colonists that they began to refuse to put up with controls they had long accepted as loyal British subjects, albeit sometimes unhappy ones.[103] The second dynamic was the fact that, by 1760, the colonists were thinking of themselves as Americans following two decades of transformation at home. Their America was changing, and so were they. This cultural phenomenon, which some would argue began with the first planting of colonies in British America, accelerated in the period 1740-60, aided, of course, by the outcome of the War for Empire.[104] The best term to describe what was happening in America is alienation of affection.

Washington's election in 1758 brought him together with these forces as they gathered in the Virginia House of Burgesses. That body did not meet continuously but, rather, at the call of the royal governor. Americans, like the gentry rebels in the English civil wars during the mid-1600s, however, also believed that they met as a right and not merely as a matter of royal pleasure. Washington's role in the House of Burgesses was relatively minor. It is known that he was neither an orator nor a brilliant writer. Yet he was an important figure, with a sizable following. He was also a member who had personal experience in the west and a very keen personal interest in western lands. His bitter experience with the British army was valuable, as was his experience in the very lucrative tobacco business. Like others of his legislative peers, he soon come to feel pressed, as a businessman, by debt brought about by the shortage of sufficient British specie with which to conduct business, and by indebtedness to British merchants and business agents, or factors. In other words, Washington was feeling the same economic pressures that other Virginians were, and these were promising to only get worse under the new colonial system. Also like the men he served with in the House of Burgesses, Washington was growing increasingly disaffected with the attitude British authorities expressed and demonstrated toward their American subjects, particularly regarding British imperial legislation during the 1760s.

The Proclamation Line imposed along the frontier in 1763 offended many colonials, including Washington, who possessed western land interests and promoted westward expansion. The Currency Act of 1764 exacerbated the problems arising from a lack of British specie in the colonies, while the Stamp Act of 1765 outraged a great many Virginians because it proposed to levy an internal tax on the colonists for revenue purposes alone. Virginians, and others, rejected Parliament's authority to levy an internal tax on them since they were not represented in Parliament. They argued that they could only be deprived of their property (be taxed) by their own vote in their own legislatures. In this they had the support of a significant number of Whigs in the Parliament, who represented the loyal opposition to King George III's party of Tories. The Americans were, in fact, beginning to think of themselves as American Whigs. The Stamp Act was repealed in 1766, in response to active protests by the Sons of Liberty, Patrick Henry's Virginia Resolutions, the non-importation of British goods (which hurt British merchants), and resolves that were adopted by the Stamp Act Congress in October. The Declaratory Act that was then enacted in its place was viewed as an unimportant British face-saving measure.

Rutyna: GEORGE WASHINGTON

Under the presumption that the Americans objected only to internal taxes, the Townshend Acts of June 1767 raised another storm of protest by imposing a series of external taxes on the colonists, placing duties on such American imports as lead, paint, glass, paper, and tea. The Americans' position had "changed," however, and they responded with vigorous non-importation activities until all save the tax on tea were repealed. At this point, Washington rose to play his first important role in the House of Burgesses, calling for a "colony-wide boycott of enumerated English manufactured goods, to include a cessation of the slave trade . . . This was an important moment in Washington's public career, for he now became an acknowledged leader in the resistance movement within Virginia's planter class."[105]

The extent of Washington's alienation at this time was expressed in an April 5, 1769, letter to George Mason, in which he wrote: "At a time when our lordly Masters in Great Britain will be satisfied with nothing less than the depreciation of American freedom, it seems highly necessary that some thing [sic] shou'd [sic] be done to avert the stroke and maintain the liberty which we have derived from our Ancestors; but the [best] manner of doing it to answer the purpose effectually is the point in question." In the next paragraph, Washington suggested to Mason that "no man shou'd [sic] scruple, or hesitate a moment to use a-ms [sic] in defence [sic] of so valuable a blessing [as liberty], on which all the good and evil of life depends; is clearly my opinion; yet A-ms [sic] I wou'd [sic] beg leave to add, should be the last resource; the denier [last] resort."[106] Still a moderate, Washington's reference to "our Ancestors" may well have been intended to put a point on William Pitt's 1766 speech in Parliament in opposition to the Stamp Act, during which he shouted: "The Americans are our sons, not our bastards!"

From 1770 to 1775, matters simply grew worse, as the words got sharper and the responses became more violent and destructive. The Boston Massacre of 1770, followed by the seizure and burning of the British revenue cutter "Gaspee" in 1772, the Boston Tea Party in December 1773, and the retaliatory British imposition of the Coercive Acts in 1774, brought matters to the point of armed resistance and reaction. The colonists called the Coercive Acts "outrageous" and Intolerable Acts, combining them with the Quebec Act in their protests against them.[107] The Boston Tea Party disturbed Washington, mainly because he thought it would only provoke the British to stern measures. His reaction to the Intolerable Acts was intense, however, referring to them as "an unexampled testimony of the most despotic system of tyranny that was ever practiced in a free government." For Washington, "opposition had become an absolute duty."[108]

When Royal Governor John Murray, Earl of Dunmore, suspended the Assembly, the members simply moved their business elsewhere and later met as a Revolutionary Convention. The royal governor had tired of their protests and resolutions. They urged the other colonies to join in a Continental Congress, and then met on August 1, 1774 in the First Virginia Revolutionary State Convention to express support for the citizens of Boston. They hesitated, however, to completely condemn the authority of Parliament to make laws governing them, but they did choose delegates to the forthcoming Continental Congress, and encouraged non-importation.[109] The delegates to the Revolutionary Convention elected seven delegates to go to the Continental Congress, including George Washington, who finished third in the balloting. Patrick Henry finished "far behind him and the young Thomas Jefferson failed of election."[110] That alone says something about the regard in which Washington was held.

A Second Revolutionary State Convention was held on March 20, 1775 in the city of Richmond. The First Continental Congress had, in the meantime, already assembled on September 5, 1774 in Philadelphia. "The March convention, dominated by members of the House of Burgesses, approved the work of the Continental Congress, but foremost in the minds of the delegates was the problem of defense."[111] It was at this meeting, in St. John's Church, that Patrick Henry made his famous "Liberty or Death" speech, and the Virginians made preparations to defend their "country."

In July 1774 Washington presided over a meeting of the "Freeholders and Inhabitants" of Fairfax County. Robert Harrison was his clerk and George Mason is believed to have been his ghostwriter or, at the very least, his editor. The resolves were twenty-four in number. The first "*resolved* that this Colony and Dominion of Virginia can not be considered as a conquered Country; and if it was, that the present Inhabitants are the Descendants not of the Conquered, but of the Conquerors." The ninth resolve spoke to the intent of the people: "*Resolved* that it is our greatest Wish and Inclination, as well as Interest, to continue our Connection with, and Dependance [sic] upon the British Government, but tho'[sic] we are it's [sic] Subjects, we will use every Means which Heaven hath given us to prevent our becoming it's [sic] Slaves."[112]

The First Continental Congress was a moderate assembly, denouncing the hated Intolerable Acts, rejecting Joseph Galloway's conservative plan for union with Britain, discussing theories of government, dispatching resolutions and declarations of American rights to the Home Government, and resuming non-importation by forming a Continental Association. Washington played only a supporting, quiet role. By the time the Second Continental Congress met on May 10, 1775, however, the battles of Lexington and Concord had already been fought. The venerable Peyton Randolph of Virginia was chosen to chair the congress, and another Virginian, Patrick Henry, radicalized the meeting with his sharp oratory, declaring "government is dissolved" and eliminating the distinctions between men from different colonies, exclaiming: "I am not a Virginian, but an American."[113]

Washington appeared at the congress dressed in his Virginia militia uniform, and in so doing put everyone on notice that he was available, ready, willing, and able. John Adams, a key New England figure, did not know Washington very well, but did not think much of him either. He thought Washington had delivered the "Liberty or Death" speech in Richmond, for example. He also took a dim view of Washington's lack of education and polish. Perhaps one reason Adams felt as he did was that Mrs. Abigail Adams was a great admirer of Washington. One joke that Adams apparently liked to tell about George was that the reason he got along so well, and advanced so quickly, was that he was taller than anyone else in the room. In any event, Adams knew very well that New England was being seen as a hotbed of sedition and treason, and that the leadership of any defensive force would have to fall to a Virginian. Who else was there? After some discussions pro and con, Washington was chosen to command the Continental Army that was created.[114]

The Commander-in-Chief

During the period between 2003 and 2005, no fewer than seven very good books about George Washington were published. These join a great number of standards, and even some revered classics, such as Douglas Southall Freeman's *George Washington: A Biography*, published in seven volumes (1948-57). Four of these new books deal extensively with Washington as commander-in-chief during the War for American Independence.[115] One is a biography,[116] one is a study of Washington and slavery,[117] and one is a study of Mr. Washington as a republican thinker and president.[118]

Many authors who comment on Washington's abilities as a military commander are fond of pointing out his weaknesses and the conclusion that he lost more battles than he won. The books alluded to above show him in a more positive, respectful, and still human light. What seems to be the consensus among most of these particular historians is that, despite all of his faults (and they were numerous), he was still the only and best man for the job. He was not a great soldier, and never had been. As Flexner tells it: "The debate [as to how good a soldier he was] has overlooked the fact that Washington was never really a soldier. He was a civilian in arms."[119] The fact that he admired Alexander the Great did not make him an Alexander, of course, or a Julius Caesar, or a Charles XII of Sweden, or a Frederick II The Great of Prussia.[120]

After his commissioning, Washington set out for Boston via Philadelphia and New York but, by the time he arrived there, the Battle of Bunker (Breed's) Hill had been fought at great cost to the British, who continued to hold the city. He entered the lines held by the Americans on July 2, 1775.[121] The British had won the battle, but estimates of the number of British officers killed run high, although it is always hard to credit casualty numbers. In the months that followed, Washington met with thirty-five year-old Colonel Benedict Arnold and they plotted a daring raid into Quebec for December 31, 1775 and January 1, 1776 (as it turned out). It was a bold strategy to shake the British and foment Canadian unrest. The attack did not succeed in capturing the city, but it did serve to spread anxiety among Canadians.[122]

The invasion of Canada was not a great plan. For one thing, it was contrary to the American strategy to fight a defensive war, but George functioned in attack mode most of the time and had to learn to restrain himself. Closer to home, his own officers advised him not to attack the British in Boston. "Washington had never before faced such a rebuke from his officers."[123] George then decided, with his officers' concurrence, to attack Dorchester Heights instead and an American bombardment was launched. Washington wanted to draw the British into battle, but they "spiked" Washington's cannon by evacuating the city (the last of the British troops left on March 17, 1776). Soon, Washington became the "hero" of Dorchester Heights and his supporters celebrated "the capture of Boston."[124] From that point on, everything went downhill and most of Washington's days were those of defeat.

What Washington had going for him was that he was a fairly good strategist; he was brave (if not brash); he believed himself impervious to gunfire; he had some war experience; he was ready, willing, and able to fight; he hated to lose; he was quick off the mark; he was aggressive and willing to attack; he was usually decisive; he had contempt for the British; he was a good administrator and politician; he was loyal, dedicated, and he cared for his men.[125] However, says his most recent biographer, he had " . . . a truly monumental ego with a massive personal agenda . . ."[126] Washington's slide to oblivion was halted at Trenton and Princeton (December 31, 1775 and January 1, 1776) in what have been called brilliant battles and the collective "turning point" in the war. David Hackett Fischer says: "in the New Jersey campaign, American troops repeatedly defeated larger and better trained regular forces in many different types of warfare . . . professional observers judged the entire performance to be one of the most brilliant in military history."[127]

David McCullough refers to the Battle of Trenton as "the first great cause for hope, a brave and truly 'brilliant stroke,'"[128] even while saying of Washington that, "he was not a brilliant strategist or tactician."[129] In addition to Trenton and Princeton, the Americans also enjoyed a great victory at Saratoga. The rest of the New York campaign, however, was a disaster, as were Washington's losses at Brandywine and Germantown. The British took Philadelphia near the end of 1777.

Washington was forced into a winter encampment at Valley Forge, which, in a sense, turned out to be a great American victory simply because the American forces survived. Edward Lengel says that, before December 1776, Washington's men "neither liked nor trusted him;" that after Trenton and Princeton they trusted him more and liked him only slightly better; but that, after Valley Forge, mired in the dark and frozen depression of defeat, "the Continentals [were] ready to follow him anywhere."[130] Earlier, his men were "thrilled" by his courage, but before Valley Forge he really did not interact well with them. At Valley Forge, they bonded as never before. The very fact that he stayed with them while other officers went home truly impressed them. In fact, Martha came to join him in winter quarters there, as was her custom wherever he was, because he went home to Mount Vernon for only a few days during the entire war.[131]

In a way, Washington was at his best when conditions were at their worst. This demonstrated his great character coming to the fore, and this is why he was great—not because he was a great one-man army. He constantly prodded others (even the Continental Congress) to do their duty, to perform. To everyone he wrote, and presumably to everyone with whom he talked, like his men, he stressed "perseverance," courage, spirit, and patience.[132] In other words, Washington was the great personal magnetic force at the vortex of the struggle that kept it from flying apart in all directions at any time. His "secret weapon" was to endure, and to constantly encourage his associates to do likewise.[133]

The Trenton and Princeton campaigns, which were big gambles, "prompted American leaders to invent a new way of war."[134] They would now gamble on shifting the focus of the war from north to south, and "once Washington shifted his focus from New York to the south, he never looked back."[135] Washington himself never again commanded a battle after Monmouth Court House, New Jersey, in June 1778, the culmination of a complex and controversial campaign, until he commanded the Yorktown campaign. With the support of the French, who had allied with the Americans in 1778 following the victory of General Horatio Gates at Saratoga the previous year, Washington moved on Yorktown. On October 19, 1781, he achieved a great strategic victory there, which doubtless was owed to luck as much as to strategy. The victory was accomplished, in the main, because of the timely arrival of a French fleet, under the command of Admiral François Joseph Paul, Comte de Grasse, at the entrance to the Chesapeake Bay that effectively prevented the retreat of British General Charles Cornwallis from Yorktown by sea. Converging American and French land forces laid siege to Yorktown, beginning on September 28, and attacked redoubts No. 9 and 10 on October 14. Three days later, the British raised a white flag. The British commander asked for a twenty-four-hour truce to work out terms of surrender. Washington gave him two hours. After the formal terms were signed, the surrender ceremony took place on October 19, 1781. As Flexner noted:

> Never a man to place his fate in trust, [Washington] had learned to mistrust everything emanating from London. Even the term 'negotiations' troubled him. What was there to negotiate? The British had tried to destroy him and his army, but he had destroyed them. He wanted the personal satisfaction that came with an unqualified, unconditional surrender. He wanted them to say that they had lost and he had won. He wanted his vaunted superiors to admit that they were his inferiors.[136]

For all practical purposes, the war was over and American Independence was won. There still remained the matter of winning the peace, of course, in Paris, where the great powers considered the Americans lambs who they wanted to shear before it was too late. To avoid that, the Americans made a separate peace with Great Britain in the Treaty of Paris (1783), and snatched victory from the almost certain jaws of diplomatic defeat. That, however, was a different kind of battle, for different heroes to wage.

In the end, Washington could perhaps have become a military dictator, or even a king. The so-called Newburgh Conspiracy afforded him that opportunity, based on his broad-based popularity and the avid support of the army. His "Newburgh Address," in March 1783, renounced any such aspirations on his part, in what Ellis has called "his most eloquent oration."[137] In June 1783, Washington dispatched his last "Circular Letter to the States," which Ellis describes as "the most poignant piece of writing he ever composed," which envisioned a vast continental empire in which the "Citizens of America" were the "Sole Lords and Proprietors."[138] This was the Promised Land to which he had brought them, and it was to be theirs, not his. George III had once been heard to say that, if Washington resisted the monarchial mantle and retired, as he always said he would, he would be "the greatest man in the world."[139] Was he not?

After bidding his troops goodbye in "an emotional ceremony" at Newburgh in November 1783, and again in a "teary-eyed" speech to his officers at Fraunces Tavern in New York, Washington made his final farewell to the Confederation Congress, meeting in Annapolis, on December 22, 1783. About this last, Joseph Ellis says: "The man who had known how to stay the course now showed that he also understood how to leave it."[140]

Washington the Republican

Washington, the "unifying symbol of the cause," was a republican in political philosophy, a republican Patriot King, "the true patriot writ large."[141] Glenn A. Phelps agrees, saying both that Washington was the "one national symbol of the struggle for independence" and that "Washington was a thoroughgoing republican both before and after the war."[142] Phelps further explains that Washington was a "conservative," which meant that he believed in the ideas that "consent clearly had to come from the people," that government was not just for the few but for the many, and that "the people's representatives had to be chosen by a broadly based electorate."[143] Conservative also meant, however, that Washington "could never bring himself to accept the notion that all men were equally endowed with virtue, experience, and disinterestedness." In the final analysis, "political liberty was a natural right and therefore held equally by all men; but political virtue was neither inherent nor held in equal measure by all men," and it was virtue more than natural right that should guide the actions of men and governments.[144] The fly in that ointment, however, is that it was too often the self-righteous, self-anointed few who determined that they alone were the only ones fit to guide. "In Washington's estimation there could be no democracy in the organization of a republican army [or in a republican state ?] for democracy took no account of the social values that *he* most cherished: order, discipline, virtue, and *most of all, deference.*"[145] Was not "virtue" equal to "disinterestedness," and, in fact, part of the formula for virtue? Were liberty, justice, and equality for all, part of the "deference" *he* "most cherished"? George Washington was clearly an eighteenth-century man,[146] and for that we certainly may not fault him, but we need not embrace all of his social values either. Nor need we throw the baby out with the bath water.

What Washington clearly preferred was what Gordon Wood calls "Enlightened Paternalism" of the sort that Plato envisioned for his republic. George also knew about the Roman Republic, and at least some of what had been written about it. That was part of the milieu in which he had grown to manhood. Many of his enlightened peers, both in Virginia (like Jefferson, as well as others) and throughout the colonies, spoke and wrote about the Roman Republic and, even if George had not read most of the original works, he read about them in the newspapers, which he read extensively.[147] He also learned about republican ideals from his friends in the House of Burgesses, the Continental Congress, and from the writings and speeches of the British Whigs. An American republic, modeled on the Roman, would become the first established in roughly 2,000 years. That was an attractive goal.

Washington, like many of his peers, had economic interests at stake in the War for American Independence but, in the end, it came down to a constitutional issue and a fight for the political survival and success of Virginia's and America's ruling class. It was they the British were really challenging.[148] George, as time passed, simply came to resent British attitudes toward the "inferior" Americans, as expressed, for example, by Hugh Earl Percy, vice admiral of North America after 1764: "The people here [in the colonies] are a set of sly, artful, hypocritical rascals, cruel and cowards. I must own I cannot but despise them completely."[149]

"Cruel and cowards"? It was the British that had executed American prisoners after the fall of New York.[150] Washington expressly forbade any such treatment of British or Hessian prisoners.[151] In short, Washington and his fellow Americans had suffered a lifetime of military and political abuse at the hands of British bureaucrats and they had had enough. They had governed themselves for years and would not allow the British to enslave and tyrannize them by revoking or infringing the freedoms that they had come to enjoy, and demand, as free-born Englishmen; nay, as free-born Americans. The Americans became staunch republicans and antiroyalists, antimonarchists, and therefore ceased to be subjects of the king of Great Britain. Thomas Paine made common sense to them because their own experience told them that what he said was true. They articulated his ideas, as well as their belief in natural rights, in the Declaration of Independence, and they fought an eight-year war for those principles, not simply to break away from Great Britain in a revolution, but also to establish a new American nation.

These republican ideals gestated in Washington during his semi-retirement from active public life during the so-called Critical Period, until he was again called to public service, first by a few close friends, then by the 1787 Constitutional Convention in Philadelphia. He went to the convention with some reluctance because of his position as national president of the Society of the Cincinnati, the only veterans' organization in existence after the War for American Independence. He feared that people might think he was trying to "storm" the convention, so to speak. It was already a widely held belief, however, that, if a republic were to be established to supercede the confederation (which some wanted and some did not), it was a foregone conclusion that he would be called on to serve as president. As for himself, Washington had long believed that the legitimate object of the "revolution" was the establishment of a new, strong, and stable union of all the states, a United States of America. Some of the more radical supporters of the independence movement had something more democratic in mind. That is why Thomas Paine came to write to George that he prayed for his "imminent death," and then wondered "whether the world will be puzzled to decide whether you are an apostate or an imposter, whether you have abandoned good principles, or whether you ever had any."[152] Jefferson's relationship with Washington likewise suffered because of their differences over what the legitimate object of the war had been. There never had been a clear consensus; there were revolutions within the revolution—one for home rule as well as others to decide who should rule at home.

Washington was elected to preside over the Constitutional Convention that met from May 28, 1787, through September 17, 1787. Aside from whatever conversations he had privately or with the Virginia delegation, he spoke to the convention itself only once, on the last day, concerning a slight but important alteration in a measure that provided for representatives to represent 30,000 people in preference to 40,000.[153] As expected, in 1789 and again in 1793, Washington was elected to serve as president of the United States. On both occasions, he was elected unanimously.[154] He was what Thomas Flexner has called the indispensable man.

Washington the Slave Owner

It is useful here to address briefly the issue concerning George Washington as an owner of Negro slaves. He did buy, sell, and trade slaves. However, like Jefferson, he never sold away family members without their consent. In that alone, and in the fact that, in his will, he manumitted his slaves upon Martha's death, he was ahead of his time. At that time, no one had so manumitted as many personally held slaves with a single pen stroke. None of that, however, mitigates the fact that slavery was an evil and disgraceful institution engaged in for short-term economic gain and long-term disregard for human rights. Slavery, however, had been established in Virginia almost three-quarters of a century before Washington was born: It was an inherited evil. It was part of the world he lived in, but was not of his making, and it was a time and place very different from our own.

From a late-eighteenth-century point-of-view, Negro slavery had grown into something with which most men of that generation simply did not know how to deal. As for Washington, he personally rejected it.[155]

> He also stipulated that, once freed, his slaves must not be simply abandoned to their fate. All the old and infirm slaves "shall be comfortably cloathed [sic] and fed by my heirs while they live." The very young slaves should be supported until they reached adulthood, which he defined as twenty-five years, and taught to read and as well as [sic] "brought up to some useful occupation." His final instruction concerned Billy Lee, who had been hobbling around Mount Vernon for over a decade on two badly damaged knees. He should be freed outright upon Washington's death and provided with a small annuity along with room and board, "as a testimony to my sense of his attachment to me, and for his faithful services during the Revolutionary War".[156]

Washington was, of course, the richest man in Virginia. Many of his neighbors were less well off and were frightened to death of what might happen if hundreds of thousands of slaves were released without being provided for as Washington graciously provided for his. Some have likened it to having a wolf by the ears. It was not a position one wanted to be in at all, and it was also one in which it was unthinkable to let go of the wolf's ears.[157] It was, in fact, a dilemma of the first order.

Henry Wiencek, in *An Imperfect God*, ponders the "mystery" by which George Washington became a revolutionary.[158] He says that, "by 1769 slaveholding was twisting the masters into ontological and epistemological knots."[159] Slavery was like the ghost at everyone's dinner table, one author has suggested. To use a different metaphor, slavery was like the elephant in the room that no one wanted to discuss.

The freeing of slaves was not something that was done in the British Empire before the War for American Independence. During the war itself, it was believed that it would be unthinkable to loose thousands of perhaps hostile slaves behind American lines. The British soon offered freedom to blacks as an incentive to revolt and join them in fighting the Americans. Some thought also was given to what might happen if the war did not go because of economic failure to maintain a viable agricultural system in the colonies. Many of these problems might have been resolved, of course, by following the plans set down by Washington for the enlightened treatment of his slaves both while he had them and after he manumitted them, which was at least sixty years before the Civil War in America.[160]

Notes

1. Edward G. Lengel, *General George Washington: A Military Life* (New York: Random House, 2005), xiii. Lengel is associate professor of history at the University of Virginia and associate editor of *The Papers of George Washington*.

2. William W. Abbot, "An Uncommon Awareness of Self: The Papers of George Washington," *George Washington Reconsidered*, Don Higginbotham, ed. (Charlottesville: University of Virginia Press, 2001), 279. Abbot is James Madison professor of history emeritus at the University of Virginia and emeritus editor of *The Papers of George Washington*.

3. *Ibid.*, 280, 285 n. The quotation is from G.W. to Reverend William Gordon, October 23, 1782, in George Washington, *The Writings of George Washington* 25, John C. Fitzpatrick, ed. (Washington, D.C.: U.S. Government Printing Office, 1931-44), 287-89. The same source also has two letters from G.W. to Lt. Col. Richard Varick, both dated May 25, 1781, in *Ibid.* 22, 112, 113-15. In the first, Washington appointed Varick as his "Secretary at Head Quarters," and, in the second, he gave Varick explicit instructions as to how the work was to be carried out.

4. Abbot, "An Uncommon Awareness of Self": 276-86.

5. Douglass Adair, *Fame and the Founding Fathers: Essays by Douglass Adair*, Trevor Colbourn, ed. (New York: W.W. Norton & Company [published for the Institute of Early American History and Culture at Williamsburg, VA], 1974), 8.

6. Gordon S. Wood, "The Greatness of George Washington," in *George Washington Reconsidered*, 310.

7. *Ibid.*, 310-11.

8. *Ibid.*, 310.

9. Arthur M. Schlesinger, Jr., *The Disuniting of America: Reflections on a Multicultural Society* (New York: W.W. Norton & Company, 1992), *passim*. The author of the present essay has taught history for over twenty-five years, all but one of them at the university level, and has some experience with the curriculum issues raised by Schlesinger. The writer also understands very well the distinction between "United States" and "America/American" but sometimes uses the terms interchangeably for the sake of the text and not out of any Eurocentrist, racist, or nationalist bias.

10. Mrs. Robert E. Lee IV, "Restoring George Washington to an Honored Place in America," *Mount Vernon Ladies' Association Newsletter* (Merrifield, VA: 2004): 2. The emphasis is in the original.

11. Washington's last will and testament provided that his slaves be freed by manumission upon the death of his wife Martha.

12. Don Higginbotham, "Afterword," in *George Washington Reconsidered*, 327.

13. Schlesinger, 18.

14. *Ibid.*, 43.

15. *Ibid.*, 24-25.

16. Marcus Cunliffe, *George Washington: Man and Monument*, rev. ed. (New York: New American Library, A Mentor Book, 1958 [reprinted 1982]), 22-24. Augustine first married Jane Butler in 1715. They had a son, Lawrence, who was named for his grandfather and great-grandfather. George's birthday was February 11, 1731/32 (Old Style), but the date became February 22, 1732, when the New Style, Gregorian calendar was adopted throughout the British Empire in September 1752.

17. *Ibid.*, 24.

18. Bernard Mayo, *Myths and Men* (Athens: University of Georgia Press, 1959), 27-30. Washington died in December 1799, and Weems, ever the bookseller, published the first edition of Washington's biography early in 1800. The fifth edition was published in 1806.

19. *Ibid.*, 25-48.

20. Cunliffe, 28-29. Admiral Vernon was himself held up as a hero by Lawrence Washington, who acquitted himself well in the Cartagena Expedition but did not achieve heroic deeds. Many of the Americans who died during the campaign died of yellow fever. Lawrence himself returned to Virginia with the "seeds" of the tuberculosis that was to weaken him and eventually claim his life, according to W.E. Woodward, *George Washington, the Image and the Man* (New York: Liveright, 1926 [subsequent printings, 1946 and 1972]), 32.

21. Wilmer L. Hall, ed., *Executive Journals of the Council of Colonial Virginia* 5 (Richmond: Commonwealth of Virginia, 1945), 117. In the eighteenth century, claiming land was one thing, but far more important was "seating" it, which meant establishing a habitation on it, be it ever so humble. This was part of the doctrine of "effective occupation" that was of greater legal importance than were mere claims or documents. Augustine Washington, Jr., ("Austin") was given the property at Pope's Creek before his father "Gus" (Augustine, Sr.) died. George would inherit Ferry Farm upon his father's death.

22. Cunliffe, 24.

23. *Ibid.*, 24-28, 26 n. Some of the skill and craftsmanship Washington later displayed as a writer was no doubt due to his employment of skilled secretaries. Woodward, 14-29, provides more detail about the young Washington's education, telling us that neither his father nor his mother was very intellectual, and that his father was "land poor" (meaning that he had most of his capital tied up in land) and lacked ready cash to expend on educating George were the lad so inclined. We suspect strongly that the boy was so inclined but that circumstances intervened before his time came, which precluded his pursuing the education that was deemed obligatory for the future leaders of his class. Lack of funds as well as her own desire to keep young George close at hand may also have prevented his mother from sending him away. She had five children to care for, including George. Woodward confesses that Washington was one of his "cherished heroes" from the outset, and that his admiration for his subject grew as the work progressed, but he was among Washington's earliest biographers to try to humanize his subject. He says that Mary Ball was an orphan from Virginia, the daughter of Colonel Joseph Ball (p. 14). In *The Writings of George Washington* 1, 1-5, Fitzpatrick alludes to, and addresses in notes, some Washington copybooks and schoolbooks touching on a number of subjects, such as geometry, geometrical definitions, surveying, solid measure, gauging, and geographical definitions. George was good in arithmetic, which he may have studied at a school near his home, and it is assumed that his half-brother Lawrence may have tutored him or had him tutored.

24. Cunliffe, 28.

25. Lawrence and Anne were married on July 26, 1743. The story of the Fairfax family was unique in Virginia history. The family estates were descended from Thomas Lord Fairfax by virtue of a royal proprietary grant from King Charles II to Thomas Lord Culpeper, governor and captain general of Virginia in 1680 and 1682-83. Culpeper bequeathed his lands to his daughter, Catherine, who married the Fifth Lord Fairfax. The Sixth Lord Fairfax was Culpeper's grandson and the heir to his titles and estates (1719). Fairfax himself came to the colony of Virginia, in 1746 or 1747, to settle somewhere, anywhere he pleased, on the 4,500,000 to 6,000,000 acres to which he held title. His lands extended from the entire Northern Neck to the mountains and Shenandoah Valley, and eventually encompassed what were to become about twenty-four Virginia (and, later, West Virginia) counties. During his stay at Belvoir, which was owned by his cousin and agent in Virginia, Colonel William Fairfax, the father of Anne Fairfax Washington, Lord Fairfax, met George and took a strong liking to him. George William, the son of William Fairfax and the brother of Anne, at the same time became one of George's best friends, as did Bryan Fairfax, also the son of Colonel William Fairfax. See, among others: Richard L. Morton, *Colonial Virginia* 2 (Chapel Hill: University of North Carolina Press, 1960), 545-48, 548 n.; James MacGregor Burns and Susan Dunn, *George Washington* (New York: Times Books/Henry Holt and Company [The American Presidents Series], 2004), 7-8; Joseph J. Ellis, *His Excellency, George Washington* (New York: Alfred A. Knopf, 2004), 9-10; James Thomas Flexner, *Washington: The Indispensable Man* (Boston: Little, Brown and Company, Back Bay Books, 1974), 5-7; Woodward, 29-36; and, Cunliffe, 30-32. Several aspects of the Washington-Fairfax story are worthy of interest but are beyond the purview of the present essay.

26. Flexner, 5-6; Cunliffe, 25, 28, 168 n.

27. Lengel, xxxvi.

28. *Ibid.*, 11-12. Flexner, 6-7, suggests that it may have been the Fairfaxes who proposed that George join the British navy.

29. Paul K. Longmore, *The Invention of George Washington* (Charlottesville: University of Virginia Press, 1999), 15-16, the quotation is from p. 16.

30. *Ibid.*, 6-7; Ellis, *His Excellency,* 9; Burns and Dunn, in a chapter entitled: "Blind Ambition," 5-6; Wood, 314-15.

31. George Washington, "Journey Over the Mountains, 1748," in *The Writings of George Washington* 1, 5-13; Ellis, *His Excellency,* 10-11; Lengel, 13-14. Lengel states here that Washington saw his first Indian while on this expedition.

32. G.W. to Lawrence Washington, May 5, 1749, in *The Writings of George Washington* 1, 13-14. George discussed the settling of his mother in this letter.

33. Lengel, 15.

34. Robert E. and B. Katherine Brown, *Virginia, 1705-1786: Democracy or Aristocracy?* (East Lansing: Michigan State University Press, 1964), 227-39, and *passim*; Charles S. Sydnor, *American Revolutionaries in the Making: Political Practices in Washington's Virginia* (New York: Free Press, Macmillan Publishing Co., Inc., 1952), 60-85, and *passim.*

35. Wood, 311-15.

36. Ellis, *His Excellency,* 11; Flexner, 7; Lengel, 15. Lengel suggests that the number of acres involved in this purchase was 2,300 as opposed to Ellis's and Flexner's 1,459, if indeed it was the same transaction.

37. Burns and Dunn, 8.

38. Lengel, 15. Lawrence had previously gone to England in search of better health, but to no avail.

39. George Washington, *The Diaries of George Washington, 1748-1799*, John C. Fitzpatrick, ed., vol. 1, *1748-1770* (Boston: Houghton Mifflin Company, 1925), 15-36. The diary commences on October 4, 1751, about page ten of the original manuscript, because some early pages were lost or badly mutilated according to Fitzpatrick's notes.

40. *Ibid.*, 22-29, 36, including the notes.

41. Ellis, *His Excellency,* 10.

42. Hall, 412-13. The board had decided that the responsibilities of adjutant were so great that they should be divided among four officers rather than one.

43. Ellis, *His Excellency,* 12; Lengel, 17.

44. Flexner, 8-9; Lengel, 17-18. The rank of major was that normally assigned to the position of adjutant.

45. *The Writings of George Washington* 1, 22 n, 45. Once again, Washington's friends in high places assisted in his reassignment.

46. Flexner, 9.

47. Richard A. Rutyna and Peter C. Stewart, *The History of Freemasonry in Virginia* (Lanham, MD.: University Press of America, 1998), 61-64, 102-3.

48. *Ibid.*, 45, 108-9.

49. Hall, 295. George Fairfax was among the other members. Lengel, 19, points out that, in 1751, Lawrence Washington was president of the company, which came to command some 500,000 acres.

50. Lengel,19.

51. *The Writings of George Washington* 1, 22-23

52. Ellis, *His Excellency,* 19.

53. Virginius Dabney, *Virginia, The New Dominion: A History from 1607 to the Present* (New York: Doubleday and Co., Inc., 1971), 209.

54. Ellis, *His Excellency,* 11-12, including the quotation. In an interesting new development, Libby Copeland, a writer for *The Washington Post*, published an article, entitled: "George as a buff young man" (September 5, 2005), suggesting that "George Washington may have been kind of hot." She was discussing a project then being undertaken by Jeffrey Schwartz, at the University of Pittsburgh, to employ "forensic" techniques to create statues of Washington at ages 19, 45, and 57, working with known features and working backward to recreate a skeleton and then flesh it out. A preliminary finding reports that, at 19 ,Washington was a "good looking" young man.

55. Edmund S. Morgan, "The Aloof American," in *George Washington Reconsidered*, 287-307.

56. *The Writings of George Washington* 1, 23-25, 24-25 (for the speech).

57. Flexner, 11.

58. *The Writings of George Washington* 1, 25-27.

59. *Ibid.*, 27; Lengel, 24-29.

60. Lengel, 31; *The Writings of George Washington* 1, 30.

61. Lengel, 30-34. "Disingenuous" or not, it cannot be said that Washington had not "warned" Dinwiddie of his lack of experience.

62. *Ibid.*, 36.

63. *Ibid.*, 34-38, the quotation is on p. 37; Flexner, 15-16; *The Writings of George Washington*, "Journal of [the] March Toward the Ohio," 1, 36-58, including letters to Governor Dinwiddie and various others (see, pp. 55-56 for the account of the killing of Jumonville). Among the letters is one to Colonel Joshua Fry, in which Washington reported the results of the battle to his superior officer. Fry had fallen from his horse and suffered a serious injury earlier, had never joined the fray with the French, and died on May 31, 1754. Command of the expedition thus officially passed to Washington and Dinwiddie promoted him to colonel of provincial forces, June 4, 1754. See, also: Longmore, 20-23.

64. Lengel, 38; Flexner, 18.

65. Flexner, 16-17, for the quotation; Lengel, 38; Woodward, 62-64; Morton, 651-56. Morton explains (p. 652) that, after the death of Colonel Joshua Fry, Colonel James Innes was given command of "all the forces operating in Virginia," and that Washington was promoted to colonel and given command of the First Virginia Regiment and the position of second-in-command to Innes. He also says (p. 656) that: "There is no doubt that Washington's inexperience and rashness were partly responsible for the disaster at Great Meadows." See, also: Ellis, *His Excellency,* 16-18.

66. Flexner, 18

67. Morton, 661.

68. Longmore, 19-21.

69. *Ibid.*, 15-16.

70. *The Writings of George Washington* 1, 70, 70-71 n 31. There had been only one Virginian killed in the skirmish.

71. Longmore, 21.

72. Clinton Rossiter, *The First American Revolution* (a revised version of *Seedtime of the Republic*) (New York: Harcourt, Brace and Company), the quotation is the foreword, and is truncated, 4-5. John Adams used words like these on a number of occasions in his writings, including those to Thomas Jefferson.

73. Flexner, 20-26; Ellis, *His Excellency,* 19-24.

74. Flexner, 27-28; Longmore, 31-33.

75. Flexner, 29-33. Washington seems to have suffered, in both this and the earlier instance, from dysentery, but Flexner suggests that he may also have had a touch of tuberculosis that he must have contracted earlier from Lawrence.

76. *Ibid.,* 33-34; Ellis, *His Excellency,* 31-35. Ellis makes the point (p. 29) that Washington was becoming adept at playing politics, "while claiming total disinterest in the game." There was some skirmishing with the French before Washington actually occupied the deserted fort, and George had clearly expected opposition when he advanced on the fort. To insure stealth, Washington even had all the dogs in the regiment killed before he advanced.

77. Flexner, 34-35.

78. Robin Reilly, *Wolfe of Quebec* (London: Cassell & Co., 1960), *passim*, and esp. 163-316.

79. Ellis, *His Excellency,* 28. Washington's falling-out with Dinwiddie, and his mixed "admiration" and contempt for Lord John Campbell, Earl of Loudoun, not to mention his difficulties with the Virginia House of Burgesses, would seem to suggest that this "abiding respect" came to Washington as a delayed response.

80. *Ibid,* 30, for the quotation, and also 28-35.

81. Longmore, 27-28. George's supporters included William Fairfax, George William Fairfax, and John Carlyle, among other prominent persons.

82. Morton, 718-22. It was not necessary for one to live in the county one was chosen to represent. "Treating" the voters was not at all unusual. After everyone got sufficiently relaxed, the vote was taken by a show of hands or by ayes and nays.

83. Longmore, 56-67; Cunliffe, viii.

84. Longmore, 86-87.

85. *Ibid.,* 3-4; Ellis, *His Excellency,* 45, emphasis added by the present writer.

86. Bishop William Meade, *Old Churches, Ministers and Families of Virginia* 2 (Philadelphia: J.B. Lippincott Company, 1804), 243.

87. *Ibid.,* 247.

88. *Ibid.,* 244.

89. *Ibid.,* 254-55.

90. Burns and Dunn, 51-53

91. Sydnor, 64-83.

92. *Ibid.,* 100-6.

93.The term "peers" is used in this essay to mean colleagues, associates, or those roughly equal to one's self, and is not used in the technical British sense.

94. *The Writings of George Washington* 1, 34 (G.W. to Richard Corbin, March 1754), 35 (G.W. to Robert Dinwiddie, March 20, 1754), 107-8 (G.W. to Robert Orme, March 15, 1755); *The Writings of George Washington* 2, 172-74 (G.W. to Brigadier General

John Stanwix, April 10, 1758), 176-77 (G.W. to Colonel Thomas Gage, April 12, 1758), to cite but a few examples.

95. *The Writings of George Washington* 1, 128-31 (G.W .to John Augustine Washington, May 28, 1755).

96. Ellis, *His Excellency,* 38.

97. *Ibid.*, 38-39. The quotation is on p. 38.

98. *Ibid.*, 35, 39.

99. Flexner, 39-50; Ellis, *His Excellency,* 35-39, 41-43; Cormac O'Brien, "Martha Washington," *Secret Lives of the First Ladies* (Philadelphia: Quirk Press, 2005), 11-17. Discussion of George Washington's possible sterility would not have enhanced his "macho" image at all. Could such a condition have been caused by his early bout with small pox? There has also been some speculation that George's marriage to Martha was loveless, and that he was deeply in love with Sally Fairfax, the wife of his good friend, William Fairfax. There is no evidence of anything more than George's unrequited love for the slightly older Sally, to whom he wrote a few mash notes. Patsy Custis died in 1773, after suffering from epilepsy her whole life. Jackie died in 1781 of "camp fever" while in the army.

100. Ellis, *His Excellency,* 40.

101. *The Diaries of George Washington, 1748-1799,* 1, 107-455. There does not seem to be a single notation here concerning British-American politics; all is routine rural.

102. Flexner, 51, 52, and for the quotations, 54-55.

103. Lawrence Henry Gipson, *The Coming of the Revolution, 1763-1775* (New York: Harper & Brothers [The New American Nation Series], 1954), xi-xiv, and *passim.* See also Walter L. Dorn, *Competition for Empire, 1740-1763* (New York: Harper & Row, 1963), *passim,* for the European issues and background.

104. Rhys Isaac, *The Transformation of Virginia, 1740-1790* (Chapel Hill: University of North Carolina Press [for the Institute of Early American History and Culture, Williamsburg, VA], 1982), 320-57, and *passim*; Carl Bridenbaugh, *The Spirit of '76: The Growth of American Patriotism Before Independence, 1607-1776* (London: Oxford University Press, 1975), 73-105.

105. Ellis, *His Excellency,* 61. George Mason, who preferred to stay home at Gunston Hall and allow Washington to make the presentation, had, in fact, written the Washington proposal. It is not clear that the Americans ever accepted the right of Parliament to levy external taxes on them as a matter of right. The Virginia Resolves, which Washington introduced, and which the House adopted unanimously, were clear in stating that the sole authority for taxing Virginians belonged to the governor and assembly of Virginia.

106. *The Writings of George Washington* 2, 500-1. Note Washington's easy use of the word American in the quotation. See also Bridenbaugh, 106-40.

107. Bridenbaugh, 141-54.

108. Flexner, 58 (see also, 57-61).

109. William W. Abbot, *A Virginia Chronology 1585-1783* (Williamsburg: Virginia 350th Anniversary Celebration Corporation, 1957), 66-67. Ellis, *His Excellency,* 61, says that George wrote to friend George William Fairfax in London and "vowed" that the cause of Boston would never become the cause of America. The Fairfaxes remained

Loyalists throughout the war, and their property in Virginia went unmolested. That was not very unusual, however, because, as a general rule, many Loyalists or their families remained in Norfolk and elsewhere in Virginia and neither they nor their properties were seriously molested unless they took up arms or tried to return to their homes after having taken up arms.

110. Flexner, 58.

111. Abbot, 67.

112. Fairfax County Resolves, July 18, 1774, maintained by Jon Roland of the Constitution Society (Internet: constitution.org/bcp/Fairfax_res.htm, 2003), 1,2 of 5. Ellis, *His Excellency,* 63, thinks, very appropriately, that George Mason had a great influence in shaping Washington's thought. He also states that Washington thought the British crossed a line when they occupied Boston, and that war became a real possibility because of it.

113. Lynn Montross, *The Reluctant Rebels: The Story of the Continental Congress, 1774-1789* (New York: Harper & Brothers Publishers, 1950), 3-40, 41-42 (for the quotations). There never was a Third Continental Congress, as the second simply went on, with occasional breaks, for about fourteen years.

114. *Ibid.*, 43-73, and *passim.* Washington was overcome with modesty. He had left the room when his name was being discussed (other leaders were discussed and passed over) and is said to have looked as if stricken when he was selected. He no doubt thought about his lovely Mount Vernon. Geographic factors were considered as important as experience in the selection process.

115. Bruce Chadwick, *George Washington's War: The Forging of a Revolutionary Leader and the American Presidency* (Naperville, IL: Sourcebooks, Inc., 2004); David Hackett Fischer, *Washington's Crossing* (New York: Oxford University Press, 2004); David McCullough, *1776* (New York: Simon & Schuster, 2005); and Lengel.

116. Ellis.

117. Henry Wiencek, *An Imperfect God: George Washington, His Slaves, and the Creation of America* (New York: Farrar, Straus and Giroux, 2003).

118. Burns and Dunn.

119. Flexner, 178-180 (the quotation is on p. 179).

120. Longmore, 60.

121. Lengel, 105-13.

122. *Ibid.*, 113-18.

123. *Ibid.*, 120.

124. *Ibid.*, 127.

125. *Ibid.*, 369.

126. Ellis, *His Excellency,* 271, for the quotation.

127. McCullough, 290. A good portion of this book is devoted to an analysis of the battles of Trenton and Princeton, which are portrayed as the "turning point" in the war. See Fischer, 367, for the quotation "in the New Jersey campaign . . . ." The focus of this book is primarily on the battles of Trenton and Princeton.

128. McCullough, 291.

129. *Ibid.*, 293.

130. Lengel, 368-69.

131. *Ibid.*

132. McCullough, 293-94.

133. *Ibid.*

134. Fischer, 367.

135. Ellis, *His Excellency,* 134.

136. Flexner, 156-64; Lengel, 330-44; Ellis, 130-38. Washington had the very capable help of several excellent commanders in his army, including: General Nathaniel Greene; Inspector General Friedrich Wilhelm Augustus von Steuben; General Marie Joseph Paul Yves Roch Gilbert du Motier, Marquis de Lafayette; and others.

137. Ellis, *His Excellency,* 143-44.

138. *Ibid.,* 144-45.

139. *Ibid.,* 139.

140. *Ibid.,* 146. The Confederation Congress had superceded the Second Continental Congress under the Articles of Confederation (the first constitution, as it were) proposed in 1777 and adopted in 1781.

141. Longmore, 204, 208. "Republican" is here spelled with a lower case " r " signifying a political theory or ideal, and does not refer to any political party of any period.

142. Glenn A. Phelps, "The Republican General," in *George Washington Reconsidered,* 166-97, 167 for the quotation.

143. *Ibid.,* 168.

144. *Ibid.*

145. *Ibid.,* 170-71. The emphasis in the quotation is added by the present writer.

146. Gordon S. Wood, *The Radicalism of the American Revolution* (New York: Random House, Vintage Books, 1991), 93-145, for background.

147. *Ibid.,* 145-168. Longmore, 213-226. See also Bailyn, 25-26.

148. Thad W. Tate, "The Coming of the Revolution in Virginia: Britain's Challenge to Virginia's Ruling Class, 1763-1776, *The William and Mary Quarterly,* 3rd Series, 19, no. 3 (July 1962): 323-43.

149. Chadwick, 71, for the quotation from Percy.

150. Fischer, 98, 103, 113.

151. *Ibid.,* 238-40, 255, 258-59, 376-79.

152. Ellis, *His Excellency,* 245, quoting Paine.

153. Rutyna and Stewart, 123-24.

154. The following books devote considerable space to Washington's presidency from 1789 through his great 1796 Farewell Address: Lengel, 352-71; Flexner, 212-402; Wood, 209-325; Chadwick, 463-500; Burns and Dunn, 31-145; Ellis, 188-271; Ellis, *Founding Brothers: The Revolutionary Generation* (New York: Alfred A. Knopf, 2004), *passim.*

155. Ellis, *His Excellency,* 263.

156. *Ibid.*

157. John Chester Miller, *The Wolf By the Ears: Thomas Jefferson and Slavery* (New York: New American Library, Meridian, 1977), *passim*; Robert McColley, *Slavery and Jeffersonian Virginia,* 2nd ed. (Urbana: University of Illinois Press, 1973), *passim*; Henry Wiencek, *An Imperfect God: George Washington, His Slaves, and the Creation of America* (New York: Farrar, Straus and Giroux, 2003), *passim.*

158. Wiencek, 157.
159. *Ibid.*, 160.
160. See the following: Ellis, *Founding Brothers*, 81-119, and *passim*; Dorothy Twohig, "Washington's Role in the Controversy over Slavery," in *George Washington Reconsidered*, 115-38; Chadwick, 403-31.

Molly Pitcher

Ellen E. Dodge
Butler County Community College of Pennsylvania

Although the name "Molly Pitcher" looms large in the local history of Cumberland County, Pennsylvania, there was never a person named Molly Pitcher. The heroine celebrated for her heroic deeds during the American Revolution and who, as a resident of Carlisle, Pennsylvania, died there in 1832, was Mary Ludwig Hays McCauley. She was a genuine folk heroine. Married to William Hays at the time of the Battle of Monmouth, she later married John McCauley.

It was not until years after her death that she achieved the status of heroine. In 1876 public-spirited citizens arranged to have a stone inscribed "Molly Pitcher" for her then unmarked grave, and in 1916 the Commonwealth of Pennsylvania erected a large monument in her memory. One public-spirited citizen, Jeremiah Zeamer, editor of Carlisle's newspaper, *American Volunteer,* campaigned before 1916 against honoring Mary McCauley to no avail.[1]

Zeamer had a point. Because no one had taken her biography seriously until after her death, evidence is sketchy and conflicting. The story as we usually read about it is as follows: On June 28, 1778, in sweltering weather, American and British forces met in battle at Monmouth Courthouse, New Jersey. Molly Hays was involved in the battle by carrying her pitcher of water to quench the throats of the American artillerymen, including her husband, William Hays. William fell wounded in the battle and his doughty wife dropped her pitcher, cleaned the gun barrel to ready it for the next firing, and continued to fire it herself.

There are no contemporary military records of such a feat, although two accounts remembered by participants in the battle appeared decades later. According to one, the woman—then unidentified—had an enemy cannonball pass between her spread legs in such a way as to destroy the lower part of her petticoat. She is supposed to have said, according to veteran-of-the-battle Joseph Martin, that she was lucky that the cannonball had not passed a little higher. The story became part of the legend.

While the cannonball story seems contrived, perhaps it is not. Molly in her younger days might have been a bit bawdy. In his campaign to keep the woman with the pitcher from being recognized by the commonwealth, Zeamer wrote to Congressman M. E. Olmstead that a townswoman had remembered Mary McCauley as "a vulgar, very profane, drunken old woman."[2]

In 1822, ten years before Molly's death, the Pennsylvania legislature voted to grant $40 per year to her, not as a soldier's widow, but for her own actions in the Revolutionary War. This award by the state legislature in itself gives credence to her story.[3]

There are details of Molly's life that are not known. She was born perhaps in 1754 but there seems to be no record of her birthplace. One account, related by Martha Washington's grandson, George Washington Parke Custis—who was not present at the battle—has it that Molly's husband William died at Monmouth. However, records do show that he lived out the rest of his life in Carlisle and died in 1786. She later married McCauley.[4]

It should not be considered strange that a woman appeared with an army. There were many such, not soldiers, but women who performed the necessary tasks of cooking, sewing, and laundering. They were known as "camp followers." It was customary for an army to authorize three to six women per company to receive rations for themselves in return for services. Women were also hired as nurses to tend to the wounded.[5]

To complicate further the story of the woman with the pitcher who became known as Molly Pitcher, the candidacy of one Margaret Corbin has been put forth. Her story is similar to that of Mary Ludwig Hays McCauley. When her husband was killed at Fort Washington in New York, she took over his artillery duties and suffered disability from her part in the battle. It may have been from Corbin's story that Custis assumed that Mary's husband died in battle.

There indeed are other stories of Revolutionary War heroines. Molly and Margaret were not the only ones. Whether or not the story is factually true does not negate its importance. The endurance of a legend says something about the culture of the people who believe it. If this story is not completely factual, it is not the only such story in history.

Notes

1. D. W. Thompson and Merri Lou Schaumann, "Goodbye, Molly Pitcher," *Cumberland County History* (Summer 1989): 3, 4, 18.

2. *Ibid.,* 20.

3. *The American Revolution, 1775-1783: An Encyclopedia* (New York: Garland Publishing Company, Inc., 1983), 986.

4. Thompson and Schaumann, 18, 11.

5. Major General Jeanne Holm, *Women in the Military: An Unfinished Revolution* (Novato, CA: Presidio Press, 1982), 4, 5.

Toussaint Louverture
and the Haitian Revolution

David Geggus
University of Florida

According to the British *Annual Register* for 1802, the major public figure of that year was a small, elderly West Indian who had spent half of his life as a slave. The public career of Toussaint Louverture lasted barely a decade and had just come to an end. Deported that summer from the Caribbean, where he ruled the French colony of Saint-Domingue, Toussaint died in a French prison in April 1803. A few weeks before, William Wordsworth published in the London *Morning Post* his sonnet, "To Toussaint L'Ouverture." Brief biographies had already appeared in France, England, South Carolina, and Sweden. Another soon followed, by the abolitionist James Stephen, that went through four English and Irish editions in a year and began: "Every body has heard of Toussaint, the famous Negro general." The German press hailed him as "a highly admirable, truly great man, whose sad fate one wants to mourn."[1]

Toussaint was popular with France's enemies because he had stood up to Napoleon Bonaparte, and he was celebrated by abolitionists and radicals as a symbol of antislavery. As a leader of the largest and most destructive of American slave uprisings, he was generally feared in colonialist circles, and his first French biographers vilified him as a sanguinary and duplicitous tyrant. However, the fact that some Southern slave owners praised him for his respectful attitude toward whites and for imposing forced labor on the former slaves of Saint-Domingue suggests some of the man's complexity.[2] Toussaint's modern biographers have offered diverse portraits that include Erwin Rüsch's charismatic opportunist, C.L.R. James's humane and statesmanlike black Jacobin, and Pierre Pluchon's conservative black racist.[3] All agree that Toussaint was the dominant figure of the Haitian Revolution of 1791-1804, which ended slavery in the Caribbean's wealthiest colony and created the Americas' second independent state. His contribution to both these achievements, however, remains controversial, as does his role in the initial uprising from which they emerged.

Early Life

The colony of Saint-Domingue, where Toussaint was born probably in 1746, was the world's major exporter of tropical produce for most of the eighteenth century. A dynamo of the Atlantic economy, by 1790 it was generating at least two-fifths of France's foreign trade and absorbing one-tenth of U.S. exports as well as more African slaves than anywhere in the Americas. On the brutally productive sugar estates of its coastal plains and the coffee plantations being cut out of its mountain forests, most slaves lived short lives and rarely had children who reached adulthood. Yet between the early 1770s and the outbreak of the French Revolution, its enslaved population doubled to nearly one-half million.

Toussaint's experience of slavery was unusual. The eldest child of African parents, he was raised with numerous siblings on the Bréda sugar plantation at Haut-du-Cap in northern Saint-Domingue. His father, a war captive sold to European traders, seems to have been singled out by the plantation owner for favored treatment, because his fellow slaves treated him as a man of high status. Apparently christened Hyppolite, he was the son of Gao Guinou, commander of the army of Dahomey, a powerful West African kingdom. This prestigious lineage probably served Toussaint well throughout his life, as did the pleasure he took (unusual for American-born slaves) in speaking his parents' Aja-Fon language. Such "Arada" slaves, as the French called them, from what is now Togo and Benin, were numerous in Saint-Domingue during this period and, although by the time of the revolution they accounted for only 1 in 13 adult slaves, they played a predominant role in shaping Haitian popular culture. Spared from laboring in the cane fields, Toussaint worked with the plantation livestock as stable-lad and, later, coachman. Using herbalist knowledge passed on by his father, he gained a reputation as a horse doctor, and in old age he was still an indefatigable rider.[4]

Coachmen were the most glamorous figures in the slave community. Sharply dressed, they enjoyed unusual mobility and had frequent contact with their owners and white society. This gave Toussaint a basic command of French in addition to the French creole that was the lingua franca of Saint-Domingue, which, as later sources tell us, he could speak with mesmeric effect. Growing up on the outskirts of the major seaport of Cap-Français, Saint-Domingue's largest town, also gave him broader horizons than the average rural slave. Although white society in the colony had a profane and fast-living reputation, Toussaint belonged to the last generation of slaves exposed to the proselytizing of the Jesuits before their expulsion from the French Caribbean in the mid-1760s. This presumably was when he acquired the piety for which he was later famous and the smattering of Latin phrases he liked to drop. His slave godfather taught him to read—a great rarity—but he did not learn to sign his name until some time between 1779 and 1791.[5]

116

Toussaint's early years thus taught him how to move between different social worlds: African, creole, and French. The social skills this required may help explain why contemporaries subsequently claimed one of his dominant characteristics to be a virtuoso use of deception. This trait is certainly relevant to the startling discovery, made only in the 1970s, that, when the Haitian Revolution began, Toussaint was no longer a member of the "slave elite" but had been free for many years and was both a landowner and a slaveowner.[6] During his rise to power in 1791-92, some contemporaries certainly thought he was a slave and Toussaint seems to have fostered this illusion with remarkable success. For historians, the more conservative features of his later life suddenly became easier to explain, and his bizarre claim to Napoleon to have had a fortune of 648,000 francs before the revolution appeared to make more sense.[7] His most recent biographer, Pierre Pluchon, cast him as "a man of the Ancien régime," a sort of black colonist.

Toussaint's literacy and Christianity, his liking for European culture, and his support for forced labor and plantation agriculture are indeed all less surprising when we know that, from the age of 25 or so, he lived as a propertied free man. However, the revisionism goes too far and obscures some basic points. The evidence shows Toussaint owning merely one slave, whom he freed in 1776, and leasing another 13 on a very small coffee plantation that he briefly rented from his son-in-law. His only land purchase cataloged in Saint-Domingue's voluminous notarial archives was for three undeveloped acres adjoining the Bréda plantation. Here he continued to live, working for Bayon de Libertat, who ran the estate for the Bréda family heirs. Perhaps he continued as coachman, but more certainly he acted as overseer when the very active Bayon began building his own plantation in the 1780s a dozen miles away. In August 1791, on the eve of the slave insurrection, he was described as directing the slaves in putting out a fire in the cane fields.[8] Toussaint's continuing association with his old plantation no doubt encouraged the perception that he remained a slave.

More than this, however, his wife, children, and brothers were still slaves and being inventoried as part of the estate. Although historians usually depict Suzanne Baptiste as a literate free black woman who married Toussaint around 1780, she was, in fact, the laundress in the plantation house, and there is no record of their ever marrying.[9] There is thus no question of Toussaint having a large fortune, or he would have bought his family's freedom. Saint-Domingue was exceptional in having a substantial nonwhite planter class, but it tended to be freeborn and of mixed racial descent, and a fortune of 600,000 francs would have made Toussaint one of its wealthiest. Instead, he was fairly typical of the colony's black freedmen, who made up the lowest stratum of the free people of color and still lived in the penumbra of slavery. More needs to be known about the sociology of this group, but evidence suggests that, in the Haitian Revolution,

117

free blacks exhibited two contrary tendencies: They were more likely to combine with either slaves or whites than with other free people of color.[10]   Important slave conspiracies and rebellions were led by free blacks in Venezuela in 1795, Havana in 1812, and South Carolina in 1822. Toussaint Bréda's involvement in the huge Saint-Domingue uprising of 1791 remains the great mystery of the Haitian Revolution.

The 1791 Slave Revolt

The revolution began at the apex of Saint-Domingue society in 1789 as a movement for self-government and free trade among wealthy colonists who were encouraged by the promise of reform in France. They were soon challenged by poorer whites demanding their own political voice and by free people of color seeking an end to racial discrimination. These conflicts simmered for two years, interacting with the unfolding revolution in Paris. In August 1791, when the white population was riven by rumors of secession and counterrevolution, free coloreds launched an insurrection in the colony's west province, where they outnumbered whites, while the slaves around Cap-Français began a devastating rebellion that swept through the northern plain and into the surrounding mountains.[11]   The two simultaneous uprisings were unconnected, but each contributed to the other's success by paralyzing white resistance. Whites fled pell-mell from the countryside, and within weeks hundreds were killed and more than a thousand plantations were burned. An improvised cordon of camps managed to contain the slave revolt within the north province, but military sorties from Cap-Français and Port-au-Prince proved ineffective against the insurgents' guerrilla tactics. The fighting was vicious. Throughout the revolution, the slaughter of non-combatants and the use of torture and mutilation were widespread; both white and black soldiers made collections of severed heads.

Conservative colonists asserted that the slaves, led astray by libertarian ideology, were calling for the Rights of Man. Far more evident among the rebels, however, was their use of royalist symbols and a church and king rhetoric. Like many other slave insurgents in this age of revolution and abolitonism, they demanded a liberty, or sometimes just "three free days" (per week), that they claimed the king had already granted them but that the colonists were covering up.[12]   Numerous past events, embellished by rumor and viewed through the lens of wishful thinking, lent plausibility to such beliefs, but there is little doubt that they were deliberately shaped by astute leaders to mobilize support. The uprising began a few weeks after news arrived of Louis XVI's flight to Varrennes, which marked his rejection of the French Revolution. Since most colonists were prorevolutionary, it seems the slaves' strategy was to declare their friendship for their enemy's enemy. They also sought the support of the extremely conservative

Spanish of neighboring Santo Domingo, with whom they were soon covertly trading plunder for munitions. Recent scholarship has also stressed the monarchical ideologies many slaves had known in Africa.

White radicals, however, soon came to suspect that the slaves and free coloreds were tools of their royalist opponents in the administration and military, who hoped that turmoil in Saint Domingue would provoke a counterrevolution in France. These suspicions sent the governor to the guillotine in 1793, and they are taken seriously by some historians today. Yet it is fairly clear that slave leaders like Jeannot, the *médecin-général*, who pretended to be in league with certain officers and colonists, were merely trying to exploit these suspicions to further divide their opponents, as well as boost their followers' confidence, and perhaps gain legitimacy in the eyes of the Spanish.[13]

Toussaint's role in the uprising has for two centuries been depicted in two contrasting narratives. The best known presents Toussaint as the loyal slave preserving order on the Haut-du-Cap plantation for several months before deciding to join the insurgents. He then drove Mme Bayon de Libertat to safety and left for the rebel camp, where he became an advisor to the number two leader, Georges Biassou. The fact Toussaint does not appear in the historical record of the revolution until December 1791 lends support to this account.[14] In the second version, he played a key role, that of a trusted intermediary recruited by a group of white counterrevolutionaries to organize the rebellion. Being cautious and slight of stature, he chose as leaders physically imposing men, who were slave-drivers and coachmen, but he himself kept in the background. This version, favored by most Haitian historians, appeared in an 1801 report by François Kerverseau, a French general serving in Saint-Domingue.[15]

Pierre Pluchon, author of several Louverture biographies, argued that this was a false rumor that Toussaint encouraged at the height of his power so as to write himself back into the revolution's founding moments.[16] If the story was just self-serving propaganda, however, one wonders why the black leader, then an official of the French Republic, did not invent for himself a more glorious role than that of tool of the counterrevolution. Unexploited Spanish sources in fact reveal that this story dates from at least the summer of 1793 and that it originated with Georges Biassou, Toussaint's superior.[17] Locked in a power struggle with Jean-François, the principal leader of the insurgent slaves, Biassou wanted to convince their Spanish allies to recognize him as supreme commander. The argument is rather absurd: Toussaint supposedly received a written commission from a random group of royalists, including a judge and a journalist, but he proved too hesitant and so handed over to Biassou. The supporting documents Biassou produced were obviously clumsy forgeries. Yet they may well represent the illiterate Biassou's attempt to substantiate a story the wily Toussaint had concocted on the eve of the 1791 revolt. Otherwise, it is hard to

119

understand why the self-proclaimed Generalissimo Biassou would seek to establish his primacy by reference to his subaltern, unless he had really been the architect of the slave uprising.

La Liberté Générale

All this leaves unsettled the motives and goals of Toussaint and of the slave insurgents in general, which is an equally controversial issue. When Toussaint first appeared as a public figure, in the fourth month of the insurrection, it was as one of several free men of color in the rebel slaves' camp seeking to negotiate a peace on behalf of Jean-François and Biassou. He held no military rank at that time but appeared to be an influential figure. Several eyewitnesses depicted him as keen to end the rebellion and return most of the insurgents to slavery. He in fact persuaded Jean-François to reduce his demand that 300 leaders be freed to only 50. He also intervened to protect white prisoners, whom he escorted to safety.[18] The negotiations broke down because of the intransigence of the planters and the refusal of the rebels, mainly African, to accept the compromise peace their creole leaders were secretly discussing.[19] Historians generally assert that, once these negotiations failed, Toussaint became an unwavering champion of "general liberty," as the complete ending of slavery was called.[20] Eight months later, however, in summer 1792, we find him and Jean-François making renewed overtures that would have restored slavery in exchange for peace and amnesty.[21]

Both attempts at negotiation occurred when the colonists were expecting large military reinforcements from Europe. The slave leaders' actions might thus be interpreted as pragmatically flexible rather than callous betrayals. On the other hand, their compromises and royalist affectations, and the fact that Jean-François and Biassou rounded up women and children on the plantations for sale to the Spanish, suggest the slave insurrection was more a premodern rebellion than a revolution inspired by libertarian ideals. Historians have had trouble making sense of the diverse pronouncements supposedly made by different slave leaders and their followers. None has noticed that the only letter by Jean-François and Biassou that demands an end to slavery looks very much like it was forged by their royalist opponent, Colonel Cambefort, so as to discredit his radical critics.[22] The two other main leaders, Jeannot and Boukman, who both were killed in early November 1791, appear to have been more militant. In Toussaint's case, however, there is no documentary evidence connecting him to the goal of abolishing slavery until the eve of its abolition in August 1793.

For Pierre Pluchon, Toussaint's behavior reflected his status as propertied freeman; it showed the gap that separated him from the rural masses. I would contend, however, it is precisely Toussaint's free status that offers the strongest argument for his commitment to improving the lot of the slaves. Without such a commitment, it is difficult to explain why he remained with the insurgent slaves after the December 1791 negotiations failed. He could have accepted the amnesty offered by the National Assembly, as did many free men of color. When France finally abolished racial discrimination in April 1792, most free colored insurgents achieved an uneasy reconciliation with the whites, with whom they then began to combine their efforts in suppressing insurgent slaves in different parts of the colony.

During the following year, as the veteran fighters in the northern mountains faced increasing pressure from troops sent from France, Toussaint Bréda emerged as a military leader with his own group of followers. Usually he was the subordinate of *Viceroi* Biassou, the hard-drinking ex-slave driver; sometimes he served with *Grand Amiral* Jean-François, the handsome and elegant former coachman. Documents from this period variously call him *maréchal, lieutenant-général* or *général d'armée.* In spring 1793, the position of the rebel slaves dramatically improved when the French Republic, after executing Louis XVI, declared war on Spain and England. The Spanish government, hoping to conquer Saint Domingue in a cut-price campaign, offered the insurgents munitions and food, with uniforms and pay for their officers and freedom and land for themselves and their families. The slave regime, though seriously weakened, was still functioning in most parts of Saint Domingue. The Spanish planned to take it over using ex-slave mercenaries and revive it. By early June, the fighters of Jean-François, Biassou, and Toussaint, had become the *tropas auxiliares* of Carlos IV.

Facing invasion by the two main colonial powers, the French administration in Saint-Domingue also needed black soldiers and, after offering piecemeal concessions, found that the only way it could outbid the Spanish was to free all the slaves. Contemporaries described the emancipation proclamation of August 29, 1793, as "an electric shock."[23] It was the first time slavery had been abolished in a major slave society. Antislavery discourse had been a peripheral and strictly theoretical feature of the Enlightenment and played only a marginal role in the early French Revolution. The official responsible for the decree, Civil Commissioner Sonthonax, who had an antislavery background, had no authorization for the measure, but he did know that hostility to slavery was increasing in Paris as the Jacobins became ascendant.

It was against this background that Toussaint adopted, in early August, the name Louverture ("the opening") with its cryptic connotation of a new beginning. In a letter to free colored opponents dated August 25, he declared himself "the first to stand up for" general emancipation, a cause he had "always supported . . . and having begun, I will finish." Four days later, in a similar letter, he dictated the lines almost all his biographers cite, which began: "I am Toussaint Louverture . . . I want liberty and equality to reign in Saint Domingue."[24] Most historians treat these two documents as defining the man and his mission; some see in them proof that he was the instigator of the 1791 uprising. Conservative historians, like Rüsch and Pluchon, however, ignore them as being of no significance. For Pluchon, the "real" Toussaint was revealed in other letters with a very royalist tone that said nothing of emancipation, which he continued to send to his opponents up to this time.[25] The letters of August 25 and 29 were certainly less dramatic than one would judge from the edited extracts historians usually cite. Their references to emancipation, in fact, were made among a mélange of arguments that mix racial solidarity and the restoration of the monarchy, stability for plantation agriculture, divine punishment, and vengeance for Vincent Ogé (a martyred hero of the free coloreds). They, nonetheless, were the first documentary linkage between the black general and the ideal of abolishing slavery.[26]

The letters were thus hardly insignificant, but neither were they proof of a long-standing commitment to general emancipation. Toussaint's evocation of liberty and equality at this time looks very much like a response to Sonthonax's move toward outright abolition. In mid-July, the commissioner was already telling black leaders that emancipation was on the way, indeed inevitable.[27] Toussaint may have taken his lead from these developments and decided to rewrite his role in the revolution. This was precisely the time Georges Biassou passed on to the Spanish the story of Toussaint's participation in a counterrevolutionary plot, which similarly made him the instigator of the slave uprising. However, the unflattering picture of Toussaint in Biassou's documents makes it unlikely that the two men were launching a joint propaganda campaign. A more reasonable inference, perhaps, is that he was indeed the instigator. As for his libertarian credentials, no document connects him with the idea of general emancipation until it was almost a reality, but it is dubious that anyone would orchestrate such a massively destructive rebellion for merely reformist goals. The fact that Toussaint was already free, and did not lead the rebellion, weakens the argument he was motivated by self-interest and ambition. He distinguished himself from Jean-François and Biassou in not rounding up slaves for sale to the Spanish; and, unlike them, he began in August 1793 quietly giving lip-service to the idea of freedom for all, claiming always to have fought for it. The altruistic picture of the black leader is thus slightly more convincing than the cynical and conservative ones, although it is nowhere near as solidly based as most of its proponents have imagined.

For eight months after Sonthonax's emancipation proclamation, Toussaint continued to fight for the proslavery Spanish against the republican French. Several factors might explain this. The commissioner's position in Saint-Domingue was precarious, as was that of the French Republic in Europe with fighting foreign invasions and civil war. There was no point in backing the losing side. While Toussaint may have been restrained by his royalist inclinations, as he said at the time, or seduced by the attractions of Spanish service, his forces were not yet large enough to challenge the army Spain was expected to assemble, or the other black generals. Finally, the choice between the proslavery Spanish and the abolitionist Republirans was not quite as Manichean as it might appear. While the freedom Sonthonax offered was little more than remunerated serfdom, the Spanish in 1793 were in no position to force blacks back into plantation work in those areas where they had abandoned it. Blacks in Saint Domingue therefore spent the fall of 1793 waiting to see whether the Convention in Paris would ratify Sonthonax's decree and how Spanish policy would develop once planters sought to return to their estates.

As soon as he entered Spanish service, Toussaint revealed himself as a highly astute military leader, adept at ambush and at totally confusing opponents. Spanish officials found him pious, prudent, honorable, and dignified.[28] While his superior, Biassou, lived it up in the frontier towns of Santo Domingo, Toussaint won a series of victories in the northern mountains against the French and free men of color. He proved both ruthless and humane, capable of making barbarous threats but of sparing even those who had double-crossed him. This policy reaped rewards. White and free-colored property owners surrendered to him, knowing his reputation for mercy and his interest in preserving the plantation regime. His conquest of new regions little affected by the slave revolt nonetheless opened up new opportunities for recruiting. As arms and ammunition fell into his hands, so his tiny army grew. Lances and machetes were exchanged for muskets. Free colored and even French soldiers joined its ranks and helped train its levies. At the end of the year, he broke through the cordon separating the north and west provinces and took the port of Gonaïves. It became an important source of foreign supplies for the rest of the revolution.

Not until April 1794 do French or Spanish sources suggest that Toussaint favored a broader scheme of emancipation than the one the Spanish supported. For the cynics, this confirms that his pronouncements of the previous August were meaningless and that, when he abandoned the Spanish for the French in spring 1794, his decision had nothing to do with libertarian ideals but resulted from personal calculation. There had long been friction between the leading black generals. The vain and powerful Jean-François had once held Toussaint captive and he caused the death of his younger brother Pierre. Biassou had been stealing the supplies of Toussaint's troops and selling as slaves their wives and children. Although Spanish officials recognized the superior talents of the freedman, they tended to side with his two rivals as these conflicts came to a head in 1794. At the same time, the French Republic went on the offensive in Europe and began to look like a more attractive ally, while the Spanish and British invasions of Saint-Domingue sputtered. Resistance came from various quarters: From plantation blacks who had not taken up arms but who now refused to be coerced back into the fields; from free coloreds disenchanted with their treatment by the Spanish; and from some of the black mercenary troops as well, who deserted to the French. It was behind this movement that Toussaint decided to fling his weight around the beginning of May 1794.[29]

The altruistic case for Toussaint's *volte-face* from royalism to republicanism links it to the decree of February 4, 1794, by which the French Convention ratified Sonthonax's initiative and abolished slavery in all France's colonies. This became the official version: Toussaint rallied to the republic once revolutionary France adopted antislavery. The problem with this argument is that, when Toussaint declared his allegiance to the French general Laveaux in May, the decree was still unknown in Saint Domingue owing to the wartime dearth of shipping. The problem is not insuperable, however, for Toussaint's about-face was a drawn-out, devious affair. For several months after he informed Laveaux he was fighting hard for the republic, he emained largely on the defensive, assuring the Spanish that such hostilities as occurred (including several massacres of colonists) should be blamed on his disobedient subordinates. He tried to allay the suspicions of Jean-François and also promised his allegiance to the British forces who were threatening him from the south. In the meantime, news trickled through from Europe of the abolition of slavery and of French victories, while in Saint-Domingue the spring rains brought fevers that decimated the Spanish and British troops. Cunningly choosing his moment, Toussaint then fell on each of his opponents in turn with devastating effect.

Whether motivated by idealism or ambition, Toussaint's reversal of alliances was cautious and protracted, and it was not a single-handed initiative. Nor did it rescue an entirely powerless republican regime from strong invading armies, which is the traditional interpretation. The free colored commander of Cap-Français, Jean-Louis Villatte, easily routed the Spanish army's long-delayed invasion in May. The *volte-face* was nonetheless a decisive turning point in the Haitian Revolution. Black militancy and the libertarian ideology of the French Revolution were now melded, and the cause of slave emancipation had found a leader of genius. The balance of power tipped against the alliance of slave owners and foreign invaders. French rule in Saint Domingue would be saved for almost a decade, but real power shifted rapidly to the free men of color and the former slaves who were becoming their rivals.

The Rise of Toussaint, 1794-1798

During the following four years of almost constant warfare, Toussaint's ragged soldiers continually lacked food, clothing, and ammunition. They died by the hundreds attacking the well-entrenched positions of the British and Spanish, but

124

in the process was forged a formidable army. The rank and file were in large measure Africans; the officer corps was a mixture of black ex-slaves, *anciens libres* (as free colored were called now that all were free), and a few whites. Already prominent by the end of 1794 were the youthful Moïse, from the Bréda plantation, whom Toussaint called his nephew, and the grimly energetic Jean-Jacques Dessalines, both creole ex-slaves. Toussaint kept up his remarkable double game with the Spanish until October and continued to draw supplies from them, which they delivered out of fear rather than ignorance.[30] He then drove them in a rapid campaign from their frontier towns on the central savanna. Defeated in Europe and the Caribbean, Spain withdrew from the war in July 1795, surrendering Santo Domingo to France. Biassou, Jean-François, and nearly 800 of their followers and family members went into pensioned exile in different parts of the Spanish empire.[31] In the northeast mountains a few remnants of their armies fought on in the king's name until 1797.

The British and their planter allies, who occupied most of the central part of the colony, now became Toussaint's principal opponents. For nearly four years, the floodplain of the Artibonite valley acted as a no-man's land, across which Toussaint repeatedly led his forces, trying to dislodge the redcoats from their positions in Saint-Marc and Mirebalais that barred the route south to the capital, Port-au-Prince. In the most sheltered parts of the occupied zone, the plantations were kept in production using slave labor, but the British position was always precarious. During the five-year occupation of Saint Domingue, the British lost 15,000 of the 25,000 troops they sent there, primarily to yellow fever and malaria. They were constantly harried by the *anciens libres* led by André Rigaud, who controlled most of the southern peninsula. Rigaud was a goldsmith, son of a French official and his African wife, and an enthusiastic republican. Unlike many free colored, he had supported slave emancipation, but he was foremost a supporter of his own caste, the freeborn intermediate group of mixed racial descent. A considerable cultural divide separated such men from the former slaves coming to power in parts of the north, where free men of color controlled much of the littoral in an uneasy relationship with the French general and governor, Étienne Laveaux, and his few surviving European troops.

During this long struggle against the British, Toussaint's influence within the republican zone grew steadily at the expense of *anciens libres,* ex-slave rivals, and the white representatives of France. Early in 1796 the northern *anciens libres,* led by Villatte, attempted to overthrow Governor Laveaux. It apparently was a caste-based bid for independence, said to have been secretly supported by André Rigaud in the south. According to some sources, Toussaint knew of the planned coup and, with supreme cunning, even encouraged its instigators. But once it had broken out, he intervened in force and crushed it.[32] The French government was left in no doubt on whom it depended for keeping Saint

Domingue in French hands. Toussaint, the ex-slave, was proclaimed deputy-governor in April 1796 and, the following year, commander in chief.

Dissension remained rife in the republican zone for the rest of the year. The efforts of Sonthonax and a new civil commission to centralize control of the war and the economy aroused the hostility of local *ancien libre* leaders long accustomed to autonomy. Ex-slaves, who saw their future as independent peasants, resented the forced labor system that tied them to their old estates and government efforts to conscript young males as soldiers. Attempts to increase the productivity of surviving plantations spread fears of a plot to restore slavery. The northwest peninsula, where plantations had suffered comparatively little, and whose coffee was sold to American traders for food and munitions, saw a series of rebellions in which black cultivators killed most of the remaining white colonists in the region. More whites were massacred in the south, when Rigaud expelled Sonthonax's tactless officials and unofficially broke with France.

The republic was to weather these crises only at the cost of seeing more power pass into the hands of Toussaint Louverture. Pacifying the blacks of the northwest with his homespun diplomacy, he neutralized the rivalry of the African general Pierre-Michel, hero of the northeast campaigns and a favorite of Sonthonax. Earlier rivals of Toussaint had already disappeared. With the aristocratic Governor Laveaux, Toussaint had formed a remarkably close friendship, referring to him in his correspondence as "Papa," although the two men were about the same age.[33] By summer 1796, however, Toussaint was intimating that Laveaux could best serve Saint-Domingue in Paris, where angry planters were demanding the restoration of Caribbean slavery. Laveaux was promptly elected a deputy for Saint-Domingue and returned home to France. Next it was the turn of Commissioner Sonthonax. In the following summer, Toussaint suddenly accused him of plotting to make Saint Domingue independent. Although still popular with the blacks, he also was forced to depart.

Smitten with life in the West Indies and threatened by political reaction in Paris, Sonthonax may conceivably have wished to see Saint-Domingue sever ties with France. Nevertheless, Toussaint's accusation suggests a neat sense of irony. While continuing to play the role of a loyal servant of the French Republic, he eliminated one by one all his rivals within the colony. The French government becaming alarmed and in 1798 dispatched a new plenipotentiary, General Hédouville. In six months, he, too was deftly outmaneuvered, although with all due courtesy, and driven out of Saint Domingue by a supposedly spontaneous uprising.

The growth of Toussaint's power was inexorable. By 1799 observers in France, England, and the United States suspected that he would seek to make Saint-Domingue independent.[34] Most Haitian historians argue that this was his aim. Yet it was a step he would never take, although henceforth he acted more like an independent ruler than a colonial official.

126

Supreme Power, 1798-1802

Toussaint's expulsion of Sonthonax facilitated a rapprochement with Rigaud, which enabled the two men to cooperate in driving out the British over the course of 1798. Thereafter, only Rigaud himself stood between Toussaint and complete domination of Saint Domingue. With about 20,000 soldiers, Toussaint's army was twice as large as Rigaud's, and he could, in addition, call on thousands of plantation workers armed with pikes or muskets distributed by Sonthonax in 1796. Rigaud controlled all of the southern peninsula; Toussaint, all of the north and west. Once their common enemy was eliminated, relations between them rapidly deteriorated. Still regarded today as a sensitive issue by Haitians, the conflict between Toussaint and Rigaud was basically a regional power struggle, but it tended to divide the light-skinned *anciens libres* from the new class of black military officers. Many of Toussaint's light-skinned officers, although they had been with him for years, sided with Rigaud; and when Toussaint invaded the south, they staged rebellions against him. The fighting was desperate, and Toussaint's reprisals were brutal, although prudently delegated to subordinates.[35] Rigaud and most of the leaders fled to France.

By the middle of 1800, Toussaint ruled supreme in Saint Domingue and of necessity was recognized as its governor. A small, wiry man, very black, with mobile, penetrating eyes, he greatly impressed most who met him, even those who thought him ugly. He had lost in battle his upper set of front teeth and spoke with a nasal twang, but his presence was commanding and suggested enormous self-control. Whether socializing with white planters or pacifying angry plantation workers, his manner was reserved but dignified. In private, the whites might mock his rusticity (his headscarf, his limited French) or his "pretensions" (his huge watch chains, his moralizing piety), but in his presence no one laughed. Although Toussaint maintained the external pomp of previous colonial governors and he acquired much landed property, his private life was frugal. Wary of being poisoned, he ate little, and he slept only a few hours each night, invariably working late with his secretaries. His prodigious activity astonished people, as did the air of mystery he deliberately cultivated.[36]

With the war ended in the south, Toussaint then set about rebuilding the colony and restoring its shattered economy. He thought it essential to revive the plantation regime to restore Saint Domingue's prosperity. With no export economy, there would be no revenue to maintain his army, which was the guarantor of black freedom, and the gains of the revolution would be at the mercy of France's unstable politics. Toussaint therefore continued with the schemes of Commissioner Sonthonax, whereby the ex-slaves were compelled to work on the plantations in return for a share of the produce. It was a difficult policy to implement because increasingly the blacks preferred to establish smallholdings of their own and had little desire to work for wages. Toussaint, however, refused to break up the great estates. He used the army to impose the forced labor regime and sanctioned the use of corporal punishment. He outlawed Vodou, the emergent folk religion that was a vehicle for resistance, and he even supported the reintroduction of the slave trade to replenish the workforce. Since most estates had been abandoned by their owners, they were leased out, usually to army officers and other privileged figures in the new regime. Toussaint also encouraged the return of white planters from exile to take charge of their properties and to work toward the creation of a new Saint-Domingue.

The return of the planters, of course, raised grave suspicions among the plantation blacks and also among some of Toussaint's officers. They also resented his white advisers and the pleasure he evidently took in inviting planters and merchants to his social gatherings. A naturally taciturn man, he seemed to be becoming increasingly remote. C.L.R. James, Toussaint's most famous biographer, treated this growing distance from the masses as a character flaw, the hubris of a tragic hero moving toward his downfall.[37] Pierre Pluchon related it to his prerevolutionary past as a man of property, a slave owner.[38] These tensions were given violent expression when the very popular General Moïse staged a revolt in the northern plain, which caused the deaths of many of the returned planters. When Toussaint had him executed, many thought his policies were going awry.[39] It is usually argued that Toussaint thought the technical expertise of the whites and their social polish were necessary to the rebuilding of the colony, and that he therefore was committed to a multiracial Saint Domingue. Pierre Pluchon's interpretation is that, although Toussaint encouraged the whites to return, he rarely gave them back their estates. These tended to remain in the hands of his army officers, who constituted a new, black, landholding class. The return of the planters served to camouflage this development, and also to provide hostages.[40]

It is by no means clear how successful Toussaint was in reviving the plantation economy. Export figures for the twelve months following the war against Rigaud (1800-1) show coffee production at two-thirds the 1789 level, raw sugar down by four-fifths, and semirefined sugar, the most valuable item, almost nonexistent. Much of the produce probably came from areas preserved by the British. On the other hand, it is likely that trade figures were deliberately understated to allow the amassing of secret funds and the stockpiling of munitions. The administrative confusion and the autonomy of local army commanders, of which white officials complained, probably fulfilled the same function. According to his critics, Toussaint kept his generals' loyalty by allowing them to amass personal fortunes. Their troops went unpaid but the soldiers, in turn, were allowed to exercise a petty tyranny over the cultivators, whose provision grounds were subject to army requisitions. Only on the generals' plantations, however, were the labor laws effectively applied. Other commentators painted a more enthusiastic picture of the regime, insisting that a new spirit was abroad in the colony. Race prejudice was diminishing fast. Towns were being rebuilt. Justice was administered impartially. Even some schools were established (although this was a French initiative). All one can say with certainty is that the new regime was given very little time to prove itself.

Late in 1799, France, like Saint Domingue, also acquired a military strongman for a ruler. Napoleon Bonaparte and Toussaint Louverture had much in common. Both were seen as defenders of basic revolutionary gains of the previous decade, particularly of new land settlements. Both were autocrats who extinguished all political liberty in their respective countries. Both were destroyed by their own ambition. In July 1801, shortly before Bonaparte proclaimed himself consul for life, Toussaint promulgated a constitution for Saint Domingue that flagrantly concentrated all power in his hands and made him governor for life, with the right to choose his successor. Drawn up by planters with a secessionist background, the document came within a hair's breadth of a declaration of independence. Toussaint had anticipated by 160 years the concept of associated statehood. He justified the move, ironically, by referring to Bonaparte's removal of the colonies from the protection of the French constitution and his proclamation that they were henceforth to be ruled by "special laws." The first consul was infuriated. He, however, had already determined that French rule should be restored in what had been France's most valuable possession.

Some historians contend that Bonaparte initially considered cooperating with Toussaint, and long delayed a decision about restoring slavery; others assert that he was always eager to restore the colonial status quo.[41] By spring 1801, it was apparent that, under its black governor, Saint Domingue would be of little use to France, as it was de facto already an independent state. Although France was at war with Great Britain, and unofficially with the United States, too (the Quasi-War of 1798-1800), Toussaint made a secret commercial treaty and nonaggression pact with both of these powers. This involved expelling French privateers from the colony. His purpose was to preserve the trade on which Saint Domingue, and his army, depended. The United States supplied vital foodstuffs, livestock, and munitions; the British navy controlled the sea-lanes, and would otherwise have blockaded Saint Domingue. This is why, when the French government and *anciens libres* tried to foment a slave rebellion in Jamaica and sent agents there from Saint Domingue, Toussaint covertly betrayed the plot to the Jamaican administration.[42] Whatever his interest in black liberation, he needed to keep on good terms with his neighbors so as to preserve his autonomy. In January 1801, Toussaint suddenly annexed, without reference to France, the adjoining colony of Santo Domingo, which was then French territory. Suspicious of French intentions, he aimed to deny a potential invasion force use of Santo

Domingo's harbors. The ex-slave thereby became master of the entire island of Hispaniola. Within a few weeks, blacks in the hills of western Venezuela, five hundred miles to the south, were singing his name.[43] It was the high point of his career.

If Bonaparte had ever had doubts about his relations with Toussaint, they were now gone. Toussaint seems to have miscalculated. If he was willing to antagonize Napoleon to this degree, some say, he should have gone all out and declared complete independence, rallying the black masses behind him. Instead, he kept up the fiction of loyalty to France, sending envoys to Napoleon to explain each act of defiance. He continued to assure local whites of his goodwill and to admonish the blacks on the necessity of hard work. The ambivalence of his double game to critically weakened black resistance to the coming invasion.

Toussaint's failure to declare independence was doubtless due to a number of factors. Along with caution and the need for white administrative personnel, the most important was probably fear of alienating the slaveholding Americans and British, who could cut off the trade on which he relied. Yves Bénot's argument that he needed France's protection against these powers is less convincing, as is C.L.R. James's stress on Toussaint's faith in republican France and his commitment to its ideals.[44] By stopping short of de jure independence, Toussaint evidently thought that Napoleon would negotiate rather than fight. Perhaps he overrated the military lessons he had taught the Spanish and British. Perhaps he even believed that the British navy would prevent a French fleet from crossing the Atlantic. The British, however, would support the black governor's rule only so long as it weakened France's war effort, and the Anglo-French war was now drawing to a temporary close. The British government feared both Toussaint and Napoleon, but regarded the latter as the lesser of two evils. To see the two embroiled in internecine conflict was a perfect compromise solution to a threatening situation. In October 1801, as soon as peace preliminaries were signed, the British gave their assent to an invasion of Saint-Domingue.[45]

Downfall

Napoleon's brother-in-law, General Leclerc, landed in Saint-Domingue at the beginning of February 1802 with some 10,000 soldiers. By sending out a large force in the healthy winter months and deploying it rapidly, Napoleon avoided the worst mistakes of the British and Spanish. His troops also were far superior to those previously sent there, and their numbers were doubled within two months. Leclerc's orders were, nevertheless, to seize the colony by ruse, winning over, where possible, the black generals. Only later, once he had allayed their suspicions, was he to disarm their soldiers and then deport all the black officers.[46]

Uncertain of French intentions, the blacks failed to offer any concerted resistance and Leclerc quickly occupied all the colony's ports. Cap-Français, under the eye of Toussaint, was burned by its commander, Henry Christophe, as was Saint-Marc by Dessalines, but several of the generals surrendered without a fight. They were now planters themselves and had property to protect. Toussaint, Christophe, and Dessalines took to the mountains, fighting heroic rearguard actions and destroying all that they left behind. Battle casualties were heavy and, from the beginning, the war was marked by terrible atrocities on both sides. Parts of the rural population, fearing the return of slavery, gradually rallied to the black army and produced guerrilla leaders of their own. As successive generals surrendered, however, their troops were turned against those who still held out. Christophe's surrender led to that of Toussaint early in May. While he retired to private life on one of his plantations, the other generals were maintained in their posts and used by the French to mop up remaining guerrilla resistance.

Perhaps all three leaders were biding their time, knowing that, by summer, the French troops would be decimated by disease. Nevertheless, when within a month Toussaint was accused of plotting rebellion, it was Dessalines and Christophe who helped denounce him. The old leader was kidnapped, hastily deported, and died in a French dungeon in April 1803. On leaving the colony, he declared that the French had felled only the trunk of the tree of liberty; it had strong roots and would grow again.[47] Within months, as it became clear that the French intended to restore slavery and racial discrimination, they faced massive resistance and the desertion of most of their collaborators. Jean-Jacques Dessalines, in alliance with the *anciens libres*, declared the independence of Haiti on January 1, 1804.

As with his relationship to slave emancipation and the slave revolt that led to it, Toussaint's contribution to Haitian independence was enormous but indirect. It was a cause he never openly supported, even in his desperate struggle against Leclerc's invasion force. Yet he laid the groundwork for its achievement by building the black army, expelling foreign invaders, weakening the *anciens libres*, negotiating treaties with the British and Americans that permitted the stockpiling of munitions, and by creating an autonomous colonial state that pointed the way to national self-determination.

Toussaint Louverture was thus a strange type of radical. A pious autocrat, who imposed a forced labor regime supported by corporal punishment and a revived slave trade, his economic vision was that of the planter class, while his politics were those of old regime authoritarianism. Perhaps a black nationalist, many have seen him as too wedded to European culture. Haitians remember him as the architect of their freedom from slavery and colonial rule, and as the first of a long line of dictators.

Notes

1. David Geggus, "British Opinion and the Emergence of Haiti, 1791-1805," in *Slavery and British Society, 1776-1848,* James Walvin, ed. (London: Macmillan, 1982), 140-141; [Charles-Yves] Cousin d'Avallon, *Histoire de Toussaint-Louverture*; [Louis] Dubroca, *Vie de Toussaint-Louverture* (Paris, 1802), which was quickly translated into English and Swedish; Karin Schüller, "From Liberalism to Racism: German Historians, Journalists, and the Haitian Revolution from the Late Eighteenth to the Early Twentieth Century," in *The Impact of the Haitian Revolution in the Atlantic World*, David P. Geggus, ed. (Columbia: University of South Carolina Press, 2001), 28. The preferred spelling of his name is "Louverture" since that is how he signed it himself.

2. Alfred Hunt, *Haiti's Influence on Antebellum America: Slumbering Volcano in the Caribbean* (Baton Rouge: Louisiana State University Press, 1988), 86-87.

3. Erwin Rüsch, *Die Revolution von Saint Domingue* (Hamburg: Friedrichsen, De Gruyter, 1930); C.L.R. James, *The Black Jacobins: Toussaint L'Ouverture and the San Domingo Revolution*, 2nd ed. (New York: Vintage, 1963); Pierre Pluchon, *Toussaint Louverture: Uun révolutionnaire noir d'Ancien régime* (Paris: Fayard, 1989).

4. The evidence on Toussaint's early life is sparse and often misrepresented. It is reviewed in David Geggus, "Les débuts de Toussaint Louverture," *Généalogie et Histoire de la Caraïbe* 170 (2004): 4173-74, and *id.*, "Toussaint Louverture avant et après le soulèvement de 1791," forthcoming in *La traite, l'esclavage colonial, la Révolution de Saint-Domingue et les droits de l'homme*, Franklin Midi, ed. (Montreal: CIDHICA).

5. Some nineteenth-century historians refer to him as Pierre-Dominique or François-Dominique. One or the other may have been his baptismal name, but I have found no evidence of their being used in his lifetime.

6. Gabriel Debien, Marie-Antoinette Menier, and Jean Fouchard, "Toussaint Louverture avant 1789: Légendes et réalités," *Conjonction* 134 (1977): 67-80. The authors date Toussaint's emancipation from 1776, but they wrongly interpreted their key source. He was probably freed between 1769 and 1772. See David Geggus, "Toussaint Louverture and the Slaves of the Bréda Plantations," *Journal of Caribbean History* 20 (1986): 30-48; *id.*, "Les débuts."

7. Centre des Archives d'Outre-mer, Aix-en-Provence (hereafter: CAOM), E 1991, letter of 8 Oct. 1802.

8. Geggus, "Toussaint Louverture and the Slaves of the Bréda Plantations," 44. Since Toussaint once said that he owed his freedom to Bayon, who had lived in the northern plain since the 1740s, it is possible Bayon had purchased and freed Toussaint even before the period he worked for the Bréda heirs (1772-89).

9. David Geggus, "La famille de Toussaint Louverture," *Généalogie et Histoire de la Caraïbe* 174 (2004): 4319-20. Toussaint had children by several women and, as late as 1782, he was, in fact, married to a woman named Cécile, a local free black and former Bréda slave.

10. David Geggus, *Haitian Revolutionary Studies* (Bloomington: Indiana University Press, 2002), 117-18. Dominique Rogers's superb dissertation, "Les libres de couleur dans les capitales de Saint-Domingue" (Thèse de doctorat de l'université, Université de

Bordeaux 3, 1999), downplays the significance of phenotypical difference but is not entirely convincing in this regard.

11. The major recent studies are: Carolyn Fick, *The Making of Haiti: The Saint Domingue Revolution from Below* (Knoxville: University of Tennessee Press, 1990); and Laurent Dubois, *Avengers of the New World America: The Story of the Haitian Revolution* (Cambridge, MA: Harvard University Press, 2004).

12. David Geggus, "Slavery, War, and Revolution in the Greater Caribbean, 1789-1815," in *A Turbulent Time: The French Revolution and the Greater Caribbean*, D.B. Gaspar and D. Geggus, eds. (Bloomington: Indiana University Press, 1997), 7-11.

13. See enclosures in Archivo General de Indias, Seville, Audiencia de Santo Domingo 954 (hereafter: AGI, SD), García to Bajamar, 25 Nov. and 25 Dec. 1791; Jean-Philippe Garran Coulon, *Rapport sur les troubles de Saint-Domingue* 2 (Paris, 1797-99), 210; Gros, *Isle Saint-Domingue, Province du Nord* (Paris, 1793), 8. Many historians have thought the *médecin-général* was Toussaint, merely because of his reputed knowledge of herbs. It was, however, one of the titles of the sadistic sorcerer Jeannot. Executed early on by his rival, Jean-François, his military merits have been overlooked.

14. However, the story about Mme Bayon probably confuses her real and far more dramatic escape in August from Limbé a dozen miles away, where she really lived. Her protector was another slave leader, Paul Belin. See Public Record Office, London (hereafter: PRO), WO 1/58, f. 1-11; *A Particular Account of the Commencement and Progress of the Insurrection of the Negroes in St. Domingo* (London, 1792), 7. Toussaint's delay may have been due to the fact that his wife had recently given birth to their son, Saint-Jean.

15 CAOM, CC9B/23, rapport du général Kerverseau au Ministre, 20 fructidor an IX (7 Sept.1801). This version is also used in Madison Smartt Bell's best-selling novel, *All Souls' Rising* (New York: Pantheon, 1995).

16. Pierre Pluchon, *Toussaint Louverture d'après le général Kerverseau* (Port-au-Prince: Le Natal, nd), 20. In this late work, the brilliantly cynical Pluchon produced a very original synthesis of the two versions, suggesting that Toussaint had nothing to do with the uprising until counterrevolutionaries asked him to infiltrate the rebels' ranks, so as to guide the rebellion toward a negotiated settlement.

17. Some of this material is reproduced in Geggus, "Toussaint Louverture avant et après le soulèvement."

18. David Geggus, "Toussaint Louverture et l'abolition de l'esclavage à Saint-Domingue," in *Les abolitions dans les Amériques,* Liliane Chauleau, ed. (Fort de France: Société des Amis des Archives, 2001), 111.

19. Colonial radicals, however, blamed the failure on counterrevolutionary interference. A best-selling pamphlet by a former white prisoner named Gros retailed a story of how Jean-François broke off discussions after receiving a nocturnal visit from a royalist officer. Scholars have taken the episode seriously without recognizing that the story was hearsay that originated solely with Toussaint. My suggestion is that Toussaint, accepting the negotiations had failed, once again played the "counterrevolutionary card" to divide his opponents. See Gros, *Isle Saint-Domingue, 27-28.*

20. *E.g.*, James, 107-8; Aimé Césaire, *Toussaint Louverture: La Révolution française et le problème colonial* (Paris: Présence Africaine, 1962), 173.

21. AGI, SD 955, García to Bajamar, 25 Sept. 1792.

22. Biassou, Jean-François, Belair to the General Assembly, etc., July 1792, in Joseph-Paul-Augustin Cambefort, *Quatrième partie du Mémoire justificatif* (Paris, 1793), 4-11. The mixture of stylish, high flown language and crude errors of grammar and spelling resembles none of the varieties of language found in other documents that issued from the rebels' camps, which were generally written by free colored aides de camp or white captives. The letter is known only in printed versions; an original has not been found.

23. The decree freed slaves only in the North Province, but it was soon extended to the rest of the colony. In February 1794, after receiving deputies sent from Saint-Domingue, the Convention in Paris extended abolition to all of France's colonies.

24. Archives Nationales, Paris (hereafter: AN), Section Moderne, AE II/1375, letter by Toussaint Louverture, 25 Aug. 1793; AN, AA 53/1490, letter by Toussaint Louverture, 29 Aug. 1793.

25. Rüsch, 86-93; Pluchon, 92-104. See also: AN, AA 55/1511, "Réponse sentimentale," 27 Aug. 1793; Garran-Coulon, *Rapport*, 4:47.

26. Some time before mid-June 1793, Toussaint had made overtures to the French general Laveaux, but the common assertion that he called for an end to slavery derives from a fraudulent citation by the historian Gragnon-Lacoste. See Geggus, *Haitian Revolutionary Studies*, 126.

27. AN, Dxxv/43/415, letters to Pierrot, 13 July 1793, and to Duvigneau, 18 July 1793.

28. He was mentioned in ministerial correspondence as early as March 1792, when he spent three days with his officers attending the Easter masses in the frontier town of Daxabon, praising Spanish church organization and making great efforts to obtain a copy of a pastoral letter by the Archbishop of Santo Domingo to send to Cap-Français. Knowing the text described the slave insurgents as instruments of divine punishment, Toussaint probably was seeking to worsen Franco-Spanish relations, and succeeded. See AGI, SD 1110, Portillo to Bajamar, 14 March and 25 Sept. 1792.

29. Geggus, *Haitian Revolutionary Studies*, 128-34.

30. AGI, SD 1089, Cabello to García, 7 Oct. 1794; Archivo General de Simancas, Guerra Moderna 7161, García to Campo de Alange 6 Aug. 1794. García called him "a creole black full of maxims, who knows how to keep his hand hidden."

31. Geggus, *Haitian Revolutionary Studies*, 179-203.

32. Pluchon, 121-32.

33. Bibliothèque Nationale, Paris, Manuscrits, Fonds français 12102-4.

34. AN, 195 Mi 1, dossier 8, item 10. Some Federalists, such as Alexander Hamilton, favored such a development.

35. PRO, CO 245/1, 26 Nov. 1799, Cathcart to Maitland; F.-Richard de Tussac, *Flore des Antilles* 1 (Paris, 1808), 43.

36. One of the best contemporary portraits available in print comes from Michel Etienne Descourtilz, *Voyages d'un naturaliste et ses observations* (Paris, 1809). Despite his public prudishness, he reputedly had secret liaisons with numerous white women. This is reported not just in the well-known memoirs of Jacques de Norvins and Pamphile de Lacroix but also earlier in J.A. Albert, *Des véritables causes qui ont amené la ruine de la colonie de Saint-Domingue* (Paris, 1815), 65.

37. One might think that James's identifying of Toussaint Louverture with the Jacobins was meant to suggest a comparison between the relationship of the slave leadership and masses, on the one hand, and that of middle-class Jacobins and *sansculotte* workers, on the other. That this was not James's intention is shown by the following extract (p. 286): "Robespierre's problem was inevitable; he was bourgeois, the masses were communist. But between Toussaint and his people there was no fundamental difference of outlook or aim."

38. The explanatory power of looking at Toussaint from this angle should not be exaggerated. Jean-Jacques Dessalines and Henry Christophe, both slaves until the revolution, followed similar policies as head of state, whereas the freeborn Alexandre Pétion was less authoritarian as president.

39. The botanists Descourtilz and Tussac, of whom the latter lived close to the Haut-du-Cap Bréda estate, both thought that Toussaint was behind the revolt and used it to eliminate an opponent of his plans for independence. This seems highly improbable. See Descourtilz, *Voyages* 3, 279; Tussac, *Flore* 1, 41-42.

40. *Toussaint Louverture*, 424-29.

41. Cf.: *Ibid.*,446-53; Yves Bénot, *La démence coloniale sous Napoléon* (Paris: La Découverte, 1991), 21-31; Claude B. Auguste, Marcel B. Auguste, *L'expédition Leclerc, 1801-1803* (Port-au-Prince: Deschamps, 1986), 7-8.

42. "Letters of Toussaint Louverture and of Edward Stevens, 1798-1800," *American Historical Review* 16 (1910): 83; Gabriel Debien, Pierre Pluchon, "Un plan d'invasion de la Jamaïque," *Revue de la Société Haïtienne d'Histoire et de Géographie* 36 (1978): 3-72.

43. David Geggus, "The Influence of the Haitian Revolution on Blacks in Latin America and the Caribbean," in *Blacks, Coloureds and National Identity in Nineteenth-Century Latin America*, Nancy Naro, ed. (London: Institute of Latin American Studies, 2003), 40-41.

44. Pluchon,296; Bénot, 25-31; James, 282, 288, 290.

45. David Geggus, "The Great Powers and the Haitian Revolution," *Tordesillas y sus consecuencias: La política de las grandes potencias europeas respecto a América Latina (1494-1898)*, Bernd Schröter and Karin Schüller, eds. (Frankfurt: Vervuert, 1995), 113-25; *id.*, "L'expédition Leclerc et l'opinion anglo-américaine," in *1802 en Guadeloupe et à Saint-Domingue: Réalités et Mémoire* (Gourbeyre: Société d'histoire de la Guadeloupe, 2003), 119-26.

46. Leclerc's instructions are reprinted in Gustav Roloff, *Die Kolonialpolitik Napoleons I* (Munich: Oldenbourg, 1899), 244-54.

47. Thomas Madiou, *Histoire d'Haïti* 2 (Port-au-Prince: Deschamps, 1989), 327.

Padre Miguel Hidalgo:
Mexican Revolutionary, 1810-1811

Edward T. Brett
La Roche College

Introduction

On January 17, 1811, the rebel forces of Ignacio de Allende and Padre Miguel Hidalgo suffered their worst of several consecutive defeats at the Battle of Puenta de Calderón. Their revolution had started with a string of victories and great hope for a speedy, successful conclusion, but it had soon degenerated into one disaster after another, all of which seemed to result from their own ineptitude rather than their enemy's prowess. Now, following their latest defeat, they decided to move what was left of their forces northward to Texas. The two rebel leaders had previously instructed two of their officers to go to San Antonio to try to recruit new soldiers for their cause. The two emissaries were then to enter the United States and travel to Washington, DC, where it was hoped that they might gain U.S. support for their revolution. The plan was poorly thought out and had virtually no chance of success. Why would the U.S., which had little empathy for Catholicism or downtrodden Indians, risk the wrath of several European countries by supporting an Indian insurgency led by a priest? The fact that Hidalgo and Allende thought that the North American government might be supportive is illustrative of their naiveté and lack of foresight. Be that as it may, Allende and Hidalgo now sent word to their emissaries to delay their U.S. mission and await the arrival of the rebel army at San Antonio. Some historians speculate that Allende may have decided to accompany them to Washington, which was why the rebel army was moving toward Texas. We will never know for sure because royalist authorities captured the two secret agents before the insurgent army had time to reach San Antonio, and news of their fate forced Allende and Hidalgo to alter their plans.

The two men decided that it was now best to split their forces and to continue separately toward Monclova, a town southwest of San Antonio that they incorrectly assumed was securely in the hands of their ally, Francisco Ignacio

Elizondo. They were wrong. Elizondo was an ambitious *criollo* who had joined the rebel cause when he thought it expedient, but, unbeknown to Allende and Hidalgo, he had decided to switch sides when he concluded that the royalists had gained the upper hand in the struggle for Mexico. Once informed that the two rebel leaders were now heading toward his town, Elizondo devised an ambush plan that he thought would ingratiate him with his new allies. He sent word to Hidalgo and Allende suggesting that their troops reunite at Baján, just south of Monclova, where there were wells that would enable the insurgent forces to replenish their water supply. He further advised the rebel leaders to break their troops up into small contingents and then send each group, one at a time, to the wells. He informed the gullible rebels that there was not enough water in the wells to meet the needs of the whole army if all came at once. Thus, it would be better if the soldiers came at intervals, thereby allowing time for the wells to replenish themselves. The credulous insurgents saw no reason to suspect a trap and decided to comply. As each rebel contingent approached the wells, it was captured by royalist troops who were waiting in ambush. About half of the rebel forces were captured in this manner before their leaders realized what was happening. Among these were both Hidalgo and Allende. The latter was quickly tried, found guilty of treason, and executed. Since Hidalgo was a priest, however, he was handed over to the Inquisition, which declared him a heretic and defrocked him before returning him to secular authorities. He was executed by a firing squad on July 31, 1811.

Although the military ineptitude and incompetence of Hidalgo almost verges at times on the comical, he nonetheless was one of the very few Spaniards who had empathy for the oppressed masses of Mexico. His vision of justice for them did not end with his death. His name would be invoked and his vision resurrected time and time again by the downtrodden Indians of Mexico as they struggled for a better life. This is why today, almost 200 years after his death, he is still held in reverence and almost universally regarded as one of the greatest heroes of Mexican history.

Bourbon Reform

To fully comprehend the complexities of the Hidalgo-led revolt in New Spain (Mexico), one must first go back to the beginning of the eighteenth century, when a new dynasty of Bourbon kings replaced the inept Habsburgs as rulers of Spain. Since the late sixteenth century, Spain had been steadily declining and, by 1700, it had become so weak that it no longer was able to play more than an ancillary role in the give and take of European power politics. Part of the problem was the archaic colonial system. It was inefficient and laden with a corrupt tradition of patronage. If Spain was to improve its status *vis-à-vis* other European countries, its colonial system had to be replaced with something better. Consequently, throughout most of the eighteenth century, the Bourbons made economic and administrative reform a high priority.[1]

King Philip V (1700-46) took the first step when he transferred primary responsibility for governing the colonies from the corrupt Council of the Indies to the newly created and better managed Ministry of the Navy and the Indies. Next, several measures were taken by Philip and his successors, Ferdinand VI (1746-59) and Charles III (1759-88), to modernize trade policy and break the commercial monopoly of the Merchant Guild (*Consulado*) of Cádiz. Whereas in the past all colonial trade was restricted to four American ports, now all ports were permitted to take part in commerce. Likewise, exports could now be shipped to any port in Spain as well as to other Spanish colonial ports. Hitherto, all American shipping had to pass through Seville, which was controlled by the Cádiz Merchant Guild, whose members therefore reaped the lion's share of all colonial trade profits and were in a position to inflate costs for their services. The opening up of additional American ports, along with the break-up of the Cádiz monopoly, brought about the desired effect in that it increased colonial trade dramatically, so much so that New Spain not only enjoyed greater prosperity than ever before at the close of the eighteenth century, but had become Spain's most prosperous colony by far. Indeed, by 1810 New Spain was producing 75 percent of all profits from Spain's colonial empire.[2]

The Spanish crown also needed to reform its unwieldy colonial administrative system so that it could acquire more revenue through an efficient taxation process. This was done by the able Charles III, who introduced the French *intendant* model, which replaced the unruly, decentralized system of governors, *corregidores*, and *alcaldes mayores*. The king also mitigated the long-held practice of choosing high-ranking government officials on the basis of their political connections. Competence and experience were now factors that were taken into consideration.[3] This not withstanding, virtually all of these officials, as in the past, were from the Spanish-born *peninsular* (or *gachupin*) class. This was much resented by the *criollos*, that is, colonial Spaniards who were born in America and who, as a consequence of their birth, were excluded from high-ranking governmental and ecclesiastical positions. After Charles III's death, his incompetent successor, Charles IV (1788-1808), reverted to the previous policy of appointing incompetent *peninsulares* with political connections to important colonial jobs. This foolish move only served to intensify the long-held resentment of *criollos* toward the Spanish-born colonials and the monarchy that favored them with unfair advantages. This became an important factor in the preliminary events that led up to Padre Hidalgo's revolt.

In New Spain on the eve of the Hidalgo uprising there were over a million *criollos* and about 15,000 *peninsulares*, nearly a seventy-to-one ratio that certainly

138

did not bode well for the crown.[4] Moreover, many *criollos*, wealthier now as a result of the Bourbon reforms, sent their sons to Europe for education or travel. There they became familiar with the republican ideals that had been formulated by the intellectuals of the Enlightenment. When they returned to America, they created discussion groups, through which they spread the radical European ideas to other creoles, who now had an ideology to go along with their resentment of a monarchy that favored the hated *peninsulares*.

But the *criollos* were not the only ones with cause for resentment. Over 80 percent of the Mexican population was composed of Indians and *mestizos*, people of mixed European and indigenous ancestry. The Bourbon prosperity that helped create so much wealth for the rival *criollos* and *peninsulares* had virtually no effect on them. Together, they lived in poverty, were kept illiterate, and owned almost no land. They worked as day laborers, but wages were extremely low, so much so that they made just enough to stay alive, and many fell into debt peonage with no hope of ever paying their way out. The Indians especially suffered. Over the decades, their lands had been steadily stripped from them. They faced fierce discrimination and were forbidden to wear European clothing. Moreover, despite their extreme poverty, they had to pay tribute to the crown. Kept in a state of ignorance, these two classes of paupers lacked any kind of organization or leadership and therefore were incapable of producing serious revolution on their own. If led by a *criollo* leader, however, they could be a serious danger to the crown. That leader became Padre Hidalgo.

Miguel Hidalgo's Early Years

Miguel Hidalgo y Costilla was born on May 8, 1753 on the hacienda San Diego Corralejo, near Pénjamo, southwest of Guanajuato. His parents were moderately well-to-do *criollos*, who were wealthy enough to own five slaves.[5] His father, Cristóbal Hidalgo Costilla, was overseer (*mayordomo*) of the hacienda. His mother, Ana María Gallaga y Villaseñor, died when Miguel was eight, while giving birth to her fifth son. Miguel's oldest brother, José Joaquin, eventually become a priest, and another brother, Mariano, later joined Miguel in his uprising. His other siblings were José María and Manuel.[6]

Shortly after his mother's death, Miguel was sent to live with his uncle, José Manuel Villaseñor, who was a priest. This seems to indicate that his father intended a career in the church for him. At any rate, he received the basics of education while with his uncle.[7] Aside from this short period, he spent the rest of his first twelve years on the hacienda, where he came in close daily contact with the Indian peons who labored there. Historian Hubert Miller postulates that this contact may have caused him to develop sympathy for oppressed indigenous people.[8]

139

When Miguel was twelve, his father sent him and his older brother, José Joaquin, to Valladolid (today Morelia) to study with the Jesuits at the College of San Francisco Javier. Historian Hugh Hamill notes that this school was relatively mediocre until the renowned Jesuit educator, Francisco Javier Clavigero, was assigned there. Although he was sent elsewhere shortly before the Hidalgo brothers arrived, by then he had thoroughly renovated the curriculum, phasing out much of the traditional scholasticism that was still being taught at the time in most of New Spain. In its place he introduced courses based on the new rationalism and scientific methods then in vogue in Europe.[9] Even though he was quite young, Miguel was greatly influenced by these modern methods of education, and they would affect the rest of his life as student, educator, pastor, and revolutionary.

Unfortunately, however, in February 1767, King Charles III expelled the Society of Jesus from Spain and its empire and, as a consequence, the College of San Francisco Javier was closed. Since Miguel had to wait for a new school year to begin before continuing his studies at another school, he returned home. During this interim period, his father had to spend an extensive amount of time in the village of Tejupilco, near Toluca, and he decided to take Miguel with him. This proved to be significant for the fourteen-year-old because it brought him into close contact with the Otomí Indians. As Hamill notes: "Having nothing else to do, the boy spent most of his time talking with them and made considerable progress in learning to speak their language."[10]

In October his father sent him and his brother back to Valladolid, where they were enrolled in the diocesan College of San Nicolás Obispo. There he studied traditional Thomistic philosophy and theology, rhetoric, Latin, and the Otomí Indian language, but outside the formal curriculum he also learned French, Italian, and the Tarascán and Nahuatl Indian languages. His prowess in languages, especially the Indian tongues, proved of enormous value to him later in his career.[11]

Miguel's excellent academic record earned him a scholarship to the University of Mexico City, where he received his bachelor of arts degree in 1770. A bachelor's degree in theology followed in 1773. On September 8, 1778, at the age of twenty-six, he was ordained a priest. He and his brother, José Joaquin, who had also been ordained, continued their theological studies at the university, where they now worked toward their doctorates. Although José Joaquin successfully completed this degree, Miguel did not. This is odd since he did finish his dissertation and it was awarded a prize of twelve silver medals by the dean of Valladolid Cathedral for the best thesis on the study of theology. Moreover, it later served as the basis for curriculum reform at the College of San Nicolás Obispo.

Indeed, when all is said and done, it seems that Hidalgo did not receive his degree simply because he never bothered to defend his dissertation before his doctoral board. This, says Miller, is probably because he disagreed with the conservative theological views of some of his professors.[12] Hamill is a bit more emphatic. He claims that Hidalgo looked with disdain on the antiquated and unchallenging academic system of the time and, therefore—probably to make a point—seems to have refused to take his doctoral exams.[13]

Hidalgo's study, *Disertación sobre el verdadero bymétodo de estudiar Teología Escolástica*, was an attack on the way theology was taught at the time in New Spain. He argued that it was insufficient to limit theological study to traditional Thomism. The latter must be accompanied by what he called positivist theology, that is, a study of the historical development of theological concepts. His arguments were greatly influenced by the writings of Jesuit theologians, who employed more contemporary methods of scholarship in their work, but he seems to have gone farther than them in his de-emphasis of scholasticism. Be that as it may, modern-day scholars all agree that Hidalgo's theology "was both sound and bold" but far from radical,[14] and that there was certainly nothing in his dissertation that could be considered heretical.[15] It seems, however, that Padre Hidalgo's scorn for "the system" and his willingness to take what some might call reckless steps to make his point says much about his personality. His conduct in the 1810-11 revolt that would cost him his life seems to fit this same pattern.

In 1776, two years before his ordination and seven years before he completed his dissertation, Hidalgo was assigned to teach grammar, theology, and philosophy at his old school, the College of San Nicolás Obispo. He was considered an excellent teacher and, following the completion of his theological studies, he was awarded an endowed chair. This brought with it an increase in salary that he used to invest in three haciendas.[16] Eventually, he was appointed rector, a position that allowed him to reform the curriculum in accordance with the Jesuit-inspired reforms he had long advocated.

On February 2, 1792, he resigned as rector. Hamill states that opposition to his curriculum innovations may have played a part in his decision. Another factor could have been his personal life. There is evidence that he may have been addicted to gambling, and there is no doubt that he was a womanizer. During his years at San Nicolás he had a son, Joaquin, with Bibiana Lucuero, and two other children, Augustina and Lino Mariano, with Manuela Ramos Pichardo. As Miller correctly notes, however, clerical celibacy was lax in Spanish America at this time, and it was not out of the ordinary for a priest to have a mistress.[17]

Padre Hidalgo's demotion from academia to pastoral ministry, if indeed it was a demotion, does not seem to have affected his ability to adapt well to different circumstances, for in all of his pastoral assignments he seems to have been well loved and respected by his parishioners. His first parish was San Felipe de Jesús in Colima, south of Guadalajara, where he was assigned on January 24, 1793.

Franciscan friars had long ministered to the parish and his major charge was to make sure that the transition to a diocesan parish was accomplished without conflict. Tact was necessary since parishioners felt a strong loyalty to his Franciscan predecessors. He seems to have achieved his goal without problem and, consequently, eight months after his arrival, he was reassigned to another parish, also named San Felipe, in the Guanajuato area, northwest of Dolores.[18]

At his new parish Hidalgo organized a parish orchestra that played at church services but also at concerts and dances that he organized for locals. He also created a literary club at his rectory. He translated dramas of the French playwrights Racine and Moliere into Spanish and had them performed by locals. This is interesting since these plays were filled with satirical criticism of the clergy and aristocracy. Moreover, his new mistress, Josefa Quintana, served as his leading actress. She bore two more of the priest's children, Micaela and María Josefa. Hidalgo's cultural enterprises were both unusual and noteworthy in that they were open to and attracted people from all classes.[19] Thus, the activities of his literary club again portray a priest with a strong commitment to social equality and one not afraid to criticize authorities, be they from the nobility or his own clerical caste.

In January 1800 Padre Hidalgo took a leave of absence from his parish to attend to business on his hacienda and at nearby mines where he had investments. During Holy Week, he assisted at a parish in the nearby town of Taximoroa. Here he joined in a discussion group with several other priests. True to his usual lack of caution, he questioned several traditional beliefs of Catholicism—the virgin birth of Christ, the practice of confessing one's sins to a priest, transubstantiation, papal infallibility, priestly celibacy, and even the sinfulness of sexual relations outside of marriage. One of the priests in the group reported his comments to the Holy Office in Valladolid and soon the Inquisition in Mexico City began investigating him for heresy. Although the inquisitors decided that the accusations against him could not be substantiated and therefore exonerated him, the testimony against him nevertheless was put on file and later resurrected for use against him after he commenced his revolt.[20]

On September 19, 1803, his brother, Padre José Joaquin, died. He had been pastor of Nuestra Señora parish in Dolores, a prosperous town of 15,000 people, and Miguel asked to be reassigned to take his place. His request was approved and he took over Nuestra Señora the following month. He was fifty years old at the time.

Upon his arrival at his new parish, Hidalgo immediately began projects aimed at mitigating the poverty of his impoverished parishioners while also developing their social awareness. As he had done in his last parish, he turned his residence into a place where parishioners met to discuss questions of history, culture, and social justice. What is unusual and truly amazing, however, is that he encouraged the uneducated, especially Indians, to participate along with the educated.[21] Such discussion groups had some things in common with the *comunidad de base* (Christian base community) movement of the late twentieth century, where small groups of Latin American poor people met to read the Bible and apply it to their current situation. Although Hidalgo's group was not centered on Bible study or, for that matter, even religious questions, its discussions nevertheless were aimed at eradicating the fatalism of the poor while raising their social consciousness. In this respect, its goal was the same as the latter-day *comunidades de base*.

Hidalgo also concerned himself with promoting economic projects for his Indian parishioners. He helped them organize a brick and tile making venture, a pottery business, carpentry and shoemaking shops, a tannery, a bee keeping enterprise, a weaving cooperative, a wine making enterprise, and even a silk producing business. He also helped his parishioners in marketing their products. Some of these ventures were successful while others were not, in part because of his poor administrative skills. However, as historian Hubert Miller points out: "in all of these endeavors, he showed his deep concern for the material well-being of his parishioners, especially the Indians."[22] This concern obviously was a major factor in gaining the people's trust and helps to explain why so many Indians, who were almost always suspicious of *criollos*, were willing to follow this sacerdotal member of that despised class.

The French Invasion of Spain and Its Effect on New Spain

As has been shown above, there was much discontent in New Spain during the early years of the nineteenth century. The *criollos* resented the favor shown by the crown to the hated *peninsulares*, while the Indians and *mestizos*, having no reason to see a difference between these two subgroups of the Spanish upper class, hated them both and made no distinction between them. Despite this discontent, however, there was no reason to think that it would turn into rebellion. The lower classes were too unorganized and uneducated to produce leaders who could carry out a serious revolution. Moreover, as historians Meyer and Sherman note, in spite of their grumbling, serious consideration of armed rebellion against Spain was entertained by only a small number of *criollos*. While royal favor to the *peninsulares* curtailed *criollo* power and wealth, the reforms of the Bourbon monarchs enabled American-born Spaniards to be better off than ever before. Equally important, the *criollos* perpetually feared the possibility of a revolt by the oppressed lower class majority and depended on the military power provided by the crown for security. Meyer and Sherman are thus no doubt correct when they claim that conditions had been more ripe for rebellion in 1700, prior to the Bourbon reforms, than in 1800.[23] A new factor was needed in the Spanish

American equation if revolution were to become a real possibility. Events taking place in war-torn Europe soon produced that factor.

As stated above, in 1788 the able Charles III died and his son Charles IV became king. The latter quickly proved to be an incompetent monarch who showed little interest in affairs of state. He allowed his wife's secret paramour, the twenty-five year-old Manuel de Godoy, to become prime minister. Meanwhile, Napoleon Bonaparte implemented his Continental System on November 21, 1806, forbidding continental Europe to trade with England, with whom he was at war. In 1807 he invaded Portugal and in 1808 Spain to make sure that England could not trade with them. He next forced Charles IV to abdicate. Then, with the connivance of Godoy, he had Charles and his son and successor, Ferdinand, go to France, where they were kept as virtual prisoners. When Napoleon then named his own brother Joseph king of Spain, he outraged the Spanish population, which rose in insurrection. By late September 1808, some Spanish rebels formed a government-in-exile, soon called the *Junta Suprema*, in Seville. In 1810 it was moved to the fortified city of Cádiz. From there, its members claimed the right to rule Spain in the name of Ferdinand until the latter could be returned to the throne.

When news of the above-mentioned events reached New Spain, there was disagreement between the *peninsulares* and *criollos* on how to respond. All were unanimous in rejecting the rule of Joseph Bonaparte. The *peninsulares*, however, felt that, in the absence of the legitimate King Ferdinand, it was only logical that the viceroy should assume rule and that he be assisted by the king's royal officials in New Spain, all of whom would operate in close cooperation with the *Junta Suprema* in Spain. In other words, what they were calling for was a government that would maintain the pre-Bonaparte status quo. The *peninsulares*, who had always dominated colonial government, would continue to do so.

The *criollos*, not surprisingly, rejected this idea, favoring instead a solution that would give them more power. They argued for a sort of shared governance of the viceroy and a *junta* composed of provincial officials who, of course, would be *criollos*. Furthermore, unlike in the *peninsular* plan where royal officials would be little more than caretakers managing the king's business affairs in his absence, the *criollos* envisioned an activist government able to make changes when they felt they were needed. In other words, they wanted a government where they would be in a position to pass legislation that could enhance their power and wealth at the expense of the *peninsulares*.

A clash between the *peninsulares* and the *criollos* was inevitable, especially when the viceroy in New Spain, José de Iturrigaray, although Spanish-born, decided to side with the creoles in an attempt to curry their favor. He seems to have thought that, with creole support, he might eventually be in a position to declare Mexican independence with himself as king.[24] The *peninsulares* saw the viceroy's treachery as criminal and, with the help of General Gabriel Yermo, seized him and sent him to Veracruz, from where he was later shipped to Spain to be imprisoned. They also arrested some of the *criollo* members of the Mexico City *cabildo*. The *peninsulares* now capped their victory by declaring as viceroy the eighty-year-old and senile field marshal, Pedro Garibay. The old man promptly decreed that the *Junta Suprema* in Spain was the sole legal authority with power to legislate for New Spain in the absence of King Ferdinand. He next abolished several taxes that had cut into the profits of both the *peninsular* and urban *criollo* merchants but, in so doing he inadvertently upset the *Junta Suprema*, which needed those tax revenues to finance the war against the French. The *Junta* promptly replaced him with a new viceroy, Archbishop Francisco Xavier de Lizana y Beaumont.

While the more urbane *criollos* in Mexico City complained but remained relatively passive in the face of such political instability, the same could not be said for their counterparts in the rural provinces. Independent-minded and more isolated from *peninsular* authority, many formed conspiratorial group in their locals under the guise of "literary clubs." In September 1809, the government in the capital uncovered one such group in Valladolid that had been plotting to overthrow the government. It was led by Mariano de Michelena, a *criollo* military officer, and included priests and Indians, among others. The conspirators defended their actions by claiming that the *peninsular*-dominated government was illegitimate since it had used force to overthrow a legitimate viceroy. Their claim was not without some merit in the eyes of Archbishop-Viceroy Lizana. Consequently, he proceeded to treat them with leniency. The *peninsulares*, in turn, used their influence with the wealthy merchants of the *Junta Suprema* in Cádiz to have him removed from office. The new viceroy, Francisco Xavier Venegas, only arrived in Mexico City on September 24, 1810, two days prior to Hidalgo's call for revolution.[25] Meanwhile, a drought throughout New Spain in 1809 had caused a shortage of corn, which, in turn, caused food prices to rise dramatically and many workers to be laid off.[26]

Hidalgo and the Querétaro Conspiracy

Although we do not know precisely when Hidalgo came to support Mexican independence, we do know that he was on close terms with many of the Valladolid conspirators and seems to have attended secret meetings with *criollo* conspirators in Guanajuato. Some time after his arrival in Dolores, he came to know, and develop a close relationship with, Ignacio de Allende, a captain in the Queen's Cavalry Regiment in Guanajuato. Allende introduced him to a group of creole conspirators to which he belonged. Other significant members included: Juan de Aldama, a fellow military officer; Miguel Domínguez, a former *corregidor* of Querétaro; his wife Doña Josefa Ortiz de Domínguez; Epigmenio González, a grocer; and José Marino Galván, a postal clerk. The group had formed a "literary club" and met at the home of Padre José Sánchez in Querétaro, where they planned an uprising aimed at toppling the *peninsulares* from power.[27] By late summer 1810 Hidalgo had joined their group. The priest was brought into the plot for a specific purpose. Since the Indians trusted him, he was to convince them to become foot soldiers in the uprising.[28]

Almost all of the conspirators had nothing but disdain for the Indians but, for their revolt to succeed, they realized that they needed large numbers of Native Americans and *mestizos* to serve as cannon fodder for their cause. The *criollo* conspirators wanted their own American-born subclass to replace the *peninsulares* in the Mexican power structure (there is no evidence to indicate that they wanted to break from Spain). Once they obtained their goal, they would have no more use for the downtrodden masses that had fought for them and, therefore, they planned to abandon them. They had no thoughts of creating a genuine socio-economic revolution and, indeed, had always feared such a possibility since it would mean that they would lose much of their own wealth and power. Thus, the *criollo* conspirators, although they probably did not realize it at the time, had objectives that differed from those of Hidalgo. It would become apparent, once the uprising was underway, that the priest was a revolutionary in the full sense of the word, in that he wanted an independent Mexican nation with rights for the lower classes.

The Querétaro group set December 8, 1810 as the day to begin their revolt. This coincided with the fair in San Juan de los Lagos, and the conspirators reasoned that they therefore would be guaranteed a large audience when they announced their uprising. Hidalgo spent the summer months learning about weaponry and instructed his Indian followers to make machetes, spears, and slings. He wanted to be well prepared when the targeted December day arrived.

The conspirators were, of course, sworn to secrecy, but one of their members, the postal clerk José Marino Galván, told his boss of the plot and the latter reported it to government officials in Mexico City. Similar reports from others soon followed, and on September 13 the authorities decided to send troops to Querétaro to nip the revolt in the bud. When they searched the house of the grocer Epigmenio González, they uncovered a large stockpile of weapons and arrested him. Josefa Ortiz de Domínguez, however, found out what was happening and sent Ignacio Pérez to the town of San Miguel el Grande to inform Ignacio de Allende, the leader of the conspiracy. Allende, however, was nowhere to be found, so Pérez notified the leader's fellow soldier, Juan de Aldama, who immediately fled to Dolores to warn Hidalgo. He arrived at the priest's residence at about two o'clock in the morning on September 16 and found that Allende was already there, along with Hidalgo's brother, Mariano, and cousin, José Santos Villa. The three, by chance, had been visiting Hidalgo. The group agreed with Hidalgo that the best course of action was to begin the uprising at once, before soldiers could arrive to arrest them. Moreover, the thirty-one soldiers stationed in Dolores were under the command of Mariano Abasolo, a staunch ally of Hidalgo and, therefore, they could be counted on to join the rebellion. At 5:00 a.m. Hidalgo rang the church bells, summoning his parishioners earlier than usual for Mass. Since it was a Sunday market day, many Indians and *mestizos* had come to town from the surrounding areas to set up for the selling of their goods. Consequently, there were a large number of people who gathered at the church once they heard the bell.

Hidalgo's speech, known to history as the *Grito de Dolores*, was probably extemporaneous since there undoubtedly was little time to prepare it. Nevertheless, it was definitely mesmerizing to the poor peasants who heard it. Although there is no record of the fiery priest's exact words, we know that he challenged his poverty-stricken listeners to rise up against the hated Spanish, and we can be almost certain that he promised an end to the tribute that they were required to pay to the crown. He then ended with a passionate cry including one or all of the following: "Long live Ferdinand VII, long live America, long live religion, and death to bad government!" According to some sources, the crowd responded with the retort: "Death to the *gachupines* (*peninsulares*)!"[29] The revolution was now underway.

Hidalgo Goes to War

Hidalgo armed his 600 or so followers and ordered them to free those who were incarcerated in the local jail so that they could join the movement. He next commanded his Indian charges to arrest and imprison the area's *peninsulares*. It is telling that his followers either were unable or unwilling to distinguish between wealthy *peninsulares* and *criollos*, for they arrested both. As will soon become apparent, actions such as this did not bode well for the success of Hidalgo's revolution since, in the long run, they caused it to lose the allegiance of the American-born Spaniards.

The rag-tag army was now ready to march the twenty miles from Dolores to San Miguel el Grande, the home base of Allende and Aldama. Hundreds of Indians and *mestizos* joined the rebels along the way. When they passed through the hamlet of Atotonilco, Hidalgo took the banner of Our Lady of Guadalupe from the local church and gave it to his Indians to carry into war. Historian Brian R. Hamnet well sums up the significance of this action:

147

> It seems . . . that once Hidalgo had taken the banner of Guadalupe from the Shrine of Atotonilco and placed it at the head of his forces, the dissident priest became transformed into a revolutionary prophet in the leadership of a Marian crusade, the chosen person to whom the Mother of God communicated.[30]

This was a stroke of genius. The invocation of the Indian-like, dark-skinned virgin of Guadalupe, who about 300 years earlier was said to have shown compassion for the downtrodden Indians of Mexico when she appeared to Juan Diego, one of their own, would now show compassion to them again and, through her chosen prophet, Padre Hidalgo, would lead them to victory. Indeed, a few days later, when the Archbishop of Mexico City condemned the revolution, he invoked the *Virgin de los Remedios* (Virgin of Recourse), thereby anointing her patroness of the royal cause. In the war of the dueling virgin-mothers, however, the *Virgin de los Remedios* was no match for her counterpart. Whereas the dark-skinned, humbly robed Our Lady of Guadalupe reflected the devotional preferences of the general body of the faithful, the white-skinned, gold brocaded *Virgin de los Remedios* only reflected the mindset of the institutional church and, like the *peninsular* bishops who invoked her, was alien to the masses. From this time on, Our Lady of Guadalupe would be the symbol for oppressed peasants in Mexico whenever they rose up to fight for their dignity. She became synonymous with Indian nationalism and has remained so until the present.

By the evening of September 16, Hidalgo and his followers reached San Miguel. Since Allende was in charge of the soldiers stationed there, the city was turned over to the insurrectionists without a fight. As night descended, however, the unexpected happened. Hidalgo's Indian and *mestizo* followers turned into an uncontrollable mob. Roaming through the streets, they looted, killed Spaniards, and destroyed property. No distinction was made between *criollos* and *peninsulares*; they released their pent-up frustrations equally against both. Hidalgo unsuccessfully tried to stop them. After much carnage, Allende and his soldiers finally restored order. This episode marked the beginning of what eventually led to a split between the two revolutionary leaders. The undisciplined rampage of Hidalgo's dark-skinned mob caused Allende to argue that his own regiment of well-trained *criollo* soldiers, the Regiment of the Queen, should take control of the insurgency. Hidalgo disagreed. As historian Hubert Miller explains: Hidalgo, lacking totally in military experience, "saw warfare in terms of large mass movements, which by sheer weight of numbers could overwhelm smaller forces" even when the latter were better armed and disciplined.[31] More important, as Miller notes, "Allende was not a revolutionist in the same sense as was the padre. The creole officer feared a socio-economic revolution and mob violence." He understood that the revolution could not succeed without the support of the *criollos*. Thus, he reasoned that mob violence would eventually

148

result in this hitherto sympathetic subclass of Spaniards joining forces with the *peninsulares,* whom they hated, to protect themselves from the masses whom they feared.[32] At this early stage of the insurgency, however, Allende agreed to defer to the will of Hidalgo, albeit reluctantly.

Allende and Hidalgo next marched south toward Celaya, picking up new recruits from the poor classes along the way. At Celaya they again faced no resistance and, at the request of the revolutionary leaders, the municipal government, *ayuntamiento,* granted them official titles to create a sense of legitimacy for the insurrection. Hidalgo was declared captain general and defender of the nation. Allende was named lieutenant general, and his associates, Juan de Aldama and Mariano de Abasolo, each was given the rank of field marshal. Just as in San Miguel el Grande, however, Hidalgo's irregular army again looted and pillaged until Allende restored order. Official titles aside, the split that developed between Hidalgo and his *criollo* officers was growing wider.

On September 23 Padre Hidalgo and Allende decided to move on to Guanajuato rather than to the closer but better defended Querétaro. Guanajuato was a silver mining center and the rebels reasoned that the wealth from this industry could help finance the insurgency. When the rebel army left Celaya, its leaders commanded a fighting force of about 25,000 men. As the rebel force passed through the towns of Salamanca and Irapuato on route to Guanajuato, one of the largest cities in Spanish America, new recruits, many of them impoverished Indian mine workers, came forth in droves, so much so that, by the time that the rebels reached their destination, their army had more than doubled in size.

It is worth noting that, two days before his forces left Celaya, Hidalgo sent a messenger to the *intendant* of Guanajuato, Juan Antonio Riaño, informing him that he was marching on his city to free Mexico from 300 years of humiliating colonial rule. He promised the *intendant* that, should he surrender Guanajuato without a fight, all *peninsulares* would be granted safe passage from the city and all property would be protected. Should he decide to resist, however, this pledge would be negated and the city would suffer dire consequences. Hidalgo suggested that Riaño, who had only 500 soldiers to defend a city of 66,000 people, appoint a negotiating team to meet with rebel officers to bring about a peaceful surrender of the city.

Hidalgo's message to the *intendant* is intriguing. In it he made it clear that his primary goal was more than just to replace *peninsular* power with that of the *criollos*, it was to free Mexico from 300 years of Spanish colonialism. Thus, it seems that the priest was no longer disguising the fact that his motives differed radically from that of his creole associates. The message also raises some titillating questions: Could Hidalgo have been so repulsed by the violence that took place after the taking of San Miguel el Grande and Celaya that he was trying to avoid a similar occurrence in the much larger city of Guanajuato? Was he shying away from the mob violence that inevitably followed a genuine socio-economic uprising? Finally, does his message shed light on his later puzzling decision to divert his forces from Mexico City when it was probably his for the taking? Historians have long grappled with these questions but have been unable to come to any conclusions that are more than speculative.

At any rate, Riaño immediately rejected Hidalgo's offer. He already was aware of the violent aftermath of the rebel capture of both San Miguel el Grande and Celaya, and he was wise enough to know that Hidalgo was not able to back up his guarantee should Guanajuato capitulate. Thus, he decided to fight, even though his forces were greatly outnumbered and he did not have the backing of most of the population of his city. It should further be pointed out that Hidalgo and Riaño were friends who had participated together in "literary club" discussions in Guanajuato.[33] Thus, one would think that the *intendant's* response to the padre's offer would be positive. His fear of lower class mob violence, however, seems to have been the factor that caused him to throw in his lot with the royalists and call on them to send him military support. Therefore, we again see that mob violence, coupled with *criollo* distain for the indigenous population, proved to be a more serious threat to Hidalgo's movement than the royal forces sent against it.

Riaño positioned his men in the Alhóndiga de Granaditas, the public granary, since it had thick walls that were hard to penetrate. He reasoned that this fortress-like building would enable his small force to hold out until reinforcements could arrive from the capital. On September 28, Hidalgo's troops attacked. For the first time in the uprising, they would have to fight to gain their objective. Riaño immediately ordered his soldiers to open fire. The Indians, poorly armed, untrained in military tactics, and lacking discipline, were cut down in droves. They died by the hundreds.

Before the second attack began, Riaño decided to position a small number of his men outside the granary so as to better protect the building. It was a fatal mistake, for, just as he was about to reenter the fortress, a random musket ball struck him in the head, killing him instantly. This caused confusion in the ranks of his troops but they, nevertheless, held out for a while longer. Finally, one of Hidalgo's men, a miner named Juan José María Martínez, volunteered to set fire to the main entrance to the granary. He tied a large stone to his back to protect himself from royalist gunfire above and crept up to his target, carrying soft pine torches that were used in the mines. Although wounded, he managed to burn down the door and thereby gain for himself a place in history. Hidalgo's forces immediately rushed into the granary and slaughtered most of its defenders. The battle was won but about 2,000 rebels were killed in the process. Since only some 300 royalist defenders died in the battle, the rebels lost almost seven men for every enemy killed. With such a large army, however, and one that grew daily from new, impoverished Indian and *mestizo* recruits, it was a ratio that Hidalgo felt was acceptable.

Following the battle, the insurgents in a drunken orgy stripped Riaño and several of the other dead defenders and dragged their naked bodies through the streets. This was the prelude to two days of looting and destruction that far exceeded those at San Miguel and Celaya. On this occasion, however, Hidalgo seems not to have protested such conduct by his followers. Evidently, he reasoned that such violence was a necessary price that the revolutionary leaders would have to pay to maintain the allegiance of the lower classes. On this point Allende strongly disagreed and, consequently, the breach between the two top leaders of the uprising grew closer to the breaking point.

Lucas Alamán, who was eighteen years old at the time, witnessed what took place and later recorded it in his monumental, five-volume *Historia de México* (1849-53). He tells his readers that the pillage inflicted on Guanajuato by Hidalgo's forces that day was more merciless than what would have been expected had a foreign army conquered the city.[34] Alamán, whose family lost much of its property in the sacking of Guanajuato, painted a disturbing picture of drunken Indian followers of Padre Hidalgo looting stores and destroying mining equipment, while also smashing in house doors and chasing helpless women across rooftops as they fled for their lives and virtue. This negative portrayal became standard fare in Mexican schools throughout the nineteenth century and only changed with the Mexican Revolution of the following century, when Hidalgo was transformed from monster into hero.[35]

After taking Guanajuato, Hidalgo ordered the city council to swear allegiance to the rebellion but they refused, claiming that their loyalty was only to King Ferdinand VII.[36] No doubt the unbridled violence that followed the battle was a major factor in the city council's decision. At any rate, the rebel priest replaced the recalcitrant office holders with people who supported him, thus securing official approval of his cause. It was becoming more apparent with each passing day, however, that, because of the misconduct of the lower class followers of Hidalgo, the revolution was rapidly losing the support of the *criollos,* and this was especially troubling to Allende.

On October 8, Hidalgo and Allende split their forces in two and marched toward Valladolid, capturing Zacatecas and San Luis Potosí along the way. On October 17, after their rendezvous, their army had grown to over 60,000. Leaders in Valladolid loyal to Spain fled the city after receiving news of the coming of the insurgents. For this reason, the city was taken without a fight. On October 19, Hidalgo issued a proclamation that declared the abolition of slavery and the Spanish tribute system.

Those *criollos* who remained in the city pledged loyalty to the rebel cause, but many were evidently insincere since they later switched sides when royalist forces arrived and it was safe to do so. One young *criollo* officer who fled to avoid being put in the position of having to support Hidalgo or face incarceration was Lieutenant Agustín de Iturbide, the man who, ironically, would later complete the war for independence from Spain begun by Hidalgo.[37] It was Iturbide who eventually took command of all royal military forces in New Spain and, in 1821, after years of fighting for the crown, switched sides and joined his adversaries. He then declared Mexico free from Spain, and had himself crowned emperor.

The Church and the Revolution

Another person who fled Valladolid just prior to Hidalgo's arrival was Bishop-elect Manuel Abad y Queipo of Michoacán. (Valladolid was the diocesan seat of Michoacán.) On September 24, following the fall of his episcopal see, he issued a notification of excommunication against Hidalgo and his creole officers, declaring their rebellion immoral on the grounds that the Catholic church condemned rebellion, assassination, and the oppression of innocent people. Two weeks later, he issued another edict in which he condemned Hidalgo for attempting to persuade the Indians that they were the rightful owners of the land that the Spanish took from them and that they therefore had the right to regain that land through conquest. Archbishop Francisco Xavier Lizana y Beaumont of Mexico City soon added his name to the excommunication edict, as did the bishops of Puebla and Guadalajara. Following this, the Inquisition in Mexico City did its part by issuing an official, formal indictment, in which it resurrected the heresy charges that had long ago been brought against the priest but dismissed for lack of evidence.[38]

Hidalgo, however, proved that he could give as well as he got when it came to the political use of religion. After incorporating into his army the eight divisions that Bishop Abad y Queipo had recruited to defend the city, he confiscated the funds that the prelate had left in his treasury when he fled. He then appointed a fellow revolutionary priest to govern the Michoacán diocese in the bishop's absence and had the cleric immediately lift his excommunication. All priests in the areas under rebel control were then ordered to proclaim the innocence of Hidalgo from the pulpit.[39]

Since virtually all bishops and high-ranking priests in Mexico were *peninsulares,* they opposed the revolution. A surprisingly large numbers of priests, however, although certainly not the majority, disobeyed the orders of their prelates and threw their lot in with the excommunicated Hidalgo. Historian Nancy M. Farriss has closely researched this topic. From her study of government documents, personal accounts and memoirs, and correspondence of insurgents, she has compiled a list of 401 priests—244 secular and 157 religious order—who played an active part in the revolutionary movement. She notes, however, that official reports included only those priests who were captured in battle or convicted of subversion. In other words, they fail to take into account the many priests who must have escaped detection while collaborating with the rebels or who fought in the rebel forces but were too obscure for mention. She concludes, therefore, that the actual number of revolutionary priests must have been much higher than the 401 on her list.[40] Farriss, however, further contends that clergy numbers do not tell the whole story:

> [Priests] were the leaders [of the revolt], both militarily and political, and their choice of allegiance was often decisive in determining that of large sectors of the population. Entire villages remained loyal or joined the insurrection according to the dictates of the parish priest, and many curates followed Hidalgo's famous example, "pronouncing" for the revolution and leading their parishioners [in that cause].[41]

Brian Hamnet agrees, noting "the role of parish priests . . . in recruiting for the uprising cannot be overlooked."[42]

Priests, however, did more than just recruit and lead their parishioners. They were involved, says Farriss, in every facet of the revolution: Creole clerics helped to direct the course of the rebellion, to lead the ideological warfare against the royalists conducted through the medium of the insurgent press, and to define the confused and amorphous political aspirations of the revolution in manifestoes and constitutional decrees.[43] Padre Francisco Severo Maldonado, for instance, served as an important propagandist for the revolutionary cause.[44]

Moreover, no other Latin American country contributed as many priests to the early nineteenth-century revolutionary cause as did Mexico. Nor did any other nation produce as many sacerdotal military officers. Such clergy were called *cabecillas* and some, most notably Mariano Matamoros, José Izquierdo, José Navarrete, Pablo Delgado, and Fray Luis de Herrera, held high military rank. Indeed, it was a priest, José María Morelos, who took over the leadership of the rebel forces after the capture of Hidalgo and carried his cause on for another four years.[45]

From the above, we can conclude that a substantial segment of the lower clergy identified more with the poor masses they served than they did with their hierarchical superiors. The latter, from the elite *peninsular* subclass, had virtually no personal contact with the lower classes. They likewise had little in common with the lower clergy, who saw them as foreign allies of the elite oppressors of the people. This explains why episcopal decrees of excommunication had no effect on rebel priests, nor did the dictates of their religious superiors or the Inquisition.[46] Whereas many *criollos* were initially sympathetic with Hidalgo's uprising, but eventually turned against it when they realized that the cleric's aim was a genuine popular revolution, a significant minority of the lower clergy had the same radical ideals as the fiery priest from Dolores and, therefore, remained true to his cause even after his execution. Indeed, Lucas Alamán, who witnessed the sacking of Guanajuato, goes so far as to say in his *Historia de México* that, had no priests participated in the 1810 revolt, it would not have happened.[47] Historian Karl M. Schmitt goes almost as far: "[H]ad the lower clergy opposed the insurrection in mass, the rebellion of 1810 would have been only a minor affair, and the whole course of the Mexican movement for independence would have been changed."[48] On the other hand, Hubert Miller cautions against giving too much credit to the lower clergy for the success of the revolt. He points out that many priests were adroit at shifting sides. When Hidalgo came through their parishes they backed him, but when royalist forces came afterward, they took to their pulpits to condemn the revolutionary priest.[49] Be that as it may, the fact remains that the lower clergy played a crucial role in Hidalgo's movement and that, without clerical support, it would have quickly fizzled out.

The Road to Mexico City

On October 20, the rebel army left Valladolid. Its next objective was the biggest prize of all, Mexico City. When it reached Acámbaro on October 22, Allende and other *criollo* officers implored Hidalgo to hold up and take time out to train his inexperienced forces before engaging the better armed and disciplined royal forces that defended the capital. He refused, contending that his enormous numerical advantage would give him victory despite the military negatives of his men. He did, however, make one concession. He reorganized his army, dividing it into eighty regiments of a thousand soldiers each.[50] Once this was done, he and his men left Acámbaro, traveling southwest for about a hundred miles, where they took Toluca without a fight. Meanwhile, Francisco Venegas, the new viceroy in Mexico City, ordered Lieutenant Colonel Torcuato Trujillo to take his army of 2,500 troops to intercept the rebel forces before they reached the capital. On October 29 at Monte de las Cruces, to the east of Toluca and less than sixteen miles from Mexico City, the two armies met in combat. Trujillo stationed his soldiers on the rim of the valley, giving them the advantage of the terrain to go with their superior artillery. The battle continued well into the next day. Royalist forces inflicted very heavy casualties on Hidalgo's untrained soldiers but, in the process, Trujillo lost about 2,000 of his 2,500 men. Fearing eventual annihilation if his army stayed put, the lieutenant colonel retreated to the capital. Thus, Mexico City had only about 500 soldiers left to defend it against the tens of thousands that fought for Hidalgo.[51] It seemed like the capital was there for the priest's taking but, inexplicably, he chose to retreat rather than attack.

154

For generations, historians have tried to explain Hidalgo's decision. While some have postulated that he may have decided to retreat to avoid the wide scale carnage that would surely follow a rebel victory at Mexico City,[52] this does not seem to hold up under historical scrutiny. Although it is true that he did try to mitigate the looting and violence that followed the capture of San Miguel el Grande and Celaya, he does not seem to have done so following his later victories. Hamill correctly points out that, once it became clear to Hidalgo that the vast majority of *criollos* were unwilling to support a genuine revolution that threatened to overturn the status quo, the priest saw no reason to attempt to check the violent behavior of his followers.[53] Indeed, Hidalgo seems to have concluded that, by trying to restrain the violent behavior of his lower class followers, he risked losing their support and that was a risk he was unwilling to take.

Other reasons that have been offered to explain his decision to retreat seem more plausible. At Monte de las Cruces, his army had faced disciplined soldiers and state of the art artillery for the first time, and Hidalgo was certainly shaken by the heavy losses that resulted. Moreover, he was low on ammunition and his hitherto inexperienced soldiers, frightened by the bloody realities of battle, were deserting by the thousands, thereby leaving him to wonder if others would do the same once the siege of Mexico City got underway. Perhaps the most important factor in Hidalgo's decision to retreat, however, was the fact that he simply had no idea that the capital was so weakly defended.

At any rate, following the victory at Monte de las Cruces, Hidalgo moved his army closer to Mexico City. Although Allende exhorted him to attack at once, he hesitated and, instead, sent a message to Venegas, urging the viceroy to surrender the capital so as to avoid the slaughter that would be inflicted on those within the city should they decide to fight. Like Riaño at Valladolid, however, the viceroy rejected Hidalgo's offer and prepared for battle. Only then did the priest-general give the order to retreat, doing so over the strong objection of Allende and the other *criollo* officers.

As his forces moved in a northwest direction, his rag-tag soldiers, with their expectation of post-battle plunder dashed, began to desert in droves. Within a few days, the rebel army was reduced in size from 80,000 to about half that number. To make matters worse, Hidalgo's retreat provided royalist General Félix Calleja with the necessary time to move his army of 7,000 well equipped men to the capital before it fell. It is worth noting that Calleja's forces consisted largely of *criollos* fighting under the command of a *peninsular* general.[54] This is significant for it demonstrates that the creole sub-class would fight under the hated *peninsulares* before it would countenance a genuine revolution.

On November 7, Calleja's troops unexpectedly crossed paths with the retreating rebel forces at Aculco. With their army in disarray, Hidalgo and Allende were ill prepared to battle such a formidable foe. They therefore decided to feign an attack to give their army cover for an orderly retreat. Not surprisingly, the plan failed because of the lack of discipline within the rebel ranks. The retreat turned into a disaster for Hidalgo. Calleja captured virtually all of his enemy's artillery, baggage, and livestock and his army suffered only one casualty in the process.[55]

Guanajuato and Puente do Calderon

With the insurgents demoralized and in disarray, Calleja prepared to follow up his victory at Aculco with an attack on rebel-held Guanajuato. Allende argued that his and Hidalgo's best recourse was to retreat with their forces to this city and to prepare its defense. Hidalgo disagreed, opting instead for a plan to withdraw to Valladolid. Unable to agree, the rebel forces were split, with part following Hidalgo and the rest accompanying Allende. On reaching Valladolid, however, Hidalgo received some rare good news. A fellow rebel officer, José Antonio Torres, had just taken Guadalajara. Reasoning that, by joining Torres he would be safe from Calleja's army and would, therefore, have the time to recruit new men, Hidalgo quickly left Valladolid and traveled unimpeded about 200 miles westward to Guadalajara. Before he left, however, he allowed his soldiers to execute about sixty *peninsulares* whom they had captured. Meanwhile, Allende's soldiers were too few to defend Guanajuato without Hidalgo's forces. Consequently, as Calleja neared the city, the *criollo* revolutionary leader had no choice but to flee and allow the royalists to take Guanajuato without a fight.

While in Guadalajara, Hidalgo issued several decrees in an attempt to re-stimulate Indian recruitment. He called for the abolition of slavery, a reduction of various taxes, and an end to rent fees and tribute that Indians were still forced to pay to the crown. What perhaps was most noteworthy, however, was his radical call for a return of all lands that had been illegally taken from the Indians.[56] Evidently his proclamations had the intended effect, since by January he had attracted enough Indians and *mestizos* to raise the number of his troops to 80,000.[57] When a *peninsular* plot to overthrow him was uncovered, he executed the ringleaders. All in all, from November to January, the rebels put over 300 *peninsulares* and *criollos* to death.[58] Allende, who had arrived with his soldiers in early December, opposed these executions, claiming that they would further alienate the creoles, but his protest fell on Hidalgo's deaf ears.

So disgusted was Allende at Hidalgo's overall conduct in the revolution that, in January, he conspired with other insurgents to poison the priest, reasoning that it was the only way to save the revolution. He even went so far as to seek assurances from a church official that such an action was justified. Realizing the animosity that the *criollo* leaders had for him, however, Hidalgo was cautious and the poisoning plot never reached fruition.[59]

156

In January, General Calleja, with an army of 6,000 soldiers, marched on Guadalajara, intending to capture the city and destroy the combined forces of Hidalgo and Allende once and for all. With overwhelming numerical superiority, Hidalgo wanted to take the offensive and make one massive strike that he reasoned would overwhelm the royalist army, just as it had done at the Battle of Monte de las Cruces outside of Mexico City. As in the past, Allende vehemently disagreed with these tactics, arguing that, should the attack fail, the result would be mass chaos followed by a rout of the rebel forces. Instead, he wanted to break up the insurgent army into six or more units, which would strike at the enemy one at a time. Again, as in the past, Hidalgo refused to change his strategy.[60] The battle took place on January 17 at Puente de Calderón on the Rio Lerma, 29 miles north of Guadalajara. It lasted six hours and was finally determined by a battlefield accident, when, by mere chance, a royalist artillery shot hit an ammunition wagon of the insurgents. The explosion that resulted caused a grass fire that enveloped Hidalgo's army in a thick cloud of smoke. Panic ensued and the rebel forces broke ranks and fled in all directions. As Allende predicted, the mass confusion resulted in a rout. Approximately 1,200 rebels were killed, while the forces of Calleja suffered only about fifty dead. Hidalgo and Allende fled north with the remains of their army, stopping at the Hacienda de San Blas del Pabellón. There Allende and the other *criollo* officers blamed the priest for all of their recent failures and removed him from command, replacing him with Allende (although it was decided that this change should be kept secret from the rebel army).[61] Allende, Hidalgo, and the other rebel leaders now moved north, hoping to obtain new recruits and arms in Coahuila and Texas. It was, however, too late. Their cause was already lost, and it was only a matter of time before they were captured.

By March, many *criollo* provincial rebel officers, hearing of Hidalgo's defeats, began to switch sides, turning cities and towns over to the royalists without a fight. One of these was the aforementioned Francisco Ignacio Elizondo, who engineered the capture of Hidalgo, Allende, and the bulk of the revolutionary leadership at the Baján wells near Monclova in Coahuila, thereby ending the first phase of the war for Mexican independence.

Conclusion

Padre Miguel Hidalgo was certainly a flawed man. He was definitely not a "good priest" in the traditional sense. He had numerous mistresses and at least five illegitimate children. He was dismissive of church doctrine and promoted literary works that were critical of the church and its clergy. He was said to have devoted little time to prayer but much to partying and secular issues. He was equally flawed as a military leader. He refused to listen to the advice of his

157

fellow officers, even though he had no expertise in military tactics and no combat experience. He seemed incapable of long-term planning and made important decisions on the spur of the moment with no thought of their consequences. His inability or unwillingness to control the behavior of his Indian and *mestizo* followers cost his movement the crucial support of the *criollo* subclass. Likewise, his inexplicable decision to retreat rather than attack a poorly defended Mexico City, more than anything else, doomed the uprising to failure.

On the other hand, however, Padre Hidalgo seems to have had an understanding of and a sympathy for the lower classes that was unmatched by other Spaniards of his social class. He did not seem to view his exile from academe and his reassignment to pastoral work among mostly Indians as a demotion. Indeed, he threw himself into working for the amelioration of his impoverished parishioners, creating numerous economic projects for them and allowing then to attend the discussion sessions at his home. More important, once the revolt began, Hidalgo articulated a vision of a new kind of state. It would be one that was free from European domination and interference; one in which there would be no slavery and Indians would no longer be burdened with the forced payment of tribute to the crown. It would likewise be one in which the indigenous population would again own agricultural land that they could farm to feed their families. Hidalgo's revolution and dream were kept alive by another priest, the *mestizo* José Morelos, who continued to battle the Spanish elites for another four years. During this time, he further articulated and developed Hidalgo's blueprint for a Mexico with justice for the masses. With his capture and execution in November 1815, however, the only true revolutionary movement in the wars for Latin American independence came to an end. Fighting continued until 1821, when Augustín de Iturbide broke with the crown and finally created an independent Mexico. This fighting, however, was restricted to the upper class *criollos* and *peninsulares* and its outcome had little effect, if any, on the masses.

Following independence, Mexico soon degenerated into a state of intermittent warfare between conservative and liberal *caudillos* (dictators). The Indian and *mestizo* population continued to be oppressed and exploited and their lack of land and rights was of little concern to the elites that fought among themselves for power. This changed, however, with the rise of Emiliano Zapata and other lesser figures in the Mexican Revolution of the early twentieth century. These revolutionaries resurrected the names of Padre Hidalgo and the Virgin of Guadalupe to inspire their Indian soldiers as they fought tenaciously and successfully for land and other rights that had long been denied them. As time went on, however, Indian gains were gradually eroded. Consequently, they rose up in revolt again in Chiapas, in the mid 1990s, and fought with the Zapatista National Liberation Army (EZLN). Again, the leaders of this revolt resurrected the names and memories of Hidalgo and Our Lady of Guadalupe. As time goes on, new Indian uprisings will again burst forth, and again the indigenous people will fight under the banners of Hidalgo and the Virgin. This will continue until the poor masses of Mexico finally obtain their rights and the dignity that has been denied them for so long.

Notes

1. For Bourbon reforms, see: John R. Fisher, *Commercial Relations Between Spain and Spanish America in the Era of Free Trade, 1778-1796* (Liverpool: Center for Latin American Studies [University of Liverpool Monograph Series, no. 13], 1985); D.A. Brading, *Miners and Merchants in Bourbon Mexico, 1763-1810* (Cambridge: University of Cambridge Press, 1971); Jacques A. Barbier, "The Culmination of the Bourbon Reforms," *Hispanic American Historical Review* 57 (1977): 51-68, and Allan J. Kuethe, and Lowell Blaisdell, "French Influence and the Origins of the Bourbon Colonial Reorganization," *Hispanic American Historical Review* 71 (1991): 579-607.

2. Hugh M. Hamill, Jr., *The Hidalgo Revolt: Prelude to Mexican Independence* (Gainesville: University of Florida Press, 1966), 1; Michael C. Meyer and William L. Sherman, *The Course of Mexican History* (New York: Oxford University Press, 1983), 255.

3. Hubert J. Miller, *Padre Miguel Hidalgo: Father of Mexican Independence* (Edinburg, TX: Pan American University Press, 1986), 1-2.

4. Meyer and Sherman, 271.

5. Hamill, 54.

6. *Ibid.*, 36-38, 54; Miller, 17.

7. Miller, 17.

8. *Ibid.*

9. Hamill, 55-56.

10. *Ibid.*, 57.

11. *Ibid.*

12. Miller, 18.

13. Hamill, 58-60.

14. *Ibid.*, 62.

15. Gabriel Méndez Plancarte, "Hidalgo Reformador Intellectual," *Abside* 17 (April/June 1952): 135-70. See also Miller, 17-19.

16. Hamill, 64; Miller, 19.

17. Hamill, 65-67.

18. *Ibid.*, 68.

19. *Ibid.*, 69; Miller, 21.

20. Hamill, 73-79; Miller, 22; Meyer and Sherman, 286.

21. Hamill, 82.

22. Miller, 24. See also: Hamill, 80-88; Meyer and Sherman, 286.
23. Meyer and Sherman, 276.
24. *Ibid.*, 281.
25. Hamill, 117.
26. Meyer and Sherman, 281.
27. Hamill, 101-8.
28. *Ibid.*, 111.
29. *Ibid.*, 118-23; Miller, 15-16; Luis Castillo Ledón, *Hidalgo: La vida del héroe* 2 (Mexico: Talleres Gráficos de la Nación, 1949), 6; Meyer and Sherman, 285-88.
30. Brian R. Hamnet, *Roots of Insurgency: Mexican Regions, 1750-1824* (Cambridge: Cambridge University Press, 1986), 16.
31. Miller, 29.
32. *Ibid.*, 30.
33. Hamill, 118.
34. Lucas Alamán, *Historia de México* 1 (Mexico: Editorial Jus, 1942), 403-4.
35. Whereas Alamán's negative account lacks impartiality, the same is true for revisionist Luis Castillo Ledón, who, in his two-volume *Hidalgo: La vida del héroe* (Mexico: Talleres Gráficos de la Nación, 1948-49), overlooks his hero's shortcomings. In 1966, Hugh M. Hamill, Jr., while making use of the scholarship of both Alamán and Castillo Ledón, corrected the record with a more balanced account in his *Hidalgo Revolt: Prelude to Mexican Independence*, 137-41.
36. Hamill, 146.
37. *Ibid.*, 171-72.
38. *Ibid.*, 152-59.
39. Miller, 36.
40. N.M. Farriss, *Crown and Clergy in Colonial Mexico, 1759-1821: The Crisis of Ecclesiastical Privilege* (London: The Athlone Press, 1968), 198-99.
41. *Ibid.*, 199.
42. Hamnet, 126.
43. Farriss, 199-200.
44. Hamill, 170, 191-92.
45. Miller, 36. For Morelos, see Wilber H. Timmons, *Morelos of Mexico: Priest Soldier Statesman* (El Paso: Texas Western College Press, 1963).
46. Farriss, 202.
47. Cited in Miller, *op cit.*
48. Karl M. Schmitt, "The Clergy and the Independencia of New Spain," *Hispanic American Historical Review*, 34 (August 1954): 311.
49. Miller, 37.
50. *Ibid.*, 39-40.
51. Hamill, 126; Miller, 40.
52. See, for example, Meyer and Sherman, 290.
53. Hamill, 182.
54. Miller, 41-42.
55. Hamill, 180.
56. *Ibid.*, 194-96.

57. *Ibid.*, 198.
58. Miller, 44, 49; Castillo Ledón, 144.
59. Hamill, 200.
60. *Ibid* , 201.
61. *Ibid.*, 204-5.

José Francisco de San Martín:
The Good Soldier

Joan E. Supplee
Baylor University

Mi juventud fue sacrificada al servicio de los españoles, mi edad media al de mi patria, creo que tengo el derecho a disponer de mi vejez.

(I gave my youth to the Spanish, my maturity to the nation, and I think I have earned the right to spend my old age as I please.)

—José Francisco de San Martín[1]

José Francisco de San Martín used a distinguished military career in the Old World to become a hero of the nineteenth-century wars for independence in the New. After serving in the Spanish military for 22 years, Lieutenant Colonel San Martín resigned his commission to fight for the independence of his native Argentina. His South American campaigns included one of the most daring military operations since Hannibal's army crossed the Alps. General San Martín led his army through high mountain passes across the crest of the Andes Mountains to surprise and overwhelm his Spanish enemies. He participated in the liberation of Chile and Peru from Spanish rule and in 1822 offered to join his forces with those of General Simón Bolívar to complete the liberation of South America. Rather than divide the armies when Bolívar refused, San Martín retired from the battlefield at age 44. Limiting his political ambitions, he soon retired from public life, pledging not to "become the executioner of my own countrymen" as had other military commanders.[2] He sought a peaceful retirement on the family hacienda, but political rivals drove him into exile. He finally settled in the south of France and never returned to his native Argentina.

162

Supplee: JOSÉ FRANCISCO DE SAN MARTÍN

Mi juventud fue sacrificada al servicio de los españoles . . .

Like many of the details of José Francisco de San Martín's early life, uncertainty surrounds his birth date. Most authors assert that he was born on February 25, 1778, the youngest son of Spanish parents, Lieutenant Juan de San Martín y Gómez from Cervato de la Cueza and Gregoria Matorras y del Ser from Paredes de Nava. Lieutenant San Martín of the Spanish infantry served as the military governor of the town of Yapeyú, in the sparsely settled missions region in the current province of Corrientes. The family soon relocated to Buenos Aires where José Francisco attended school. His father received permission to return to Spain to take a position with the general staff at the southern port of Málaga. The three older San Martín brothers followed their father into military service as cadets in the Soria Regiment. In 1786, his parents enrolled their youngest son in the Seminario de Nobles de Madrid (Madrid Seminary for Nobles). The school prepared sons of the nobility and senior military officers for the king's service. On July 1, 1798, José Francisco de San Martín submitted his written request for enrollment as a cadet "following the example of his father and brothers . . . to pursue a distinguished military career."[3]

San Martín began his service to the Spanish against the Ottomans in 1789 as a cadet in the Murcia Infantry Regiment and soon saw his first action in North Africa in the battle of Melilla. His regiment later assisted in the defense of Orán, which was besieged by the *bey* of Máscara. There San Martín survived the month long battle that reduced the fortress to ruins and led to the capitulation of the Murcia Regiment and its return to Spain following the surrender.

His regiment next saw action in a campaign against the French in 1793 under the command of General Ricardos. The Murcia Regiment moved up to the Pyrenees Mountains and advanced with the main Spanish line. When the French counterattacked in 1794, San Martín was with a unit cut off by the French advance and forced to surrender at Port Vendre. With the signing of the Peace of Basel in 1795, he was released from French custody and returned to Spain.[4] During this campaign, he was promoted several times for valor on the battlefield, reaching the rank of second lieutenant in 1795.

He resumed his career against the British in 1796, when the Spanish signed an alliance with France and sought to dislodge the British from Gibraltar. In 1797, San Martín's regiment fought unsuccessfully as part of the Spanish fleet against the British at Cape St. Vicente. The following year, the British ship *Lion* engaged the Spanish off the coast of Cartegena, capturing the frigate *Santa Dorotea* and with it San Martín's regiment. His release came this time as part of a prisoner exchange.

Rejoining his regiment in 1801, San Martín participated in a campaign against the Portuguese. His unit helped to capture the fortress of Olivares, which

163

pressured Portugal to sign a treaty excluding the English from its ports. He returned to Spain to help reinforce the blockade of Gibraltar. In 1804, he was in the port of Cádiz assisting with an epidemic. To advance his opportunities for promotion, he transferred to the *Voluntarios del Campo Mayor*, a light infantry battalion, and made second captain of the *Voluntarios* in 1804.[5] His cavalry unit then served with the forces that invaded Portugal for a second time.

In 1808, as the Spanish crown fell victim to Napoleon's intrigues, San Martín was once again in Cádiz. While he was standing guard duty, a local mob demanding protection from the French sailors stormed the regiment's headquarters and killed its commander, General Francisco María Solano Ortiz de Rozas. For the rest of his life, San Martín distrusted mobs and popular violence and commemorated Solano's sacrifice by carrying a miniature with the General's image.[6]

In 1808, with the French invasion of the Spanish peninsula, San Martín's military career advanced quickly. After distinguishing himself in fighting against the French at Arjonilla, he was promoted to captain of the Bourbon Regiment. That regiment participated in the defeat of Napoleon's troops at Bailén on July 19, 1808, marking the first major defeat for Napoleon and enabling the Spanish Army of Andalusia to retake Madrid. For his role in the action, San Martín received the rank of lieutenant colonel and a gold medal. Soon after, he fell gravely ill, suffering with ulcers and asthma. Some have speculated that he contracted tuberculosis during this period. When he recovered, he joined the Army of Catalonia and continued to fight with the allied forces of Spain, Portugal, and England. At the battle of Albuera, he fought under the command of British General William Carr Beresford, who, as a colonel in 1806, had captured and detained San Martín in Buenos Aires. By 1811, at age 33, San Martín's service to the Spanish crown culminated with the rank of adjutant-general and command of a regiment of dragoons.[7]

Following the second siege of Badajoz, he applied for permission to resign his commission and travel to America. His commanding officer said of the request: "This officer has served well for twenty-two years and he has special commendations for his service in war, especially the present one, which do him credit and have earned him a high reputation. . . . For my part I believe the reasons for requesting his retirement and transfer to Lima to be well founded."[8] San Martín resigned his commission and left Spain on September 6, 1811.

. . . *mi edad media al de mi patria* . . .

Events in Argentina called San Martín home. The Napoleonic wars had reduced British trade and Prime Minister William Pitt decided that either the Spanish American colonies should receive independence or that the British would seize strategic ports in the region. Francisco de Miranda, a Venezuelan and former Spanish officer who had spent years in exile in Britain campaigning for Spanish American independence, favored the former. The British first experimented with the latter. In 1806 and again in 1807, the British attempted to take the port of Buenos Aires. While neither attempt resulted in success for the British, they did much to encourage the citizens of the port to rethink their connection to the Spanish crown. Because the Spanish viceroy chose to flee rather than defend the city, the *porteños* (residents of Buenos Aires) organized militias and drove out first the British forces and then the Spanish viceroy when he tried to return. Emboldened by this action, they forced the Spanish crown to grant them free trade while looking forward to the day of political independence.

Napoleon's activities in Spain provided the final impetus for the *porteños* to seize political control. When the French army captured Sevilla and threatened the last center of resistance in Cádiz, the *porteños* called a *cabildo abierto* (an open town meeting) on May 25, 1810 to plan their response. They created a *junta* composed of members of the *porteño* elite to rule in the name of deposed King Ferdinand VII. Prodded by Mariano Moreno, the *junta* moved toward independence, exiling Spanish officials and refusing to recognize the authority of the Regency in Spain. Forces countering this movement forced Moreno out of the *junta* in 1811. He died on his way to take up a diplomatic post in Britain, the same year that San Martín resigned his commission in the Spanish army.

San Martín kept up with the events occurring in his homeland. During the fighting around Cádiz in 1808, he had joined a Masonic lodge, the Rational Knights, with connections to a London organization, founded by Francisco de Miranda. Miranda worked to bring together Spanish American exiles and British politicians, including William Pitt, who had an interest in Spanish American independence. The membership also included Matías Zapiola (a Spanish naval officer who recruited San Martín for the Rational Knight), Andrés Bello, Tomás Guido, Manuel Moreno, Carlos Maria de Alvear, and Juan Martín de Pueyrredón.

In addition to his activities with the Rational Knights, San Martín made the acquaintance of Lord James Duff of the British secret service. Lord Duff introduced San Martín to other revolutionaries in Cádiz and encouraged his resignation from Spanish service. Duff also arranged passage and a fake passport for San Martín, who left Cádiz on September 14, 1811 for London. This was quite a coup for Duff: San Martín was the highest ranking officer in the Spanish army to fight with the American rebels.

San Martín stayed briefly in England to meet with others who had gathered at the former home of Miranda, including several Argentines, to promote independence. They also conferred with British politicians interested in encouraging Latin American independence. By January 1812, San Martín had embarked on the British vessel, the *George Canning*, bound for Buenos Aires.

165

The situation in Buenos Aires had shifted with the death of Moreno and the departure of Manuel Belgrano from the *junta*. Belgrano took over command of the northern army and, in September 1811, an unstable Triumvirate replaced the *junta*. The Triumvirate met with San Martín in Buenos Aires in March 1812. It recognized San Martín's rank as lieutenant colonel and charged him with training a force to fight the Spanish in Peru. San Martín created the Mounted Grenadiers and spent most of 1812 training and drilling the troops on the banks of the Río de la Plata.[9]

While San Martín organized and trained his troops, the political situation continued to evolve in Buenos Aires. In June, the Triumvirate suppressed a royalist coup attempt but faced even more difficult challenges from forces demanding independence. San Martín played a pivotal role in this challenge. Not long after landing in Buenos Aires, he and fellow conspirator, Carlos María de Alvear, organized a secret lodge, similar to that in Cádiz. The Lautaro Lodge pledged its members to the cause of independence and to strict secrecy. Lower members of the lodge did not know who the leaders where. Lodge members worked to control key institutions in the government. When news of General Belgrano's defeat of the royalist forces in Tucumán reached Buenos Aires in October 1812, the lodge demanded a seat for one of its members on the Triumvirate. The town council refused. The city garrison, including San Martín and his cavalry, then appeared in the main plaza to pressure the town council to accede to the demands of the lodge. It soon did. The council appointed a new Triumvirate approved by the lodge and called for an assembly to draft a constitution for the United Provinces.[10] San Martín used his forces to pressure the town council to move toward independence.

When not occupied with the cause of Argentine independence, San Martín, a bachelor of 34 years, pursued a young member of a prominent local family, María de los Remedios de Escalada de la Quintana. They were married in Buenos Aires on September 12, 1812. Argentine independence became a family affair. María's brothers joined San Martín's grenadiers while she raised money to arm and equip the troops in Buenos Aires.[11]

San Martín's Grenadiers faced their first test of battle in 1813. The Triumvirate ordered San Martín's troops north to resist the Spanish pressure on Rosario and disruption of trade on the Paraná River. He failed to intercept the Spanish in time to save Rosario, but he later surprised and defeated them at the convent of San Lorenzo, despite the Spaniards' superior numbers. The Grenadiers first victory demonstrated San Martín's ability to train American soldiers in European cavalry techniques. It also enhanced San Martín's stature in the political circles of Buenos Aires and put royalists in Montevideo on the defensive.

While San Martín's forces distinguished themselves at San Lorenzo, Spanish forces successfully resisted the troops under General Belgrano's command. Two defeats in rapid succession—Vilcapugio in October 1813 and Ayohuma the following month—put Buenos Aires on the defensive. Upon his return from San Lorenzo, the Triumvirate charged San Martín with defending the city, but he sought a more active role: Leadership of an expedition against Montevideo. A friend of dubious loyalty, Alvear maneuvered to secure that assignment for himself while having San Martín named major general of the Northern Auxiliary Army, with orders to relieve Belgrano's beleaguered forces. Always the dutiful soldier, San Martín left Buenos Aires in December 1813 with a force of artillery and 250 of his grenadiers. Alvear speculated at the time that San Martín would not return.[12]

The northern assignment altered San Martín's strategy for winning independence. He was discouraged by what he found as he assumed command of Belgrano's forces in January 1814; Spanish attacks had shattered the army. Lacking hospital supplies and money for wages, uniforms, and training, San Martín despaired of progress on the northern front. As he rebuilt the army, he reworked his plans for the campaign ahead. Because Spanish forces in the silver producing areas of Upper Peru were well entrenched, San Martín developed a "continental" alternative in March 1814. Rather than north, he struck out to the west across the mountains into Santiago, from where he could then move against Lima from the sea. Gauchos under the command of Martín Güemes of Salta would hold back Royalists in the north while San Martín outflanked them.

While concealing his plans from all but a few friends in the Lautaro Lodge, he implemented them almost immediately. In April 1814, he took a leave of absence for health reasons at a ranch in Córdoba and petitioned the government to appoint him governor of the province of Cuyo, a post more appropriate for his health. Cuyo also guarded the passes to Chile. In September, the government in Buenos Aires acceded to his request and San Martín moved to the city of Mendoza, capital of Cuyo province.

As San Martín settled into Mendoza, the situation on the other side of the mountains deteriorated for the patriots. In October 1814, a royal army from Peru landed in Chile and defeated them at Rancagua. Under the command of José Miguel Carreras, the defeated army retreated across the mountains to Mendoza. With the royalists occupying Santiago, the threat of an invasion across the mountains from Chile preoccupied San Martín and the government in Buenos Aires.

San Martín threw himself into the governorship of the region. He established a college, worked on irrigation projects, built roads to the principle towns in Cuyo, beautified the city of Mendoza, and, after the arrival of his wife, inaugurated a lively social life in the city. San Martín described this period in his life as one of the happiest; his only child, Mercedes Tomasa, was born on August 24, 1816. His civic projects endeared San Martín to the inhabitants of Cuyo and, particularly, to the citizens of Mendoza.[13]

167

His local popularity saved the continental plan. Political fortunes shifted in Buenos Aires in 1815 and brought to power the young and ambitious Carlos María de Alvear. With the help of a squadron under British mercenary Captain William Brown, Alvear defeated the royalists at Montevideo and used the victory to assume leadership of the United Provinces of the Río de la Plata in January 1815. The ascension to power of an old rival led San Martín to petition the government to relieve him of his governorship, ostensibly for reasons of health. Alvear used the opportunity to appoint a new governor for Cuyo. The Mendocinos had other ideas. Refusing to recognize the new governor, they demanded San Martín's reinstatement. Other cities in Cuyo followed suit and forced the reinstatement. In April, Alvear himself resigned, forced out by a revolt of the forces in Buenos Aires.[14] Alvear's resignation cleared the way for San Martín's plan for a campaign in Chile.

The political and military situation still challenged San Martín. Patriot forces across the continent were in retreat in 1815 and, with the restoration of Ferdinand VII in Spain, reinforcements arrived in Venezuela to battle Bolívar's forces. Chile remained under the control of a royalist force from Peru. In November 1815, the Army of the North faced another defeat at the hands of the Spanish at Sipe-Sipe, and the government considered pulling men from San Martín's forces to reinforce the line in the north. To forestall this plan and preserve his own vision for the liberation of South America, San Martín hosted a banquet in Mendoza, to which he invited his officers and prominent citizens. His intentions became clear as he raised a glass "to the first shot fired against the oppressors of Chile on the other side of the Andes."[15] The instability of the government of the United Provinces did not deter San Martín. In fact, his military plan could save the government.

The power vacuum in Buenos Aires allowed San Martín to influence the delegation sent to a congress in Tucumán to reorganize the United Provinces in 1816. He urged the delegates to take decisive action, but the delegates hesitated. In a series of letters to his friend Tomás Godoy Cruz, a representative to the congress and a member of the Lautaro Lodge, he reiterated the call for independence: "How long must we wait to declare our independence? . . . Courage! Ventures were intended for brave men. Our path is clear."[16] In May, after discussing the candidacies of San Martín and Belgrano, the congress selected as its supreme director, Juan Martín de Pueyrredón. San Martín dispatched his aide-de-camp and engineer, José Antonio Álvarez Condarco, to explain the battle plan to Pueyrredón and get his support. The supreme director ordered Buenos Aires to send as much help as possible to the expedition. On July 9, 1816, the Congress of Tucumán declared the United Provinces of the Río de la Plata independent. The declaration both relieved and disappointed San Martín: "Congress has delivered the master stroke with the declaration of independence.

I only wish that at the same time some brief explanation might have been given of the just reason that the Americans had for their action."[17] The declaration nevertheless gave San Martín and his brothers in the Lautaro Lodge the victory for which they had been working for nearly a decade.

In July 1816, San Martín's plan became the plan of the United Provinces. Pueyrredón met with him in Córdoba for two days of secret meetings to arrange more supplies for the army. When he got to Buenos Aires, Pueyrredón sent as much aid as he could.[18] At one point, he wrote to San Martín that he was sending "the World, the Flesh and the Devil . . . Don't ask me for anything more."[19] In August, Pueyrredón named San Martín general of the Army of the Andes.

San Martín rallied the citizens of Cuyo to support the effort. Preparations required more than two years. Fray Luis Beltrán prepared the foundry, organizing 300 laborers to supply cannon, shot, bullets, and other equipment needed to transport an army across the Andes. They established a gunpowder factory and a textile mill for uniforms. The government granted the army a budget of 8,000 pesos per month, but more was soon needed. María de Remedios organized fund raising; women of the local elite donated their jewels to the cause.[20]

Final preparations were made in September 1816. General San Martín moved his army to the camp at Plumerillo, north of Mendoza, for final training. He divided his forces into three main units. One was placed under the command of the Chilean Bernardo O'Higgins (who San Martín supported over the Carrera brothers), and another was led by General Miguel Estanislao Soler. General Juan Gregorio de Las Heras commanded the third main unit. San Martín organized additional smaller units to divert attention from the main forces.

The expedition was ready in January 1817. San Martín prepared the ground by using spies and misinformation to confuse the Spanish commander, General Marcó de Pont, about the route of the army's advance. On January 5, the Army of the Andes marched through Mendoza as San Martín called on the Virgin of Carmen to protect his troops. In total, San Martín led an impressive force: 5,500 men, 10,600 saddle and pack mules, 1,600 horses, 700 head of cattle, 500 wheeled carriages, two 6-inch howitzers, and ten 4-inch field pieces. They carried food and supplies for twenty days. The main force moved out of Mendoza on July 9. It took nearly a month for the army to travel 150 miles and traverse a pass 12,000 feet above sea level. Thousands of mules and hundreds of horses died in the crossing, along with more than 100 soldiers. Despite the conditions, the three units reunited in Aconcagua valley at the village of San Felipe.

The battle came on February 12 1817. Too late to send reinforcements, the Spanish commander, Marcó del Pont, planning for an attack from the south, realized that San Martín was approaching from the north. San Martín re-divided his troops under O'Higgins and Soler and sent them against the Spanish at Chacabuco. O'Higgins's initial attack was almost repelled until Soler's men

169

outflanked the Spanish left wing. The Spanish line broke and retreated toward Santiago. San Martín's troops, however, failed to follow up. While some of the defeated force escaped to fight again in Chile, the patriot army's victory was impressive. For the loss of 129 soldiers, San Martín's force reduced the Spanish force by more than 1,100 killed, wounded, or captured.

The capture of Santiago was easier. While the American troops recuperated after the battle, news reached their camp of a Spanish withdrawal from Santiago to the port Valparaíso, for a retreat by sea to Peru. San Martín's cavalry intercepted part of the Spanish force, but 500 soldiers escaped. On February 14, San Martín and the Army of the Andes occupied Santiago.

The capture of Santiago failed to end the royalist resistance in Chile, particularly in the south. While patriots crossing from the north, and dispatched from Santiago, gained control in the north, southern royalists took control of the port of Talcahuano, where they could be resupplied by sea. San Martín dispatched General Las Heras's force to suppress the royalists.

San Martín left subordinates in charge of quelling the remaining resistance while he turned his attention to the political situation in Chile and the continuation of his continental plan. He installed his loyal ally O'Higgins as supreme director of Santiago, established a local Lautaro Lodge to help secure Chile for the patriot cause, and began a training camp for new recruits. The town council's gift to San Martín of 10,000 gold pesos was donated for the construction of a public library.[21] San Martín then made plans to return to Buenos Aires to obtain the funds needed to build a fleet for the campaign against Spanish and royalist forces in Lima.

After securing funds for the Lima campaign from the Pueyrredón government, in May 1817 San Martín returned to Santiago as conditions for the patriots deteriorated. When Las Heras proved incapable of suppressing the royalist insurgents in the south, O'Higgins turned over command of Santiago to another Argentine member of the Lautaro Lodge, ordered the court martial of Las Heras, and took a force of 800 men south to finish the job. O'Higgins also became bogged down and the royalist garrison at Talcahuano continued to receive reinforcements by sea. Instead of resolving this problem, however, San Martín busied himself with preparations for the Peru invasion, establishing his headquarters and training facilities near the port of Valparaíso. In Santiago, political factions emerged that were hostile to the Argentine colonel who O'Higgins had left in control of the city, and Chileans chaffed under the taxation scheme used to raise money for the Peruvian expedition. José María Carrera, unhappy with San Martín's selection of O'Higgins as a commander, worked to undermine his position in Chile. Along with his brothers in exile in Mendoza, Carrera promised to retake Chile for the Chileans, to exile O'Higgins, and punish San Martín as a criminal.[22] At the same time, royalist sympathizers worked to prepare Chile for a new invasion from Peru.

Supplee: JOSÉ FRANCISCO DE SAN MARTÍN

At the end of 1817, a new threat appeared on the horizon. Viceroy Joaquín de Pezuela raised a force of 3,300 men, under General Mariano Osorio, and dispatched it to reinforce Talcahuano. Osorio planned to draw the patriot forces away from Santiago toward the south and then quickly move his force by sea to Valparaíso and against an undefended Santiago. San Martín's spies in Peru informed him of these plans as the force departed for Chile. Alarmed, San Martín urged O'Higgins to raise the siege of Talcahuano and move north. He withdrew to the city of Talca in January 1817 and, in defiance of the Spanish threat, declared Chilean independence on February 12, 1817.

To meet the threat, San Martín first reinforced Valparaíso and then marched south with troops to join O'Higgins. Revising his plans, General Osorio landed at Talcahuano and marched his forces out to meet the gathering patriot army. His troops encountered those of San Martín and O'Higgins on March 18, 1817. Realizing that the patriot forces far outnumbered his troops, Osorio ordered a halt the following day just outside Talca. Meanwhile, San Martín's troops assembled on the nearby plains of Cancha Rayada. During the night of the 19th, the royalists launched a surprise attack and completely routed the patriot army. O'Higgins's troops panicked after their general fell wounded. The panic spread all the way to Santiago, where residents despaired that all was lost. A supporter of the Carreras, Manuel Rodriguez, rallied the city, organized its defense, and prevented a general flight across the Andes in terror.[23]

The defeat at Cancha Rayada had several results. First, O'Higgins and San Martín returned to reestablish order in Santiago. Osorio's delayed approach to the city left them time to prepare an effective defense. A patriot force of some 5,000 men and 21 artillery pieces met Osorio's 5,300 soldiers with fewer field guns. In early April, Osorio moved his troops to the plains outside of Santiago, by the Maipú River. The clash came on April 5, 1817. San Martín's forces charged first. The royalists drove them back but could not hold when the patriots, with reserves and cavalry, resumed the attack. Outflanked, the royalist center collapsed and the patriot cavalry reduced the retreating force. Osorio lost all but 200 men. This battle marked the end of the royalist cause in Chile and freed San Martín to execute the final step in his continental plan.

The preparations for the assault on the royalist stronghold in Lima took San Martín another two years. He followed up the victory at Maipú with yet another trip to Buenos Aires to get support for his plans. Control of the seas proved the main challenge; Viceroy Pezuela's fleet controlled the Pacific coastline. The United Provinces had little to offer when it came to naval preparations, and geography precluded an overland campaign to Peru. San Martín had to secure the sea to transport his troops and to prevent the Spanish from landing reinforcements.

The Chileans shouldered the responsibility for the Pacific fleet. Manuel Blanco Encalada, a Chilean who had served in the Spanish navy, took command but was soon replaced by the flamboyant Lord Thomas Cochrane, late of the British navy. A talented naval officer, Cochrane had run afoul of military and civil authorities in Britain. In 1818, he began to assemble and train a patriot navy in Santiago. Within two years,he cobbled together a fleet of ships capable of raiding and harrying Spanish ships up and down the Chilean coast.[24] Although he and San Martín clashed, Cochrane and his fleet were critical for the invasion of Peru.

The unstable political and financial situation in Chile and the United Provinces hindered and, at times, endangered San Martín's project. The victory at Maipú secured the Chileans from Spanish attack but left them weary of Argentine influence in their affairs. They particularly distrusted the Lautaro Lodge, and resented increased taxation and state confiscation of property undertaken to outfit a fleet and finance the Peruvian expedition. When no more funds could be squeezed from the Chileans, San Martín turned to Pueyrredón and the United Provinces. He painted the blackest picture he could of the reduced fortunes of the Chilean army, but received only vague promises of aid. In frustration, he played the health card one more time and offered to resign his command. Pueyrredón buckled under the pressure and promised the aid for the Peruvian campaign if San Martín rescinded his resignation. Events, however, forced the recall of San Martín's army to defend the Río de la Plata. San Martín used this order to pressure O'Higgins to provide more support. As one of San Martín's divisions marched back toward Mendoza, O'Higgins, fearing the loss of that force, joined with the United Provinces to pledge support for the Peruvian campaign in February 1819. Chile would provide most of the financial support and 4,000 well-equipped troops. Satisfied, San Martín prepared to return to Chile.

With the financial support that he needed secured, San Martín faced a more serious setback in the United Provinces. Word had reached Buenos Aires that Ferdinand VII had gathered a force of 20,000 in Cádiz destined for the re-conquest of the Río de la Plata. Pueryrredón recalled San Martín in earnest. While he could not refuse a direct order, he delayed in Mendoza. In June, the situation deteriorated further with the resignation of Pueyrredón. In response, the United Provinces threatened to break apart and San Martín received repeated orders to return his army for the defense of Buenos Aires. Still he delayed. Finally, he took leave of his command—again citing ill health—and returned to Santiago with some of his men. As the turmoil in Buenos Aires continued, he ordered the rest of his troops in Mendoza back to Santiago. In February 1820, the congress of the United Provinces dissolved. With it went San Martín's authority. He counseled the officers of the Army of the Andes to name their own general; they unanimously selected him. With the Act of Rancagua, San Martín cut himself off from the Buenos Aires government. In May 1820, he took formal command of the Peruvian expedition. He explained his actions to the Argentines in July 1820, concluding with the promise that ". . . General San Martín will never shed the blood of his compatriots, and he will unsheathe his sword only against the enemies of South American independence."[25]

The Peruvian campaign followed San Martín's careful strategy. His spies kept him informed of the enemy's troop strength—23,000 regular troops, including nearly 8,000 defending Callao and Lima. San Martín had fewer than 5,000, at least a thousand fewer than he felt necessary. The return of Belgrano's Army of the North to Buenos Aires robbed San Martín of that force as well. He altered his plans for a direct attack on Lima, opting instead for a series of landings along the Peruvian coast to probe the enemy's defenses and perhaps reinforce his numbers with Peruvian recruits.

As the expedition set sail from Santiago on August 20, 1820, the political landscaped shifted in Peru. The revolt of the troops at Cádiz had forced Ferdinand VII to reinstate the liberal constitution of 1812. Viceroy Pezuela received orders from the new liberal government to pursue negotiations rather than combat with the insurgents. As the Peruvian expedition disembarked at the port of Pisco, San Martín accepted Pezuela's offer of an armistice and negotiations. The talks failed, but gave San Martín time to assemble his forces at Pisco.[26]

Unable to reach an agreement with the royalists, San Martín initiated his plan for Peru. Without sufficient numbers to challenge Perzuela's troops directly, he recruited Peruvians to join his cause while besieging and starving the royalists in Lima. He moved forces north of Lima at Huacho in November 1820, thereby blocking the imperial capital from receiving supplies from the agricultural north. Cochrane blockaded Callao, Lima's port, cutting it off from reinforcements and re-supply by sea. San Martín also wrote to the political leader in Peru's northern district and convinced him to join the patriot cause. As conditions deteriorated in Lima, desertions to the patriot cause augmented their ranks. In January 1821, mutinous troops deposed Viceroy Pezuela and replaced him with General José de la Serna. He proposed new negotiations with San Martín in May 1821. San Martín hoped to discredit the royalist officers who could never accept independence.[27] His plan was to stall as Peruvians increased his numbers, then maneuver the Spanish into surrendering without a direct confrontation.

This strategy brought mixed results. When the negotiations collapsed, de la Serna evacuated Lima. He and his army headed for the mountains, leaving a garrison force at Callao. San Martín faced sharp criticism for not engaging the royalist troops as they withdrew from the city. On July 10, San Martín's troops entered the capital and, on July 28, Peru declared its independence. On August 3, San Martín assumed the title of "Protector," with civil and military authority.

Royalist troops, however, still menaced the capital. De la Serna was able to reassemble his army in the highlands and, in September, he sent a force that marched past Lima on its way to occupy Callao. San Martín refused to engage it and, after a few days in Callao, the force withdrew for lack of supplies. Again, San Martín was criticized for his failure to act, although he had calculated correctly. A few days later, the Spanish garrison at Callao surrendered the port without a shot being fired. Cochrane, who had positioned his fleet to blockade the port, was among San Martín's harshest critics. He demanded that the Protector reward the navy for its role in the siege. When San Martín refused, arguing that the fleet was the responsibility of the Chilean government, Cochrane seized government funds to pay his sailors. San Martín then ordered Cochrane out of Callao, and the fleet withdrew to prey on Spanish shipping in the Pacific.[28]

Amid mounting criticism of his handling of the war, San Martín faced the task of managing the imperial city. He worked to restore law and order and to improve living conditions. Slaves were freed, indigenous tribute and forced labor were abolished, a national library was established, ports were opened to free trade, and Spanish properties were confiscated. The Order of the Sun was established to reward his officers' service and provide them with large estates.[29]

Consolidating independence in Peru proved too great a challenge as local factions conspired against the Protector and charged him with monarchism. The Spanish army in the highlands still threatened Lima while northern rebellions jeopardized national unity, replaying the earlier Argentine experience. Faced with an untrained army and without a fleet, San Martín cast about for a way to bring the campaign to a close. Simón Bolívar's success in the north and election as president of Colombia suggested a solution. He decided that, if he could join his army to that of Bolívar, together they could drive the royalist forces from South America.

San Martín made plans to discuss the unification of the two forces as Bolívar's army moved on Quito. Troops from the Peruvian expedition were sent to help and San Martín planned to rejoin them at the port of Guayaquil. Sharing some of San Martín's vision, Bolívar offered to send elements of his army to Peru if needed. In the meantime, San Martín authorized the calling of a congress to create a new national government.

The two soldiers met alone in Guayaquil on July 26-27, 1822, and neither issued a statement after the meetings. Subsequent correspondence and conversations with their aides made it clear that the two failed to agree on strategies and tactics. San Martín withdrew from Guayaquil as soon as the talks ended and returned to Callao. In Lima, a constituent congress convened in September 1822 and he resigned his office and turned power over to them. The congress later awarded him a pension, which he enjoyed in a long retirement. As he made plans to leave Peru, he told a friend: "There is not enough room for

Bolívar and me in Peru . . . let him come, if he can, taking advantage of my absence. If he succeeds in consolidating what we have won in Peru, and a little more, I shall be quite satisfied. In any case, his victory will be an American victory."[30]

. . . *creo que tengo el derecho a disponer de mi vejez.*

The Peruvian campaign ended San Martín's military career. From Peru, he returned to Chile until O'Higgins's overthrow forced him to move again. Traversing the Andes for the last time, he returned to the family estate in Mendoza. Unwelcome any longer in Chile, and uninterested in returning to Peru, accusations of treason by his enemies in Buenos Aires even prevented him from making a trip to his dying wife's bedside in August 1823. In November, he was able to return to the capital long enough to join his young daughter, Mercedes, and make preparations for exile in Europe. He returned to the Río de la Plata one last time, in 1826, but political conditions made it too dangerous for him to disembark, and he returned to Europe.

He offered his services to the nation one final time when the regime of Juan Manuel de Rosas was challenged by the British and French, but Rosas declined. San Martín lived on the outskirts of Paris until civil unrest drove him to Boulougne-sur-Mer. He died there on August 17, 1850.

San Martín's was the life of a good soldier. He served the Spanish army with distinction for twenty-two years before transferring his loyalties to his native land. The creation and execution of his continental plan marks his greatest achievement. More clearly than any of his contemporaries, he envisioned a strategy for liberating not only his homeland but the entire southern cone from European powers. More consistently than any of his contemporaries, he enlisted or maneuvered political leaders in support of that vision. In the process, he led an army of liberation through one of the most formidable mountain ranges in the southern hemisphere and into the annals of military history. He pursued national independence for his own and neighboring peoples with so little thought of personal political or financial reward that the only peace he would find in retirement was in exile. His parting words to the Peruvian Congress highlight this self-awareness: "I have fulfilled my promises to the people for whom I have fought: to achieve independence and let them decide on the election of their governments. The presence of a victorious soldier (no matter how detached) is fearsome to states that are in the process of formation."[31] After his death, those countries for which he fought formed stable, independent governments. As the good soldier, José Francisco de San Martín desired little more, but settled for nothing less.

Notes

1. Taken from a plaque in the Área Fundacional in Mendoza, dedicated by the Asociación Sanmartiniana de Mendoza; also quoted in General Secretariat, Organization of American States, *The Liberator General San Martin* (Washington, DC: OAS, 1978 [hereafter, OAS, *Liberator*]), 8.

2. As quoted in Carlos Fuentes, *The Buried Mirror Reflections on Spain and the New World* (Boston: Houghton Mifflin, 1992), 256.

3.. As quoted in OAS, *Liberator*, 1.

4. For more specific detail on the French campaign, see: J.C.J. Medford, *San Martín: The Liberator* (Oxford: Basil Blackwell, 1950), 16-17; and OAS, *op cit.*

5. For a copy of San Martín's military record up to 1804, see OAS, *Liberator*, 4.

6. Robert Harvey, *Liberators* (Woodstock: The Overlook Press, 2000), 320.

7. For more detail on his activities during the French invasion, see Medford, 21-22.

8. As quoted in Medford, 23; OAS, *Liberator*, 1.

9. John Crane, *San Martín Liberator of Argentina, Chile and Peru* (Washington: Pan American Union [American Historical Series 2], 1948), 12.

10. *Ibid.*, 34-35; Saul Flores, *San Martin "El Santo de la Espada"* (San Salvador: Ministerio de Educación General de Publicaciones, 1964), 13.

11. Harvey, 326.

12. Medford, 38.

13. For more information on San Martín's activities in Mendoza, see Ana E. Castro, "Una Década Turbulenta," in *Historia de Mendoza*, Pedro Santos Martínez, ed. (Buenos Aires: Plus Ultra, 1979), 47-55.

14. Bartolomé Mitre, *Historia de San Martín y de la emancipación Sud Americana* 1 (Buenos Aires: La Nación, 1887-88), 390; Thomas B. Davis, Jr., *Carlos de Alvear Man of Revolution* (New York: Greenwood Press, 1968), 11-12.

15. As quoted in Medford, 50.

16. Bartolomé Mitre, 639-40.

17. As quoted from a letter to Tomás Godoy Cruz from San Martín on July 16, 1816, in OAS, *Liberator*, 16.

18. David Rock, *Argentina 1516-1982* (Berkeley: University of California Press, 1985), 92.

19. This quote is repeated in several accounts, including Fuentes (p. 254) and Medford (p. 52).

20. Castro, 45-47.

21. Flores, 16-17.

22. Medford, 88-89.

23. *Ibid.*, 79.

24. For more information on Cochrane's career and activities, see Donald Thomas, *Cochrane* (New York: Viking Press, 1978).

25. OAS, *Liberator*, 21.

26. Jay Kinsbrunner, *The Spanish-American Independence Movement* (Hinsdale, IL: The Dryden Press, 1973), 64.

27. John Lynch, *The Spanish-American Revolutions, 1808-1826* (New York: W.W. Norton and Company, 1973), 176-77.

28. Medford, 108-10.

29. Lynch, 179-83.

30. As quoted in Metford, 116.

31. As quoted in OAS, *Liberator*, 7-8.

Hezekiah Niles, His *Weekly Register,* and the Atlantic Revolutionary World

Roy E. Goodman
American Philosophical Society Library

American newspapers after the revolution for the most part were dependent on the skills of the proprietor or the printers to keep the finances of the business in the black. This was far from an easy task, to be sure. By 1800 it was unlikely that a newspaper could support a proprietor even into middle age. There were about 200 papers, with fewer than a dozen tracing their roots to the revolution era. No paper south of Maryland was older than twenty years. Clearly, in America, the business of journalism was in the hands of risk taking entrepreneurs. A concentration of population was an important component in the success of a paper, but it was no guarantee for a paper's survival. The talented journalist James Thomson Callender, whose mordant articles initially supporting the Jeffersonians and then the Federalists, died a pauper. William Cobbett, perhaps America's best political writer in the early nineteenth century, failed to make a go of it as the notorious "Peter Porcupine."[1]

The juncture of politics and business was an ever growing factor for journalists. The rivalry of Alexander Hamilton and Thomas Jefferson helped establish a network of partisan newspapers prior to the first contested presidential election of 1800. The campaign found only fourteen publishers withdrawing from Federalist or Jeffersonian ties.[2] However, newspapers often circulated political information without an "axe to grind." While the claims of impartial reporting grew, America bred a press that was political rather than a press that encouraged unbiased reporting.

Long gone was the eighteenth-century press linkage of the colonial political structure with crime and sin. Independence forced the press to abandon this approach.

A different kind of news publication, a most extraordinary addition to the American press, was the formulation of Hezekiah Niles. Niles was born in 1777 near Chadds Ford in Chester County, Pennsylvania. His Quaker family fled their home in the wake of British troops. Most likely educated at the Friends

178

School in Wilmington, at the age of seventeen he was apprenticed to Benjamin Johnson, a printer, bookbinder, and bookseller. Hezekiah was an intelligent, well read youth. His skills as the quickest and most efficient typesetter in America were well known.

In 1805 Niles moved to Baltimore, where he bought and edited the *Baltimore Evening Post.* On 11 September 1811, he then issued the first edition of *Niles' Weekly Register,* which was usually referred to as *Niles' Register.* The publication offered Americans a comprehensive publication that thoroughly gathered and disseminated international and American news to an eager community of readers.

In fact, *Niles' Register* was America's first national news magazine. For the most part, it was an issue of 16 pages that was available on Saturdays, from Niles' Baltimore office, through 1836. The newspaper continued to be published after Hezekiah's death (in 1839) until 1849. It lacked any advertisements, allowing more space for news, documents, and copious editorials by the editor. A compact format saved paper and made it easy to hold. For almost half of the nineteenth century, the *Niles' Register* influenced a broad range of readers. By 1825, *Niles'* was being mailed to 700-800 post offices, although it has been claimed to have had close to 4,000 subscribers.[3] It was frequently quoted by other newspapers because of the numerous primary sources and government documents that appeared in it.

Niles was a very tolerant individual. "He stoutly defended foreign-born American citizens from attack, respected the opinions of others, decried the persecution of Jews in Europe and the hostility to them in America."[4] However, his views on England, and on monarchies in general, were far less tolerant. The belief in democracy was a guiding principle that imbued his writings, philosophy, and personal interactions. The government of the United States was the "grandest experiment" ever tried. Furthermore, "the end of government is the happiness of society." He wrote, "a free republic is the strongest system yet devised for a social compact amongst men." His response to attacks on the republic reflected this ardor. "We have many times said that we preferred even the licentiousness of freedom to the calm of despotism."[5]

America's reliance on England for books and magazines needed to be rectified. The publications of histories, geographies, encyclopedias, collections of letters and documents, and biographies by American authors were essential components of a national literature that Niles espoused.[6]

The *Register's* scope reflected the wealth of news between 1811 and 1849. Maximum coverage of the Napoleonic Wars and the War of 1812 was evident. Indian wars, foreign revolutions, and, later in the 1840's, the war between Mexico and the United States received ample print. National issues (which are not the focus of this paper) comprised perhaps two-thirds of the total stories appearing in the *Register.* Public land policy, slavery, and the tariff were major news topics.

Technological accounts frequently peppered its pages. Such internal domestic improvements as canals and railroads, the introduction of the telephone, and the steam engine were ever present. The agricultural, industrial, and technological stories from even the farthest reaches of the globe made the *Register* a truly cutting-edge publication.

Niles' keen eye for printing stories that sketched the personalities of the era was another selling point for the publication. Tsar Alexander, the Duke of Wellington, Queen Victoria, and Napoleon Bonaparte came to life beside their American contemporaries, Davy Crockett, Sam Houston, John C. Calhoun, and Andrew Jackson.

Voluminous articles from the London and New York press, including documents, proclamations, treaties, decrees, speeches, and diplomatic correspondence were deftly summarized by the editor. On occasion, foreign events comprised over one half of an issue. Initially, foreign stories appeared merely under the heading "Foreign News" or "Foreign Articles." Organizing the news by country took hold by 1817. News from abroad was often extracted from New York papers. These accounts had been translated and rewritten from the European press. Often unable to verify the accuracy of these stories, Niles alerted his readers not to accept the veracity of everything in the press. Censorship and conflicting accounts of facts always weighed on the difficult task of vetting the news, especially those accounts emanating from foreign sources.

Niles notified his audience when little of consequence occurred abroad. However, when happenings of substance arose, an extremely exacting examination of texts was processed and reported. Frequently, stories about the Holy Alliance, revolutions in various nations, or happenings in England were subject to the editor's views.[7] Napoleon's exile and death warranted much space in the *Register*. This news bore the editor's compassion for continental revolutionary activities.[8]

Newspapers in the larger American cities were quite dependent on the New York press for continental news. The *Register* was no exception. Early issues of the paper's foreign affairs section noted: "Just before this number went to press, we received London dates, via New York."[9]

Americans received news from Europe in the early nineteenth century through London. Continental happenings took close to three months to reach America.[10] In addition, there were often two to six week lags for London to receive this information from European capitals. By the 1820s and 1830s, Paris's role as a point of news dissemination grew. The importance of the cotton trade with France was a major factor in this situation. In spite of speedier ships, delays were common and frustration ran high. Hezekiah Niles noted from Baltimore in 1829: "This is the 17th January, and our [latest] European date is of the 9th November-or sixty-eight days since. We believe that never, since the establishment of the New York packets, have we been so long without news from Europe."[11]

A particularly noticeable quality of the *Register* was its virulently anti-English tenor. Early in Niles' life, he and his family endured numerous hardships at the hands of the English during the American Revolution. Antimonarchical sentiments were clearly promoted in his writings prior to establishing the *Register* and continued afterward. Economic confrontations between America and Britain added to the mix of hostility. The dumping of British goods impeded and directly hurt American manufacturers. Niles frequently promoted protectionist policies in the *Register,* warning that Britain's economic relationship with the South "would encourage civil war" if given half a chance.[12]

The Church of England's link to the government was loathed by Niles. "There is no government in Europe, that of *Turkey* and *Spain* excepted, so intolerant [sic] as the government of *Great Britain*, in religious affairs," aptly reflects this disdain.[13] British recognition of the South American republics in the 1820s prompted a short-lived, warmer tone in the *Register.* The British people, rather than the government, were credited with these events.[14] Endless examples of enmity toward Britain appeared regularly in the *Register*.[15] In the mid 1820s, however, Niles eased his mordant opposition to England and the English a bit; he reprinted President Monroe's final message to Congress and friendly editorials from the *Times* and the *Public Ledger*, written in a "kind, liberal, and manly manner."[16]

Vicious attacks on the United States flowed from English newspapers, which were reprinted in the American press along with ample rejoinders. Despite Niles' resentment of American reliance on England for ideas and literature, he amassed many pieces that bore little political content. Accounts that were simply informational or technical had little impact on Anglo-American relations.

The *Register* gave much print to the English treatment of the exiled Napoleon and England's concern with Cuba and the Floridas. Cuba's strategic location and her trade with the United States, prompted Niles to oppose its cession to Great Britain. He felt it should remain under Spanish rule or become independent.[17]

The abortive Canadian insurrections, riots, and invasions of 1837-38 offered mere accounts of the activities, and eschewed commentary. This was in keeping with William Ogden Niles's laissez-faire editorial predilections.

Coverage of Latin America in the *Register* was quite prominent. The editorial opinions of Niles clearly colored the numerous decrees, treaties, and diplomatic correspondence relating to the Spanish colonies, Brazil, and the Caribbean islands. In addition, articles with a broad range of information not easily found in other contemporary publications shed light on South America and the southern portion of the North American continent. From the outset, Niles inserted pieces like the

"Declaration of Rights by the People of Venezuela," which appeared in the first page of the second issue, to the last number, which printed several Mexican news items. Rarely were items about Central America, Mexico, and South America lacking from the *Register*.

The spin on the news was evidenced by commentaries such as: "We have cheering intelligence from *South America*. The details are scant, but include, *Montevideo* was closely besieged by the patriot army May 20—the cause of liberty is well sustained in the provinces of *Buenos Ayres*—the patriotism of *Chili* is alert and active—*Peru* is decidedly opposed to royalty. In the provinces of Caracas, the flame of liberty burns with renewed vigor; the greater part of the country appears to be in the hands of the whigs."[18] Niles, disappointed with America's tepid reception of the revolutionary struggles in Latin America noted:

> It is astonishing how indifferent the great body of the people of the United States appear as to the events in these extensive regions. This may partly arise from our ignorance of their real situation and of what is going on. It is strange that the feelings of the nation should have been so excited for the "deliverance" of old *Spain* from Bonaparte, when so little interest is excited for the *real* deliverance of the new world from the dominion of a knave, fool and bigot. The freedom of *Mexico* alone, is indeed, fifty times more important to the United States than the rescue of Spain from the hands of Napoleon was, in a commercial point of view, independent of those desires which, as republicans, we ought to have for its emancipation; and I seriously wish that circumstances were such that we could give them a helping hand. *Perish the ' legitimates,' live the people*, say I—*Up republics; down* royalty.[19]

Niles called the revolutionary groups "patriots" in editorials and most news stories, while the royalist forces were named "finished villains," "tory priests," and "murderers." Comparisons between the North American colonies' struggle with England and the South American cause was a major thread in the *Register*. Americans were not prompted to join the revolutionary forces, unless their United States citizenship was renounced. "The natural as well as the national law" required one to forfeit all claims on his country for protection.[20]

The most space given to Latin American nations were stories about Venezuela and New Granada, which united to form Columbia. Protracted struggles between royalist and revolutionary forces from 1811 and 1822 were thoroughly reported. Friendly editorial coverage regarding the prohibition of the slave trade, or the education of Columbian youths in the United States, vouch for the *Register's* friendly sentiments toward the nation.[21] Stories from the United Provinces of Rio de la Plata were among the most numerous to appear in the *Register* reports.

The swift changes in government, along with commercial and geographical news, allowed Americans to read about a region little exposed in their press. News also about Brazil reflected Niles' fear that revolt and turmoil would plague the nation.[22]

Coverage of other South American news was well represented, along with Simon Bolívar's fight against the royalists. In 1821, the "Liberator" was compared with George Washington. He was quoted as saying: "A man like me, (who) is a dangerous citizen in a popular government—is a direct menace to the national sovereignty. I wish to become a citizen, in order to be free, and that all may be so too. I prefer the title of *citizen* to that of *liberator*—because this emanates from war, and that from the laws. Exchange, sir, all my honors for that of a *good* citizen."[23]

Sources for South American stories came from United States newspapers that translated articles from the Spanish language press. In addition, the Buenos Aires papers, *Gazeta, El Censor*, and *La Prensa Argentina* were sources. The Puerto Rico *Gazette*, and Bogota *Constitucional* were examined and cited. Niles perused English language newspapers from Kingston, Jamaica, and St. Thomas occasionally for South American news.

The burgeoning Mexican War with the United States was well covered in the *Register*. The dispute over Texas's annexation from early 1842 through 1845 was a significant part of the publication. Volumes 61 through 69 were replete with documents, messages, and diplomatic correspondence. Of course, the *Register* had come under the ownership of William Ogden Niles. The stylistic and editorial policies of the publication were markedly altered.

News gathering techniques during the Mexican War developed an important fashion. American newspapers were cooperating in their efforts to bring stories to the public.[24] The conclusion of the Mexican War in 1848, and the suspension of the *Register* the next year, presented a less optimistic tone to the public on the affairs of the southern republics than had previously been the case.

The strong opinions of the editor-owner colored the news that the *Register* printed. Hezekiah Niles's dislike of England permeated the publication. His son, William Ogden Niles, offered little analysis of politics or the news on assuming the editorship of the *Register* in 1836. Rather he presented the opinions of others. By the 1840s, Jeremiah Hughes expressed friendlier feelings toward England. American public sentiment, too, had shifted to a non-combative stand for the mother country.

The *Register*, with its worldwide focus on political, commercial, agricultural, and industrial news, was superior to other contemporary American publications. The social and cultural aspects of the era were not given nearly as much attention as the former topics.

183

By the end of its long run in June 1849, the *Register* had succumbed to competition in two spheres. Technology, which greatly hastened the mail service through railroads, steamboats, and improved telegraph lines, was garnered by other news sources. No longer did the *Register* have a marked advantage in the speed with which news reached the public. Also, more affordable printing processes assisted the newspaper establishment and created a broader range of choices.

Second, the decline of partisanship among the reading public affected American journalism. Newspapers in the 1840s benefited from a rising literacy rate, along with a growing readership.

The unbiased, broad-view type journalism of Hezekiah Niles was replaced by Jeremiah Hughes's *Register* of the 1840s, fraught with its partisan Whig leanings. This partisan slant, along with the ebbing popularity of the Whigs, accelerated the *Niles'Register's* demise. George Beatty's feeble attempt to revive the *Register* in July 1848, from his new office in Philadelphia, was ineffective. Most likely because of a lack of publishing experience, coupled with the barriers cited, the *Register* ceased to appear.

For today's historian, the *Register* provides an incredible wealth of information in its thirty eight years of coverage. Through it, one can delve into a good part of the first half of the nineteenth century with the greatest of ease. Availabilty of the *Register* is not a problem either. Most university, as well as many state or public libraries, hold either the paper edition or a microfilm copy of *Niles.'* Technology has created an electronic index for the *Register*, (www.accessible.com), as well as a recently produced web-based subscription version available from National Information Services Corporation (www.nisc.com).

Surely, Hezekiah Niles would marvel at the sophistication of twenty-first-century communication networks and the internet. In a very real way, Niles helped this American revolution in news coverage by sustaining the *Register* through a very important era of world events.

Notes

1. Thomas C. Leonard, *The Power of the Press: The Birth of American Political Reporting* (Oxford: Oxford University Press, 1986), 54. See also, Jeffery L. Pasley, *"The Tyranny of Printers." Newspaper Politics in the Early American Republic* (Charlottesville and London: University of Virginia Press, 2001), for an insightful overview of the period.

2. Leonard, 55.

3. Philip R. Schmidt, *Hezekiah Niles and American Economic Nationalism: A Political Biography* (New York: Arno Press, 1982), iii.

4. Norval Neil Luxon, *Niles' Weekly Register: News Magazine of the Nineteenth Century* (Baton Rouge: Louisiana State University Press, 1947), 31.

5. *Niles' Weekly Register* (afterwards *Register*): 1 August 1812, p. 364; 30 August 1817, p. 1; 29 August 1818, p. 1; 10 February 1821, p. 387.

6. *Register:* 5 October 1816, pp. 84-85; 22 May 1819, pp. 213-14; 21 April 1821, p. 113; 27 October 1821, p. 134; 6 July 1822, p. 289; 26 May 1827, pp. 218-24; 6 October 1827, p. 83; 23 October 1830, pp. 143-44; 25 February 1832, p. 475; 13 April 1833, p. 101.

7. *Register:* 5 May 1821, p. 151, which carries the "Great and glorious news!!!" of "All Italy . . . in flames!"; and 4 September and 11 September 1830, pp. 33, 37-47, in which the toppling of the Bourbons is reported.

8. *Register:* 1 September 1821, pp. 5-8; 8 September 1821, pp. 18-20.

9. *Register*, 11 July 1812, p. 320.

10. Allan R. Pred, *Urban Growth and the Circulation of Information: The United States System of Cities, 1790-1840* (Cambridge: Harvard University Press, 1973), 26-27.

11. *Register,* 17 January 1829, p. 21.

12. William Kovarik, "The Editor who tried to Stop the Civil War: Hezekiah Niles and the New South" web article, n.d. <www.radford.edu/~wkovarik/ papers/niles.html>, 3-4.

13. *Register*, 4 September 1830, p. 18.

14. *Register,* 2 April 1825, p. 67.

15. *Register,* 5 March 1825, pp. 1-2.

16. *Register:* 5 April 1823, pp. 72-73; 6 December 1823, p. 210.

17. *Register,* 11 September 1813, p. 32; Luxon, 194-95.

18. *Register,* 4 November 1815, p. 170.

19. *Register:* 20 January 1816, p. 364; 15 March 1817, p. 34; 3 May 1817, pp. 168-69; 10 May 1817, p. 174; 18 October 1817, p. 117; 25 October 1817, p. 143; 18 April 1818, p. 132; 26 September 1818, pp. 78-79; 15 May 1819, p. 206; 21 April 1821, p. 126.

20. Luxon, 197.

21. *Ibid.*, 198-99.

22. *Register:* 18 July 1812, pp. 327, 335; 7 August 1813, p. 376; 31 December 1814, p. 285; 11 April 1818, pp. 113-16; 10 July 1819, p. 335; 31 May 1823, pp. 205-6; 14 August 1824, p. 398; 5 March 1825, pp. 1, 6-8; 7 May 1825, pp. 156-58, are examples.

23. See Victor Rosewater, *History of Cooperative News-Gathering in the United States* (New York and London: D. Appleton and Company, 1930).

Rhetoric and Ambition:
The Impolitic Foreign Policy of J.-P. Brissot

Benjamin Reilly
Visiting Assistant Professor
Carnegie Mellon University-Qatar

A prolific writer, pioneering journalist, radical activist, and political faction leader, Jacques-Pierre Brissot de Warville played a wide-ranging role in the unfolding drama of the French Revolution. It was perhaps in the field of French foreign policy, however, that he exerted his greatest impact. Indeed, this is only to be expected, since Brissot's pre-revolutionary personal experience seemed to have groomed him perfectly for a career in international politics. By the time of the revolution, Brissot had traveled widely in both Europe and the United States, published widely on both European and American affairs, and accumulated an impressive collection of contacts and acquaintances throughout the world, including such lights as Benjamin Franklin, Joseph Priestly, Jeremy Bentham, Catherine Maccauley, and George Washington. Small wonder, then, that Brissot's colleagues in the Legislative Assembly and then the National Convention allowed him to play a crucial role in the formulation of the revolution's foreign policy.

As it turned out, however, these worthy legislators misplaced their trust: Brissot's intervention in foreign affairs proved to be almost uniformly disastrous. French Revolutionary historians, normally a highly disputatious tribe, are in rare agreement about Brissot's woeful record in the field of international relations. According to Patrice Gueniffey, Brissot's policy initiatives were characterized by an "inconceivable frivolity (*légèreté*)," largely because Brissot proved himself incapable of "judging the circumstances and the men, evaluating the chances, tracing a plan of battle and foreseeing, as much as possible, its effects."[1] Other scholars have formed similar opinions about Brissot, pronouncing him "impractical, extreme, and undiplomatic,"[2] or else judging his view of international politics to be "as fantastical and as naïve as it could possibly be."[3]

Why, then, did a man with so much apparent promise in the field of international relations prove to be such a failure in actual practice? On this matter, there is far less agreement among historians. Indeed, most scholars have limited themselves to recounting his disastrous decisions without giving much consideration to the underlying reasons for his foreign policy ineptitude. This gap in revolutionary historiography is surprising, since the reasons for Brissot's diplomatic failures are of interest to modern historians in a number of ways. First of all, the sheer scale of Brissot's diplomatic disasters—his policies have been blamed for precipitating the overthrow of the French monarchy and inaugurating over two decades of nearly continuous warfare between France and its European neighbors—seems to demand a more thorough explanation than has heretofore been provided by French revolutionary historians. Second, given the highly rhetorical character of Brissot's diplomacy, a study of Brissot's motives ought to shed further light on an ongoing debate within French revolutionary historiography concerning the role played by ideology in revolutionary affairs. Simply put, was ideology merely a tool employed by revolutionary actors, as some historians argue, or was it a virtual actor itself, driving forward revolutionary events? Finally, Brissot's foreign policy initiatives are worth exploring in light of their evident similarity to present-day events: The campaign by modern-day American Neo-Conservatives to make the world safe for democracy by means of an aggressive program of diplomatic and military initiatives has some striking similarities to Brissot's crusade to strike down the tyrannical states of Europe through war and revolutionary propaganda. As we shall see, much of Brissot's career could well serve as a cautionary tale about the dangers of pursuing an ideologically-driven foreign policy agenda.

To better understand the roots of Brissot's ill-fated diplomacy, this essay will be divided into two broad but closely interrelated sections. Part one will consist of a brief biography of Brissot, with a particular focus on his ideological presumptions, his pre-revolutionary political activities, his international peregrinations, and his work as a journalist and legislator once the revolution had begun. The second part will examine, in more detail, the degree to which these background experiences explain Brissot's failed policies. In particular, this essay will consider the relationship between the ideological discourse of the French Revolution and Brissot's failed diplomacy. Were Brissot's deficiencies unique, or were they shared by other revolutionary figures with the same ideological mindset? Most important of all, was the "inconceivable frivolity" of Brissot's diplomacy attributable to Brissot himself, or was it merely a manifestation of deeply-rooted tendencies inherent in French revolutionary political culture?

Unlike many French revolutionary leaders, who hailed as often as not from the elites or the "almost-ins" of the *ancien régime*, Brissot's background was humble.[4] He was born in 1754, the thirteenth child born to a Chartres restaurant proprietor, and one of only seven children who survived infancy. By all accounts, Brissot's

187

childhood was a difficult one, largely because the traditionally religious Brissot family had little in common with the bookish Jacques-Pierre, who soon became an avid student of Enlightenment thought. Indeed, Brissot spent much of his childhood digesting the wisdom of such figures as Montaigne, Montesquieu, Voltaire, and (above all) Rousseau, who Brissot later credited with "[making] fall the blindfold from my eyes."[5] Unable to satisfy his thirst for knowledge by means of the French language alone, Brissot taught himself English, Italian, Latin, Spanish, Portuguese, and German!: Indeed, his sympathetic biographer and future political ally Jerome Pétion considered him a linguistic prodigy.[6] Brissot's language talents would later allow him to maintain vigorous correspondence with radical thinkers throughout Europe and even the infant United States. In the meantime, Brissot emulated his Enlightenment heroes by writing profusely on anything that caught his attention. The resulting writings were of dubious quality—one biographer has judged Brissot's philosophic works to be "hasty and superficial"—but they did give the young Brissot some claim to knowledge on subjects ranging from religion, to legal reform, to international affairs.[7]

Brissot's writings on international affairs, in fact, gave him his first chance to make a name for himself. In the mid-1770's, while trying to scribble a living with his pen in Paris, Brissot authored an attack on British colonial policy, entitled: *Testament politique de l'Angleterre*, which he hoped would catch the attention (and with it the patronage) of the Foreign Minister Vergennes. It did not, but it did pique the interest of Samuel Swinton, the English publisher of the French-language *Courier de l'Europe*, who was looking for an editor on the French side of the English Channel with a clear grasp of English politics. Happy to be gainfully employed, Brissot accepted the job and transplanted himself to Boulogne, on the north coast of France. Here he received a crash tutorial in the ups and downs of the newspaper business: Brissot was delighted to have an organ for his youthful idealism, but that same youthful idealism got him in trouble with the French government's censors, and that may, in turn, have been a factor in Swinton's decision to fire Brissot in 1780 (though Brissot himself claimed in his memoirs that Swinton's decision was primarily a cost-cutting measure).[8]

Brissot's career as a *philosophe* was off to an inauspicious start but, far from despairing, he applied himself energetically to new projects. Returning to Paris, Brissot purchased a degree at a law school, which was common practice in eighteenth-century France, and attempted to make a living as a lawyer. Despite his best efforts, however, Brissot failed to establish himself at the Paris bar, perhaps, in part, because his previously published work was highly critical of the French legal system and, thus, did little to endear Brissot to his would-be colleagues. Stung by rejection, Brissot responded with several essays that were even more critical of French jurisprudence and then hatched a bold new scheme:

188

The foundation of a new literary society, to be called the *Lycée*, which would serve as an intellectual meetinghouse for European radicals and reformers—and in the process, a vehicle for the moral and political regeneration of Europe.

Seeking funding for his *Lycée* project, Brissot journeyed to Switzerland, which at the time was the home to a thriving publishing industry that produced books for the French market from just across France's eastern border—and just outside the reach of the French censors and police. Brissot hardly arrived in the Swiss town of Neuchâtel, however, before departing for nearby Geneva, the birthplace of his idol, Jean-Jacques Rousseau. Brissot's motives in visiting Geneva were as much political as personal: News had reached him of an incipient civil war between the aristocratic and democratic factions in the city. Brissot of course unhesitatingly favored the democratic side and, after arriving in Geneva and meeting with that faction's leaders, he even offered the services of his pen to the democratic cause.[9] His efforts were of no avail: The democratic faction was crushed and exiled by a coalition of forces from Austria and neighboring Swiss states. Brissot may have lamented the failure of Genevan democracy, but he himself benefited enormously from his foray to Geneva, since he forged ties with wealthy Genevan exiles (especially the rich banker, Étienne Clavière) that proved to be long lasting. Indeed, the money that Clavière and others pledged to Brissot during his Swiss excursion convinced Brissot that he had sufficient backing to get his beloved *Lycée* project off the ground.

Encouraged by this promised infusion of cash, Brissot stopped in Paris just long enough to marry Félicité Dupont, an under-governess employed by the family of the Duc d'Orléans, and then set out for London to build his *Lycée*. Once in England, Brissot made the rounds in London's community of scientists, reformers, and Whig political radicals, attempting to recruit them to his ambitious project. He also set up a new monthly journal, entitled: *Correspondance universelle*, which he eventually intended to publish in French and German, as well as English, to give the *Lycée* an international audience. The *Correspondance universelle* proved to be a financial bust, however, as did the *Journal du Licée de Londres*, which Brissot printed during the same period. What is more, promised funding from Swiss sources did not materialize, meaning that the indebted Brissot had no way to repay his creditors. Perhaps the only silver lining to this portion of Brissot's career was the acquaintance he made with the future revolutionary leader, the Comte de Mirabeau, who, like Brissot was attempting to make a living with his pen in London, and who would be important to Brissot's future advancement.

In the meantime, however, Mirabeau could not prevent the penniless Brissot from being imprisoned for debt in Britain and, although he was soon bailed out by his friends and family, his situation went from bad to worse: Soon after setting off for France to seek new work, Brissot was arrested and imprisoned in the Bastille, accused of publishing (and perhaps authoring) a libelous pamphlet against French Queen Marie Antoinette. Thankfully, Brissot's incarceration lasted only two months, in part due to the intervention of the duc d'Orléans, to whom Brissot was connected through his wife. Nonetheless, in the short term, Brissot was in a perilous state: He was jobless, deeply in debt, and was obliged to abandon his beloved *Lycée* as a condition of his release. As we shall see, however, Brissot's dream of propagating revolutionary principles throughout Europe via the press did not die with the *Lycée*.

Of all the phases of Brissot's pre-revolutionary career, Brissot's return to Paris in 1784 has attracted the most scholarly attention, since it was during this period of penury that Brissot may have sought employment as a *mouche*— a police spy. The accusation was first leveled against Brissot by the royalist press in 1791, while Brissot was seeking election to the Legislative Assembly. Brissot forcibly denied the charge, but it refused to die, and was resurrected later by Brissot's old political allies Marat and Desmoulins, who parted ways with Brissot during the factional conflict between Brissot's supporters and Robespierre's backers in the National Convention. Before 1968, historians generally dismissed the police spy accusation as baseless slander, ascribing it to the overheated political atmosphere of revolution. Indeed, Brissot had also been accused at various times of being an Orléanist conspirator or a paid British agent, charges that made being a *mouche* seem almost tame by comparison.

The police spy accusation gained credibility, however, after Robert Darnton's 1968 attack on Brissot in the *Journal of Modern History*. Darnton claimed to have uncovered definitive proof of Brissot's work as a police spy in the unpublished notes of Jean-Pierre Lenoir, the lieutenant-general of the Paris police in the 1780's. According to Lenoir, Brissot offered his services to the police after his release from the Bastille and, although Lenoir himself had refused him employment, Brissot was hired by another member of Lenoir's office and served for a time as a paid spy.[10] Darnton has since bolstered Lenoir's claim with a fair amount of circumstantial evidence, documenting Brissot's long-standing pattern of prostituting his pen to dubious stock manipulation schemes, and suggesting that Brissot knew a police secretary named Martin well enough to enlist his help in smuggling forbidden books into France.[11] Frederick A. de Luna has endeavored, with a fair degree of success, to combat Darnton's insinuations and rehabilitate Brissot's reputation, but the suspicion remains.[12]

So was Brissot really a *mouche*? While most of Darnton's circumstantial evidence is weak at best, Lenoir's claim is much harder to dismiss since, although Lenoir was certainly opposed to the French Revolution, there is no evidence that he bore a grudge against Brissot in particular. Might Lenoir, however, have issues with Brissot that did not find their way into the historical record, or was Lenoir, who wrote his notes years after the fact, simply mistaken in his recollections? In the end, we just do not know. One fact, however, is incontestable: Some of those who later claimed that Brissot was a *mouche* (most notably Marat and Desmoulins) nevertheless maintained strong ties with Brissot for years, despite his relationship to the police. Indeed, Brissot served as one of four witnesses at Desmoulins' wedding in September 1790, and Brissot enjoyed a long-standing friendship and productive working partnership with Marat, championing Marat's crackpot scientific work in the 1780's and even supporting the publication of Marat's new journal in 1790.[13] Whatever Brissot's relationship with the police, it did not preclude Marat and Desmoulins from benefiting from Brissot's friendship, and it seems suspicious that these men only discovered their moral revulsion for Brissot's supposed police connections once political divisions arose between them for other reasons. The accusations that Brissot was a police spy, then, reflect as badly upon Brissot's accusers as upon Brissot himself.

In any case, for defenders of Brissot, these charges are beside the point: Brissot's character should be judged not according to the unsubstantiated accusations of a former policeman of the old regime but, rather, by the positive qualities revealed in his many philosophic works. Indeed, such works do show Brissot in a mostly favorable light. Like many *philosophes*, most notably his idol Jean-Jacques Rousseau, Brissot championed the notion of a social contract, and even adopted the then-dangerous position that the people have the right to depose a tyrannical or unworthy ruler. Brissot also adopted the common Enlightenment desire to reform the legal code and to make prevention, not retribution, the basis of the judicial system. In other regards, however, Brissot broke from his *philosophe* colleagues. Brissot, for instance, was sympathetic to the plight of women, advocating divorce rights for women and greater equality of the sexes—though he was too loyal a student of the misogynistic Rousseau to advocate female participation in the political arena.[14] Brissot also departed from the main intellectual flow of the Enlightenment in his belief in universal education. Unlike most *philosophes,* who tended to distinguish between the masses and the philosophic elites, Brissot believed that the common man should be educated in, and thus liberated by, the ideals of the Enlightenment.[15]

Brissot's belief in mass education was connected to his almost millenarian conviction that the popular press could serve as a tool for human betterment. "Philosophical books are the best vehicle for political revolutions," Brissot contended in his memoirs. But how to disseminate them? "I formed, in order to strike down despotism, a project that appeared to me to be infallible. To prepare a general insurrection against absolute governments and to enlighten ceaselessly the spirit would require, not well-reasoned and voluminous works which the people do not read, but rather small pamphlets like those propagated by Voltaire to destroy religious superstition, or else newspapers that would spread

Enlightenment everywhere."[16] Brissot wrote these words specifically in defense of his failed *Lycée* but, as we shall see, the same beliefs shaped much of his later revolutionary career, including his work in diplomacy.

In the mid-1780's, however, Brissot was forced to put these dreams aside and, as Darnton has pointed out, he was obliged by his straightened circumstances to sell his services to various dubious enterprises. His tutor in the business was his Genevan friend Clavière, who kept Brissot and his family financially afloat in exchange for the fruits of Brissot's pen. The pamphlets that Clavière commissioned were put to the service of stock manipulation schemes: Clavière would "short sell" stock (contract to sell stock he did not own) in a target company, commission a pamphlet from Brissot denouncing that company on moral grounds, wait for the stock's value to fall, and then buy shares of the stock at the reduced price to meet his obligations.

Brissot and Clavière's work had a strong political component as well. They collaborated in this period with the Comte de Mirabeau, who was now back in Paris working as a publicist for Calonne, the French minister of finance. Calonne and Mirabeau's interests dovetailed quite nicely with those of Clavière, since the companies that Brissot was directed to attack were generally those in competition for capital with state-run financial institutions. Nor was Brissot's connection with Calonne his only flirtation with *ancien régime* politics. In 1786, Brissot was offered a job as publicist for the ambitious Duc d'Orléans, perhaps by virtue to his wife's old connections with the Duc d'Orléans's family. Orleans wanted to stir the muddy waters of the monarchy with calls for reform, largely to bolster his own political position within France, and the reform-minded Brissot was only too happy to comply. Unfortunately for Brissot, however, the French government eventually took note of his anti-ministerial pamphleteering, and Brissot eventually felt compelled to flee Paris in 1787 before he could be locked away for a second time in the dreaded Bastille.[17]

The period between 1785 and 1787, then, was probably not Brissot's finest moment: He was employing his pen in the service of underhanded financial schemes, not to mention acting as a paid agent, albeit indirectly, of an absolute government he professed to abhor. Even Robert Darnton, Brissot's harshest critic, however, conceded that Brissot maintained his intellectual integrity during this period. "They [Brissot, Mirabeau, and Clavière] all meant to make money," Darnton contended, "but they also meant what they said."[18] What is more, several of Brissot's works during this period had a more genuinely altruistic character, such as the two open letters written to the Austrian emperor condemning the bloody suppression of a Transylvania peasant revolt. Brissot's continued idealism was also visible in the forceful tract in defense of the Quaker sect. Many Quaker beliefs—especially abhorrence for violence, avoidance of religious dogmatism, dislike of material ostentation, and adherence to strict moral principles—were echoed in the writings of Brissot's hero, Jean-Jacques Rousseau, and, as a consequence, Brissot found himself drawn to the Society of Friends. Indeed, Brissot's interest in Quakerism eventually gave him the opportunity to escape his somewhat sordid Parisian existence and reestablish his connections with radical thinkers outside of France. In 1787, Brissot set out for London, though he stopped on the way in Holland, where a civil war was under way between the "patriots" and the supporters of the autocratic Dutch Stathouder (Brissot favored the patriots, of course). When that rebellion was crushed by Prussian troops, Brissot continued on to London, where he re-established his contacts, first forged during the failed *Lycée* experiment of the early 1780's, with prominent English Quakers. When Brissot arrived, many Quakers were becoming increasingly interested in the plight of African slaves, and, after being invited to meetings of the newly-formed British Committee to Abolish the Slave Trade, Brissot himself became an enthusiastic convert to the abolitionist cause and promised to establish a similar society in France.

Once Brissot returned to France in 1788, he fulfilled this promise by establishing the *Société des Amis des Noirs*. Unfortunately for Brissot, this society was almost totally ineffective: In fact, the failures of the *Amis des Noirs* serve to illustrate, in miniature, many of the problems that would later plague Brissot's diplomatic initiatives. For one thing, the *Amis des Noirs* refused to focus on the problem at hand—namely, the existing slave societies in the French Caribbean—and indulged instead on denunciations of tyranny, as a general world phenomenon, or else "slavery," in an abstract Rousseauist sense. Perhaps more damaging was the organizational structure that Brissot gave his fledgling group. Rather than create a mass society with firm connections to the political elite on the British model, Brissot remained loyal to the structure of the *Lycée*, envisioning the *Amis des Noirs* as a society joining together a select body of literary men. Worst of all, Brissot put his faith in the power of the press, believing that the best way to disseminate the anti-slavery message was through pamphlets and newspapers directed to a popular audience. According to a historian of the *Amis des Noirs*, however, this tactic proved counterproductive, serving only to "alarm the opposition without stirring up a constituency for reform."[19] Blinded by moral absolutes, Brissot and his colleagues in the *Amis des Noirs* were unable to comprehend either the importance of West Indian sugar to French merchants and consumers or the intimate workings of the institution that they attacked. In the end, despite Brissot's altruistic motives, his advocacy of abolition proved to be an embarrassment for him personally and, as we shall see, a misfortune for France as well.

Brissot then decided to embark on his most ambitious international adventure to date, a tour of the newly-independent United States of America. His motives for this new voyage were complex. Brissot was inspired to go, in part, by his new abolitionist sensibilities, and hoped that first-hand observations of slavery in the United States might provide grist for his abolitionist mill. He also hoped to make contacts with the American Quaker sect, which, like its British counterpart, was beginning to embrace the cause of the enslaved Africans. Characteristically, the cash-scrapped Brissot also had financial motives: The backers of his expedition (who included Clavière) were planning to speculate on America's massive debt to France, purchasing shares of the debt at a low price in hopes that Brissot's highly favorable account of America's fiscal solvency would bump up their shares' value.[20] Perhaps most important, by this point in his slightly disreputable career as a struggling (and occasionally persecuted) writer, the disillusioned Brissot was seriously considering leaving the "intolerable tyranny of the French viziers" behind and emigrating permanently to the virgin soil of the United States.[21]

Before he could do so, however, Brissot caught word that the French Estates-General would be convoked as early as January 1789, and he quickly set out for France, unwilling to be away during such a momentous event. Once back in his native land, he threw himself into French politics, campaigning unsuccessfully to become a delegate to the Estates-General, working his way into a position of some authority in the new municipal government of Paris, and resuming his work on behalf of black slaves. Indeed, such was Brissot's importance to the French antislavery movement that the *Amis des Noirs* had virtually disbanded in his absence.[22] Perhaps most notable of all, Brissot established the *Patriot Français*, one of the first of a growing number of French daily newspapers, in the spring of 1789. Brissot's newspaper, which a sympathetic contemporary described as the "*first* sentinel who cried Constitution, Truth, Liberty,"[23] was a worthy successor to Brissot's *Lycée* project: Brissot hoped his newspaper, by disseminating knowledge within France, would be the spark for political reform, just as revolution in America had been inspired by radical gazettes. Brissot's *Patriot Français* also resembled the *Lycée* in its international scope, particularly in its consistent coverage of American affairs, a topic of keen interest to French radicals at the time. Due in part to this wide range of subject matter, the *Patriot Français* soon rose to the status of one of the revolution's most popular and influential newspapers, and Brissot's own renown rose correspondingly.

In the meantime, Brissot networked with like-minded political radicals, forming personal friendships (and personal animosities) that later shaped his career as a revolutionary legislator. Like many members of the revolutionary elite, Brissot was an early participant in the Society of Friends of the Constitution, which became known as the Jacobin Club since it was headquartered in a former Jacobin monastery. Brissot also became a contributor to the *Cercle social* publishing group, a loose association of Paris-based radical publishers. The aim of the *Cercle social* project was, in fact, strikingly similar to the goal of Brissot's

194

Lycé—spreading knowledge in the service of the cause of "universal brotherhood"—though Brissot himself seems to have been somewhat frustrated with the *Cercle social*'s inability (or disinclination) to reach a mass audience.[24] More informally, Brissot and Madame Roland organized evening meetings of like-minded political radicals who met to discuss the goings-on in the National Assembly. Interesting enough, membership in this group seems to have been largely accidental, since all participants apparently lived close to Madame Roland's home, but this gathering nonetheless included some of the heaviest hitters of the radical movement, most notably the future Paris mayor, Jerome Pétion, Brissot himself, and Maximilian Robespierre.[25]

Brissot and Robespierre later became bitter rivals, but they were still friendly during the period of the National Assembly, and the events in the summer of 1791 drove them even closer together. On 21 June, French King Louis XVI attempted to escape his semi-confinement in Paris and link up with the forces of a sympathetic general on the border with the Austrian Netherlands, only to be stopped in the village of Varennes. Most members of the National Convention, who had nearly finished the exhausting task of penning a monarchical constitution, were inclined to forgive his indiscretion, and even spread the tale that Louis had been abducted to absolve him from blame. For radicals like Brissot and Robespierre, however, the king's flight furnished absolute proof of his hostility to the revolution, and both men were converted to republicanism, though both were also reconciled to the necessity of retaining some degree of monarchy in France in the short run.[26] Brissot and Robespierre were also pushed together by the split of the original Jacobin Club: After Varennes, its original members divided themselves into left-leaning Jacobin and conservative Feuillant factions, and Brissot and Robespierre became leading figures in the new, more radical Jacobin society.

Thanks to the twin pulpits of the Jacobin Club and the *Patriot Français*, Brissot was becoming a well-known figure in the revolution and, despite the vocal opposition of the royalist press, the citizens of Paris elected him as a delegate to the Legislative Assembly in the fall of 1791. Ironically, however, Brissot suffered his first defeats in the field of foreign policy even before he took his seat in this new assembly. From the moment he returned to France in 1789, Brissot had worked as a tireless advocate for the victims of slavery and, when a deputation of all-white and somewhat royalist-leaning colonists from Saint-Domingue arrived to take part in the Estates-General, Brissot waged a campaign to have them excluded from the Estates' deliberation since they did not represent the colony's other two classes of citizens: The black slave population and the mostly-mulatto "citizens of color" [*citoyens de couleur*], who often owned slaves themselves but who were considered inferior by the white colonists. That campaign failed, but Brissot continued to champion the rights of the mulattos through the *Patriot Français* and the *Amis des Noirs*. Brissot even went so far as to praise mulatto leader Vincent Ogé as a "martyr of liberty, [and] a martyr of the law" after he was executed by the French colonial government following a failed 1790 mulatto insurrection.[27]

Brissot's advocacy for Ogé and the mulattos was well-intentioned but, as one historian has pointed out, it was probably "more eloquent than timely or politic."[28] In August 1791, a massive slave revolt overwhelmed French authority in Saint-Domingue, and horror stories of massacres and atrocities began to filter into France. Brissot's response was to heap blame not on the mulattos, who had helped to stir up slave revolt through their own insurrection, but on the whites themselves, claiming bizarrely that the white colonists had staged the insurrection to justify their quest for independence and their desire to impose "eternal slavery" on the blacks.[29] Many of Brissot's contemporaries, however, placed the blame for the revolts squarely on Brissot's shoulders. One of his opponents accused him of "seeking to hide from the moral responsibility that rests on the heads who have, by their imprudent discussions, lit the torch of discord in the colonies."[30] Desmoulins came to a similar conclusion, accusing Brissot of being "directed by the profit of England and its commerce, and to the ruin of France."[31] As we shall see, this was not the only occasion in which Brissot was charged with ignoring the circumstances of the moment in favor of his ideological convictions.

Whatever Brissot's role in the Saint-Domingue disasters may have been, he still managed to impress most members of the newly formed Legislative Assembly with his credentials in the field of foreign policy. Indeed, Brissot did look good on paper: He had traveled widely through Europe and America, had published extensively on world affairs, had numerous contacts in the European radical community, and could even boast of being an eyewitness and minor participant in the failed revolutions in Geneva and Holland. By virtue of this experience, Brissot was appointed as a member of the diplomatic committee by his colleagues in October 1791 and quickly became the dominant voice in that committee's deliberations.

The first major problem confronted by the diplomatic committee lay on France's northern border. *Émigré* nobles hostile to the revolution were building up an army in the small German state of Colbentz to restore monarchical authority in France. What is more, several other small German Rhineland sovereigns, who had formerly enjoyed some feudal rights within France, threatened to appeal to Austria for redress if the revolutionaries did not restore their revoked privileges. Brissot's proposed solution to the problem was one of limited military action: A swift and decisive intervention against the small German states, in combination with a program to rebuild the French army, would quickly end the *émigré* threat and force monarchical Europe to respect France's constitution.

196

War is a risky policy in the best of times, of course, but, at first, Brissot downplayed the dangers, especially those of possible foreign intervention on the Rhineland states' behalf. According to Brissot's 29 December speech in the Legislative Assembly, Spain was in a "paralytic state," the Dutch craved liberty, the Sardinians were weak, Prussia would not support a war against France that might strengthen Austria, and Austria was too torn by internal divisions to risk war with France. Indeed, Brissot concluded, "we have nothing to fear from war with any of these powers."[32] By January 1792, however, Brissot had gotten wind of diplomatic documents suggesting the existence of an Austrian-sponsored alliance of kings against France. As a result, Brissot adopted a far more belligerent anti-Austrian stance. Austria had refused to help with the *émigré* problem, Brissot charged, and had even signed a treaty with Prussia against France, despite France's 1756 treaty of alliance with Austria. Therefore, Brissot advocated canceling not only the 1756 treaty, but the entire existing system of international treaty alliances, since treaties were born of "ignorance and corruption," "constantly sacrifice the people to the interests of a few individuals," and were "eternal pretexts of war." "Why shouldn't we limit ourselves to a treaty of amity," Brissot asked rhetorically, "not only with our neighbors, but with the entire human species?" Before such a vision of universal fraternity could be realized, however, France would first have to strike down Europe's kings, since "they [our enemies] are kings and we are people, they are despots, and we are free . . . [and] there is no point of sincere capitulation between tyranny and liberty."[33]

On a more practical level, Brissot hoped that the war would yield positive dividends on the domestic political front. Some of those dividends would be personal: Brissot hoped a successful war would strengthen the hand of radicals within France. Brissot and his allies also hoped that war would unmask conspirators against the body politic. "Let us designate the place for traitors beforehand," Brissot's colleague Gaudet announced, "and let it be the scaffold."[34] What is more, Brissot assumed that the king would oppose a policy of war with Austria—his wife after all was an Austrian princess—and would be dethroned as a result. Much to Brissot's embarrassment, however, the king threw his support behind Brissot's war policy in hopes that war would strengthen his own position against the radical factions.

Despite the king's unexpected acquiescence to the policy, Brissot's call for war was received with great enthusiasm in the Jacobin Club and the Legislative Assembly, but the king's Minister of Foreign Affairs Delessart opposed the measure. Brissot's response demonstrates that, bookish child of the Enlightenment though he may have been, Brissot was quite capable of ruthless political maneuvering if the situation so required. Undeterred by Delessart's resistance, Brissot turned his bombast against the foreign minister himself, in hopes not only of removing an obstacle to his war policy but also to punish his master the king for his recent dismissal of the pro-war War Minister Narbonne. What is more, Brissot hoped that Delessart's dismissal might force the king to replace his current stable of conservative ministers with a radical ministry more to Brissot's liking. To this end, Brissot accused Delessart of fatal vacillation, of covering up important evidence of an Austrian plot to forge a league of tyrants against France, and of "degrading" the nation in his speeches besides.

Brissot had little hard evidence to offer against Delessart: His chief "crimes" were such things as adopting the wrong style of diplomacy, clinging to the 1756 treaty, and not being as pro-war as Brissot might have liked. Nonetheless, lack of evidence did not stop Brissot from accusing Delessart of a bewildering list of infractions, such as damaging the value of the *assignats* (France's currency), undermining France's financial credit, and "encourage[ing] domestic disorder." On the basis of this litany of woes, Brissot concluded that Delessart's conduct amounted "either to ineptitude or treason," and Brissot demanded that a decree of accusation be published against Delessart.[35] Stunned by Brissot's accusations, the Legislative Assembly acquiesced to his demands, and on 14 March the Assembly voted to submit Delessart's case to the French High Court. In the end, the decree of accusation against Delessart proved to be a decree of death: The hapless minister was still incarcerated in September and, as a result, became just one of many victims of the September Massacres.

Delessart may have suffered personal tragedy, but Brissot got what he wanted: His fingers on the levers of government. Shortly after Delessart's downfall, the king tried to placate popular opinion by replacing his old ministers with a new "patriot" ministry of proven radicals. Brissot did not join himself but did exert a great deal of influence over the selection of ministers, managing to secure the appointment of trusted friends and supporters like J.-M. Roland (Madame Roland's husband) and his old collaborator Clavière to the ministries of the interior and finances, respectively. With Delessart out of the way, the king favorable to war for his own reasons, and with radical critics of the war, such as Robespierre, temporarily in eclipse, Brissot convinced the assembly to declare war on Austria on 20 April. It is important to note that Brissot was far from the only deputy pushing for war and, indeed, the measure passed in the Legislative Assembly with only seven dissenting votes. Nonetheless, as the war's most consistent and powerful supporter, Brissot bears the lion's share of responsibility for both the war and the disasters it brought in its wake.

Historians have been nearly unanimous in their denunciation of Brissot's war policy, and for good reason. The French army, disrupted by desertions from the noble-dominated officer corps, was in no shape to fight in the spring of 1792. What is more, historians have not shared Brissot's assessment of Austria's inherent ill-will toward the revolution and have argued that the Austrians, far from plotting war against France, were resigned to the success of the French

Revolution throughout most of 1791 and even promulgated measures acquiescing to France's demands to demilitarize the *émigrés* in the Rhineland as late as 3 January 1792.[36] What is more, Brissot's prediction that Prussia would never join Austria against France proved to be a grave error, since the Prussian king immediately threw his lot in with Austria when war was declared, in hopes of being granted territory in Germany or Poland as a reward for his assistance.

Brissot could have overcome these mistakes with vigorous diplomatic initiatives and war preparations, but he chose to conduct a war of words against an internal enemy instead, launching a verbal offensive against the so-called "Austrian Committee," which (he claimed) was plotting to strengthen the king's power, foil France's foreign policy, give grace to the *émigrés*, and favor the foreign policy interests of the "house of Austria." This time around, Brissot did not even try to document his claims, arguing instead that "[in] these sorts of coalitions, these conspiracies against liberty, nothing is written; mystery envelopes the secret bases and transactions, and cloaks [*dérobe*] them from the eyes of the public: they can be studied only in the series of public acts of the coalition; and [those acts] are sufficient to prove their existence." On the basis of such spectral evidence, Brissot demanded that Montmorin, an ex-minister and current councilor of the king, be arrested on charges of high treason.[37] This time around, however, the Legislative Assembly was unimpressed and failed to act on Brissot's suggestion.

Ironically, Brissot's suspicions about an "Austrian Committee" were substantially correct: A body of ultraconservatives dedicated to the principles of absolute monarchy did exist, though Queen Marie-Antoinette, rather than Montmorin, was at its head.[38] Still, the energy Brissot invested in his campaign against the "Austrian Committee" was vastly out of proportion to the actual threat that this relatively ineffectual group represented to France. Indeed, it is hard to avoid the conclusion, especially in light of Brissot's equally opportunist attack on Delessart, that Brissot's "Austrian Committee" campaign was little more than a cynical scare tactic to further strengthen his political dominance in France. If so, it failed: Brissot's political influence was given a sharp check on 13 June when Roland and Clavière were dismissed during a squabble with the king over domestic policy. Fuming, Brissot redoubled his "Austrian Committee" attacks and launched accusations against the new foreign affairs minister, Chambonas, hoping to force him out of office and to force the king to reinstate Brissot's expelled friends. He eventually succeeded in the former but it took a popular insurrection to achieve the latter goal.

In the meantime, Brissot and his supporters looked for allies in the coming war with the Austrian Empire, though with little success. Brissot had no doubts that Britain and the United States were natural allies of France: "in time, France and England will unite, and they will be united with America . . . and liberty and peace will shortly cover the earth."[39] Indeed, Brissot was convinced that the cause of France enjoyed widespread support among the British populace and even directed diplomats to London to go over the head of the British court and appeal directly to the people and Parliament. This initiative resulted only in a sharp rebuff from the British court, which sternly informed the French diplomat in question that all diplomacy had to follow official channels, and lead to a decided chill in Anglo-French relations.[40] The French diplomatic attempt to lure Prussia out of Austria's orbit proved equally unsuccessful, as did French attempts to "revolutionize" Belgium and Holland with propaganda and to buy the allegiance of various minor German princes. In sum, French revolutionary diplomacy in early 1792 was, as one historian has noted, a "debacle."[41]

Events on the battlefield proved no less disastrous. On 29 April, the French general Dillon ordered his army to retreat after sighting Austrian troops, leading to calls of treason in the ranks and Dillon's eventual murder at the hands of his demoralized men. Much of the rest of the French army was paralyzed by lack of military discipline and by feuds between the commanding generals and the Legislative Assembly. Scenting blood, the combined Austro-Prussian force issued the so-called "Brunswick Manifesto," on 25 July, threatening terrible vengeance on Paris if the French royal family was harmed, and marched across the French border 25 days later. The commanding general boasted he would "enter [France] at Brest and leave by Toulon."[42] At first, events on the ground seemed to prove him right: The Austro-Prussian force took two crucial border forts, Longwy and Verdun, in quick succession. Paris, many believed, would be next to fall.

News of these defeats spurred the Parisian popular radicals into action. Already troubled by rising inflation, rising grain prices, and increasing scarcity of staple goods such as sugar (a scarcity that Brissot's intervention into Saint-Domingue internal affairs probably aggravated), an outraged coalition of Paris *sans-culotte* radicals and volunteer soldiers from Marseilles stormed the king's Tuilleries palace on 10 August and effectively dethroned Louis XVI. Brissot assumed that removal of the king would restore his ascendancy over revolutionary affairs, but he didn't count on the hostility of the Parisian *sans-culottes*, who remembered how Brissot's supporters had been willing to work in the ministry of the now-reviled French king. Indeed, the newly formed Commune of Paris, which seized power from the constituted municipal authorities during the 10 August insurrection, directly challenged the Brissot-dominated Legislative Assembly's authority over the country, and even managed to force the election of a new legislative body elected by universal male suffrage.

In the elections that followed, Brissot was stunned to find himself rebuffed by Parisian voters, who elected a slate of ultra-radicals instead, including Marat, Desmoulins, and Robespierre. Brissot alleged electoral fraud and intimidation, but had to resign himself to deputation in the less prestigious department of

Eure-et-Loir.[43] He was further shocked by the September Massacres of early September 1792, during which Parisian radicals, panicked by the news of the fall of Verdun, executed the bulk of the prisoners in the Paris jails over the course of six blood soaked days. What disturbed Brissot was not the massacres themselves, but the knowledge that he could have easily have been one of its victims: Marat apparently convinced officials in the Commune to sign arrest warrants for Brissot and eight of his supporters on the eve of the massacres and, if these orders hadn't been quashed by justice minister Danton, Brissot may very well have perished.

As a result of these events, the political atmosphere of the newly formed National Convention was polarized from the start between adherents of Brissot and supporters of Robespierre. Historians have traditionally labeled these two factions the "Girondins" and the "Montagnards," respectively, and have invested these groupings with various socio-economic or ideological meanings. Recent research into these factions, however, suggests that these groupings were far from cohesive party structures but, rather, were weak, transitory, and based largely on personal ties and animosities.[44] This is especially true about Brissot's supposed "Girondin" faction, which enjoyed neither internal ideological homogeneity nor deeply rooted support within the Convention.[45] As a result, this study will avoid the misleading "Girondin" and "Montagnard" labels, despite the fact that they are still in common usage among many French Revolutionary historians.

The lack of formal party structures, however, did not prevent Brissot from quickly becoming a prominent, if not dominant, voice in the new National Convention. Contemporary sources made reference to "Brissot and his coterie" or "Brissot and company," and the term "Brissotin" was coined to describe Brissot's supporters, though Brissot himself, in keeping with the anti-factional rhetoric of the time, always denied belonging to any party.[46] What is more, Brissot was rapidly invested with positions of authority in the Convention: He was chosen as one of its first secretaries on 21 September and was later picked to be a member of the constitutional committee, the committee of general defense, and (most significant for our purposes) the diplomatic committee. Thankfully, the foreign policy situation Brissot faced had improved markedly because of the French victory at Valmy on 20 September and the subsequent withdrawal of Prussian troops from French soil—a withdrawal, incidentally, that resulted from the decidedly traditional style of diplomacy employed in the field by French General Dumouriez rather than from the ideologically driven diplomacy of Brissot.[47] Dumouriez followed up this success with a victorious campaign into the Austrian Netherlands (Belgium), which was occupied in its entirety by France soon after the decisive Battle of Jemappes on 6 November. This victory, combined with French gains in Savoy, Nice, and the Rhineland German states, meant that France found itself in a highly favorable strategic situation as 1792 gave way to 1793.

201

Unfortunately for France, however, Brissot's inept diplomacy soon snatched defeat from the jaws of victory. French agents tried, and failed, to create goodwill for the revolution in Holland, and Brissot himself managed to alienate Gouverneur Morris, the minister of the United States to France, by demanding promises that Morris could not accommodate and criticizing Morris's aristocratic manners to boot.[48] Brissot and colleagues in the diplomatic committee also took a tough line against the strategically important city of Geneva—partly because of Brissot's personal hostility to the Genevan ruling oligarchy—and insisted that Geneva scrap its aristocratic constitution. When General Montesquiou, who was in charge of operations in Switzerland, threatened to upset Brissot's plans by signing a compromise settlement with Geneva on his own initiative, Brissot reacted with fury, denouncing Montesquiou's willingness to sign a deal with the oppressors of a free people, and accusing him of weakness, stock-jobbing, and pro-aristocratic sentiments besides.[49] Brissot insisted that Montesquiou's treaty be supplemented by a demand that Geneva adopt a democratic constitution. The Genevans were forced to capitulate to French demands but public opinion throughout the Swiss states became increasingly hostile to the French Revolution as a consequence.

Following France's victory at Jemappes, Brissot's diplomacy became even more uncompromising and grandiose. Flushed with success, Brissot and his colleagues framed European diplomacy in increasingly ideological terms, abandoning previous hopes for alliances with Prussia and Britain and reframing European politics as a "combat to death between French liberty and universal tyranny."[50] "We cannot be at peace," Brissot asserted, "until that time that Europe, and all Europe, is in flames."[51] To give institutional expression to this millenarian mindset, Brissot and his allies pushed a decree through the Convention declaring that France would "accord fraternity and assistance to all peoples who wish to recover their liberty and charges the executive power to give the generals the necessary orders to bring help to these peoples and defend those who have been or might be threatened [vexés] for the cause of liberty."[52] Brissot and his supporters hoped that this revolutionary-era experiment in nation building would lead to the establishment of five sister republics in Western Europe: Spain/Portugal to the south, England to the north, Italy to the southeast, the Rhineland to the northeast, and France reigning supreme in the center.[53]

To realize this vision, Brissot first advocated a preventive war against the Spanish monarchy, since he feared that the Spanish Bourbon king would inevitably come to the support of his deposed kinsman, Louis XVI. Brissot advocated the invasion of Spain combined with a simultaneous propaganda campaign to "electrify all the spirits" and to "demonstrate to Spain that the Revolution is its political resurrection."[54] In the meantime, Brissot wanted to dispatch the Spaniard-turned-revolutionary Francisco Miranda to the Spanish colonies, where "he would be able to easily break the chains forged by the [men] of Pizarro and Cortez."[55] Nothing came of these plans, but French agents were sent to Rome, Genoa, Turin, Saint-Petersburg, and even Constantinople, though with little success. (The agent sent to Rome made such a nuisance of himself that he was set upon by a pro-Papacy crowd and assassinated.) Arguing that "the conversion of public opinion in England would be as good as winning a battle," Brissot also dispatched still more agents to indoctrinate the British public with "true notions on the state of France" and to make direct contacts with the parliamentary opposition.[56] These agents, however, did nothing to stem the tide of British hostility toward France, which mounted still further in the winter of 1792-93 after the French violated the 1713 Treaty of Utrecht's ban on navigation on Belgium's Scheldt River, a move that the British took as a clear sign that the French would not respect the neutrality of Britian's ally, the Netherlands. Still another agent, Edmund Genet, was dispatched to the United States to bolster support of France and raise forces to seize the Louisiana territory from the Spanish, though nothing resulted from his bungled machinations (he had the effrontery to publicly denounce Washington) other than a distinct cooling of Franco-American relations. Brissot also began to flirt with the notion of annexing Belgium to France, thus expanding the French republic's borders to the supposedly "natural frontiers" of the Pyrenees, the Alps, the sea, and the Rhine. This proposal was never carried out, partly because of the Belgians' hostility, but Brissot and his allies did push through the annexation of Savoy on 27 November, and the incorporation of the Rhineland German states was seriously contemplated as well.

Interestingly, in the midst of these utopian dreams and majestic ambitions, Brissot sounded an uncharacteristic note of caution during the trial of King Louis XVI. In his trial opinion, Brissot insisted that Louis was worthy of death, but cautioned that the league of foreign kings, who were already "painting us as cannibals in the eyes of [their people]," would use Louis's death as a further opportunity to slander the revolution if the Convention itself ordered his execution. To avoid this, Brissot supported the motion that the king's fate be "appealed" to the French primary assemblies instead: "thus would tumble down the accusations poured out by the kings to all of Europe, [seeking] to persuade [the people] that the judgment [of Louis] is only the result of the preponderance of one handful of factionalists." On the contrary, an appeal to the people would prove that "it is the nation who pronounces, and 25 million men cannot be directed by a bunch of plotters." Brissot also hoped that a dignified national vote to ratify the king's fate would, by demonstrating that France was not the "theatre of an unceasing carnage," foil the sinister designs of the "universal coalition" of foreign powers plotting to "place [France] back under the yoke of despotism."[57] This time, however, Brissot's oratory did not carry the day, and the "appeal" proposal was defeated by a lopsided margin.

Had Brissot been converted to a more cautious style of diplomacy, or was the new tone of foreign policy moderation he adopted during the appeal debate a mere side effect of his internal political agenda, namely, his desire to weaken the Parisian radicals by giving the departments a greater voice in French government? Subsequent events suggest the latter. Indeed, Brissot's next major diplomatic initiative was perhaps the most reckless of his career. On 12 January 1793—just nine days before Louis XVI's execution—Brissot presented a report to the Convention in the name of the Committee of General Defense concerning Anglo-French relations. Although its findings reflected the work of a committee, Brissot's fingerprints were clearly visible throughout the document; its style, tone, and findings were remarkably similar to Brissot's early 1792 speeches concerning Austria. Britain was becoming increasingly hostile to France, Brissot charged, though British grievances against France were unfounded. French spies were not subverting the British, Brissot claimed, and Brissot denied that France had any hostile intentions against the Dutch (though he went on to accuse the Dutch Stadtholder of chronic mismanagement and "complete despotism"). As for the reopening of the Scheldt River, Brissot acknowledged that this was Britain's chief grievance against France but maintained that the closure of the Scheldt was a crime against "eternal justice," and that France was not bound to obey "treaties concluded between tyrants." In actuality, Brissot contended, it was France that had grievances: Britain had declared a virtual trade war against France; had begun arming her forces; and was giving comfort to French *émigrés* while the "horrors of the inquisition" were inflicted on patriotic Frenchmen in England.[58] Brissot concluded his presentation with an ultimatum to Britain, including the restoration of free trade, but predicted confidently that the British had too few allies, too much debt, and too many colonial complications to risk war with France.

Brissot's initial prediction that Britain would shrink from war proved just as fleeting as his similar 1792 predictions about Austrian timidity, however, and, by 1 February, Brissot was pushing for a pre-emptive strike. Britain, Brissot asserted, was holding up a "perfidious mask of neutrality" while actively plotting for "war against our liberty."[59] In fact, Brissot was not wrong on this point: The British attitude toward France had grown increasingly hostile throughout 1792, and calls for war with France gained even more momentum after the execution of Louis XVI. Even if war was inevitable, however, it would have been advisable for Brissot to try to delay it as long as possible, or else to divide Britain from its continental ally, the Dutch. Brissot did neither. Confident that the common people of Britain would not support their government's war with France, Brissot advocated an immediate declaration of war against both Britain and the Dutch on 1 February, and the Convention unanimously adopted the degree. France was now at war with Austria, Prussia, the Netherlands, and Britain; in addition,

Spain and Portugal had declared war on France soon after Louis's execution in January. Brissot's rhetoric of a universal war between liberty and despotism—"it is Europe entire, or at least all the tyrants of Europe, that we are now combating on the land and on the sea"—was fast becoming a self-fulfilling prophesy.[60]

Events unfolded in 1792 much as they had in 1793: Having rashly provoked war, Brissot found that France did not have sufficient military means to fight it. In the months after France's declaration of war on Britain, the British stitched together a broad (if somewhat fragile) coalition of European monarchies, stretching from Portugal to Russia, dedicated to the defeat of the French. Allied troops defeated French General Dumouriez's invasion of Holland on 1 March, and then counterattacked into Belgium, inflicting a major defeat on Dumouriez on 18 March at Neerwinden and forcing him to evacuate much of the province. When voices rose in Paris blaming Dumouriez for the disaster, he attempted to turn his army against the Convention, only to defect to Austria when his army refused to support his treason. In the meantime, Prussian armies besieged the French fortress town of Mainz, Sardinian troops made gains in the southeast, and Spanish troops captured several border forts and even invested the ancient French fortress town of Perpignan. Even more distressing were the growing threats France faced from within. When French officials tried to conscript the peasants of the Vendée into the French army in March 1793, the result was a massive popular revolt that took tens of thousands of French troops well over a year to fully suppress. Urban centers simmered with revolt as well, most noticeably France's second city, Lyon. The revolution seemed close to collapse.

As a result of these disasters, Brissot and his allies were finally chased from positions of authority over diplomatic affairs. In late March, an election was held to renew the Brissot-dominated Committee of General Defense and, although Brissot kept his seat, he and his allies lost control over this body. When this committee proved too unwieldy to deal with France's mounting problems, the Convention invested dictatorial powers on a new Committee of Public Safety to address the crisis, and the fact that none of Brissot's supporters were elected to it at all clearly demonstrates the power shift that was taking place in the Convention. Indeed, Robespierre and his supporters began to turn Brissot's tactic of denunciation against him, harping on Brissot's friendship with Dumouriez and denouncing Brissot as a crypto-royalist and conspirator against the revolution. In the meantime, Robespierre's supporters, who now had their hands on the wheel of French foreign policy, were developing a more hard-headed diplomacy, abandoning propaganda and the concept of the universal liberation of peoples in favor of more traditional diplomatic means. In one historian's words, "brutal realism would take the place of utopias."[61]

The return to *realpolitik* in external affairs, combined with the use of terror to cow internal enemies, eventually saved the revolution, but Brissot did not live to see the turning of the tide. Brissot and his allies never forgave the Parisian radicals for the September Massacres and maintained a stance of resolute hostility to the Parisian revolutionaries through the spring of 1793, to the point of calling for the creation of a departmental guard to defend the Convention against Parisian "assassins." Brissot's hostility toward the Parisians was such that he refused to accept the support of the influential Georges Danton—the same man who saved Brissot's life by quashing the warrants against him on the eve of the September Massacres—out of personal hostility and distaste for Danton's Parisian connections. The final straw, for the Parisians, was the Convention's 28 May vote to renew the work of the Committee of Twelve, a political body established by Brissot's allies in the aftermath of the September Massacres to tamp down Parisian radicalism. Outraged Parisian revolutionaries surrounded the Convention on 31 May and 1 June to demand the expulsion of 22 deputies, a group that included Brissot and some of his closest supporters. At first, these 22 deputies received relatively lenient treatment from the Convention, as even Robespierre and his supporters were dismayed by this show of Parisian political might and the consequent diminution of their own power. After the assassination of the popular Parisian radical Marat on 13 July, however, Brissot and the other expelled deputies—some of whom had fled to the provinces to stir up provincial rebellion in the interim—were accused of treason, rounded up, and hauled before hastily formed kangaroo courts. Brissot himself was accused of a sweeping list of crimes, including plotting with the British ministry to ruin the colonies and overthrow the revolution. Brissot prepared a defense but was not allowed to deliver it in court. He was found guilty despite the flimsy nature of the evidence against him. A French patriot to the last, Brissot reportedly sang the *Marseilles* on his way to the guillotine on 30 October 1793.

Given the conduct and results of French foreign policy under Brissot's direction, it is easy to see why historians have been so critical of his foreign policy initiatives. Determining the exact reasons for Brissot's foreign policy ineptitude, however, is a far more difficult task.

Some previous historians, though mostly interested in recounting rather than explaining Brissot's ineptitude, have made limited stabs at answering this question. In his work on Franco-German relations during the revolution, for instance, Sidney Biro points to the important role played by foreign radicals in Paris in "egg[ing] on" the revolutionary war party.[62] Like the Iraqi exiles of the modern day, who convinced the Bush administration that Iraq was fertile ground for American imposed democracy, these foreign radicals promised the French revolutionaries that Europe was full of groaning, discontented peoples looking to France for national liberation. Biro's work deals primarily with German radicals in Paris, but radicals from elsewhere in Europe had Brissot's ear as well, most especially Spanish, Genevan, Dutch, and British political exiles. The influence of the latter was crucial in converting Brissot to a policy of war with England. Based on his contacts with such figures as the expatriate British radical Thomas Paine and delegates from the Constitutional Society of London, Brissot and his compatriots came to believe that the British general public, if sufficiently propagandized, might bestir itself into revolution rather than consent to war against a sister republic.[63] French spies mistakenly reinforced this impression: "to the eyes of an outside observer," one wrote, "England offers precisely the same prospect as France did in 1789."[64] The result of this fatal miscalculation was 22 years of almost unceasing war between France and Great Britain.

Brissot may have gotten bad advice but this by no means absolves him of responsibility, especially since some of Brissot's contemporaries were not deceived by the self-interested chatter of the radical exiles. In a 1792 speech concerning Brissot's war policy against Austria, for example, Robespierre warned the Jacobin Club that "the most extravagant idea that can be born in the head of a statesman is to believe that it suffices for a people to enter a foreign country with weapons in hand in order to make them adopt their laws and their constitution." Arguing that "no one loves armed revolutionaries," Robespierre argued that revolution came by slow, progressive stages, and that outside attempts to impose revolution might only unite the people against France.[65] Even some radical exiles in France themselves thought Brissot's plans overblown. The Spanish expatriate revolutionary Marchena, for instance, advised Brissot against revolutionizing Spain, arguing that "a nation is always slave when it obeys another will than its own, whether that will is that of a king, or that of another people."[66] Wise words, but Brissot was not listening.

In any case, Brissot's eagerness to believe the promises of the radical exiles should probably be seen as a symptom of a wider disease: Brissot's tendency to frame revolutionary affairs in terms of a millenarian struggle between tyrants and the oppressed masses of Europe. "[war with Austria] will be a crusade for universal liberty," Brissot lectured his fellow Jacobin Club radicals in late 1791. "Each soldier will say to his enemy: Brother, I am not going to cut your throat, I am going to free you from the yoke you labor under . . . I was once a slave; I took up arms, and the tyrant vanished; look at me now that I am free; you can be so too; here is my arm in support."[67] Brissot made the same point more succinctly a year later in a speech to the National Convention: "it is not for yourself that you are going into battle," Brissot told his colleagues, "it is for all the nations of Europe."[68] Missionaries of freedom like Brissot, however, believed that the defeat of despotism required the book as well as the sword. Indeed, as children of the Enlightenment, Brissot and his political allies believed fervently in the written word's power to sweep away prejudice, superstition, and privilege, and put their faith in the "magical force" of pamphlets, hoping to use the press to open the eyes of deluded peoples and thus achieve the universal liberation of humanity.[69] Admittedly, Brissot's exaggerated faith in the transformational power of ideological discourse exceeded that of many of his compatriots, perhaps as a result of his pre-revolutionary experiences as a radical author and journalist, but the difference is only one of degree.

As a result of this bookish mindset, Brissot and other French revolutionaries approached foreign policy in a highly ideological mode, regarding diplomacy as an exercise in rhetoric rather than the art of the possible. According to French revolutionary historians Linda and Marsha Frey, Brissot was far from unique in his belief that revolutionary diplomatic practice should be guided by ideological discourse and should adopt an entirely new mode of diplomacy better suited to the manners of a free people. Throughout the revolution, the French selected their ambassadors on the grounds of ideology rather than ability, flaunted formalities, based policies on abstractions such as "natural law" or the "rights of man," insisted on open rather than backroom negotiations, and broke existing treaties if they conflicted with revolutionary convictions. Indeed, many revolutionaries considered "diplomacy" in the traditional sense as unnecessary: Jeanbon Saint-André, for instance, declared that "our diplomacy is the truth, liberty."[70] Brissot's foreign policy writings were awash in similar declarations. "French diplomacy ought to finally revert to the character of our revolution," Brissot declared, "it ought to be free, loyal and proud; simplicity, terseness [*laconisme*], and clarity ought to constitute our diplomatic style."[71] Revolutionary France had no need for the tools of the trade of "old diplomacy": Espionage, pens-for-hire (a profession Brissot knew all too well), and secret liaisons. It was high time, Brissot argued, to leave behind the "profound myster[ies]" of the "Machiavellianism of the courts of Europe."[72] Unfortunately for Brissot and his compatriots, however, this sharp break with traditional diplomatic practice served only to further unite the crowned heads of Europe against the dangers posed by French "incendiaries" and the "epidemic" of revolution.[73]

Should Brissot's failures be excused on the grounds that his diplomatic practices merely echoed the millenarian tenor of the time? To a degree, perhaps, but some of Brissot's own contemporaries were clearheaded enough to reject his undiplomatic style of diplomacy. Chief among them was Robespierre, who thought Brissot's war policy folly. "You would have our army stroll triumphantly into the lands of all neighboring peoples," Robespierre asked Brissot, "you would establish everywhere municipalities, directories, national assemblies . . . as if the destiny of empires is directed by figures of rhetoric." As for Brissot's contention that war would be quick and successful, Robespierre hoped it was correct, but warned his contemporaries that Brissot's optimistic outlook "has not at any rate been proven, and given this doubt, we ought not hazard our liberty."[74] Desmoulins raised similar concerns about Brissot's advocacy of war:

"is it good policy . . . to break treaties, to make war against all the powers, and to annex [*municipaliser*] Europe?"[75] Brissot's war policy may have been popular, then, but it was far from unchallenged.

In any case, Brissot himself was not entirely loyal to his own universalistic rhetoric. Some of his foreign policy mistakes can be attributed, not his desire for universal fraternity, but to his decidedly old regime sense of French nationalism. As one historian has noted, Brissot and his supporters had trouble deciding between the ideology of "universal confraternity" of European peoples and more traditional expansionist policies designed to augment "the grandeur of France."[76] As a result, Brissot and his allies continuously flirted with the notion of annexation of conquered territory, and even consented to follow the old regime practice of draining conquered territories of resources to pay for the war, thus calling into doubt the benefits of French "liberation." Small wonder, then, that the initial popularity of the French in their conquered territories quickly turned to dislike or outright resistance. Since Brissot's latent nationalism emerged relatively late in his foreign policy career, Brissot's nationalism can serve as only a partial explanation for his foreign policy ineptitude. However, nationalism does explain, in part, why Brissot's inept policies proved so popular: Brissot's call for war with Europe's kings appealed greatly to the "purely Gallic conquering spirit" that still resided, despite the Enlightenment, in the breasts of Brissot's contemporaries.[77]

Perhaps the fatal flaw of Brissot's diplomatic practice, however, was his predilection to infuse his foreign policy writings with charges of factional conspiracy. Indeed, accusations of treason were a constant theme in Brissot's foreign policy writing: Over time, the white planters of Saint-Domingue, the hapless Delassart, the Austrian Committee, General Montesquiou, and even Robespierre himself became targets of Brissot's acid pen. Brissot's foreign policy rhetoric, then, had a double-edged quality to it, striking out against not only foreign plotters but also traitors within the revolution itself. Whatever Brissot's intentions, the effect was to weaken France, since Brissot's wild accusations served only to paralyze a nation and polarize discourse at a time of national crisis. This is especially true of Brissot's ill-conceived Austrian Committee campaign, which distracted the attention of the revolutionary leadership at a time when it should have been focused on preparations for war. Brissot's accusations of conspiracy against the Parisian "cannibals," though understandable given his post-September Massacre fears, had a similar effect, dividing a formerly united radical coalition on the eve of a war with the combined armies of Europe.

To some extent, Brissot's penchant for conspiracy theory was typical of the age. Historians have long recognized that the "paranoid style"—a tendency to ascribe misfortunes to the ill will of pernicious schemers—was deeply embedded in political culture of the eighteenth century. Building on earlier work by Barnard

Bailyn and Richard Hofstadter, the American colonial historian Gordon Wood has argued that this mindset was the result of the fusion of two eighteenth-century intellectual trends: An older moralizing focus on human intentions and the new Enlightenment/Newtonian notion of a self-sustaining clockwork universe. As a result, American Whig political radicals assumed that "all human actions and events could now be scientifically seen as the product of men's intentions," and consequently early American political discourse was replete with accusations of conspiracy.[78] The "paranoid style," however, was by no means limited to the United States, and revolutionary historians have noted a similar French tendency to adopt the language of conspiracy. Interesting enough, French revolutionary historians have posited somewhat different intellectual roots for the same general phenomenon. In his formulation, François Furet explained the French tendency toward "democratic absolutism" as the merger of the new "democratic sociability" of the revolution with the absolutism of the old regime.[79] Still, the result was the same: Like their American counterparts, French revolutionary political actors adopted a "Manichean" world view, divided into only two elements, "patriotism and treason; the people and the plots of aristocrats."[80] Small wonder, Furet concluded, that the French Revolution proved unable to achieve stability and eventually descended into terror.

Furet's "Manichean" thesis has proven to be quite influential in French revolutionary scholarship. Lynn Hunt has similarly argued that "the rhetoric of conspiracy permeated revolutionary discourse at every political level," and that the ever-escalating calls for public vigilance ultimately culminated in the national bloodletting of the Terror.[81] Susan Dunn has gone even farther, claiming that the French revolutionaries were too "spellbound" to the "myth and rhetoric of unity" to accept the legitimacy of organized opposition to the sitting government.[82] As a result, Dunn argues, the French were obliged to adopt a discourse of accusation and exclusion, as opposed to the Americans, who valued oppositional voices and never developed a conspiratorial rhetoric (a conclusion that Gordon Wood would probably contest). The "Manichean" thesis has not gone unchallenged. In a recent article, Timothy Tackett has taken issue with the supposed ideological roots of the French propensity toward conspiracy theory, and has argued instead that it was a rational response to "a series of very real conspiracies and threatened conspiracies," most especially the king's flight to Varennes in the summer of 1791.[83] Nonetheless, the notion that revolutionary ideology imparted a conspiratorial tone to French revolutionary discourse remains well established in French revolutionary historiography.

Once again, did Brissot's flawed diplomacy merely echo the tenor of the time? Perhaps, but it is important to note that "Manichean" rhetoric was far from ubiquitous during the French Revolution. My own work on the king's trial suggests that, even when debating the divisive issue of an "appeal to the people" on the king's fate, about 75 percent of French deputies speaking on the issue chose not to employ the language of factional conspiracy, and 19 percent of the deputies actively employed explicitly anti-Manichean, inclusive language in their trial opinions. "It is all only too true," the deputy Lambert lamented, "that out of all the opinions expressed to this day on Louis XVI's judgment, the majority of orators have been more disposed to decry those who are not of their opinion, by outrageous caricatures [*personnalités*], by odious imputations of royalism, demagoguery, and corruption, than to discuss the true state of the question."[84] Lambert's colleague, Ichon, struck a similar note, imploring his colleagues to leave behind "all the systems of fabricated slander which hurt the public interest; abandon all the denunciations so often repeated, which ordinarily have no other result than to produce scandalous debates inside the Convention."[85] Given the fact that a substantial number of his own contemporaries self-consciously rejected the "Manichean" mode of discourse, Brissot's own preference for accusatory rhetoric was just as likely to be the result of deliberate choice than some sort of subliminal mandate inherent in revolutionary ideology.

Indeed, one could go even further, and argue that Brissot's case turns the "Manichean" argument of Furet and others completely on its head. Brissot and his compatriots, as the theory goes, were driven toward the language of conspiracy by the internal logic of revolutionary political discourse. What if Brissot himself, however, was responsible for the increasingly conspiratorial tone of revolutionary discourse? Diplomatic historian H.-A. Goetz-Bernstein has contended exactly that: Brissot, he asserted, was "the inventor of that system of combat that would become familiar to all parties [of the revolution] . . . the accusation of conspiracy."[86] Such tactics had been used before, Goetz-Bernstein conceded, but Brissot surpassed all previous such examples with the gravity of his charges and the wildness of his claims. Brissot's accusations produced a trail of victims, but such casualties were incidental. In each case, Brissot's real objective was the acquisition or retention of political power through the elimination or intimidation of possible opponents. Delessart, for instance, was targeted to compel the king to restore Brissot's allies to ministerial office. The Austrian Committee accusations served to draw attention from a failing war policy. In each case, Brissot doubtless believed he was serving the interests of the revolution. As Goetz-Bernstein pointed out, however, Brissot's self-serving use of the rhetoric of conspiracy set an example that later French leaders harnessed to their own political ambitions. In that sense, Brissot's own conviction and execution for treason in October 1793 has a certain irony to it. Brissot, in the end, was slain by a weapon he himself had forged.

Goetz-Bernstein is probably overstating his case. Given the wide prevalence of conspiracy theory in eighteenth-century radical rhetoric, both inside and outside of France, it seems clear that Brissot's accusations reflected, as much as initiated, wider revolutionary trends. Nonetheless, Goetz-Bernstein's work is a needed reminder about the importance of assessing human agency while evaluating historical events. There can be no doubt that Brissot's foreign policy decisions were influenced by the ideological tendencies of the French Revolution: Millenarian universalism, belief in the transformational power of texts, nationalism, and "Manichean" mindsets all help to explain the missteps that plagued Brissot's career. Ideology's role in revolutionary events, however, was far from determinative. As we have seen, many of Brissot's contemporaries came to sharply different conclusions on foreign policy matters, despite their shared Enlightenment intellectual influences.[87] It is perhaps more accurate to compare ideology's function in the French Revolution to a rough framework, which set basic guidelines for discussion and tended to channel discourse into well-worn paths, but which nonetheless allowed for considerable room for maneuver by specific revolutionary actors in their quest to achieve their goals.

Unfortunately for the French, however, Brissot's most consistent goal throughout the revolution seems to have been self-aggrandizement. Some of Brissot's early political projects seem to have been guided by real altruism, especially his advocacy of the mulatto cause in Saint-Domingue. However, once the revolution began, and particularly once Brissot reached elected office, altruism gave way to political considerations. Indeed, the unifying theme of Brissot's foreign policy initiatives—his calls for war against Austria, his vendetta against the Genevan aristocrats, and even his demand for an "appeal to the people," in the king's trial—was a clear desire for personal political benefit at the expense of his rivals. His ideological mindset certainly magnified his mistakes but, ultimately, the most compelling explanation for his foreign policy failures lay with Brissot's own political ambitions.

Notes

1. Patrice Gueniffey, "Brissot," in *La Gironde et les Girondins,* François Furet and Mona Ozouf, eds. (Paris, 1991), 439-40.

2.. Elloise Ellery, *Brissot de Warville: A Study in the History of the French Revolution* (New York: AMS Press, 1915 [reprint ed., 1970]), 257.

3. H.-A. Goetz-Bernstein, *La Diplomatie de la Gironde: Jacques-Pierre Brissot* (Paris, 1912).

4. See Lynn Hunt, *Politics, Culture, and Class in the French Revolution* (Berkeley: University of California Press, 1984), 205.

5. J.-P. Brissot, *Mémoires* 1 (Paris, 1911), 38.

6. J. Pétion, *Mémoires Inédits de Pétion et Mémoires de Buzot et de Barbaroux* (Paris, 1866), 524.

7. Suzanne D'Huart, *Brissot: La Girond au Pouvoir* (Paris: Éditions Robert Laffort, 1986), 234.

8. Brissot, *Mémoires* 1, 170.

9. Ellery, 22.

10. Robert Darnton, "The Grub Street Style of Revolution: J.-P. Brissot, Police Spy," *The Journal of Modern History* (Sept. 1968): 318.

11. Robert Darnton, "The Brissot Dossier," *French Historical Studies* (Spring, 1991): 196, 201-4.

12. See: Frederick A. de Luna, "The Dean Street Style of Revolution: J.-P. Brissot, Jeune Philosophe," *French Historical Studies* (Spring 1991); and *id.*, "Of Poor Devils and 'Low Intellectual History,'" *French Historical Studies* (Spring 1991).

13. Leigh Whaley, *Radicals: Politics and Republicanism in the French Revolution* (London: Sutton Publishing, 2000), 15, 35.

14. Ellery, 162.

15. See Leonore Loft, *Passion, Politics, and Philosophie: Rediscovering J.-P. Brissot* (Westport, CT: Greenwood Press, 2002), for excellent summaries of Brissot's philosophical works.

16. Brissot, *Memoires* 1, 238.

17. See: Loft, 11-13; Darton, "The Brissot Dossier," 201-4.

18. Darnton, *Ibid.*, 204.

19. Daniel Resnick, "The *Société des Amis des Noirs* and the Abolition of Slavery," *French Historical Studies* (Autumn, 1972): 563.

20. Not surprisingly, Brissot commits an entire chapter of his *New Travels in the United States* to the debt, concluding that "from this picture of the debt and the finances of the United States, you can see, my friend, that the greatest hopes are justified, that order, simplification, and economy are being practiced everywhere, and the only thing the Americans now need in order to acquire completely sound fiscal credit is more confidence in their own strength and more courage to . . . balance their budget." J.-P. Brissot, *New Travels in the United States* (Cambridge, MA: Belknap Press, 1964), 388.

21. *Ibid.*, 212.

22. Resnick, 562.

23. Ellery, 116.

24. *Ibid.*, 161.

25. Whaley, 31.

26. *Ibid.*, 40; Ellery, 174.

27. J.-P. Brissot, *Discours sur les causes des troubles de Saint-Domingue* (Paris: Imprimerie Nationale, 1791), 40.

28. Ellery, 202.

29. Brissot, *Discours . . . Saint-Domingue*, 15.

30. Charles Tarbé, *Réplique à J.-P. Brissot, sur les troubles de Saint-Domingue* (Paris, 1791), 18.

31. Goetz-Bernstein, 276.

32. J.-P. Brissot, *Discours sur les dispositions des Puissances étrangeres, relativement à la France, et sur les préparatifs de guerre ordonnés par le Roi* (Paris: Imprimerie Nationale, 1791), 10-28.

33. J.-P. Brissot, *Discours sur la nécessité d'exiger une satisfaction de l'Empereur, et de romper le Traité du premier Mai 1756* (Paris: Imprimerie Nationale, 1792), 5-17.

34. Georges Lefebvre, *The French Revolution* 1, (New York: Colombia University Press, 1962), 219.

35. J.-P. Brissot, *Discours contre M. Delessart, Ministre des affaires étrangères* (Paris: Imprimerie Nationale, 1792), 17-35.

36. Sisney Seymour Biro, *The German Policy of Revolutionary France: A Study in French Diplomacy during the War of the First Coalition, 1792-1797* (Cambridge, MA: Harvard University Press, 1957), 52.

37. J.-P. Brissot, *Discours sur la denunciation contre le comité Autrichien, et contra M. Montmorin, ci-devant Ministre de Affaires Étrangères* (Paris: Imprimerie Nationale, 1792), 2-12.

38. Goetz-Bernstein, 215.

39. Brissot, *Discours . . . le Traité du premier Mai 1756*, 25.

40. Goetz-Bernstein, 201.

41. *Ibid.*, 204.

42. Biro, 74.

43. Whaley, 86.

44. See Whaley, vii-x.

45. See Benjamin Reilly, "Polling the Opinions: A Reexamination of Mountain, Plain, and Gironde in the National Convention," *French History* (Spring 2004): 53-73.

46. Ellery, 303.

47. Biro, 84.

48. Goetz-Bernstein, 295.

49. *Archives Parlementaires* 53, 503-5.

50. J.-P. Brissot, *Discours sur le procès de Louis* (Paris: Imprimerie Nationale, 1793), 5.

51. Brissot to Sevran, 26 November 1792, in J.-P. Brissot, *Correspondance et Papiers* (Paris, 1912), 313.

52. Goetz-Bernstein, 326.

53. *Ibid.*, 331.

54. Brissot to Sevran, *op cit.*

55. *Ibid.*, 312.

56. Brissot to Lebrun, 15 December 1792, in Brissot, *Correspondance et Papiers*, 300. See also, Goetz-Bernstein, 293.

57. Brissot, *Discours sur le procès de Louis*, 2-3, 7.

58. *Archives Parlementaires* 57, 19-21.

59. *Moniteur Universale*, no. 33, p. 331.

60. *Ibid.*, p. 332.

61. Goetz-Bernstein, 395.

62. Biro, 62.

63. See: Goetz-Bernstein, 364-65; T. C. W. Blanning, *The Origins of the French Revolutionary Wars* (New York: Longman, 1986), 146-47, 152-53.

64. Blanning, 153.

65. *Ouvres de Maximilian Robespierre* 7, Marc Bouloiseau, Albert Soboul, and Georges Lefebvre, eds. (Paris: Presses Universitaires de France, 1950), 81.

66. Goetz-Bernstein, 325-26.

67. Blanning, 111.

68. *Moniteur Universale*, no. 33, p. 332.

69. Goetz-Bernstein, 302.

70. Linda Frey and Marsha Frey, "'The Reign of the Charlatans is Over': The French Revolutionary Attack on Diplomatic Practice," *Journal of Modern History* (Dec. 1993): 716.

71. *Archives Parlementaires* 53, 504.

72. *Ibid.* 57, 20.

73. Frey and Frey, 720-21.

74. *Ouvres de Maximilian Robespierre* 7, 80-81.

75. Camille Desmoulins, "Jean-Pierre Brissot Démasqué," 45.

76. Goetz-Bernstein, 331.

77. *Ibid.*, 328

78. Gordon S. Wood, "Conspiracy and the Paranoid Style: Causality and Deceit in the Eighteenth Century," *William and Mary Quarterly* (July 1982): 416.

79. François Furet, *Penser la Révolution française* (Paris: Gallimard, 1978), 69.

80. *Ibid.,* 110.

81. Hunt, 41.

82. Susan Dunn, *Sister Revolutions: French Lightning, American Light* (New York: Faber and Faber, 1999), 87.

83. Timothy Tackett, "Conspiracy Obsession in a Time of Revolution: French Elites and the Origins of the Terror, 1789-1792," *American Historical Review* (June 2000): 711.

84. Benjamin Reilly, "Ideology on Trial: Testing a Theory of Revolutionary Political Culture," *French History* (March 2005): 36.

85. *Ibid.*

86. Goetz-Bernstein, 158.

87. On the topic of the revolutionary elite's pre-revolutionary political influences, see Norman Hampson, *Will and Circumstance: Montesquieu, Rousseau, and the French Revolution* (Norman: University of Oklahoma Press, 1983).

215

Byron:
A Poetic Revolutionary in the Century of Words

Jonathan Gross
DePaul University

Poets, not legislators, control our perception of history. Shelley noted this in "Ozymandias" and in his justly famous essay, *Defense of Poetry*. Poets, he wrote, were the unacknowledged legislators of the world. Raymond Williams, commenting on this passage, noted that the emphasis was on the word "unacknowledged."[1] Like Williams, Byron would have denied Shelley's claim that art was so efficacious. "Acts—acts on the part of the government, and *not* the writings against them, have caused the past convulsions, and are tending to the future," he wrote in a note to *The Two Foscari*. "I look upon such as inevitable, though no revolutionist . . . But that a revolution is inevitable, I repeat."[2] The French Revolution occurred not because of the power of poetry, Byron added, but because "the government exacted too much and the people could neither give nor bear more."[3] Though he disowned the title of revolutionary (like many other labels placed on him), the dissemination of his picture, paintings of him, and translations of his poetry made his ideas far more widely understood and admired than the policies enacted by foreign ministers such as Prince Clemens von Metternich or Robert Stewart, Lord Castlereagh.

Byron's poetry and political thought, often in its most controversial aspects, inspired Pushkin, Lermontov, Berlioz, Delacroix, and Turner. One drop of ink could change the minds of millions, Byron noted (*CPW* 5: 3: 793) Reluctantly, Prince Clemens von Metternich agreed. "Public opinion is one of the most powerful weapons, which like religion, penetrates the most hidden corners where administrative measures lose their influence," Metternich wrote in 1808. "To despise public opinion is like despising moral principles . . . Public opinion requires a cult all its own . . . Posterity will hardly believe that we regarded silence as an effective weapon in this, the century of words."[4] Henry Kissinger, however, who wrote his doctoral dissertation on Metternich and Castlereagh, defended the need for silence among conservative thinkers. "Conservatism in a revolutionary situation must fight revolution anonymously," Kissinger wrote, "by what it is, not by what it says."[5]

While Henry Kissinger dismissed all political revolutionaries as "insatiable" in their demands—ahistorically linking Prometheus, Napoleon, Hitler, and Mao Zedong (while ignoring Thomas Jefferson, Patrick Henry, and George Washington),[6] Byron made the case for revolution "as inevitable" in compelling ways. In 1823, he defended George Washington as "a watchword, such as ne'er / Shall sink while there's an echo left to air" (*CPW* 7: 250). "America is a Model of force and freedom & moderation—with all the coarseness and rudeness of it's people," he wrote to Hobhouse (Oct. 12, 1821; 8: 240). Though rarely taken seriously as a thinker, even by fellow writers like Goethe and Emerson, Byron has much to teach a new century that has seen "legitimate" states defeat revolutionary powers through détente, arms escalation, congress diplomacy, and post-cold war interventionism (1992-2005).

Byron's revolutionary thought would not have been possible without his travels abroad. The poem that made Byron famous, *Childe Harold's Pilgrimage*, opened with an epigraph from *Le Cosmopolite*, addressing the importance of seeing other countries: "Je haissais ma patrie. Toutes les impertinences des peuples divers, parmi lesquels j'ai vecu, m'ont reconcilie avec elle. Quand je n'auarais tire d'autre benefice de mes voyages que celui-la, je n'en regretterais ni les frais ni les fatigies" (*CPW* 2: 3). If Monbron's hero became reconciled to his own country by traveling in others, Byron's hero had the opposite response: He saw the limits of English foreign policy all the more clearly as a result of traveling abroad. Childe Harold was an exile from England, one whose discomfort with his homeland was both personal and political. If Harold was a revolutionary, he was, like Camus's exiles, existential: His struggle with his country was like his struggle with his God.

For two years, Byron visited Spain, Portugal, and Italy, but the countries that had the most important influence on him were Albania, Greece, and Turkey. While abroad, he witnessed the effects of the Peninsular War on the continent, noting how English foreign policy looked in action. Surveying the destruction caused by a foreign policy that gave away at the negotiating table what had been won on the battlefield, Byron became skeptical about the game of international politics. He noted how brave soldiers became the dupes of men like Castlereagh, whose performances at the Convention of Cintra and then the Walcheren Expedition were so disastrous that the former led to a public outcry (Wordsworth wrote a poem on the subject) and the latter to a duel with George Canning.[7] For Byron, Wellington was merely the "best of cutthroats" (*CPW* 5: 9: 25)—an all-too-effective tool of Castlereagh's misguided foreign policy. In his journey to Spain and Portugal, catalogued in *Childe Harold's Pilgrimage*, Byron saw the wishes of the people betrayed by corrupt kings and court intrigue. He celebrated the "Maid of Saragossa," by contrast, a woman who operated a cannon after her husband was killed (*CPW* 2: 1: 573), giving meaning to his death. He urged Spanish men to be worthy of such women. By personalizing his politics, Byron made revolutionary causes seem human, extending his argument to Greece and Rome. "Fair Greece! Sad relic of departed worth," he wrote. Both Greece and Rome were once great civilizations that had become enslaved by the intrigues of cabinet diplomacy. Byron, however, saw their failures in human terms, as failures of nerve. "Who would be free themselves must strike the blow," he wrote (*CPW* 2: 721). His historical erudition allowed him to see the map of Europe in revolutionary terms: Continually, he measured present debasement against past achievements. In *Don Juan* (1819) and subsequent cantos of *Childe Harold's Pilgrimage* (published in 1816 and 1818, respectively), he dreamed that Greece could be free, for "I could not deem myself a slave" (*DJ, CPW* 5: 3: 86: 706).

Such sentiments struck a chord even as early as 1812, when Byron returned from his travels to publish the first two cantos of *Childe Harold's Pilgrimage*. England was in a protracted war with France, interrupted only by a series of treaties that seemed to show no meaningful correlation to the battles fought. William Pitt had died by 1805, along with Lord Nelson. In place of such heroic figures were a series of political temporizers—Addington (1801-2); the Ministry of all the Talents (1805-6)—followed by a prime minister, Perceval, so unpopular he was shot in the street. Friends betrayed friends: The Prince Regent courted the Whigs for three decades only to retain George III's ministers when he assumed temporary powers. As Byron put it in a poem to Lady Melbourne on Sept. 21, 1813: "'Tis said indifference marks the present time, what matters who is in or out of place, the bad, the useless—or the base."[8] Byron confessed that his brief career in the House of Lords was attenuated by the very "indifference" that he bemoaned in others. "I had been sent for in great haste to a Ball which I quitted I confess somewhat reluctantly to emancipate five Millions of people" (9: 28). The cause of Catholic emancipation, the "five Millions" Byron alluded to in his diary, had stalled at home because of George III's commitment to a Protestant ascendancy (Pitt resigned over George III's intransigence on this issue in 1801). Political reform had made no progress, and England was fighting a reactionary war against a man (Napoleon) who claimed to be on the side of progress, extending (however misguidedly) the "ideals" of the French Revolution by overthrowing monarchical power. Napoleon betrayed the French Revolution, but he was the next best thing for poets (Leigh Hunt, Percy Shelley, and Byron) who found their work censored by reactionary regimes at home and abroad.

The age in which Byron lived saw an explosion of print culture: Individuals fought for the right to represent themselves. Poems, plays, and novels were not only a branch of the fine arts, but a wing of social action. A mere glance at the titles of Byron's work indicates how historical events inspired his muse. Byron wrote on the Peninsular War, on *Sardanapalus* (the Assyrian King), on the Doge Marino Faliero—most of his plays were allegories intended to comment on political events in England. To turn to the second stanza of *Don Juan* is to recognize how well-read this poet was in the newspaper culture of his time, how often he interpreted the present through the lens of the past:

> Vernon, the butcher Cumberland, Wolfe, Hawke,
> Prince Ferdinand, Granby, Burgoyne, Keppel, Howe,
> Evil and good, have had their tithe of talk,
> And fill'd their sign-posts, then, like Wellesley now;
> Each in their turn like Banquo's monarchs stalk,
> Followers of fame, "nine farrow" of that sow:
> France, too, had Buonaparte and Dumourier
> Recorded in the Moniteur and Courier. (*CPW* 5: 1: 2).

As his final triple rhyme suggests, Byron was as interested in how newspapers represented heroism, as he was in heroic deeds themselves. By writing newspaper verse, and publishing his "Ode to Napoleon" in the *Morning Courier*, Byron became an historian himself, shaping the impression of Napoleon that we have received.

Conservative statesmen who had to contend with Napoleon were contemptuous of fictional representations of the man. "I am a man of prose, and not of poetry," Metternich wrote. "My point of departure is the quiet contemplation of the affairs of this world, not those of the other of which I know nothing and which are the object of faith which is in strict opposition to knowledge."[9] Metternich left it to Byron to compare Napoleon, unfavorably, to Cincinnatus or George Washington. "In the social world," Metternich wrote, "one must act cold-bloodedly based on observation and without hatred or prejudice . . . I was born to make history not to write novels."[10]

Metternich's opposition between fact and fiction, however, was too stark, for no one was more critical of Napoleon than Byron:

> And Earth hath spilt her blood for him,
> Who thus can hoard his own!
> And Monarchs bow'd the trembling limb,
> And thank'd him for a throne!
> Fair Freedom! We may hold thee dear,
> When thus thy mightiest foes their fear
> In humblest guise have shown.
> Oh! Ne'er may tyrant leave behind
> A brighter name to lure mankind!

> Thine evil deeds are writ in gore,
> Nor written thus in vain—
> Thy triumphs tell of fame no more,
> Or deepen every stain:
> If thou hadst died as honour dies,
> Some new Napoleon might arise,
> To shame the world again—
> But who would soar the solar height,
> To set in such a starless night? (*CPW* 5: 1: 2).

By hoarding his own blood, Napoleon proved himself a coward, supplicating his enemies for his life. Byron measured Napoleon against Roman, Spanish, and other heroes and re-labeled the man he once admired a "throneless homicide."

Henry Kissinger saw Prometheus as Aeschylus painted him: A failed revolutionary appropriately punished. The romantics had a different interpretation: "Thy godlike crime was to be kind," Byron noted in his poem entitled, "Prometheus." Goethe wrote a similar effusion in 1771 and Shelley described Prometheus as "the type of the highest perfection of moral and intellectual nature, impelled by the purest and the truest motives to the best and noblest ends."[11] Kissinger's reading of the Prometheus legend, which can be found in the "Fires of Prometheus" chapter of *Nuclear Weapons and Foreign Policy*, allows him to warn Americans that thermonuclear war was inevitable if they did not follow the containment policies of Castlereagh.[12] Unlike Prometheus, who, in Kissinger's curious misreading, was prevented from stealing the fire of the Gods, "our generation has succeeded in stealing the fire of the gods and it is doomed to live with the horror of its achievement." For the discovery of atomic weapons recalls the logic of Nemesis: That history punishes man by fulfilling his wishes too completely.

If Prometheus was a failed revolutionary in Kissinger's book (or a revolutionary who exemplified the blessings of failure), Napoleon was a failed Prometheus in Byron's view, one who chose to capitulate rather than suffer. After comparing Napoleon to Cato and other figures, Byron saved the most damning comparison for last.

> Or like the thief of fire from heaven,
> Wilt thou withstand the shock?
> And share with him, the unforgiven,
> His vulture and his rock!
> Foredoomed by God—by man accurst,
> And that last act, though not thy worst,
> The very Fiend's arch mock;
> He in his fall preserv'd his pride
> And if a mortal, had as proudly died! (*CPW* 3: 259)

For the romantics, if not for Kissinger, Prometheus was a hero precisely because he was a thief. If only Napoleon had stolen democracy from divinely ordained monarchs, just as Prometheus stole fire from the gods. In Byron's poem, however, Napoleon is not revolutionary enough.

Byron's "Ode to Napoleon Bonaparte" was written at a moment of pique after the battle of Waterloo. His renunciation of Napoleon, however, must be seen in the context of a wider admiration. Edward Tangye Lean, in *The Napoleonists*, suggests that the absence of a father figure, or a father who could not be rebelled against (as in the case of Hazlitt), led several English intellectuals to identify with the French ruler no matter how despotic he became.[13] Whatever his motives, Byron defended Napoleon's bust as a fifteen-year-old schoolboy. At Harrow, he followed his career closely in his letters and journals of 1813 (even mentioning him, repeatedly, in letters to his prospective wife). He rode in a carriage modeled on Napoleon's when he left England in 1816; approved of Napoleon's lack of *bonhomie* in a letter to Hobhouse ("How should he, who knows mankind well, do other than despise and abhor them?" he wrote); and in *Childe Harold III:* "twas wise to feel, not so / To wear it ever on thy lip and brow" (*CPW* 2: 3: 40). After his mother-in-law's death in 1822, he styled himself "Noel Byron," or just NB, the initials he had come to share with Napoleon. In *Don Juan* he called himself "the grand Napoleon of the realms of rhyme" (*CPW* 5: 11: 55).

The nature of Byron's appreciation of Napoleon is perhaps best shown in a letter in which he compared himself to a dandy (Beau Brummell), a gambler (Scrope Davies), and a radical orator (Hobhouse). "Brummell—at *Calais*—Scrope at Bruges—Bonaparte at St. Helena—and you in—your new apartments—and I at Ravenna—only think so many great men! there has been nothing like it since Themistocles at Magnesia—and Marius at Carthage" (March 3, 1820; 10: 50). Kissinger called Castlereagh and Metternich "great," but Byon defined this quality somewhat differently. He would rather have been Brummell than Bonaparte, according to one account, as if the two were equally significant.[14] For a serious revolutionary, the equation of Brummell and Bonaparte would seem absurd—an instance of Byronic perversity—if the connection had not been explained by Albert Camus. Camus saw dandyism as a social act of defiance: "La rebellion humaine finit en revolution metaphysique. Elle marche du paraitre au faire, du dandy au revolutionnaire." The French dandy moved from parodying revolution to making it.[15] Perhaps Byron found Brummell's revolution less destructive of human life than Napoleon's.

In any case, Byron was pleased to see himself competing with Napoleon for space in the newspapers: If Brummell would effect a revolution in dress, and Napoleon in deeds, Byron would lead one in words. When eight lines of his "Lines to a Lady Weeping" were reprinted (Feb. 11, 1814; 4: 53), he boasted of the event in a letter to Lady Melbourne: "Did you ever know any thing like this? at a time when peace & war—& Emperors & Napoleons—and the destinies of the things they have made of mankind are trembling in the balance—the Government Gazettes can devote half their attention & columns day after day to 8 lines written two years ago—& now republished only—(by an Individual) & suggest them for the consideration of Parliament probably about the same period with the treaty of Peace.—I really begin to think myself a most important personage" (Feb. 11, 1814; 4: 53).[16] Later Byron noted that "Buonaparte's recent advantage has usurped the column generally devoted to the cause of a personage who, however unimportant, appears to be very obnoxious" (Feb. 14, 1814; 4: 60). Though he pretended to be appalled by the equal space given to a poet and a politician, Byron recognized that he bore some resemblance to Napoleon. Most of his references to the French general refer to Napoleon as if he were an alter ego. "I can't help suspecting that my little Pagod will play them some trick still," he informed Lady Melbourne, "if Wellington or one hero had beaten another—it would be nothing—but to be worried by brutes—& conquered by recruiting sergeants—why there is not a *character* amongst them" (April 8, 1814; 4: 90). Later he noted that he wanted his books "if only to lend them to Napoleon in the 'island of Elba' during his retirement" (April 9, 1818; 4: 91).

Like Napoleon, Byron attracted the attention of the press because he was a "character." The fall of Napoleon seemed to coincide with the rise of Byron. "Oh—by the by, I had nearly forgot," he told Thomas Moore as nonchalantly as possible, on the same day that he wrote to Murray:

> There is a long Poem, an "Anti-Byron," coming out, to prove that I have formed a conspiracy to overthrow, by *rhyme*, all religion and government, and have already made great progress. I never felt myself important, till I saw and heard of my being such a little Voltaire as to induce such a production. Murray would not publish it, for which he was a fool, and so I told him. (April 9, 1814; 4: 93)

Like Byron, whose amoral work inspired an "Anti-Byron," Napoleon would affect a moral "revolution" by challenging the doctrine of divine right to the throne (Jan. 12, 1814; 4: 27).

When Napolen abdicated, Byron wondered whether his hero was worthy of him. "Ah! my poor little pagod, Napoleon, has walked off his pedestal," he wrote, continuing his April 9, 1814 letter to Moore:

> He has abdicated, they say. This would draw molten brass from the eyes of Zatanai. What! "kiss the ground before young Malcolm's feet, and then be baited by the rabble's curse!" I cannot bear such a crouching catastrophe. I must stick to Sylla, for my modern favorites

222

don't do,—their resignations are of a different kind. (April 9, 1814; 4: 93)

Eleven days later, Byron regretted the fall of Napoleon and the loss of the spirit of individualism he represented. "Buonaparte has fallen," he wrote to Annabella, "I regret it—the restoration of the despicable Bourbons—the triumph of tameness over talent—and the utter wreck of a mind which I thought superior even to Fortune—it has utterly confounded and baffled me—and unfolded more than 'was dreamt of in my philosophy'" (April 20, 1814; 4: 101). The allusion to *Hamlet* is telling, for Byron saw himself as a man of thought, and Napoleon as a man of action.

In this same letter to Annabella, Byron portrayed England's conflict with Napoleon as a struggle between mediocre kings with legitimate titles and a talented general without one. "Every hope of a republic is over," he wrote to Thomas Moore, "and we must go on under the old system. But I am sick at heart of politics and slaughters; and the luck which Providence is pleased to lavish on Lord ** (Castlereagh) is only a proof of the little value the gods set upon prosperity, when they permit such **s as he and that drunken corporal, old Blucher, to bully their betters" (July 7, 1815; 4: 302).

While Byron viewed Castlereagh as untalented, Henry Kissinger's portrait of Castlereagh was far more positive. "It was this man, more than any other," Kissinger wrote, "who forged again a European connection for Britain, who maintained the Coalition, and negotiated the settlement which in its main outlines was to last for over fifty years. Psychologists may well ponder how it came about that this Irish peer, whose career had given no indication of profound conceptions, should become the most European of British statesmen."[17] The very inhuman qualities of Castlereagh that so disturbed Byron and Shelley became points of praise for Kissinger. "Icy and reserved, Castlereagh walked his solitary path, as humanly unapproachable as his policy came to be incomprehensible to the majority of his countrymen." Though Kissinger's portrait recalled, however superficially, Shelley's "I met Murder on the way / He had a face like Castlereagh—Very smooth he looked, yet grim,"[18] Kissinger challenged the romantic view of Castlereagh as misguided. "It was said of him that he was like a splendid summit of polished frost, icy, beautiful, aloof, of a stature that nobody could reach and few would care to. It was not until his tragic death that the world was to learn the price of solitude."[19] Byron viewed Castlereagh as a reactionary opponent of revolution; Kissinger saw him as the architect of the longest peace Europe had known in two centuries. To come to terms with Byron and Kissinger's differing assessments of Castlereagh's career sheds light on the revolutionary character of Byron's political thought, and might also show why Byron's revolutionary politics was so appealing to his contemporaries.

Byron's view of Lord Castlereagh was perhaps most apparent in his introduction to Canto 6 of *Don Juan*. There Byron described Castlereagh as "the most despotic in intention, and the weakest in intellect, that ever tyrannized over a country. It is the first time indeed since the Normans that England has been insulted by a *minister* (at least) who could not speak English, and that parliament permitted itself to be dictated to in the language of Mrs. Malaprop." As Byron was writing his poem, England's leading statesman committed suicide rather than be exposed (or blackmailed, we are not sure which) as a homosexual.[20] Byron suggested that this was no reason to overlook the effects of his policies:

> Of the manner of his death little need be said, except that if a poor radical, such as Waddington or Watson, had cut his throat, he would have been buried in a cross road, with the usual appurtenances of the stake and mallet. But the minister was an elegant lunatic—a sentimental suicide—he merely cut the carotid artery, (blessings on their learning!) and lo! The pageant, and the Abbey! And "the syllables of dolour yelled forth" by the newspapers. (*CPW* 5: 6)

For Byron, no greater proof of the destructive qualities of Castlereagh's foreign policy could be shown than the manner of Castlereagh's death.[21] "It may at least serve as some consolation to the nations, that their oppressors are not happy," he wrote. "—Let us hear no more of this man; and let Ireland remove the ashes of her Grattan from the sanctuary of Westminster. Shall the patriot of humanity repose by the Werther of politics!!!" By linking Castlereagh to the hero of Goethe's novel, *The Sorrows of Young Werther,* Byron suggested that there was something emotionally immature about Castlereagh, as if (like Werther himself) he had never quite grown up. By calling him the "Werther of politics," Byron implied that Castlereagh's policies were destructive not only for himself but for England.

The tone of this passionate introduction to Canto 6—angry yet rational, *ad hominem* yet principled, accusatory yet insightful—exemplifies the kind of politics of feeling Byron employed throughout his writing. In tone and attitude, it recalls the suppressed dedication to *Don Juan,* in which Byron referred to Castlereagh as "an intellectual eunuch." A great admirer of Milton, Byron wondered if the seventeenth-century English poet, also a Calvinist (like Byron), would "adore a sultan? . . . obey / the Intellectual eunuch Castlereagh?" At first, Byron's phrase would seem to be a mere *ad hominem* attack. In his reference to Bob Southey as a "dry bob" and Wordsworth as a balding poet (*CPW* 5: "Dedication," 1), however, Byron clearly meant to link the private and the public. No sooner did he say that the public had nothing to do with Castlereagh's private life, than he alluded to it, suggesting that a lack of sexual direction marked Castlereagh's political self-betrayals; these self-betrayals ended in his suicide to escape accusations of homosexuality. Unlike Charles James Fox—a libertine in public and private life—William Pitt and Lord Castlereagh struggled to live exemplary private lives, resembling the monarch they served, George III.

While George III displayed a bigoted intolerance toward Catholics, he was beloved by his countrymen for his private virtues. Byron doubted whether such a distinction were possible. Byron felt that the private lives of George III and Castlereagh were unfairly used to justify their disastrous public policies. By contrast, Byron wrote that "[M]y politics are to me like a young mistress to an old man[:] the worse they grow the fonder I become of them" (Jan. 22, 1814; 4: 37). A closer look at Castlereagh's private character, Byron argued, revealed a desexualized political figure, more sinister (because inhuman) than the married and decorous man the public thought they knew:

> Cold-blooded, smooth-faced, placid miscreant!
> Dabbling its sleek young hands in Erin's gore,
> And thus for wider carnage taught to pant,
> Transferr'd to gorge upon a sister shore,
> The vulgarest tool that Tyranny could want,
> With just enough of talent, and no more,
> To lengthen fetters by another fix'd
> And offer poison long already mix'd. (*CPW* 5: "Dedication," 12)

For Byron, Castlereagh's role in suppressing the Irish rebellion of 1798 was particularly egregious. Half-Irish himself, Castlereagh betrayed his own people for his political advancement. It was not only his policies, however, that Byron objected to, it was his use of language:

> An orator of such set trash of phrase
> Ineffably—legitimately vile,
> That even its grossest flatterers dare not praise,
> Nor foes—all nations—condescend to smile;
> Not even a sprightly blunder's spark can blaze
> From that Ixion grindstone's ceaseless toil,
> That turns and turns to give the world a notion
> Of endless torments and perpetual motion. (*CPW* 5: "Dedication," 13)

Ixion was condemned to grind a stone for eternity for seducing Zeus's wife, although Zeus had also seduced Ixion's. Castlereagh's punishment, like Ixion's, exemplified the moral hypocrisy of the legal system he worked to uphold. Merely following a king's orders and maintaining "legitimate sovereigns" was morally myopic.

To complete his portrait of Castlereagh, Byron elaborated on his reference to the eunuch-like qualities Castlereagh possessed, employing the pronoun "its" rather than "he" or "she" to underscore his point that he carried out the policies of others and did not "procreate" his own:

> A bungler even in its disgusting trade,
> And botching, patching, leaving still behind
> Something of which its masters are afraid,
> States to be curb'd, and thoughts to be confined,
> Conspiracy or Congress to be made—
> Cobbling at manacles for all mankind—
> A tinkering slave-maker, who mends old chains,
> With God and man's abhorrence for its gains.
> If we may judge of matter by the mind.
> Emasculated to the marrow it hath,
> But two objects, how to serve, and bind,
> Deeming the chain it wears even men may fit,
> Eutropius of its many masters, —blind
> To worth as freedom, wisdom as to wit,
> Fearless—because *no* feeling dwells in ice,
> Its very courage stagnates to a vice. (*CPW* 5: "Dedication," 14)

This image of Castlereagh as a eunuch, guarding a harem, reemerged in Canto 5, when Byron gave Castlereagh a cameo appearance as the character Baba, thus underscoring Byron's comparison between English and Turkish forms of despotism.

In the stanzas above, Byron drew on his reader's knowledge of Dante's *Inferno* (Canto 34), where Satan appeared in the bottom-most ring of hell, surrounded by ice.[22] Castlereagh's foreign policy was a direct result of his "cold" demeanor, his inability (like Satan) to feel for others (even his own Irish countrymen). Metternich would defend the cold-blooded rationalism of his statecraft. Byron and Shelley saw such behavior as morally bankrupt. Having left England in 1816, Byron understood how England's foreign policy affected Italy. Byron had fought with the Italian Carbonari. England sacrificed Italian freedom to the bonds of Austrian legitimacy, annexing Northern Italy to Austrian rule to maintain peace. He faulted Castlereagh for such a policy:

> Where shall I turn me not to *view* its bonds,
> For I will never *feel* them;—Italy!
> Thy late reviving Roman soul desponds
> Beneath the lie this State-thing breathed o'er thee—
> Thy clanking chain, and Erin's yet green wounds,
> Have voices, -tongues to cry aloud for me.

> Europe has slaves, allies, kings, armies still,
> And Southey lives to sing them very ill. (*CPW* 5: "Dedication," 16)

Byron returned to his theme that bad politics creates bad poetry: "Southey lives to sing them very ill"; Southey was as mediocre a poet as Castlereagh was a foreign minister. Castlereagh's outdated foreign policy resembled the character of Mrs. Malaprop from Sheridan's "Rivals," whose misuse of the English language created the humor of that drama.

Unlike Kissinger, who praised legitimacy and legitimate orders, Byron described Castlereagh as "ineffably—legitimately vile" ("Dedication," 98). He did not hesitate to use the word "legitimate" sarcastically throughout *Don Juan*: "But oh, thou grand legitimate Alexander," he wrote in Canto 6 (*CPW* 5: 6: 1737). "No harm unto a right legitimate head," he observed two cantos later (*CPW* 5: 6: 79). In Canto 9, the Duke of Wellington was praised for having "repair'd Legitimacy's crutch," but the praise was, again, sarcastic. For Byron, legitimacy had "born votaries," mediocrities who stood to gain by supporting established powers (*CPW* 5: 5: 1023), no matter how incompetent (George III) or corrupt (Louis XVI).

Henry Kissinger noted that a legitimate power "is one that accepts international agreements; it implies the acceptance of the framework of the international order by all major powers."[23] A "revolutionary" power, by contrast, was "by definition a power that cannot be satisfied . . . The distinguishing feature of a revolutionary power is not that it feels threatened . . . *but that nothing can reassure it.*"[24] If legitimacy was the only recipe for world peace, revolutionary figures posed an untenable danger. They were dangerous because the governments that they build cannot last. In Metternich's view, "Revolution was an assertion of will and of power," Kissinger wrote, "but the essence of existence was proportion, its expression was law, and its mechanism was equilibrium."[25] The conflict between Napoleon and Metternich, genius and mediocrity, was recast by Kissinger as one between the man of will and the man of reason. "Napoleon and I spent years together," Metternich wrote in 1820, "as if at a game of chess, carefully watching each other; I to checkmate him, he to crush me together with the chess figures."[26] Kissinger's study unmasked the danger of revolutionaries, noting how idealism in politics has led to mass slaughter.

Byron saw matters rather differently. It was unfeeling diplomats, abusing the English language (and other languages)—it was the metaphysical condition of man himself—that accounted for most of the misery and wars that had been fought. Byron explored the quest for "fame" that led soldiers into battle, and the disillusionment that inevitably resulted. In a number of his poems and plays, especially the unjustly neglected "The Deformed Transformed," Byron portrayed revolutionaries as dyspeptic personalities whose private idiosyncrasies affected

227

their public conduct. Marino Faliero's impatience, Don Juan's "mobility," Arnold's "hunchback," and Childe Harold's brooding personality inevitably precipitated their involvement in world events. Where Kissinger saw world events run by "great" rational men who distrust popular opinion,[27] Byron saw that the irrational urges and child-like motives of "the great" made war inevitable.

Kissinger presented the world as a series of binary oppositions— revolutionary and legitimate, for example—rarely noting how one's own position *vis-à-vis* these terms could affect the definition that emerged. To the Soviet Union, American capitalism threatened to control Western Europe. Soviet Communism, Kissinger argued, was equally intent on expansion. This oppositional thinking, unmasked in Edward Said's *Orientalism*, continues today, with commentators representing the contrast with Iraq as one between the *Lexus and the Olive Tree*.[28] Instead, Byron, who had actually lived in the Ottoman Empire, noted shades of gray, of difference. He thought virtue was rather on the side of the Turks, who believed in the god they worshipped, rather than merely paying lip service to religion, as he criticized the English for doing in the latter cantos of *Don Juan* ("You are *not* a moral people and you know it," he wrote, "Without the aid of too sincere a poet" [11: 688]).

Though there were many travel books besides Byron's, most, like Monbron's *Le Cosmopolite*, left the person preferring their own country to those he or she visited. Robert Southey's *Letters from England*, for example, portrayed Portugal in a pejorative manner, mocked Jews in England for their loud services and for having no concept of an afterlife, and indulged in jingoistic observations about foreign countries.[29] Byron could be cynical about Jewish financiers in "The Age of Bronze," but his poetry betrayed a pluralism (in *Hebrew Melodies,* for example) that was rarely found in his contemporaries, such as Southey. Byron's *Childe Harold's Pilgrimage*, like *Don Juan*, was a travel narrative in a different sense.

What made Byron revolutionary for his age, then, was his ability to see history from two points of view. Keats referred to this as negative capability, and thought Shakespeare exemplified it most effectively. For Byron, it meant recognizing both Spanish cowardice and Spanish heroism; Greek abasement and Greek potential; Italian triviality and Italian spirit; Jewish stubbornness ("Believe the Jews, those unbelievers, who / Must be believed though they believe not you" [*CPW* 5: 5: 62: 495]), and Jewish sublimity. Byron thought of himself as a kind of coach for exiles and émigrés, accepting a gift of matzos from Isaac Nathan before he left England, and championing revolutionary movements in Portugal, Spain, and Greece. He supported and stockpiled weapons for the Italian Carbonari.[30] In 1823, at the age of 35, Byron sailed for the liberation of Greece with a war chest of 200,000 *piastres*—"twice as much as Napoleon had for the liberation of Italy," he noted in his journal.[31] He was the Kleist of poets (Dec. 27, 1823; 11: 85).

228

As an intellectual revolutionary, however, he was also intent on reinterpreting the historical record. Here is one example:

> Oh Wellington! (Or "Vilainton", for Fame
> Sounds the heroic syllables both ways.
> France could not even conquer your great name,
> But punned it down to this facetious phrase—
> Beating or beaten she will laugh the same.)
> You have obtained great pensions and much praise;
> Glory like yours should any dare gainsay,
> Humanity would rise and thunder "Nay!"   (*CPW* 5: 9: 1)

A hero to England, Wellington was a "villain" to the French. A close look at his exploits makes one wonder whether he deserved a monument and a pension (Byron's poem is full of poets and politicians who do not deserve the public salaries they received). In this stanza, Byron's poem allowed him to say and unsay his praise for Wellington. The homonym on "Nay" recalled General "Ney" who, because of his failure to join Napoleon at the proper time, caused Napoleon to lose the Battle of Waterloo. As if to prove Byron's point, Byron's publisher misspelled "Ney" as "Nay." Byron's dislike of Wellington dated from the Peninsular War, when he felt that the Irish general was over-praised for his contributions at the Battle of Talavera (July 1809).

As a revolutionary, Byron was particularly suspicious of newspapers and the accuracy of the print culture in which he participated. He questioned whether newspaper notices were worth the self-sacrifice of dying for one's country. "I wonder (although Mars no doubt's a god I / Praise) if a man's name in a *bulletin* / May make up for a *bullet in* his body?" (7: 21). Later in the poem, the narrator recounts the fate of one man, who died in battle and found his name "printed Grove, although his name was Grose" (*CPW* 5: 8: 18: 144). Misspellings were only one instance of the general misrepresentation of valor.[32] In describing the siege of Ismail, which was an account of Russia's effort to conquer a Turkish stronghold, Byron underscored how a journalist's (or poetic narrator's) nationalist sympathies could color the historical record:

> Then there were Frenchmen, gallant, young and gay,
> But I'm too great a patriot to record
> Their Gallic names upon a glorious day.
> I'd rather tell ten lies than say a word
> Of truth. Such truths are treason; they betray
> Their country, and as traitors are abhorred
> Who name the French in English, save to show
> How peace should make John Bull the Frenchman's foe. (*CPW* 5: 7:
> 22: 169-234)

Any glance at English and French histories of Napoleon supports Byron's assertion about how nationalist bias affected historiography. If French bravery was difficult to record for this English historian, Russian names (at the level of pronunciation) were even worse, which was one reason why they might not be transmitted to posterity:

> The Russians now were ready to attack.
> But oh, ye goddesses of war and glory!
> How shall I spell the name of each Cossack—
> Who were immortal, could one tell their story?
> Alas, what to their memory can lack?
> Achilles' self was not more grim and gory
> Than thousands of this new and polished nation,
> Whose names want nothing but—pronunciation.
>
> Still I'll record a few, if but to increase
> Our euphony. (*CPW* 5: 7: 14: 105-12)

Pronunciation, it turns out, governs matters great and small. Don Juan, the Spanish hero, was pronounced Don "Jew-one" by the English, thus giving his identity a different inflection. Similarly, the historian who endorsed Wellington's heroism (saying "Nay" to "ney-sayers") unconsciously articulated the name of the very man who deserved Wellington's honors (General Ney). Similarly, Wellington was "Vilainton" according to a popular French song. Pronunciation, like rhyme, has the anarchic effect of exposing truths and concealing them. Thus Byron's narrator's great gift, and perhaps his curse, was that he could speak many languages, so that his poem became a "tower of Babel (babble)." The poet's cosmopolitan perspective, its self-ironizing moments, made his poem revolutionary because it was indeterminate. Even cosmopolitanism, however, became problematic in this revolutionary poem. The more Byron's narrator tried to praise the heroes of foreign countries, for example, the more he showed how difficult it was to do so, without sounding ridiculous:

> There were Strongenoff and Stokonof,
> Meknop, Serge Lwow, Arseniew, of modern Greece,
> And Tschitsshakoff and Roguenoff and Chokenoff
> And others of twelve consonants apiece.
> And more might be found out, if I could poke enough
> Into gazettes; but Fame (capricious strumpet),
> It seems, has got an ear as well as trumpet.
>
> And cannot tune those discords of narration,
> Which may be names at Moscow, into rhyme. (*CPW* 5: 7: 15-16, 114-22)

230

The English language literally makes the enunciation of Russian heroism an impossible feat ("there were several worth commemoration . . . ending in ischskin, ousckin, iffskchy, ouski, / Of whom we can insert but Rousamouski" [7: 16-17]).

Later in the poem, the narrator comments on the ways in which soldiers find their actions left out of history books:

> "If" (says the historian here) "I could report
> All that the Russians did upon this day,
> I think that several volumes would fall short,
> And I should still have many things to say";
> And so he says no more, but pays his court
> To some distinguished strangers in that fray:
> The Prince de Ligne and Langeron and Damas,
> Names great as any that the role of Fame has.
>
> This being the case may show us what fame is.
> For out of these three preux chevaliers, how
> Many of common readers give a guess
> That such existed? And they may live now
> For aught we know. Renown's all hit or miss;
> There's fortune even in fame, we must allow. (*CPW* 5: 7: 32-33:249-64)

Byron's bisexuality, as I have argued elsewhere,[33] may well have led him to question standards of heterosexual normality, even as it affected newspaper accounts of Castlereagh's suicide or Wellington's valor/villainy. The sense that there was one way of reading history, and not a secret history, was something he abhorred. Such a belief came from an overweening nationalism, which, like any bigotry, could only be cured by traveling.

In many of his poems and plays, Byron celebrated the eccentric individual (*Marino Faliero, Sardanapalus*) whose seemingly irrational behavior exposed a great truth about the hypocrisy of the society in which he lived. In Italy, it meant that Byron took an interest in Marino Faliero's rebellion against his own social class, which demonstrated the impotence of the Venetian oligarchy (and, by implication, of the Whig lords back in England); Sardanapalus' refusal to engage in wars of conquest exposed Napoleon and Louis XVI's low estimate of the value of their citizens' lives. Byron recognized the perversity of his own political position. "Born an aristocrat, what have I to gain from a revolution?" he asked in his appendix to *The Two Foscari*. At the same time, he understood that the "King-times were fast finishing," as he put it in a diary entry (Jan. 13, 1821), and he saw no merit in propping up outdated political systems. Byron was not a fervent political progressive, a meliorist like Shelley. His Calvinism influenced his belief that political systems could never make man happy. Poverty was misery all over the earth, he noted, and democracy was a mere "aristocracy of blackguards."[34] Nevertheless, he would have disagreed, profoundly, with Kissinger's notion that a revolutionary was one whose political claims could never be satisfied. Byron, like modern theorists of nation-states, saw incompetent governments and the aggressive actions of debt ridden nations as the cause of war—not the idealistic projects of revolutionaries. In this he had the implicit agreement of Thomas Jefferson, who viewed balancing the government's debt as the most important way of avoiding foreign wars. Pitt's notorious "sinking fund" made wars of conquest possible; debt, which could finance and mobilize armies, enabled politicians to rev up the war machine. Pitt received no compensation for "ruining Great Britain gratis," Byron quipped (*CPW* 5: 9: 8:).[35] By starving the government of cash, Jefferson hoped to clip the wings of those with dreams of foreign conquest.

Jefferson, an astute diplomat who served as ambassador to France before the outbreak of the French Revolution and negotiated the Louisiana Purchase, was nowhere to be found in Kissinger's 800-page study; George Washington merited only 3 pages. Jefferson, however, like Byron, understood the role passion played in politics. He had a more complex understanding of the human dimension to politics than Kissinger, who saw war and peace (unlike Tolstoy) as historical events best managed by tacticians, the triumph of the head over the heart. "If our country, when pressed with wrongs at the point of the bayonet, had been governed by its heads instead of its hearts, where should we have been now?" Jefferson asked. "Hanging on a gallows as high as Haman's. You began to calculate, and to compare wealth and numbers: we threw up a few pulsations of our blood; we supplied enthusiasm against wealth and numbers; we put our existence to the hazard, when the hazard seemed against us, and we saved our country" (375).

Thomas Jefferson, James Monroe, and James Livingston were perhaps America's most successful foreign diplomats because they could take advantage of geopolitical opportunities without losing sight of American values. They did not engage in "collaboration," a policy Kissinger praised in Metternich. Instead, Byron found in Americans, like Daniel Boone, a symbol of self-reliance and re-invention. Boone had fought with George Washington, "Whose every battle-field is holy ground" (*CPW* 5: 8: 5) in the French and Indian War. Byron honored the Americans enough to board the USS Constitution in 1821 as the guest of Commodore Jacob Jones. He noted that "The Yankees are individually great friends of mine. I wish to be well thought of on the other side of the Atlantic," where over 150,000 copies of his works had been sold by 1840. Toward this end, he presented a copy of his works to Joseph Coolidge, Thomas Jefferson's future son-in-law.[36]

Castlereagh, by contrast, became a nemesis to Byron because his successful diplomatic career advanced by virtue of English "cant," a quality Byron complained about in his two letters on the merits of Alexander Pope's poetry (The Pope-Bowles controversy). The same opponents who branded Jefferson, Priestley, and Paine atheists, called Byron by the

> hackneyed and lavished title of Blasphemer—which, with Radical, Liberal,
> Jacobin, Reformer, &c. are the changes which the hirelings are daily ringing in
> the ears of those who will listen—should be welcome to all who recollect on
> whom it was originally bestowed. Socrates and Jesus Christ were put to death
> publicly as *blasphemers*, and so have been and may be many who dare to oppose
> the most notorious abuses of the name of God and the mind of man. (*CPW* 5: 297)

The true blasphemers, Byron argued, were men like Robert Southey, who thought they understood the topography of heaven and those who belonged there (*CPW* 6: 223). Byron's poems, "Prometheus" and "The Prisoner of Chillon," showed how patient endurance of wrongs was the true sign of heroism. Paine, like Byron's prisoner of Chillon, cooled his heels in a French jail by the order of Robespierre himself, until Jefferson granted him safe passage back to the United States in a naval frigate. Jefferson himself was so taunted by New England Federalists and Connecticut Congregationalists for his atheism that he constructed his own bible to prove his piety, and to show, as Byron did in "Cain," the nature of his rational brand of Christianity. "Mr. Southey accuses us [Shelley and Byron] of attacking the religion of the country, and is he abetting it by writing lives of *Wesley*?" Byron asked. "One mode of worship is merely destroyed by another . . . The church of England, if overthrown, will be swept away by the sectarians and not by the skeptics. People are too wise, too well informed, too certain of their own immense importance in the realms of space, ever to submit to the impiety of doubt" (*CPW* 6: 224). With regard to Castlereagh, (and in his preface to Canto 6 of *Don Juan*), Byron argued that:

> persecution is not refutation, nor even triumph: the "wretched infidel," as he is called, is probably happier in his prison than the proudest of his assailants. With his opinions I have nothing to do—they may be right or wrong—but he has suffered for them, and that very suffering for conscience's sake will make more proselytes to deism than the example of heterodox prelates to Christianity, suicide statesmen to

oppression or overpensioned homicides to the impious alliance which
insults the world with the name "Holy"! (*CPW* 5: 297)

For Byron it was impossible not to link the private morality that would condemn
Shelley as an atheist, Hunt as a libeler, and Don Juan as a blasphemer to the
statecraft of Czar Alexander's Holy Alliance, which used a false notion of
sanctimonious piety to justify taking away the freedom of Muslims:

> I have no wish to trample on the dishonoured or the dead; but it
> would be well if the adherents to the classes from whence those
> persons sprung should abate a little of the *cant* which is the crying
> sin of this double-dealing and false-speaking time of selfish spoilers,
> and—but enough for the present.
>
> Pisa, July, 1822. (*CPW* 5: 297)

"Cant" was a key term for Byron, as important as "revolutionary" was for
Kissinger. By "cant," Byron meant words unattached to deeds. "Cant" prevailed
at state funerals. Castlereagh's funeral provided one example; George III's
another.

In "The Vision of Judgment," Byron contrasted Southey's political vision
with his own. Paid by George III as his poet laureate, R. Southey wrote an
unctuous poem, "A Vision of Judgment," praising the English king and admitting
him into heaven. "There is something at once ludicrous and blasphemous in this
arrogant scribbler of all work sitting down to deal damnation and destruction
upon his fellow creatures," Byron wrote, "with Wat Tyler, the Apotheosis of
George the Third, and the Elegy on Martin the regicide, all shuffled together in
his writing desk" (225). Byron responded to Southey's poem, in a note to *The
Two Foscari,* because the poet laureate had accused Byron and Shelley of being
involved in a "league of incest," along with other unflattering insinuations,
referring to them as members of the "Satanic School of Poetry."[37] Not content
with this "appendix" to his play, Byron wrote a whole poem refuting Southey's
charge and mocking him in the process. Byron's revolutionary reaction was to
redefine heaven as a place where God and Mephistopheles debated about souls
and the actions of statesmen, rather than merely judging them *ex cathedra.* George
Washington, Benjamin Franklin, and Horne Tooke were to be called as witnesses
against George III, in Byron's humorous account. Southey's poem was entitled,
"A Vision of Judgment": Byron corrected Southey's vision by making it more
definitive ("the" rather than "a"). He argues that George III, "although no tyrant,
[was] one / Who shielded tyrants": A better farmer ne'er brush'd dew from
lawn, / A worse king never left a realm undone!" His funeral became an exercise
in moral hypocrisy:

> Of all
> The fools who flock'd to swell or see the show,
> Who cared about the corpse? The funeral
> Made the attraction, and the black the woe.
> There throbb'd not there a thought which pierced the pall;
> And when the gorgeous coffin was laid low,
> It seem'd the mockery of hell to fold
> The rottenness of eighty years in gold. (*CPW* 6: 237)

For George III: "The funeral / Made the attraction, and the black the woe."

Byron's comments on Castlereagh's death—that a gaudy celebration of a person's death can obscure the bad deeds they did in their life—prefigured Hazlitt's description of Byron's death in Missolonghi, Greece. Hazlitt had contributed to The *Liberal*, a journal Byron edited with Leigh Hunt (1821). Like Matthew Arnold, William Hazlitt admired Byron's attack on English "cant" and hypocrisy. Hazlitt, however, was very critical of Byron's aristocratic hauteur and what he called his "preposterous liberalism." He wrote a definitive essay comparing him, disparagingly, with Walter Scott, in a chapter of his important volume, *The Spirit of the Age*. When news of Byron's death reached England, Hazlitt chose not to revise his essay but to leave it as it stood. "We were not silent during the author's life-time, either for his reproof or encouragement (such as we could give, and he did not disdain to accept) nor can we now turn undertakers' men to fix the glittering plate upon his coffin, or fall into the procession of popular woe" (Hazlitt, *Spirit of the Age*).[38] Hazlitt recognized, as Byron had observed of Castelreagh and George III, that a man's funeral or place of burial could not change the meaning of his life.

Public opinion belongs to posterity, so, in the end, it did not matter whether Byron was buried in Westminster Abbey or at Newstead, though a public furor ultimately prevented Byron's burial in the same church as Castlereagh. "The poet's cemetery is the human mind, in which he sows the seeds of never-ending thought," Hazlitt wrote, movingly, "—his monument is to be found in his works. Lord Byron is dead: he also died a martyr to his zeal in the cause of freedom, for the last, best hopes of man. Let that be his excuse and his epitaph!" Unlike a king, Byron did not need "public opinion" on his side. He would be judged by "the seeds of never-ending thought," which cannot (like a poet laureate's words) be bought. Though he never wished to be a mere scribbler, and did not think of himself as a revolutionary, Byron's verse and revolutionary views triumphed in what Metternich perceptively called "the century of words."[39]

Notes

1. "Defense of Poetry," *Shelley's Poetry and Prose*, Neil Fraistat and Donald Reiman, eds. (New York: Norton, 2001), 271-93; Raymond Williams, *Keywords: A Vocabulary of Culture and Society* (New York: Oxford University Press, 1985), 35.

2. *Byron's Letters and Journals* 6, Leslie Marchand, ed. (Cambridge: Harvard Belknap, 1972), 223. (Hereafter referred to as *BLJ* [vol.], [page number].)

3. *Byron: The Complete Poetical Works* 5, Jerome McGann, ed. (Oxford: Oxford University Press, 1985-91), canto 6, line 223. (Hereafter referred to as *CPW* [vol.]: [canto]: [line].)

4. Henry Kissinger, *A World Restored* (Boston: Houghton Mifflin, 1962), 16-17.

5. *Ibid.*, 9.

6. Henry Kissinger, *Nuclear Weapons and Foreign Policy* (Garden City: Doubleday, 1958), 65-85, 322-24.

7. Byron called Canning a "genius" (*CPW* 5: 719); see also *BLJ* 10, 83. It is worth mentioning here that (*contra* Kissinger) Henry Adams, *The History of the United States of America during the Administrations of Jefferson and Madison*, abridged ed., Ernest Samuels, ed. (Chicago: University of Chicago Press, 1967), 163-64, lists Talleyrand's diplomacy (at least in America) as a failure and notes Godoy's talents.

8. 'Tis said— *Indifference* marks the present time,
   Then hear the reason—though 'tis told in rhyme—
   A King who *can't*—a Prince of Wales who *don't*—
   Patriots who *shan't*, and Ministers who *won't*—
   What matters who are *in* or *out* of place
   The *Mad*—the *Bad*—the *Useless*—or the *Base*?
   Sept. 21, 13; 3: 117.

9. Kissinger, *A World Restored*, 10.

10. *Ibid.*, 10.

11. "Preface" to *Prometheus Unbound*, in *Shelley's Poetry and Prose*, 270.

12. Kissinger, *Nuclear Weapons*, 65.

13. Tangean Lean, *The Napoleonists* (Oxford: Oxford University Press, 1970), 70-89.

14. Carlo Maria Franzero, *Beau Brummell: His Life and Times* (New York: John Day Company, 1958), 68. "I liked the Dandies—they were always very civil to *me*" (9: 22). Byron also affected the impudent wit of Brummell, whom he quoted in his journals as stating that the two plagiarized each others' *bon mots* (9: 22).

15. Ellen Moers, *The Dandy from Brumell to Beerbohm* (New York: Viking, 1960), 230.

16. What made the poem so effective ("Lines to a Lady Weeping") in 1812, but especially in 1814 when it was republished, was its tendency to personalize politics. Politics "with me is a feeling," Byron wrote (Feb. 11, 1814; 4: 38), and this feeling was best exemplified by the poem he wrote to humanize the Prince Regent's betrayal of his Whig friends.

Weep daughter of a royal
line,
A Sire's disgrace, a realm's
decay;'
Ah, happy! If each tear of
thine
Could wash a father's fault
away!

Weep for thy tears are
Virtue's tears
Auspicious   to   these
suffering isles;
And be each drop in future
years
Repaid thee by they people's
smiles. *(CPW* 3: 10)

17. Kissinger, *A World Restored*, 34.
18. Shelley, "Masque of Anarchy," in *Shelley's Poetry and Prose*, 234.
19. Kissinger, *op cit.*, 30.
20. Louis Crompton, *Byron and Greek Love* (London: GMP, 1998), 302-6. "Accusations of homosexuality seem to have played a significant part in the events leading to his death" (p. 303). Crompton refers to "the calm, almost inhuman, imperturbability of his public demeanor" (p. 300).
21. No such allowances were made for Byron or Shelley, the former of whom was considered insane by his own wife and yet denied from seeing his child by Lord Eldon; for some, madness was no defense.
22. Dante Alighieri, *La Divina Commedia*, Fredi Chiappelli, ed. (Milan: Mursia, 1965): 34: 181.
23. Kissinger, *A World Restored*, 2.
24. *Ibid.,* 2.
25. *Ibid.,* 10.
26. *Ibid.,* 26.
27. *Ibid.,* 5. "That Europe rescued stability from seeming chaos was primarily the result of the work of two great men: of Castlereagh, the British Foreign secretary, who negotiated the international settlement, and of Austria's minister, Metternich, who legitimized it."
28. Edward Said, *Orientalism* (New York: Vintage, 1978), 46-48; Thomas L. Friedman, *The Lexus and the Olive Tree: Understanding Globalization* (New York: Farrar Straus & Giroux, 1999). Even Salon.com jumps on the band wagon in their review of 1999. There is hardly a page in the book without an "underlineable" passage. For example: "In the Cold War, the most frequently asked question was: 'How big is your missile?' In globalization, the most frequently asked question is: 'How fast is your modem?'" It is hard to believe that such grand questions pass for analysis or that an editorialist, so ethnocentric, writes for the *New York Times.*

29. Robert Southey, *Letters from England* (Oxford: Oxford University Press, 1951), 392-98.

30. "In the mean time, my lower apartments are full of their bayonets, fusils, cartridges, and what not," he wrote. "I suppose that they consider me as a depot, to be sacrificed, in case of accidents. It is no great matter, supposing that Italy could be liberated, who or what is sacrificed. It is a grand object—the very *poetry* of politics. Only think a free Italy!!!" (Feb. 18, 1821; 8: 47).

31. Lean, 89.

32. Alistair Horne, *How Far to Austerlitz?: Napoleon 1805-1815* (New York: St. Martin's, 1996); Alan Schom, *Napoleon* (New York: Harpercollins, 1998).

33. *Byron: The Erotic Liberal* (Baltimore: Rowman & Littlefield, 2001).

34. "It is still more difficult to say which form of Government is the *worst*—all are so bad. As for democracy, it is the worst of the whole; for what is (*in fact*) democracy? an Aristocracy of Blackguards" (October 21, 1821, 7: 231).

35. Adams, 50.

36. Peter Accardo, "Byron in Nineteenth-Century American Culture," Catalogue of an exhibition organized by the Houghton Library, Harvard University, for the 27th International Byron Society Conference, August-October 2001 (Newark: Byron Society of America, 2001), 22.

37. "A Vision of Judgment," *The Poetical Works of Robert Southey, Complete in One Volume* (London: Longman, Brown, Green, and Longmans, 1844). "The school which they have set up may properly be called the Satanic school; for though their productions breathe the spirit of Belial in their lascivious parts, and the spirit of Moloch in those loathsome images of atrocities and horrors which they delight to represent, they are more especially characterized by a Satanic spirit of pride and audacious impiety, which still betray the wretched feeling of hopelessness wherewith it is allied" (p. 769).

38. "Lord Byron," in *The Complete Works of William Hazlitt,* P.P. Howe, ed. (after the edition of A.R. Waller and Arnold Glover) (Toronto: J.M. Dent and Sons, 1930-34).

39. Kissinger, A *World Restored,* 9.

Alexander Pushkin, the Decembrists, and Russian Freemasonry

Lauren G. Leighton
University of Illinois at Chicago

Masonry in Russia has been troubled by a history of ups and downs. Beginning in the 1730s and reaching a peak in the 1760s and 1770s, when Russians were armed with patents and charters from European obediences, lodges were opened from the Baltic through Siberia.[1] Practical and speculative Masonry flourished without discrimination, to the point that the Enlightenment thinkers organized around the poet and publicist Nikolai Novikov were so carried away by esoteric knowledge that they are known as the Moscow Mystical Masons.[2] These believers gladly mortgaged their estates to purchase, study, and translate rare documents whose revelations of powerful secrets they coveted.[3] Not the least felicitous result of their devotion is that Russian archives have recently been acknowledged to be among the richest holders of esoteric documents.[4] Masonry was not a passing Russian fancy: Pioneering scholarship in the 1970s and 1980s revealed an eighteenth-century literature steeped in Masonic symbolism.[5]

This vital Masonic culture came to an abrupt halt in 1794 when Catherine II banned the craft. The ban was continued by Paul I, but in 1803 Alexander I encouraged the reopening of the lodges and in 1809 gave official approval. In 1815, the Grand Directorial Lodge, first constituted in the 1760s, began work again under the strict Swedish system. By this time, however, the Free and Accepted rites prevailed in Europe; tolerance, reform, and reason were the new order. The Russians followed suit by founding a new Grand Lodge of Astraea, authorized to work in accordance with the ancient English system. By 1820, Astraea was dominant with twenty-five lodges in its obedience.[6] Unhappily, by this time Alexander was under the sway of mystic religionists who convinced him that Masonry was a threat, and in 1822 he ordered the lodges closed again. In 1826, following Alexander's death and the failure of the uprising of noblemen known as the Revolt of 14 December 1825, Nicholas I reaffirmed the order. Masonry ceased to assert active influence on Russian culture for the remainder of the nineteenth century. Those Masons who remained faithful were obliged to work in silence.

Attempts have recently been made to document a continuing nineteenth-century movement, but, for the most part, evidence was adduced in bits and pieces and unconvincingly argued.[7] The only apparent Masons in the later century were collectors of manuscripts, and we owe them an immeasurable debt for preserving many of the documents that enriched the Moscow archives. It is not clear, however, by what authority they signed themselves as Masons except that they belonged to leading eighteenth- and early nineteenth-century Masonic families.[8] In the early twentieth century, Masonry became an active ingredient of the Modernist movement. Not unexpectedly, extravagant avant-garde poets and artists were attracted to speculative Masonry and esotericism, especially occultism.[9] Between 1906 and 1909, lodges were opened by Masons with political interests, in particular Anglophile liberals of the Cadet Party (Constitutional Democrats) in the short-lived *duma* (parliament).[10] The Cadets and other activists have been accused of causing the February Revolution of 1917 and implementing British foreign policy under the influence of English Masons, thereby creating the conditions that enabled the Bolsheviks to take power in October. Some Cadets and members of the provisional government were educated at Oxbridge and initiated into the craft there, but most historians do not take the "February Revolution conspiracy" accusations seriously.[11]

After 1917, Russian Masonry flourished in the first wave of the emigration, especially in Paris under the obediences of the Grand Orient Française and the Grand Loge National Française. Many prominent cultural figures of the emigration were drawn to Masonry, and this interest did not wane when the lodges were reopened after the Nazi occupation and the craft attracted the postwar, second-wave émigrés. The early émigré Masons have also been accused of conspiratorial adventurism leading to the success of the October Revolution, but these claims, too, seem larger than available evidence suggests.[12] It would seem inconceivable that Masonry survived after 1917 in the Soviet Union. Thanks to recent Russian research, this possibility must be seriously considered. Documents in the archives of the OGPU (predecessor of the KGB) show that "occult Masonry" experienced a "renaissance" in the 1920s, and, in the 1930s, a United Brotherhood of Labor ("Red Masons") offered its services to Stalin (and was accordingly liquidated).[13] These were not necessarily authorized Masonic organizations, but they show that the Russian attraction to Masonry remained a viable historical factor after the Bolsheviks came to power.

Russians have been remarkably serious Masons. The hopes that they placed in Masonic ideals were exceptional. Someday social scientists will have to research the reasons for this strong dedication. That the attraction was real was demonstrated again in the 1970s when émigrés of the third wave rushed to be initiated into the craft and founded lodges of their own in Europe, North America, and Israel. After the Soviet Union fell in 1991, Russians again rushed to the craft. In 1990, contact was established between the Grand Orient Francaise and Russians in Moscow, and, in 1991, the first five Russians were initiated in a ceremony outside of Moscow. Several lodges were opened under the obedience of the Grand Orient in 1991-92, but in 1992 they went over to the Grand Loge National Française. A Grand Lodge of Russia was constituted by the Grand Loge on 24 June 1995, and its obedience on the entire territory of the Russian Federation has been recognized by over seventy grand lodges. By the late the 1990s, its original five working lodges had become twelve (including the A.S. Pushkin lodge in Moscow). At least one Moscow lodge works in English; lodges in Moscow and Petersburg have welcomed foreign brothers; at least one foreign lodge has been opened in Moscow; and the Grand Lodge has connections with American and other Masons. The number of lodges now working under other auspices and the number of new Masons are not known, but lodges are at work in orients all the way to Vladivostok. Lodges have been opened in other former Soviet republics, including Armenia and the three Baltic countries, and Ukrainians have proved to be as attracted as Russians.[14]

The new Russian Masons seem to have been attracted for three basic reasons. First, many new lodges are said to be gathering places for new rich Russians interested in developing business contacts with each other and foreign businessmen. Second, many find the craft and its symbolism intellectually engaging, while others are responsive to the Masonic idea of achieving moral and spiritual perfection through degrees of study.[15] A third category of new Masons comprises enthusiasts who are attracted to ceremony and a hope that secret knowledge will be revealed to them. Serious Masons and true believers carried away by esotericism together characterize a fourth category, namely those who write about Masonry. It is not possible to distinguish Masonic scholars from those who have not been initiated, but the devotion of unsophisticated writers is often undisguised.

In modern Russia anti-Masonry is virulent. According to V.F. Ivanov, in a work first published in China in 1934 and recently republished with significant effect in Moscow, the history of Russian Masonry is synonymous with the history of the entire intelligentsia. Masons caused every crime against the Russian people, its beloved autocracy, and its Orthodox Church from the time of Peter the Great to 1917 and later. In the world at large, "atheistic," "internationalist" Masons were behind every "catastrophe," from the Reformation and Humanism to the American and French Revolutions, to the principle of separation of church and state to the founding of a super-state intended to subordinate all countries to the League of Nations.[16] Russians are suspicious of Masonry not because they have had experience of it—the Masonic movements that flourished in the past never became mass social phenomena—but because the havoc wrought on their consciousness by the too swift revelations of *glasnost* and later disoriented even stable, sophisticated persons. Fear and hatred seem to have been instilled in the 1970s-80s, when the Communist Party mounted a propaganda campaign against Masonry as a major foreign threat to Soviet institutions.[17] As a result, many Russians easily believed accusations during *glasnost* that, for example, Gorbachev made so many concessions to the West because he was controlled by his "Masonic Masters," Reagan and Bush. The main cause of hatred, however, was the ubiquitous *Protocols of the Elders of Zion*. The infamous document was first circulated in the Tsarist empire by the secret police (*Okhrana*). The final version of the *Protocols* was written over a period of time by secret police agents, religious fanatics, and far-right charlatans connected to the court of Nicholas II. It was disseminated again during the Civil War in the 1920s by extremist White Guards, who had no difficulty adding "Bolsheviks" to the "International Jewish-Masonic Conspiracy."[18] Little wonder, then, that, during *glasnost*, the *Protocols* were again used as a propaganda weapon by Russian nationalists, fascists, and others to indoctrinate those who sought simple answers against the evils of "foreign," "cosmopolitan," and, inevitably, "Zionist-Masonic" enemies of the Russian people.

We are too close in time to fully understand the chaotic period of the rise and fall of democracy after the demise of the Soviet Union in 1990, but, so far as Masonry is concerned, the movement seems to have come to a head in the year 1999, which was devoted to the 200th anniversary of the birth of Russia's great national poet, Aleksandr Pushkin. Until recently, very little was known about Pushkin as a freemason because in the Soviet period study of the subject was forbidden. What we do know was first established in the 1960s and 1970s by American Russianists. Their work was met with great skepticism but, beginning with *glasnost*, Russian Pushkinists began to appreciate the role of Masonic symbolism in Pushkin's works. In a very short time, they successfully broadened the inventory of his Masonic works beyond what had been established abroad. In the 1990s, they were joined by amateurs who found in Pushkin either the greatest Mason who ever lived or a victim of Masonic conspirators. During his anniversary year, Pushkin became, in effect, a microcosm of the revival of Masonry in Russia in our time. A study of attitudes toward Pushkin as a Mason, with attention to efforts by Russian and Western scholars to introduce scholarly objectivity into the question, reveals the character of the Masonic revival presently underway in Russia.

The sheer bulk of recent research on Masonry in Russia is remarkable. Where study of Masonic culture was limited under both tsars and Soviets, and ignored or dismissed by many Western Russianists, it is now a major source of new knowledge.[19] So far as Pushkin is at issue, we now know that he was surrounded throughout his life by Masonic influences.[20] His father and his uncle, the poet V.L. Pushkin, were Masons. His neoclassical education at the Lyceum of Tsarskoe

242

selo was based on the Masonic principles of Enlighteners who designed the curriculum there. Most of the eighteenth-century Russian poets who shaped his early reception of literature were serious Masons who developed Masonic symbolism in their works. Many of his fellow writers in the Romantic period were Masons whose commitment ranged from serious, to simple enjoyment of banquets, to hope for social advancement (as treated, for example, by Tolstoy in *War and Peace*). Two strong influences on his generation—the sentimentalist writer and national historian, N.M. Karamzin, and the early Romantic poet, Vasilii Zhukovskii—disapproved of ceremony at the expense of active observance of moral principles. But Iu. M. Lotman has shown that Karamzin ceased his lodge work under the influence of Wieland, Klopstock, Lessing, Flesser, and other Masons who, during his tour of Europe, convinced him that Masonry should be practiced without ceremony by a "secret union of sages"—poets who by their art raised the general level of culture and education. In Lotman's view, the "brotherhood of poets" who, in the 1810s, formed a Society of Arzamas—and admitted young Pushkin to membership—was not only a gathering of funsters who parodied, among other sanctities, Masonic ceremonialism, but also a group who practiced Masonry in the service of mankind.[21]

Despite all we have learned about Pushkin as a Mason, the evidence in recorded words is scant. In his diary kept during state service in Kishinev, Bessarabia, he noted that, on 4 May 1821, "I was initiated by the Masons." In a letter to Zhukovskii, dated January 1826, responding to the older poet's inquiries on behalf of Nicholas I after the failure of the Revolt of 14 December 1825, he confessed that: "I was a Mason in the Kish[inev] lodge [of Ovid], that is, in the one because of which all the lodges in Russia were destroyed. Lastly, I had connections with the greater part of the present conspirators."[22] So far as the latter item is concerned, Pushkin perhaps exaggerated a bit—the activity of a lodge in a remote area of the Russian Empire was hardly the reason for the ban on all Masonry. As for his initiation, it is possible that he was attracted to Ovid by interesting people there, including the political oppositionist General M.F. Orlov, the radical poet Vladimir Raevskii, and the Decembrist leader Pavel Pestel'. The Masons listed there, however, were, for the most part, local officials and merchants, whereas the truly interesting people in Kishinev—at that time a hotbed of anti-tsarist sentiment and enthusiasm for the Greek Revolution—were in the early Decembrist Union of Welfare led by Orlov.[23] For that matter, the Lodge of Ovid was not recognized by the Grand Lodge of Astraea until at least 7 July 1821, two months after Pushkin's initiation, and perhaps not even formally admitted by the time that the lodges were closed in August 1822. We do not know whether Pushkin ever worked beyond the apprentice degree, and it is not likely he could have earned elevation before leaving Kishinev in December 1821.[24] He might possibly have participated in forbidden Masonic meetings in the late 1820s-30s, perhaps in foreign embassies but, as of this time, we have no evidence that he worked as a Mason after leaving Kishinev.

Fortunately, we know considerably more about Pushkin as a Mason from his literary works, specifically from discovery and verification of Masonic symbolism and other phenomena derived by analysis of his texts. The inventory of Masonry in the works of Aleksandr Pushkin has been established by the German Russianist, Markus Wolf, and by the head of the Pushkin Cabinet of the Institute of Russian Literature in Petersburg, Sergei Fomichev.[25] To this inventory, M.D. Filin has added an almost convincing argument for encoded (hidden) Masonic symbolism in "Message to Siberia" ("*Poslanie v Sibir'*," 1826)—Pushkin's expression of solidarity with exiled Decembrist comrades.[26] The first evidence of Masonry in his works was established by Professor Harry Weber in an article on the prose tale, "The Queen of Spades" ("*Pikovaia dama*," 1833), as a parody of the Masonic rite of initiation. The main protagonist Germann's confrontation with the old countess in quest of a "secret of the three cards," which will enable him to make his fortune at Faro, is shown to follow the pattern of the rite. The accoutrement of the countess's Petersburg mansion was a virtual description of a Masonic lodge (objects, decor, arrangement of furniture) and the tale had numerous discreet references to and links with Masonic symbolism.[27]

Weber's work was ratified by Leighton, who, in a series of articles revised as chapters of my monograph on the esoteric tradition in Russia, deciphered the tale's numerological system, decoded significant cryptograms based on the Cabala system, known as *gematria*, elaborated other textual elements, and traced Pushkin's knowledge of these skills to Masonic sources.[28] Work in this direction was continued by two German Pushkinists, Schmid and Nerre.[29] Masonic elements in the works of Pushkin (and others) often turn out to be so obvious as to cause wonder that they were not noticed previously. This was certainly the case with Weber's discovery of Pushkin's parody of the rite of initiation in "The Queen of Spades." Germann pleaded for the secret of the three cards in the pattern of the initiate's plea for the master of the lodge to reveal the secrets of the order, and he even verbalized the Masonic formula by begging on bended knee "in the name of my children, grandchildren, and great-grandchildren." Such was also the case with Nerre's discovery that Pushkin opened his prose tale, "The Coffin-Maker" ("*Grobovshchik*," 1830) with a clever hint at the Masonic virtue of love of death—at the gate of the coffin-maker's establishment a "plump Cupid" carried an inverted torch, the symbol of death—and thereafter developed Masonic symbolism in other ways.[30]

Wolf and Fomichev list a combined maximum of fifteen works in which Masonry was relevant. Among these was the Little Tragedy, "Mozart and Salieri" ("*Motsart i Sal'eri*," 1830). Pushkin was drawn to the legend that Mozart was poisoned by Salieri, and in this work he treated it as true. His Salieri had dedicated

244

his life to study and mastery of music. Music required reverent devotion. The frivolous Mozart was unworthy of music—his talent combined with disrespect was a threat to art. Over a bottle of wine, Mozart demonstrated both his lack of respect and the ease with which he created, and thereby sealed his fate. When he left after becoming ill from the poison administered by Salieri, the latter pondered a bitter irony: Perhaps it was true that a creative genius could not commit murder? (In Pushkin's words: "Genius and evil are two incompatible things.") Pushkin had been called a Russian Mozart, and he shared with Mozart a common dilemma, namely that he was the creative—and frivolous—genius of his time who overshadowed his contemporaries. This biographical subtext of "Mozart and Salieri," and Pushkin's belief that creative power was a gift to be developed and not something to be acquired by either devotion or study, were the meaning of the Little Tragedy. Masonry did not play a role, but was relevant to Pushkin's interest in the other legend of Mozart, namely that he was murdered by Masons incensed over his irreverent treatment of the craft and betrayal of its secrets in *The Magic Flute.* Much has been made of this awareness as proof that Pushkin was disturbed by the idea that Masons murdered those who betrayed their oath by revealing the secrets of the craft.[31]

Most of Pushkin's works in which Masonry figures are lyric poems addressed to Masons or based in some way on Masonic meaning. One of his poems, "The Prophet" ("*Prorok,*" 1826), has attracted special attention among those presently interested in Pushkin as a Mason and borne the weight of evidence either of the poet's dedication to the craft or his fate as a victim of Masonic vengeance. The poem is sufficiently important to require a reading here:

> My spirit, thirsting, wandered lost
> The grim and barren desert sand,
> And where two ancient pathways crossed
> I saw a six-winged Seraph stand;
> With touch as light as sleep or sighs
> His fingers brushed my burning eyes;
> And I beheld strange visions ablaze,
> As if with startled eagle's gaze.
> He gently touched my stricken ears—
> And roused the sounds of distant spheres:
> I heard the trembling heavens weep.
> The monsters moving through the deep.
> The flights of angels in the skies,
> The sap in valley vineyards rise.
> Then bending to my mouth he ripped
> The sinful tongue from out my lips
> And all its vain and cunning talk;
> And on the mute and lifeless stalk

245

A serpent's wise and double tongue
With right hand steeped in blood he flung.
With sword he clove my breast in two,
And he my beating heart withdrew
And thrust inside the gaping hole
A flaming shard of living coal.
I lay like death upon the sand
And heard the Voice of God command:
"Arise, O prophet! Do My Will;
Go speak what you have seen and heard,
On sea and land thy task fulfill:
To burn men's hearts with Heaven's Word."[32]

"The Prophet" is Pushkin's adaptation of Isaiah's vision and commission from God (Isaiah. 6:1-10). The poet, like the prophet, stood in the desert and contemplated the biblical choice between two ancient pathways. There he experienced a vision similar to Isaiah's, who saw God upon a throne and the seraphims, each with six wings: Then said I, Woe *is* me! For I am undone; because I *am* a man of unclean lips . . . for mine eyes have seen the King, the Lord of hosts . . . Then flew one of the seraphims unto me, having a live coal in his hand, *which* he had taken with the tongs from the altar . . . And he laid *it* upon my mouth, and said, Lo, this hath touched thy lips; and thine iniquity is taken away, and thy sin purged." The lyric is not a simple repeat of Isaiah. Pushkin's prophet is not an Isaiah, commissioned by God to preach vainly to a people doomed by their iniquity, both he and they to hear but not comprehend, to see but perceive not. He is a poet commanded to become a prophet, to be both maker and seer at once. A spirit athirst, pathways, a vision and commission, a six-winged seraphim, a live coal and a sinful tongue—these, together with the Church Slavic forms of the noun for Word and the verbs for the commission to see and hear, are the biblical essentials of this religious poem. The idea that a poet *is* a prophet, that the poet's love of beauty and the prophet's commission to speak are one—these are the elements of Pushkin's intention. They accord with his consistent emphasis on the precise meaning of words and the immanent value of poetry for its own sake.

Arguments in support of the belief that "The Prophet" is a Masonic poem are usually based on the assumption that its Masonic symbolism cannot be detected by the uninitiated. This interpretation apparently originated in the Paris Emigration in an article and a tale entitled, "The Freemason," by M.A. Osorgin.[33] The idea was endorsed by Tatiana Bakunina (Ossourguine-Bakounine) in a collection of biographies of distinguished Russian Masons recently republished in Moscow. She offered no proof other than the text of the poem itself, but her compilation of a superb bibliography and a biographical index lends her considerable authority.[34] The Masonic interpretation has been refuted by one recent specialist,[35] but it has also been taken much further by others. Here indicative is a study of Pushkin as a Mason "From Consecration to a Hymn to Rosicrucianisman." In the view of A.Ia. Zvigil'skii, "The Prophet" is the work of a Mason of the "highest degrees of consecration." Pushkin was a Masonic leader and "representative of liberal, European Masonry" in Russia who ultimately "paid with his life for his initiation."[36]

This kind of work is revisionist. Pushkin could not be discussed as a Mason in the Soviet past, he must now be treated as a devout Mason. The urge to revise has characterized new interpretations of "The Prophet" in relation to the Decembrist conspiracy. Decembrism is not the subject of the present study, but one case of Decembrist revisionism tells so much about current Russian attitudes toward Masonry that it should be considered here. Pushkin's most painful moral dilemma at the time he wrote "The Prophet," in 1826, was that he was committed by friendship and shared political convictions to Decembrist comrades. Following the failure of the Decembirst Revolt, however, he gave his allegiance to the new Tsar Nicholas I and even agreed to become court poet. Pushkinists are divided between an interpretation in which "The Prophet" was about Pushkin himself and another which posits that the poem was about "the poet" as a concept. Those who espouse the biographical interpretation find support in the condition that Pushkin did in fact stand, like the poet-prophet of his poem, "where two ancient pathways crossed."

In the view of L.M. Arinshtein, Pushkin's post-Decembrist submission to the will of Nicholas I was total, but he was afraid to jeopardize his reputation or seem to be a turncoat by professing his devotion openly. He therefore praised the tsar in poems addressed to other persons or written on seemingly unrelated themes. "The Prophet" was the poet's disguised profession of allegiance to the new tsar and an expression of gratitude for the tsar's mercy, namely, his forgiveness of Pushkin for the youthful political poems that inspired many Decembrists. Not God, but Nicholas I had responded to the wandering poet's thirsting spirit by reposing in him a "lofty moral mission." Not the six-winged fiery messenger of God, but Nicholas I had brushed the poet's burning eyes, gently touched his stricken ears, ripped the sinful tongue from out his lips. It was not God's messenger, but the emperor of Russia who cloved the poet's breast in two and thrust inside a flaming shard of living coal, made him a prophet, and sent him forth to burn men's hearts.[37]

Arinshtein and others are correct that Pushkin was not the revolutionary he was made to be in Soviet scholarship. He himself reported on several occasions that his youthful radicalism (including flirtation with atheism) was a consequence of a frivolous young man caught up in the excitement of revolutionary times. To say, however, that the Decembrist cause was never his is a revisionist over-reaction. Pushkin never repudiated his allegiance to Decembrist friends or his sympathy with their beliefs. His moral task was not to renounce, but to negotiate a twisting path from his reputation as a political radical to his standing as a mature thinker determined to honor his responsibility as Russia's major poet without betraying fallen friends. Similarly, though Pushkin's indebtedness to Nicholas became a series of affronts to his dignity, he did not renounce his allegiance to Nicholas. His conciliation with the tsar, however, did not implicate surrender of his free will, and certainly did not entail the abject servility predicated by the idea that a mortal tsar, not God or his herald, transformed a poet into a prophet. Even while confessing his initiation into the Masonic craft and his association with the Decembrist conspirators, in the letter of January 1826 to Zhukovskii, he wrote, fully aware that Nicholas would read his words: ". . . I tell you positively not to answer or vouch for me. My future behavior depends on the circumstances, on the way the government treats me, etc."[38]

Every bit as intriguing among questions about Pushkin and Masonry was an incident that became known as the legend of the two gloves. According to this legend, based on an entry in the diary of Pushkin's close friend, A I. Turgenev, before Pushkin's coffin was sealed at his funeral following his death in a duel in 1837, another of Pushkin's close friends, the poet and cultural activist, Prince P.A. Viazemskii, placed a glove in it. In a later entry, Turgenev added that Viazemskii was joined in this apparently symbolic act by another close friend, the older poet V.A. Zhukovskii. Turgenev suggested that the glove was a warning "to someone about something malevolent," that is, that vengeance for the poet's death and the vicious intrigues that led to the fatal duel could be expected. The placing of the gloves seemed definitely to implicate the symbolism of the two (or three) pairs of gloves given to new Masons during the rite of initiation. This conclusion is supported by the recent discovery in Viazemskii's belongings of one complete pair of gloves and a single white, apparently Masonic, glove. The absence of one glove suggests that, indeed, its mate was sealed in Pushkin's coffin.[39]

There are, however, some discrepancies suggesting that the Masonic connection was not as likely as it seems, or at least not serious in the sense that Masons use this word. Pushkin, Turgenev, Zhukovskii, and Viazemskii were all members of the Arzamas Brotherhood, whose proceedings parodied Masonic ceremonialism. Arzamas, not Masonic, symbolism, might be more probably intended, all the more so in that Masonic principles would proscribe vengeance and Arzamas honor might be understood to demand it. Zhukovskii received a superb Masonic education (with Turgenev, and under the tutelage of Turgenev's father), but the lodges were closed by the time that he reached maturity and he would have joined his mentor, Karamzin, in avoiding formal Masonry. As for Viazemskii, to the end of his long life he was a principled Voltairean atheist, who showed disrespect for Masonry by being initiated into a Polish lodge during diplomatic service in Warsaw simply to satisfy his curiosity. When he reported this, in a letter to Turgenev, he added that Masonry was every bit as "childish" as he expected and swore that he never again entered a Masonic temple. To this, he added that his Masonic gloves were kept with others, including several won from ladies, and he did not know if the glove he chose was Masonic.[40]

In light of this evidence, it may be suggested that the placing of a glove in the coffin was an act prompted not by serious Masonic belief, but by the knowledge that some of the principals of the fatal duel, and the scandalous intrigues that preceded it, were Masons. Here, too, however, we encounter a contradiction. It is easy to believe that the fiery liberal Prince Viazemskii would seek vengeance for Pushkin's death, but it is inconceivable that this would have motivated the devoutly religious Zhukovskii. Given that Zhukovskii was commissioned by Nicholas I to ensure that the funeral of Russia's greatest poet not be marred by further scandal, it is more likely that Zhukovskii approached the coffin to prevent Viazemskii from placing the glove; all the more so in that Pushkin died in a state of grace and charged Zhukovskii with the task of preventing his friends from avenging his death.[41]

Of course, the fact that some of the principals of the duel were Masons could not but be taken as evidence that Russia's national poet was murdered by Masons. In Filin's view, Masonry was "not Russian," anti-national, and anti-Church. For too long, such matters as Masonry had been left to "study from liberal and cosmopolitan positions that set one's teeth on edge," rather than "from the point of view of Russian national traditions and interests." He began his rehearsal of the legend of the two gloves in a coffin with the claim that "Masons—Russian and foreign—actively participated in the events culminating in the exchange of shots on Chernaya River." He admitted that "the undoubted participation of Masons in these events cannot be termed a '*Masonic conspiracy*'" against Pushkin, and he added: "In other words, we incline to the view that Masons did not take part in the affair *as a secret society*, bound together by iron discipline and unconditional submission to orders from above—they acted as private persons . . . There was no conspiracy aimed at destroying the poet and plotted in the inner sanctum of the lodge." His conclusion was equally ambiguous: "There was no organized participation by Masons in the affair. But still, something seemed to hang in the air, revealing itself in the private actions of private persons spontaneously and simultaneously drawing Pushkin and the entire duel affair inexorably into a sort of circle where a perceptibly Masonic spirit reigned." Filin then proved his case by relating the legend of the two gloves.[42]

Filin's accusations were preceded by a study of Pushkin and Masonry by the same V.F. Ivanov who exposed the Russian intelligentsia as a Masonic plot (Ivanov, V.F, *A S. Pushkin i masonstvo.* Kharbin: Tipografiia "Kha-Fyn," 1940).

According to Ivanov, the Decembrists, whose revolt of 14 December 1825 was a "Masonic revolution," failed to co-opt Pushkin. When Pushkin, "the leader of the people," proved to be a true Russian patriot and devout Orthodox believer by giving his allegiance to Nicholas I in 1826, and later planned to use his reputation as Russia's most beloved poet to foil Masonic plans, he sealed his fate. The instrument of his doom was none other than Count A.Kh. Benckendorf, founder of Nicholas's secret police, the notorious Third Section. While seeming to carry out the tsar's every command with regard to Pushkin, Benckendorf used his vast domestic and foreign powers to plan and implement each and every step of the intrigue and outright murder of the poet.[43]

Extreme views like this can be ascribed to the axiom that for every action there is a reaction. Glasnost, the fall of the Soviet Union, the looting of Russia during Yeltsin's regime—Russians and others can hardly be blamed for the disorientation that has blurred their world view in recent years. It seems impossible to avoid the dubious logic that if something is "bad," its opposite must be "good." If Communism turns out to be bad, the tsarist autocracy must have been good. If socialism is false, democracy must be perfect. If Pushkin was not, as was said so many years, an atheist, he must have been a devout believer. If he was not a revolutionary, he must have been a conservative supporter of the autocracy. Also, of course, if his initiation as a Mason was ignored during the Soviet period, then he has to have been the most serious Mason of his time. Either that or, if Masonry is considered an anti-Russian evil, he must have been destroyed for preparing to repudiate the evil.

It would seem that such views demand evidence but, despite all that we now know about Pushkin as a Mason, available evidence does not permit an answer to the most obvious question: Was he a serious Mason or was his initiation only an incident in his youth with occasional revivals of literary interest at later times in his life? If recent scholars are correct that a poem like "The Prophet" bears Masonic meaning, then we must conclude that Russia's national poet was indeed a most serious Mason. If we are to judge from the elements of parody in "The Queen of Spades," we must conclude that he not only was not a serious Mason, but he might have been a disrespectful one. Even here, however, we cannot be certain, for Pushkin was often most serious when he was or seemed to be frivolous. This witty, pun-filled, and playful tale of a card game is a model of sacred play, in which irony points to serious moral implications. So we are left with a contradictory mix of interpretations and attitudes. On the one hand are enthusiastic amateurs who are untrained in rules of evidence and prone to argue their own special case. On the other hand are revisionists who are given to see in Pushkin a secret supporter of the Russian autocracy, a devout Orthodox Christian, a highly placed Masonic authority, and so forth. Then there are patriots, who see in Masonry a vast conspiracy against Russia and in Pushkin a victim of

250

Masonic renegades.

Fortunately, we also have serious literary scholars who have introduced scholarly objectivity into the issue of Pushkin as a Mason and greatly broadened the scope of what was once seen, even by convinced specialists, as one or two interludes. This is also the condition of study of the history and current revival of Russian Masonry as a whole. Enthusiasts, revisionists, and far-right extremists have been countered by historians and social commentators who have defined tasks, refuted myths, and clarified ambiguities. At present, scholarship is still at the stage of discovery—historians and literary scholars alike are dredging the long closed archives and coming up with valuable information. If we are to judge by the integrity of these scholars' development of information into knowledge, we can expect to learn a great deal more about Russian Masonry than we have been privileged to know as yet.

Notes

1. This essay was first published as, "The Masonic Revival in Russia: The Poet Pushkin at Issue," and appeared in *Freemasonry on Both Sides of the Atlantic: Essays Concerning the Craft in the British Isles, Europe, the United States, and Mexico*, R. William Weisberger, Wallace McCleod, and S. Brent Morris, eds., (New York: East European Monograph Series of Columbia University Press, 2002), 449-67. The author has granted consent to publish this essay with a different title. The strongest influences on the early development of Russian Masonry were German and French Rosicrucians, the Order of York in Berlin, and the Grand Lodge of England. The Ancient English, Swedish, and Zinnendorf systems competed with Templarism, Rosicrucianism, and authorizations by a variety of French, German, English, and Swedish orients and orders. The most influential historians of Masonry are: A.N. Pypin, *Russkoe masonstvo. XVIII i pervaia chetvert' XIX vv.* [Russian Masonry of the 18th and First Quarter of the 19th Centuries] (Petrograd: Ogni, 1916); and G.V. Vernadskii, *Russkoe masonstvo v tsarstvovanie Ekateriny II* [Russian Masonry during the Reign of Catherine II] (Petrograd: Delo, 1917). For a brief rehearsal of their wealth of factual materials, and Herculean efforts to disentangle them, see Lauren G. Leighton, *The Esoteric Tradition in Russian Romantic Literature: Decembrism and Masonry* (University Park, PA: Penn State Press, 1994), 25-33.

2. Antoine Faivre, *L'ésoterisme au XVIII siècle en France et en Allemagne* (Paris: Seghers, 1973); "Esotericism," in *The Encyclopedia of Religion* 5 (New York: Macmillan, 1987), 155-63; *L'Ésotérisme* (Paris: Presses Universitaires de France, 1992). See also his "En Russie." *Eckartshausen et la théosophie chrétienne* (Paris: C. Klincksieck, 1969), 620-38.

3. Kenneth Craven, "The First Chamber of Novikov's Masonic Library," in *Russia and the World of the Eighteenth Century* (Columbus, OH: Slavica, 1988), 401-10.

4. This conclusion is documented by the photo-reproductions of documents in the exhibition catalogue, *500 let Gnozisa v Evrope/500 Years of Gnosis in Europe. Exhibit of Printed Books and Manuscripts from the Gnostic Tradition. Moscow and Saint-Petersburg* (Amsterdam: In de Pelikaan, 1993). The large scope of Masonic culture has recently been demonstrated again by the wealth of photo-reproductions of graphic materials, texts of archival documents, studies of a variety of subjects, and bibliographic and archival information in V.I. Sakharov, *Ieroglify vol'nykh kamenshchikov. Masonstvo i russkaia literatura XVIII-nachala XIX vekov* [Hieroglyphs of the Freemasons. Masonry and 18th-early 19th Century Russian Literature] (Moscow: Zhiraf, 2000).

5. Stephen L. Baehr, "The Masonic Component in Eighteenth-Century Russian Literature," in *Russian Literature in the Age of Catherine the Great* (Oxford: Willem A. Meeuws, 1976), 121-39; "Masonry in Russian Literature: Eighteenth Century," *Modern Encyclopedia of Russian and Soviet Literature* 3 (Gulf Breeze, FL: Academic International Press, 1987), 30-36; *The Paradise Myth in Eighteenth-Century Russia: Utopian Patterns in Early Secular Russian Literature and Culture* (Stanford, CA: Stanford University Press, 1991); Reinhard Lauer, "Russische Freimaurerdichtung in 18.jahrhundert," in *Beförderer der Aufklärung in Mittel- und Osteuropa: Freimaurer, Gesellschaften, Clubs* (Berlin: Camen, 1979); A. Levitsky, "Masonic Elements in Russian Eighteenth-Century Religious Poetry," in *Russia and the World of the Eighteenth Century* (Columbus, OH: Slavica, 1988), 419-36. A study of Russian Masonry of the time *per se* is Douglas Smith, *Working the Rough Stone: Freemasonry and Society in Eighteenth-Century Russia* (Dekalb, IL: Northern Illinois University Press, 1999).

6. Lauren G. Leighton, "Freemasonry in Russia: The Grand Lodge of Astraea, 1815-1822," *Slavonic and East European Review* 60 (April 1982): 244-61.

7. A.I. Serkov, *Istoriia russkogo masonstva, 1845-1945* [The History of Russian Masonry, 1845-1945] (Saint Petersburg: Izd. imeni N.I. Novikova, 1997), 5-6. See also his: *Istoriia russkogo masonstva posle Vtoroi mirovoi voiny* [The History of Russian Masonry after the Second World War] (Saint Petersburg: Izd. imeni N.I. Novikova, 1999); *Istoriia russkogo masonstva XIX veka* [The History of Russian Masonry in the 19th Century] (Saint Petersburg: Izd. imeni N.I. Novikova, 2000). These surveys of Masonic documents in Russian archives by the archivist Serkov are marred by inaccuracies and unpleasantly shaped by his hostility to foreigners who presume to study Russian Masonry.

8. Among the most rich collections is Fond 14, Manuscripts Division, *Arsen'ev, V. S. Sobranie masonskikh rukopisei (XVIII-XIX vv.)* [Arsen'ev, V. S. A Collection of Masonic Manuscripts (18th-19th Centuries)], Russian National Library (formerly Lenin), Moscow. Reference is to the Arsenev, Pozdeev, and Bibikov families. The Masonic (and Rosicrucian) titles appended to their names as translators of manuscripts could refer to German, rather than Russian, obediences. Initiation into European lodges was common during the "sleep" of Russian Masonry.

9. N.A. Bogomolov, *Russkaia literatura nachala XX veka i okkul'tizm* [Russian Literature of the Early 20th Century and Occultism] (Moscow: Novoe literaturnoe obozrenie, 1999).

10. For a review of recent Russian historiography on twentieth-century Russian Masonry, see V.S. Brachev, *Russkoe masonstvo XX veka* [Russian Masonry of the 20th Century] (Saint Petersburg: Stomma, 2000), 6-23.

252

11. George Katkov, *Russia, 1917, The February Revolution* (New York: Harper and Row, 1967), 163-73. The "February Revolution conspiracy" has been taken seriously by some recent Russian specialists. For an account of their views, con as well as pro, see Brachev, 16-21. The age-old flaw of Masonic conspiracy theories is again apparent: It is assumed that initiation constitutes evidence of Masonic influence even when it is clear that principals did not act in concert as Masons. Masonic solidarity had little or no effect when irreconcilable political differences were a *sine qua non* of the cataclysmic events of 1917. A.Ia. Avrekh, *Masony i revoliutsiia* [The Masons and Revolution] (Moscow: Politicheskaia literatura, 1990), has investigated assertions that Masons were active as Masons in the *duma* prior to World War I, organized the February Revolution, brought down Nicholas II, and controlled the Provisional Government. His conclusion is that Masonic influence *per se* was so negligible as to be insignificant.

12. Nina Berberova, *Liudi i lozhi: Russkie masony XX stoletiia* [People and Lodges: Russian Masons of the 20th Century] (New York: Russica, 1987), 15-62. Serkov, 42-44, savages Berberova and her Western "followers," whose works, he says, are a "display of vanity" unworthy of the word "scholarship." It is one thing to disagree with Professor Berberova, it is quite another to label her "an example of unprincipled journalism." Serkov's opinion, it must be said, is an anomaly among Russian authors of Masonic studies. For a defense of her work, see Brachev, 7-9.

13. Brachev, 197-230.

14. See *Ibid.*, 231-52; and the Grand Lodge's internet site: www.masonry.narod.ru.

15. See: O.F. Solov'ev, *Masonstvo v mirovoi politike XX veka* [Masonry in 20th-Century World Politics] (Moscow: Rosspen, 1998), 29, 210; and as quoted by Brachev, 246. Solov'ev, who attended a prominent Masonic ceremony in Moscow in November 1994, reports that there were no representatives of the new political and financial elite present. The majority of participants were scholars and intellectuals.

16. *Russkaia intelligentsiia i masonstvo ot Petra I do nashikh dnei* [The Russian Intelligentsia and Masonry from Peter I to our Time] (Moscow: Auspices of the Journal "Moskva," 1997).

17. See, for example, the English translation of L.P. Zamoiskii's, *Za fasadom masonskogo khrama*: *Behind the Facade of the Masonic Temple* (Moscow: Progress, 1989).

18. The first effective expose of the *Protocols* was provided by a member of the Russian National Committee in Paris: V.L. Burtsev, *"Protokoly sionskikh mudretsov," dokazannyi podlog* [The Protocols of the Elders of Zion, a Proven Forgery] (Paris: Société Parisienne d'Impressions, 1938). Burtsev's work has been developed by Norman Cohn, *Warrant for Genocide: The Myth of the Jewish World-Conspiracy and the Protocols of the Elders of Zion* (New York and Evanston, IL: Harper and Row, 1967). See also Walter Laqueur, *Black Hundred: The Rise of the Extreme Right in Russia* (New York: HarperCollins, 1993), 29-43.

19. In addition to Brachev, significant new studies have been provided by: S.P. Karpachëv, *Masonskaia intelligentsiia kontsa XIX-nachala XX veka* [The Masonic Intelligentsia of the Late 19th-Early 20th Centuries] (Moscow: Tsentr gumanitarnogo obrazovaniia, 1998); O.F. Solov'ev, *Russkoe masonstvo: 1730-1917* [Russian Masonry: 1730-1917] (Moscow: MGOU, 1993).

20. Factually reliable accounts of Pushkin and Masonry are: V.I. Novikov, "Pushkin," *Masonstvo i russkaia kul'tura* [Masonry and Russian Culture] (Moscow: Megakontakt, 1993), 40; "Pushkin i russkoe masonstvo" [Pushkin and Russian Masonry], in *Masonstvo i masony. Sbornik statei* 2 [*Masonry and Masons: A Collection of Articles*] (Moscow: Era, 1997); V.I. Sakharov, "Poet i 'deti vdovy': Novoe o masonskikh sviaziakh A.S. Pushkina (po arkhivnym materialam)" [The Poet and the "Children of the Widow": New Information on A.S. Pushkin's Masonic Connections (from the Archives)],*Ibid.*,151-62.

21. Iu. M. Lotman, *Karamzin* (Leningrad: Iskusstvo—SP, 1997), 59-60. Karamzin described his visits with leading Masons in *Letters of a Russian Traveller* (*Pis'ma russkogo puteshestvennika*, 1797, 1801).

22. A.S. Pushkin: *Polnoe sobranie sochinenii.* 7 [Complete Collected Works (16 vols. and a supplementary volume)] (Moscow-Leningrad: Academia, 1937-59), 303; *The Letters of Alexander Pushkin* 1, J. Thomas Shaw, ed. and trans. (Madison: University of Wisconsin Press, 1967 [3 vols. in 1]), 302.

23. S.A. Fomichev, "Pushkin i masony" [Pushkin and the Masons], in *Legendy i mify o Pushkine: Sbornik statei.* [Legends and Myths about Pushkin: A Collection of Articles] (Saint Petersburg: Gumanitarnoe agentstvo "Akademicheskii proekt," 1995), 160-64.

24. Ovid was included in the 1821 roll of the Grand Lodge of Astraea, but its members were not listed. Fomichev, 162, speculates that Ovid was officially closed on 9 December 1821, but continued to work under the obedience of the Grand Lodge of Rumania.

25. Markus Wolf, "Aspekte der Symbolik und Historie des Freimauerertums bei A. S. Puskin." *Arion: Jahrbuch der deutschen Puschkin-Gesellschaft.* bd. 2. 1992; *Freimaurertum bei Pu?kin. Einf?hrung in die russische Freimaurerei und ihre Bedeutung f?r Pu?kins literarisches Werk.* Slavistische Beitraege 355 (Munich: Peter Rehder, 1998); Fomichev, *Ibid.*

26. M.D. Filin, "Dve perchatki v grobu. 'Masonskii sled' v sud'be Pushkina" [Two Gloves in a Coffin. A "Masonic Clue" to Pushkin's Fate], in *Moskovskii pushkinist: Ezhegodnyi sbornik* 2 [Moscow Pushkinist: Annual Collection] (Moscow: Nasledie, 1996): 244-51.

27. Harry B. Weber, "'Pikovaia dama': A Case for Masonry in Russian Literature," *Slavic and East European Journal* 12 (1968): 435-47.

28. Leighton, 131-94.

29. Wolf Schmid, "Die Paromie als Narratives Kryptogramm: sur Entfaltung von Sprichwortern und Redensarten in A. S. Puskins "Hauptmannstochter," in *Kryptogramm: Zur asthetik des Verborgenen. Wiener Slawistischer Almanach,* bd. 21 (1980): 267-85; *id.,* "'Pique Dame' als poetologische Novelle," *Die Welt der Slaven,* no. 1 (1997): 1-33; E. Nerre, "Masonstvo v 'Pikovoi dame'" [Masonry in "The Queen of Spades"], in *Pushkinskoe nasledie i russkaia usadebnaia kul'tura.* [The Pushkin Legacy and Russian Manor-House Culture] (Viazma, 1992).

30. E. Nerre, "Puškins 'Grobovščik' als Parodie auf das Freimauertum." *Wiener Slawistischer Almanach,* bd. 17 (1985): 5-13.

31. See Fomichev,163-64. Fomichev refutes Zamoiskii (*op cit.*) on this and other points. If Pushkin felt he had reason to fear vengeance for his own parodies of Masonry, he certainly did not allow this to inhibit his love of literary and meta-literary play.

32. "Thirteen Pushkin Poems," James Falen, trans., *The Pushkin Journal* 1 (1993): 87.

33. "Pushkin—vol'nyi kamenshchik" [Pushkin as a Freemason], *Poslednie novosti* [Latest news], 10 February 1937.

34. *Znamenitye russkie masony* [Distinguished Russian Masons] (Moscow: Interbuk, 1991), 89-90, first published in Paris, 1935. Reference is to her *Répertoire biographique des Francs-Maçons russes* (Paris: Mouton [L'Institut d'études slaves], 1967); and Paul Bourychkine, [P.A. Buryshkin], *Bibliographie sur la Franc-Maçonnerie en Russie* (Paris and The Hague: Mouton, 1967). Index and bibliography were begun by Buryshkin and completed by Bakunina.

35. Filin, 242-43.

36. "Aleksandr Pushkin: Ot posviashcheniia do gimna rozenkreitserstva," in *Masonstvo i masony* 2 [Masonry and Masons] (Moscow: Era, 1997).

37. See *Pushkin: Neprichesannaia biografiia* [Pushkin: A Disheveled Biography], 2d ed., enl. (Moscow: Muravei, 1999), 142-47, 154-59, 160-67. For a necessary antidote to Decembrist revisionism, see F.A. Raskol'nikov, "Poet i politik v pushkinskom 'Arione'" [Poet and Politician in Pushkin's Arion"], *Russkaia literatura* [Russian Literature], no. 1 (1997): 102-6.

38. Pushkin, *Letters . . .* 1: 302. Nicholas I was known as "Nicholas Hangman" because, contrary to Pushkin's hope for mercy, he executed five of the Decembrist leaders.

39. Filin, 258-60; V.I. Sakharov, "Zagadki istorii. Masonskie perchatki P. A. Viazemskogo" [Enigmas of History. P. A. Viazemskii's Masonic Gloves], *Literaturnaia Rossiia* 27 [Literary Russia] (August 1999): 13.

40. Sakharov, *Ibid.* The author considers Viazemskii a Mason despite the contrary evidence he provides from Viazemskii's letter.

41. For a study of the circumstances of Pushkin's death, see Walter Vickery, *Death of a Poet* (Bloomington, IN: Indiana University Press, 1968). Pushkin died in January 1837 after a duel with a French adventurer, whose attentions to the poet's wife were a deliberate offense to his honor. Intrigues included an anonymous Masonic-like patent appointing him to the Order of Cuckolds and naming him Historiographer of the Order.

42. Filin, 241, 253-55.

43. V.F. Ivanov, *A.S. Pushkin i masonstvo* [A.S. Pushkin and Masonry] (Kharbin: Tipografiia "Kha-Fyn," 1940), 100-23. Benckendorf was, or had been, a Mason, and a serious one at that, but to say that the tsar's most trusted adviser was a Masonic conspirator against him is a bit much.

255

Prince Adam Jerzy Czartoryski:
Liberal Enlightener and Conservative Polish Revolutionary

R. William Weisberger
Butler County Community College, PA

The Early Career of an Enlightened Polish Prince

The life of Prince Adam Jerzy Czartoryski reveals much about the revolutionary Atlantic world. His fascinating and lengthy career between 1770 and 1861 was associated with both Enlightenment ideologies and revolutionary movements that were supportive of his ultimate aim: Namely, the creation of an independent and a workable Polish state. To achieve this goal, this aristocrat subscribed to the trans-Atlantic liberal tenets of the Enlightenment. As this essay will suggest, this Polish prince, on the one hand, embraced salient doctrines concerning constitutionalism, representative government, natural liberties, and peasant and Jewish emancipation. On the other hand, Czartoryski repudiated the use of radical and violent tactics, endorsing instead, as a conservative statesman, diplomatic strategies to create a Polish nation. Although failing to achieve Polish unity in 1830-31, during the 1840s he advocated the doctrine of federalism. Czartoryski believed that Poland and other East European nations could be established and could operate within the context of a federation.[1]

Czartoryski was born into a prominent Polish aristocratic family that was related to the Jagiełłonian dynasty, whose monarchs had ruled Lithuania and Poland between the fourteenth and sixteenth centuries. A wealthy and cultured magnate, possessing vast land holdings in both Poland and Lithuania, Prince Adam Kazimierz Czartoryski and his wife, Princess Izabela, who was the daughter of the Lithuanian treasurer, had their oldest son in Warsaw on January 14, 1770, in an era when Poland encountered intensive political turmoil, and which was followed by that nation's first partition, two years later.[2] Nannies provided the young child with tender care while his mother proved to be a comforting and understanding parent, encouraging him to be attentive, self-righteous, honorable, and studious.[3]

256

Both parents as well provided their eldest son with an opulent education; they contracted the services of eminent tutors at their Puławy home. Known as the "Polish Athens," this magnificent neoclassical edifice resembled an ancient classical temple and reflected the features of the Vitruvian style: Doric columns, atriums, rooms with rotundas, mirrors, and statutes, and numerous gardens. Puławy thus embodied the Enlightenment tenets of order and harmony and became the center of the young noble's education.[4] The education of this Polish prince was extensive during the 1780s. He studied history under the former Jesuit, Józef Koblanski, and political science with the legal scholar, Józef Szymanowski. Czartoryski also studied the classics under Ernst Groddeck and Polish literature under the eminent Franciszek Kniaznin and Julian Niemcewicz.[5] This Polish aristocrat, who was to learn from his extensive travels, emerged as a proponent of constitutional government, of natural liberties, and of Polish nationalism.[6]

During the early 1790s, Czartoryski became a liberal enlightener. Certainly the 1793 and 1795 Polish Partitions stimulated his Enlightenment thinking. The failure of the 1794 Kościuszko Rebellion greatly disappointed Czartoryki, for visions of Polish independence and the privileges of the *szlachta* (the Polish nobility) were significantly reduced as a result. In 1795, Czartoryki went to St. Petersburg to reside and became involved with Russian reformist leaders who later served on the Unofficial Committee. Czartoryki served in Vilna in 1803. Reflecting the beliefs of members of this committee, he called for Polish educational districts and for the establishment of additional *lycées* in those districts. Czartoryski, who also would serve as curator of Vilna University, favored as well the strengthening of the liberal arts and scientific programs of this institution to prepare nobles as future leaders of the Polish state.[7]

Czartoryski's 1803 work entitled, "The Political System to be Adopted by Russia," offered explanations of other salient Enlightenment concepts of this Polish prince. Distressed by the three Polish partitions, Czartoryski advocated the idea of mutual relations among major and minor states. He claimed that great and small nations should adhere to the principle of nationality to redraw the map of Europe, and that they should work in concert to create viable representative political institutions. If these circumstances were to result, the enlightener Czartoryski believed that a successful society of nations would be established in Europe, which would lead to political and economic progress.[8] Moreover, he called for the abolition of political and religious fanaticism, for Russian leadership in a Slavic federation, and for that nation's support in recreating a Polish state.[9] By 1815, Czartoryski was disappointed with the provisions of the Treaty of Vienna. Although Congress Poland was administered by Russia, major regions of the former Polish state were occupied by Austria and Prussia.[10]

257

Written during the middle years of the 1820s and published in 1830, *Essai sur la diplomatie* contained Enlightenment concepts of Czartoryski that revolved around the establishment of a unified Polish state with a constitutional government. With an executive, an assembly, and a judiciary, reconstituted Poland would function as a republic. Czartoryski maintained that Polish leaders should strive to implement natural rights; he embraced such liberties as free speech and legal justice.[11] As a liberal enlightener, he also called for religious toleration, for Jewish civic rights, and for peasant emancipation.[12]

Moreover, as an advocate of the Enlightenment concept of the heavenly city, Czartoryski espoused Sully's belief in a European league. He claimed that such an organization would enable Poland and other small European nations to cooperate with continental powers in resolving diplomatic, political, and economic issues. Lastly, as an enlightener and as an Atlanticist, Czartoryski supported the doctrine of federalism, believing that Poland could enhance her economic and diplomatic position through her participation in an East European federalist organization.[13]

A Polish Statesman at the Court of Russia

Although a liberal enlightener who worked for the cause of Polish unity, Czartoryski proved to be a discreet and a conservative leader and diplomat. His leadership achievements, in part, can be attributed to his friendship with Russian Tsar Alexander I. During the reign of Catherine II, then Grand Duke Alexander established cordial relations with the Polish prince: Czartoryski and Alexander met in the culturally refined St. Petersburg salons of the Golovins and Stroganovs. La Harpe and other eminent savants had served as tutors for both leaders. Moreover, during a discussion in 1796 in the Tauride Gardens, Czartoryski and Alexander had discovered that they shared common feelings and beliefs: They disliked Catherine and despotism and shared common views about the achievements of the French Revolution. Because of his sympathy for the aspirations of the 1794 Polish insurrectionists, Alexander earned the respect of Czartoryski. Lastly, Czartoryski, who was both intellectually and physically attracted to Alexander's wife, the Grand Duchess Elizabeth, shared with the future tsar an earnest interest in trying to implement Enlightenment tenets to reform Russia.[14]

Alexander, who became Russian tsar in 1801, in that year established the Unofficial Committee and appointed his friend Czartoryski to it. Its members were instructed to advise Alexander about reforming institutions and society in both Russia and in the imperial lands in light of Enlightenment doctrines. In February 1802, the Polish prince offered ideas for administrative reforms: He called for the transformation of the existing administrative colleges into advisory ministerial bodies; and for the senate to operate as both a supreme court and an advisory body to Alexander regarding major reports.[15] As a result of his suggestions, the tsar empowered the senate to receive annual reports and, in 1802, created eight major ministries, the most significant of which was that involved with finance. Likewise, Czartoryski took a stance on the vexing peasant question. He favored terminating the practice of giving serf lands to favorite nobles of the tsar and denounced Russian aristocrats who purchased and sold serfs as property. Alexander, however, did not institute significant reforms that would have culminated in the emancipation of the peasants.[16] Moreover, the recommendations of Czartoryki and members of the committee concerning the updating of laws in Russia and in its western possessions were not implemented by Alexander.

The influence of the Polish enlightener, however, could be detected in the realm of education. Reflecting especially the thinking of Czartoryski, Alexander's decree of February 5, 1803 provided needed educational reforms. This edict stipulated that parish, district, and provincial schools would function in the Russian empire. It also stated that the minister of education would be authorized to supervise the operations of universities in the cities of the empire. Consequently, this major educational reform produced the amelioration of programs in the liberal arts and sciences in both Russian and Polish universities and contributed greatly to fostering Polish culture in the University of Vilna.[17] In 1803, Czartoryki suggested that Jews should be permitted to attend imperial schools and universities and that this reform would encourage their assimilation within the empire. However, the 1804 tsarist liberal edict regarding Jewish education met with only partial success, since some government and Jewish leaders objected to it.[18]

Likewise, Czartoryski became a leading tsarist statesman for a short time. In late 1802, the tsar named him deputy foreign minister under Alexander Vorontsov. Prior to his retirement the next year, Vorontsov looked favorably on Czartoryski, claiming that he was well mannered, cosmopolitan, and prudent in judgment.[19] Upon Vorontsov's retirement in 1804, the tsar appointed Czartoryski as foreign minister. Attempting to promote the cause of the Third Coalition and that of an autonomous Poland, Czartoryski accentuated the importance of Russia's relationship with England. He envisioned the coalition against Napoleon as being part of a great league that would help to re-establish a Polish kingdom. After Napoleon's decisive victory at the Battle of Austerlitz, Czartoryski was constrained to resign as Russian foreign minister on July 1, 1806.[20]

For six years thereafter, Czartoryski worked for the cause of an independent Polish state in numerous ways. Despite leaving the service of the tsar, the Polish prince continued to be on cordial terms with him and frequently wrote to Alexander. As French troops were being defeated in Russia in 1812, major events were occurring in Napoleon's Duchy of Warsaw: Czartoryski's father and other aristocratic leaders of the duchy's Extraordinary Diet declared the re-establishment of Poland and summoned Poles to support the new kingdom. At this time, Czartoryski felt entrapped, since he was caught between being loyal to his father or to Alexander. In 1813, Czartoryski resolved the personal, internal conflict, expressing the belief that the newly proclaimed autonomous Polish nation, about which he had dreamed for such a long time, should seek security from Russia and look to Alexander for executive leadership. Appointed by Alexander in 1813 as its interim head, Czartoryski worked on drafting a constitution for the new Polish nation and on attempting to integrate into it former Polish regions occupied by the Prussians and the Austrians.[21]

The statesmen meeting during the 1814-1815 Congress of Vienna, however, did not comply with the numerous wishes of Czartoryski concerning the Polish state. He was disappointed to learn that Prince Hardenberg convinced the congress to acknowledge Prussian control of Posen. Moreover, Metternich won the approval of this body for Austrian hegemony over large tracts of Polish regions in Galicia. However, Czartoryski was delighted that congress statesmen had proclaimed Cracow a free city.[22]

The statesmen at Vienna gave their consent to a new Polish kingdom, known as Congress Poland. They also agreed that the kingdom would be accountable to the tsar and that it would be governed in light of the provisions of the Constitutional Bases, a document promulgated on November 27, 1815. A symbol of Czartoryski's success as an enlightener, this liberal constitution stated that Poles would be endowed with liberty and justice.[23] The *sejm* (the Polish legislature) was to consist of two houses: A senate and a house of deputies. This document further stipulated that there would be a court system, and that a state council and five ministries would function to assist in administering the kingdom. Having drafted this document that embodied American and British constitutional principles, Czartoryski thought that he would be appointed as viceroy by Alexander—a position that was the nation's chief executive officer. After the tsar appointed the Grand Duke Constantine to this position instead, Czartoryski became indignant with Alexander [24]

During the 1820s, the prince still remained involved in matters affecting his nation and also discreetly expressed his thoughts about several revolutionary movements. He traveled extensively during the early years of the decade. As a result of his trips to Italy and France, he vindicated the cause of the Greek revolutionaries. When the Philomats, who were students that belonged to a Polish secret society, revolted in Vilna in 1823 against the repressive measures of Constantine and Alexander, Czartoryski denounced their radical activities. However, he implored Alexander to ease restrictions concerning censorship in Polish universities.[25] After the 1825 Decembrist Revolution in Russia was suppressed by Tsar Nicholas I, Poles, who allegedly had contacts with the Decembrists, were investigated and arrested in 1826. They were tried for treason in 1827 in Warsaw. A member of the Polish senate, which served as the high tribunal in hearing the case, Czartoryski played a major role in persuading this body that these Poles were innocent of the charges of treason. Because of the prince's influence, the senate, by a thirty-to-one vote, found the men not guilty and consequently angered both Constantine and Nicholas. As a result of this case, Czartoryski and other Polish leaders realized that Polish relations with Russia were becoming acrimonious and could well lead to turmoil.[26]

A Conservative Revolutionary

Czartoryski's thinking about deteriorating Polish-Russian relations proved to be correct and, in late 1830, Poles in Warsaw launched a revolution directed against tsarist oppression. The 1830-31 Polish Revolution was attributed to several major causes: Nicholas's restrictive measures against the Poles; the tsar's refusal to cede regions of the Polish-Lithuanian Commonwealth to the Poles; the accelerated ascendancy of Polish nationalistic and romantic ideologies; and the outbreak in 1830 of revolutions in France and in Belgium.[27] On November 29, 1830, the Polish revolution began in Warsaw: Polish cadets and students attacked the Belvedere Palace, the home of Constantine. That same evening, Piotr Wysocki and 160 Polish cadets assailed the barracks of the Russian cavalry near Łazienki Park. Both attacks proved to be unsuccessful, stimulated other Poles to embrace the revolutionary cause, and led to the involvement of Czartoryski in the revolution.[28]

The participation of Czartoryski in the 1830-31 Revolution produced a great paradox: He denounced revolutionary activities against Russia yet became a major leader of the revolution. He served in the senate and on the administrative council, meeting several times with Constantine at Wierzbno between December 1 and 3. Constantine informed Czartoryki that he and his Russian troops would leave Poland and that the Polish leaders should move to restore order in Warsaw and in other cities of Congress Poland.[29] Czartoryski agreed for the most part with Constantine, maintaining that the Poles should be encouraged not to revolt, but he insisted that the viceroy and the tsar had for the previous five years violated Polish natural liberties. While favoring a negotiated solution with the tsar for the vexing problems in Poland, Czartoryski watched rapidly unfolding events that came to counter his aims. On December 18, leaders of the *sejm* proclaimed the events of November 29 as an "act of the nation," acknowledging that an insurrection had developed into a political and social revolution. Two days later, that body convinced General Józef Chłopicki, who favored reconciliation with Russia, to head the revolutionary army and serve as "dictator."[30]

In January 1831, Czartoryski witnessed the shaping of Polish revolutionary factions and institutions. The first faction, under the leadership of Joachim Lelewel, was the Patriotic Society, members of which were radicals advocating a belief in egalitarianism and in the creation of a Polish socialist state. Another faction was the Kalisz Group, which was under the direction of Wincenty Niemojowski. It consisted of an aristocratic elite that embraced the natural rights ideologies of moderate French revolutionary republican leaders. Lastly, the elite, of which Czartoryski was a member, consisted of both liberal and conservative nobles who wished to use diplomacy as a tactic to establish a viable constitutional monarchy in Polish lands.[31] Two major institutions operated during the revolution and were incessantly in conflict with each other: The *sejm* functioned as the revolutionary legislature and was endowed with extensive powers; while the national government operated as the executive branch and was frequently either challenged or opposed by the revolutionary assembly.[32]

In the first month of 1831, both bodies, however, agreed to two significant pieces of legislation. The Act of Deposition, which was passed on January 25 and was intended to reveal that the Polish revolution was attempting to galvanize into an envisaging socio-political movement, stipulated that Nicholas was deposed as Polish monarch. On January 30, leaders of the *sejm*, who evidently perceived Czartoryski as a sterling symbol of the Polish revolutionary cause, elected him president of the national government.[33]

In Poland's pursuit of independence, the prince in his new position encountered military problems between February and May. In the face of the *sejm*'s restraints on his activities, Czartoryski succeeded in obtaining military funding and materials. Despite the leadership and encouragement of the prince, however, the Polish war effort near Warsaw and in the eastern regions did not go well. On February 25, Chlopicki was injured and defeated in battle by the Russians at Grochów, after which he retreated to Warsaw and then resigned as commander-in-chief of the revolutionary armies. Although suffering many casualties and losing that significant battle, the Polish troops demonstrated strength and thwarted the attempt of General Dibich and the Russians to capture the Polish capital.[34] As a result of Grochów, the *sejm* appointed Jan Skrzynecki as the new commander of Polish armies.

As the revolution spread to the eastern provinces, Lithuanian troops, consisting of nobles and peasants, earned stunning victories in April against the Russians at Wawer and Iganie. These victories provided hope to Czartoryski and members of the national government. Encouraged by the prince to adopt an aggressive campaign in Lithuania in May, Skrzynecki's armies moved too slowly. Because of poor planning, the Polish general lost to Dibich and the Russians on May 26 at the Battle of Ostrołęka. That defeat prevented the Polish revolutionaries from occupying major regions in the Russian Empire.[35]

After this military setback, Czartoryski realized that the cause of the revolutionaries, which had greatly contributed to the ascendancy of Polish national consciousness, was collapsing. He had been unable to secure either recognition or aid from either Austria or France. Moreover, dissension among the leadership of the *sejm* and the national government continued during the summer of 1831, thus enabling General Ivan Paskevich to lead Russian troops into Warsaw on August 17 and to occupy the Polish capital. As the Russians suppressed the revolutionary movement in late August and September, Czartoryski, with aid from Metternich, escaped from Warsaw and rejoined his family in Cracow on September 26.[36]

Despite his aggressive yet frustrating efforts to establish an independent Polish state in 1831, Czartoryski became part of the Polish emigration movement and continued to promote the revolutionary cause of his nation from abroad for the rest of his life. He resided in London for several years, where he secured support from the radical Mason, Lord Dudley Coutts Stuart, who provided him with needed monies and who played an active role in the Literary Association of the Friends of Poland. Czartoryski then moved to Paris in 1834 and established the secret organization known as the League of National Unity to advance the Polish cause.[37] Unlike his arch opponent Lelewel, who also went to Paris and who lauded ideologies of agrarian democracy and the role of a revolutionary Polish peasantry, Czartoryski continued to advocate diplomacy directed against Russia as a vehicle to establish an autonomous Polish state. Moreover, the prince adhered to a moderate ideology encompassing a Polish constitutional monarchy. He believed that justice, natural liberties, private property, and peasant reforms should characterize a united Poland.[38]

Czartoryski at the Hotel Lambert also developed diplomatic designs and hired capable individuals for his effective network to marshal Polish policies. In conducting his anti-Russian campaign, he looked to British and French leaders. He also supported the Ottomans in their quest to thwart Russian penetration into their empire. Furthermore, he frequently became involved with intricate matters in the Balkans, believing that his leaders and agents in that region would ultimately assist in advancing the cause of Polish unity. With help from František Zach, who was an agent of Czartoryski, Prince Alexander was elected as an anti-Russian Serbian king in 1842. Lacking French support, Alexander only served as Serbian monarch until 1848.[39] Likewise, in Bulgaria during the 1840s, the activities of Czartoryski's agents to discredit the Bulgarian Orthodox Church were directed against the influence of Russia, but ultimately the efforts proved a failure.[40] In short, despite his extensive network, by the middle years of the 1840s Czartoryski met with few successes in the Balkans, where he failed, for the most part, to curb Russian power, and did little to advance the cause of Polish unity.

After the eruption of the 1846 Polish Revolution in February, Czartoryski came to its support. An opponent of the prince and a supporter of egalitarian ideologies, Edward Dembowski established in Cracow a national government on February 22 that consisted of Polish patriots. Despite his ideological differences with Dembowski, Czartoryski immediately recognized the new regime in Cracow, evidently attempting to generate a sense of Polish unity. As the revolution spread to western Galicia in February, Polish peasants in the region unexpectedly went against their aristocratic masters, killing many of them. From the standpoint of Czartoryski, this revolution proved to be disastrous for the Poles: The Austrians occupied and then annexed Cracow in November 1846. Moreover, Russian armies quickly suppressed seditious Poles in Galicia. Consequently, Russian and Austrian forces thwarted the activities of the zealous Polish revolutionaries.[41]

With the outbreak of the 1848 Revolutions, Czartoryski revealed optimism about the creation of an autonomous Polish state. He believed that a united Poland could function within a Slavic federation, in which each state would be equal. He also called for civic rights for Jews and peasants and for the summoning of a Polish delegation to assure that revolutions in major Polish regions were coordinated. Poles occupied dominant leadership positions in the national committee in Posen and, in March 1848, called for the extension of rights to Jews and peasants. They, however, refused to be associated with the Frankfurt Assembly. Because of incessant dissension between Polish and German revolutionaries in Posen, leaders in the region dissolved the national committee, thus bringing an unsuccessful end to the revolution there.[42]

Poles also were involved in the 1848 Revolutions in Galicia. During the radical stage of revolutions in this region, Poles occupied leadership positions on the Cracow Committee and the Lemberg Council. The two bodies' leaders advocated similar revolutionary doctrines: The functioning of a *sejm*; the granting of natural liberties to Jews and all nationalities in the region; the obviating of serfdom; and the creation of schools in which Polish would be the language of instruction. However, the Austrians quickly restored order to Galicia, crushing the Polish revolutionaries in Cracow in April 1848 and those in Lemberg in the following November.[43]

Disappointment and frustration continued to characterize the last eleven years of Czartoryski's lengthy career. At the Hotel Lambert, he expressed resentment in 1849 that an effective strategy had not been developed and executed to enable the creation of a united Polish state. During the early 1850s, this elderly revolutionary and statesman was heartened by Russia's defeat during the Crimean War. However, he was displeased to learn that French and British statesmen during the 1856 Paris Conference precluded issues concerning Poland. In his last speech on May 3, 1861, Czartoryski expressed deep feelings about his beloved nation, claiming that "virtue and goodness are the indomitable forces of Poland, and in them is her hope for the future."[44] He died in Paris on July 15, 1861, and his remains were brought from Montmorency to the Sieniawa parish church in Galicia in 1873, to be placed next to those of his wife and mother.[45]

Conclusion: *Czartoryski and Atlantic History*

In several ways Czartoryski contributed significantly to Atlantic history and especially to its revolutionary world during the first half of the nineteenth century. One of his major legacies concerns his promotion of pertinent trans-Atlantic tenets of the Enlightenment within the cis-Atlantic context of Eastern Europe.[46] This liberal aristocrat, who, paradoxically enough, embraced the institution of monarchy, also favored the creation of constitutional and representative government. There is another important legacy that stems from ideologies of the Enlightenment. In a unified Poland, Czartoryski wished to implement natural liberties through the judiciary and wanted to extend civic privileges to peasants, Jews, and other oppressed ethnic groups. A major legacy of Czartoryski relates to his endorsement of the concept of federation, one that he well might have known about from the eighteenth-century American revolutionary and constitutional experiences.[47]

Other achievements of Czartoryski were also significant to the study of revolutionary Atlantic history. Suppression of his revolutionary efforts to uplift various oppressed groups in the Polish lands emerged as a major theme in his long career. The failure to effectuate a successful Polish revolution through his diplomatic activities culminated in a major accomplishment: Namely, his lengthy leadership role in the government-in-exile in Paris. Finally, the thinking of this Polish aristocrat about the ideologies of nationalism and those of trans-nationalism reveals much about the importance of Czartoryski to studies regarding revolutions on both sides of the Atlantic.[48]

Notes

1. W.H. Zawadzki, *A Man of Honour: Adam Czartoryski as a Statesman of Russia and Poland, 1795-1831* (Oxford: Clarendon Press, 1993), 1-6. Pages 3-5 of this incisive biography describe conflicting scholarly perceptions of Czartoryski.

2. *Ibid,* 8-9, 16-18; Marian Kukiel, *Czartoryski and European Unity: 1770-1861* (Princeton: Princeton University, 1955), 11.

3. Zawadzki, 19; and Kukiel, *Ibid.*

4. For the classical features of Puławy, see Lorna Van Meter, "The Czartoryski Family and Stanislas Augustus Poniatowski: Promoters of Neoclassical Architecture in Poland," *East European Quarterly* 20, no. 3 (September 1986): 257-72.

5. Zawadzki, 19-20.

6. The travels of Czartoryki enabled him to meet royal and aristocratic women. He married Anna, the eighteen-year-old daughter of Prince Aleksander Sapieha, on September 25, 1817. See *Ibid.,* 275.

7. *Ibid.,* 30-32, 52-55; Kukiel, 25.

8. Kukiel, 30-31.

9. Zawadzki, 66, 79, 82-83, 90.

10. *Ibid.*, 270-72.

11. *Ibid.*, 289.

12. *Ibid.*, 290-91.

13. On Czartoryski's federalist program, see: Piotr S. Wandycz, "The Polish Precursors of Federalism," *Journal of Central European Affairs* 12 (October 1953): 346-55; M.K. Dziewanowski, "Czartoryski and his *Essai sur la diplomatie,*" *Slavic Review* 30 (September 1971): 589-605.

14. Zawadzki, 35-37.

15. *Ibid.*, 45-47.

16. *Ibid.*, 48-50.

17. *Ibid.*, 53-55.

18. *Ibid.*, 58-60.

19. Patricia K. Grimsted, *The Foreign Ministers of Alexander I: Political Attitudes and the Conduct of Russian Diplomacy, 1801-1825* (Berkeley: University of California Press, 1969), 112.

20. Charles Morley, "Czartoryski as a Polish Statesman," *Slavic Review* 30 (September 1971): 606-8.

21. Morley, 609-10; Zawadzki, 225.

22. Piotr Wandycz, *The Lands of Partitioned Poland, 1795-1918* (Seattle: University of Washington Press, 1974), 68-74.

23. Frank W. Thackeray, *Antecedents of Revolution: Alexander I and the Polish Kingdom, 1815-1825* (New York: East European Monograph Series of Columbia University Press, 1980), 14.

24. Wandycz, *Partitioned Poland*, 74-78; Thackeray, 18-21; Morley, 610-11.

25. Zawadzki, 284-286.

26. *Ibid.*, 293-96; Thackeray, 139-44; Morley, 612. However, the High Tribunal did find the Polish Decembrists guilty of lesser charges.

27. David Saunders, *Russia in the Age of Reaction and Reform, 1801-1881* (London: Longman, 1992), 177.

28. Joan S. Skurnowicz, *Romantic Nationalism and Liberalism: Joachim Lelewel and the Polish National Idea* (New York: East European Monograph Series of Columbia University Press, 1981), 58-59.

29. *Ibid.*, 60-61.

30. R.F. Leslie, *Polish Politics and the Revolution of November 1830* (London: The Athlone Press, 1956), 132-39.

31. Wandycz, *Partitioned Poland*, 110-11.

32. *Ibid.*, 109-10.

33. Zawadzki, 307.

34. *Ibid.*, 308.

35. *Ibid.*, 314-15; Leslie, 212-13; Saunders, 177; Wandycz, *Partitioned Poland*, 114-15.

36. Zawadzki, 318.

37. *Ibid.*, 329; Kukiel, 203, 217-18. For his role in promoting the cause of Polish unity through the radical Duke of Sussex, the Grand Master of British Freemasonry, see Kukiel, 224.

38. For the role of Czartoryski and other Polish exiles in Paris during the 1830s and 1840s, see Lloyd S. Kramer, *Threshold of a New World: Intellectuals and the Exile Experience in Paris, 1830-1848* (Ithaca: Cornell University Press, 1988), 52, 179-80, 229-33; Wandycz, *Partitioned Poland*, 117-22.

39. Robert A. Berry, "Czartoryski's Hotel Lambert and the Great Powers in the Balkans, 1832-1848," *The International History Review* 7, no. 1 (February 1985): 59.

40. *Ibid.*, 60-63.

41. Kukiel, 251-55; Wandycz, *Partitioned Poland*, 132-37.

42. Kukiel, 263-66; Wandycz, *Ibid.*, 137-41.

43. Wandycz, *Ibid.*, 141-50.

44. Kukiel, 311.

45. Zawadzki, 334.

46. David Armitage and Michael J. Braddick, eds., *The British Atlantic World, 1500-1800* (New York: Palgrave Macmillan, 2002), 18-25.

47. Jaroslaw Pelenski, ed., *The American and European Revolutions, 1776-1848* (Iowa City: University of Iowa Press, 1980), 118-22.

48. Peter F. Sugar and Ivo J. Lederer, eds., *Nationalism in Eastern Europe* (Seattle: University of Washington Press, 1969), 314; Thomas Bender, *Rethinking American History in a Global Age* (Berkeley: University of California Press, 2002), 25-46.

267

John Mitchel and the
Revolution of 1848 in Ireland

Anthony X. Sutherland
Jednota Press, editor

The Paris Revolution of February 1848 was greeted with enthusiasm by many national leaders in Ireland. The country had just gone through a horrific famine for three consecutive years with thousands of deaths monthly, evictions, and a landlord-tenant relationship that defied a solution. It seemed to many that Ireland was ready for a revolution like no time in its history.

Several individuals emerged in Ireland during the Revolution of 1848, most of whom were associated with the Young Ireland movement and its publication, the *Nation*. If one had to select the best representative of the 1848 movement in Ireland, however, the choice would likely go to John Mitchel, former editor of the *Nation* and principal revolutionary agitator during the turbulent months of 1848. Although Mitchel was active in journalism and politics right up to the time of his death in 1875, he is best known for his role in Irish national life during the years 1845 to 1848. He was not a politician or a street barricader but the great agitator in Ireland whose writings went on to inspire a nation brought to its knees by a famine. His writings, such as his *Jail Journal* and *Last Conquest of Ireland (Perhaps),* are considered among the great masterpieces in English literature in Ireland and read not only for information on the period but as literature as well. One of his early biographers, William Dillon, son of 1848 Irish patriot William Blake Dillon, called him the "greatest man of letters that Ireland has produced since Jonathan Swift."[1]

John Mitchel was born at Camish near Dungiven in County Derry in Ulster on November 3, 1815, a son of a Unitarian Presbyterian minister.[2] As the name might suggest, Mitchel was not Irish in origin but a descendant of Scotch-Irish Covenanters who settled in Ireland in the eighteenth century. In this respect, Mitchel was not unlike many other prominent Irish national figures, such as Wolf Tone, Robert Emmet, Thomas Davis, and Countess Constance Markievicz, who, although English in origin, became champions of Irish causes. John Mitchel's father belonged to a group of Protestants referred to as Unitarians or

"Remonstrants," a faction that broke off from the main body of Presybyterians at the Synod of Ulster in 1829, demanding more freedom of opinion in the church. His father was known as the "Melancthon of the Remonstrants" and a known sympathizer with the United Irishmen of 1798.[3] Perhaps this rebelliousness or defense of freedom found among the Remonstrants was passed on to young John Mitchel.

It was assumed that young John Mitchel would follow in his father's footsteps by joining the ministry and living out his life in a quiet parsonage in the Protestant north. This, however, was not to be. John Mitchel showed promise as a young student and at age 5 was already studying Latin. In 1830, at age 15, he entered Trinity College in Dublin and four years later received a B.A. degree. He began working as a bank clerk in Newry but after a short time left that job to begin the study of law at a solicitor's office. In 1837 he married Jenny Verner and three years later was admitted as a solicitor and took a position in Banridge. In Banridge, he often met with John Martin, a member of the Young Ireland movement and on his trips to Dublin had the opportunity to become acquainted with such other Young Irelanders as Charles Gavan Duffy and Thomas Davis. In Banridge, he frequently defended Catholics and came to appreciate the Catholic position. As one biographer wrote, "He had no sympathy with religious intolerance."[4]

Irish national life in the first part of the nineteenth century was dominated by the legacy of the United Irishman of 1798 and the Act of Union. The 1798 movement left not merely memories of bloodshed but the idea of an Irish Republic, which would become the focus of future revolutionary movements. The 1798 rebellion was followed in 1801 by the Act of Union, which ostensibly was intended to help Ireland by uniting it closer with England. It eliminated the Irish parliament and united the two established churches into the established Church of England and Ireland. Ireland was to be represented by 28 peers and four bishops in the House of Lords and 100 MPs in the House of Commons. The Union effectively destroyed Irish autonomy and was viewed in many Irish circles as the cause of the country's troubles. The Repeal Movement became the focal point of Irish agitation during most of the nineteenth century.

The leader of the Repeal Movement was Daniel O'Connell, known in Irish history as the Great Liberator for his role in achieving Catholic emancipation. In 1823 he founded the Catholic Association in Dublin and, by holding mass meetings in the country, created a mass movement for the first time in Irish history. These tactics were successful and in 1829 Catholic emancipation was finally granted. Catholics could now hold office and were no longer required to take an oath to the established church. It was an important victory for not only what it achieved, but for the way it united the population into a single successful effort.[5] On the negative side, it created a serious rift between Catholics and

Protestants by fusing Catholicism and Irish nationalism. From then on, the Irish national movement took on a Catholic character.[6]

After 1829 O'Connell transferred his energies into the Repeal Movement, hoping that the same tactics of rallies, mass meetings, and all legal means would achieve the same results. The Repeal Association was born and had as its primary goal the restoration of the Irish parliament in Dublin. Secret societies and violence were condemned, which became an issue that would cause a major division in the movement and directly involve John Mitchel.[7]

In this period, Mitchel's Ireland was a land of tremendous poverty, with literacy at 72 percent of the population, 40 percent living in one-room cottages, and over two-thirds depending on subsistence agriculture.[8] The economic situation after the Napoleonic Wars did not look that grim at first. A large number of Irish cottagers, for example, supplemented their income by making linen cloth. The industrial revolution, however, which began in England, transformed manufacturing and marked the beginning of the end of the Irish linen cottage industry. Ireland was just too close to England. Homemade cloth could not compete with mass produced cloth from English factories. With the exception of Belfast and surrounding regions, Ireland remained a backward country with few natural resources and fewer prospects.[9] The situation was aggravated by a huge surplus of labor subsisting on a potato diet. Population grew from 4,753,000 in 1791, to 6,802,000 in 1821, and to 8,000,000 in 1841. The Irish peasant was plagued with land subdivisions and rents owed to the landowner, many of whom were absentee landlords. There were only a few self-sufficient farmers in Wicklow and Wexford counties. The agricultural situation in the north was somewhat better but the vast portion of the country was impoverished.

O'Connell and his Repealers were unable to respond to these monumental challenges of poverty or to achieve any success in the political realm. The Repealers, known as Old Irelanders, were soon challenged by a new generation of leaders who confronted their tactics and role in the national movement. This new group, Young Ireland, was composed of young educated patriots who sought the country's salvation not in alliances with political parties in England, as Old Ireland attempted, but in Ireland itself and its people. The leaders of Young Ireland included: William Smith O'Brien, a Protestant landlord and descendant of one of the few native Irish aristocratic families; Charles Gavan Duffy from the Catholic middle class in Monaghan; John Blake Dillon, a Catholic lawyer; Thomas Davis, a Protestant and the soul and philosopher of the movement; and John Mitchel. The Young Ireland movement was centered around its publication, the *Nation*. Through the paper, the Young Irelanders set out to build up Irish nationality. In this respect, they were not unlike other romantic nationalists in Europe during that period. They saw the nation as a spirit and desired to create a "national spirit."[10] The first issue of the *Nation* appeared on October 15, 1843.

270

Explaining their goals, Thomas Davis wrote: "Nationality is their first object—a nationality which will not only raise our people from their poverty by securing for them the blessings of a domestic legislature, but inflame and purify them with a lofty and heroic love of country—a nationality of the spirit as well as the letter—a nationality that comes to be stamped upon our manners, our literature and our deeds—a nationality which may embrace Protestants, Catholics, Dissenters, Milesian and Cromwellian, the Irishman of a hundred generations and the stranger who is within our gates . . ."[11]

The paper enjoyed popularity unlike any previous Irish publication, with circulation said to be up to 10,000 and readership over 250,000.[12] Thomas Davis assumed the editorial duties of the *Nation* and was the leading contributor. Other writers included John Blake Dillon, Clarence Mangan, Michael Doheny, and Charles Gavan Duffy. People who became disillusioned with O'Connell's ineffectiveness were attracted to the fresh, bold ideas found in the *Nation*. Mitchel, too, while still working in Banridge, read the paper with great interest and soon sent in his own contributions. In fact, Mitchel and Davis became the two most popular writers. Davis usually wrote articles about historical figures from the distant past while Mitchel preferred more contemporary topics.[13] This renewed passion for Irish history led the Young Irelanders to propose writing a Library of Ireland, for which each member would select a topic and write a book that would be published by Gavan Duffy. Thomas Davis wrote *Memoirs of Theobald Wolf Tone*; Gavan Duffy, *National Ballads*; and Thomas MacNevin, *The History of the Volunteers of 1772*. Mitchel chose *The Life and Times of Aodh (Hugh) O'Neill, Prince of Ulster*.[14] Known as the Phalanx Project, the whole idea was criticized by O'Donnell, who compared the Young Irelanders to the revolutionaries in France in 1789 who started by writing pamphlets.[15]

The death of Thomas Davis on September 16, 1845 was a serious blow to the Young Ireland movement. Faced with the situation, Gavan Duffy invited Mitchel to move to Dublin and assume the editorial duties of the *Nation*. Mitchel accepted the offer and moved his family to Dublin and thus began the most important phase of his life. There was some misunderstanding between Duffy and Mitchel over editorial responsibilities, with Mitchel believing he could write what he wanted. Duffy was still technically the editor and publisher and he did not want to give Mitchel complete control over the paper.[16] This question, however, did not at first cause any serious problem between Duffy and Mitchel, although later they did become enemies.[17]

Mitchel was not at the helm of his new position long before he was in conflict with the authorities. An article in an English publication stated that the railroads, then being built in Ireland, would make it possible for soldiers to reach any point in Ireland within six hours, implying that any insurrection by Irish patriots would have no chance of success. In his response in the *Nation*, Mitchel explained

271

how easily rails could be fashioned into pikes and how one could destroy rails so as to prevent any troops from reaching their destination.[18] This type of writing alarmed the authorities and brought an indictment against Duffy, the official editor of the *Nation*. In the ensuing trial, in which Mitchel played the role of defender, Duffy was acquitted with the help of three Repealers in the jury. It was the first time that the crown in Ireland did not pack a jury and get a conviction.[19] The trial's only accomplishment was to make the *Nation* even more popular among the Irish public.[20]

The new ideas of Mitchel and the Young Irelanders inevitably came into conflict with O'Connell and the Old Irelanders. The idea that repeal and a native parliament were the panacea for all of Ireland's ills was losing creditability. Mitchel and others in his group joined the Repeal Association, but they became a thorn in O'Connell's side. In 1843 O'Connell's Repeal movement was gaining momentum, with many predicting that it would be the repeal year as 1839 was the year of emancipation. Throughout the summer and autumn of 1843, meetings and rallies were held all over the country. Then, in October 1843, O'Connell called for a huge rally in Clontarf outside of Dublin. It was intended to be the largest manifestation of the year, a demonstration of the people's resolve on this issue. Prime Minister Robert Peel and his government became frightened over the prospects of such a large rally, so they issued a ban and sent in more armed soldiers to discourage trouble. O'Connell, fearing bloodshed, called off the Clontarf meeting, thereby delivering a serious blow to his leadership in the Repeal movement.[21]

The Clontarf incident also brought into sharper focus the serious differences between Old Ireland and Young Ireland. O'Connell's Old Irelanders were Catholics who enjoyed support from the majority of the population while Mitchel and Young Irelanders were both Protestant and Catholic and more intellectual (and possibly somewhat anti-clerical), some of whom were slandered as atheists and enemies of O'Connell.[22] The main difference, however, was over tactics. O'Connell wished to use all legal means at his disposal and deplored any violence. The Young Irelanders were also opposed to any unnecessary violence at first but wanted to have the freedom of option and, therefore, would not commit themselves to use peaceful means exclusively. They were also opposed to an alliance with any English government, wanting instead the freedom of action to do what they considered best for the country.[23]

For O'Connell, the main issue in 1846-47 was not the horrors of the famine but how to eliminate Mitchel and the Young Irelanders from the Repeal Association.[24] At a Repeal meeting in the Rotunda in Dublin in June 1846, O'Connell demanded that all attendees sign a pledge denouncing violence as a means to achieve their goals. O'Connell, of course, fully expected Mitchel to reject this proposal. If Mitchel and the others did not sign the resolution against violence, O'Connell said they could not be members of the Repeal Association.[25] Some have regretted how unfortunate it was for the Repeal movement to be divided over a basically academic question regarding violence. At this time, Mitchel was still not in favor of physical force but did not see any point in having to sign a statement as such. He wrote: "He should feel it his duty if he knew any member who either by speaking or writing attempted to incite the people to arms or violence as a method of obtaining their liberty, while that association existed, to report such member to the committee and move his expulsion."[26]

Removed from the Repeal Association over the issue of force, Mitchel and members of Young Ireland founded a new organization, the Irish Confederation. The first meeting was held on January 13, 1847 and, within a short time, the confederation had over 10,000 members and plans to organize confederate clubs around the country.[27]

By this time, Daniel O'Connell was a sick man suffering from a brain disease but he still commanded the respect of the population and had the support of the Catholic clergy. Mitchel, however, had a different view of the "liberator." He wrote later in his *Jail Journal:* "By mere agitation, by harmless exhibition of numerical force, by imposing demonstrations (which are fatal) nonsense, and by eternally half-unsheathing a visionary sword, which friends and foes alike knew to be a phantom—he had, as he believed, coerced the British government to pass a Relief Bill, and admit Catholics to Parliament and some offices."[28] On another occasion, Mitchel wrote that "next to the British government O'Connell was the worst enemy that Ireland ever had or rather the most fatal friend."[29]

By 1846 the whole question of Repeal was no longer relevant in light of the devastating effects of the famine then being felt in many regions of the island. The potato was first introduced into Ireland possibly as early as the end of the sixteenth century and gradually came into general use in the seventeenth century. The potato was nutritious but also "the most dangerous crop."[30] It made people rely on a food that was prone to blight and poor harvests. Furthermore, there was a period in early summer when potatoes were no longer available and forced the people to purchase food for several weeks, often from unscrupulous salesmen who charged exorbitant prices. Although there were some reports at harvest time in 1845 about finding diseased potatoes, there was no undue alarm. After all, there had been numerous crop failures in the past and they had often been localized. What they did not know was that the crop failures of 1845 and the following two harvests were caused by a new disease, called late blight (*Phytophthora infestans*). When the first potatoes were dug, everything seemed normal in many parts of the country but then, in a few days, they turned rotten and became unusable. The situation was serious but not critical. The blight of 1846, on the other hand, was catastrophic in the effects it produced and was repeated again in 1847, when the potato crop failed for a third year. One cannot exaggerate the suffering caused by the famine and its impact on the population.[31] Nothing of this magnitude had taken place in Europe since the Black Death. In addition to mass starvation, there were deaths from several diseases: scurvy, dysentery (25,446 in 1847), cholera (30,000 in 1847), but the worst was typhus fever, which claimed 57,095 lives in 1847.[32] In 1841 the population stood at 8,175,124; in 1851, 6,532,385. The loss of 1,662,739 does not take into account the natural population growth.[33] According to Mitchel, 1.5 million died as a result of the famine. In his *Apology for the British Government in Ireland*, he wrote: "As for what happened to the million and a half who perished utterly, they fell for a great cause: it was to preserve the British Empire—the due payment of dividends, the price of consuls, and the dynasty of Her Most Sacred Majesty."[34]

In Mitchel's mind, God caused the blight but England was responsible for the famine.[35] His opinions on the famine were made clear in his book with the sarcastic title, *An Apology for the British Government in Ireland* (1860), and in another work, *The Last Conquest of Ireland (Perhaps)* (1861). In *Apology for the British Government in Ireland,* Mitchel attempted to make the case that England intentionally aggravated the situation as a means to eliminate the large surplus population in Ireland. Prior to the famine, the English government organized the Landlord and Tenant Commission to look into the continually vexing question of the tenant-landlord relationship. In its report, the commission recommended ways to solve the problem, which included removing about 200,000 heads of families, encouraging emigration, and denying tenant rights.[36] To Mitchel, the commission was a "fraud" made up of landlords.[37] Mitchel used this report as additional proof that England was satisfied with at least one result of the famine—the alleviation of the problems between tenant and landlord by the elimination of the excess population.

Mitchel believed that in England's mind there was a surplus of three million people in Ireland, yet, at the same time, Ireland was producing a surplus of food that went to England. Ireland was the only country in the world, according to Mitchel, with too many people and too much food at the same time. In Mitchel's word, Ireland had "too much food for her people and too many people for her food."[38] He made a strong case to the often debated argument whether there was enough food in Ireland to prevent the famine. Mitchel repeatedly claimed that food was being exported from Ireland that should have remained home. He believed there was enough food exported from Ireland during the famine to feed 18 million people.[39] "By every tide that ebbed and flowed during the year (1847) many heavy cargoes of Irish produce floated off to England; it was necessary to England in order to maintain her establishment and keep her a first rate power in the world."[40] To illustrate his point, Mitchel cited the case of a man named Boland who was found dead in his cottage, along with his two small daughters.

Sutherland: JOHN MITCHEL

"Now, what became of poor Boland's twenty acres of crops? Part of it went to
Gibraltar, to victual the garrison; part to South Africa to provision the robber-
army; part went to Spain, to pay for the landlord's wine; part to London, to pay
the interest to his honour's mortgage to the Jews. The English ate some of it—
the Chinese had their share; the Jews and the Gentiles divided amongst them,
and there was none for Boland."⁴¹ In the *Nation,* on March 7, 1846, Mitchel
wrote:

> The Irish people, always half starved, are expecting absolute famine
> day by day; they know they are doomed to months of a weed-diet
> next summer; that hungry ruin has them in the wind—and they ascribe
> to it, unanimously, not so much to the wrath of Heaven as to the
> greedy and cruel policy of England. Be it right or wrong, such is
> their feeling. They believe that the seasons as they roll are but
> ministers of English rapacity; that their starving children cannot sit
> down to their scanty meal but they see the happy-claw of England in
> their dish. They behold their own wretched food melting in rottenness
> off the face of the earth; and they see heavy-laden ships, freighted
> with the yellow corn their own hands have sown and reaped, spreading
> sail for England; they see it and with every grain of that corn goes a
> heavy curse.⁴²

Mitchel had an opportunity to see the devastation caused by the famine first
hand in 1847 when he traveled to Galway to give support to a candidate in the
parliamentary election. He wrote:

> In the depth of winter we traveled to Galway, through the very center
> of that fertile island and saw sights that will never wholly leave the
> eyes that behold them: cowering wretches, almost naked in the savage
> weather, prowling in turnip fields, and endeavoring to grub up roots
> which had been left but running to hide as the mail coach rolled by;
> very large fields where small farms had been "consolidated," showing
> dark bars of fresh mould running through them where ditches have
> been leveled; groups and families sitting and wandering on the high
> road, with falling steps and in patient eyes gazing hopelessly into
> infinite darkness; before them, around them, above them, nothing
> but darkness and despair; parties of tall, brawny men, once the flower
> of Meath and Galway, stalking by with a fierce but vacant scowl; as
> if they knew all this ought not to be, but knew not who to blame, saw
> none they could rend in their wrath; for Lord John Russell sat safe in
> Chesham Palace; and Trevelyan, the Grand Commissioner and
> factotum of the pauper-system, wove his web of red tape around them
> from afar . . . Sometimes I could see in front of the cottages, little
> children leaning against a fence when the sun shone out—for they

275

could not stand—their limbs fleshless, their bodies half naked, their faces bloated yet wrinkled, and a pale greenish hue—children who would never, it was too plain, grow up to be men and women. I saw Trevelyan's claw in the victuals of those children; his red tape would draw them to death; in his government laboratory had prepared for them the typhus poison.[43]

England's response to the famine also came under fire by Mitchel and others in his group who saw it as inadequate and starting from a bad premise. Relief measures, soup kitchens, outdoor relief, the workhouses all came under attack from Mitchel's biting pen. A particular disturbing part of the Relief Act was the infamous "Quarter Acre Clause," which stated that anyone with a quarter of an acre of land was not eligible for relief. Thus the farmer had to sell his remaining land to eat.[44] Mitchel said that the government responded to the famine with a new Coercion Bill to thwart any violence, and the repeal of the Corn Laws, which helped consumers but was harmful to the Irish farmer who used the sale of his crop to pay the landlord.[45] As a response to the first famine, the government imported corn from the United States, but it was soon obvious that this was not a solution since there were few mills to grind the American corn and people accustomed to a potato diet did not know how to prepare the new food. The corn, too, was sold at market prices according to the principle that the "economy had to be followed, not led," Mitchel wrote.[46] There was to be "no interference with the natural course of trade."[47]

The Anglican Church in Ireland, in Mitchel's opinion, also played a role in causing the country's poverty. The policy of the Anglican Church (Church of Ireland) in imposing the penal laws was not to convert the Irish Catholic peasants but to seize their lands. If they were all converted, then another means would have to found to accomplish this. In Mitchel's words, the Anglican Church "was not a missionary church, but a predatory one. Its motto was, 'not feed my sheep', but rather shear them."[48]

The year 1847 and early 1848 were pivotal not only in terms of the famine but in the evolution of Mitchel's political views, from one of passive resistance to revolution. February 1847 was the worse month in the famine, with thousands of deaths daily directly attributable to the famine. Still Mitchel, as before, sought the cooperation of the landlords. He wanted to create a truly national movement that included the landed gentry whether they be Protestant or Catholic, English or Irish.[49] During the course of 1847, however, his views went through a transition and his attitude toward the landlords changed, although he continued to hold out some hope. "We will make every reasonable effort to win them to our side. But if they are resolved to have their pound of flesh at any cost, and to make no concessions to the people; if they persist in taking their stand with England and against their own people; then we must only see what we can do without them and against them."[50] By early 1848 he was saying that the landlords had sided with England and it was useless to woo them any longer.[51] "I would this night give my right hand to bring about a combination of the various orders of Irishmen against English domination. I do believe such a union would be the salvation of all those classes of social order, and of many thousands of human lives. But I tell you, I despair of such combination."[52]

In the evolution of Mitchel's thinking at this time, an important role was played by James Finton Lalor (1807-1849), another member of the Young Ireland and an occasional contributor to the *Nation*. Unlike others in the Young Ireland movement, however, Lalor was a social revolutionary, a land reformer. Lalor believed that Ireland could be saved not by a political alliance or by Repeal itself, but by agrarian revolution, by returning the land to the peasants, making them the proprietors not tenants. "My object is to repeal the Conquest—not any part or portion but the whole and entire conquest of seven hundred years—a thing much more easily done than to repeal the Union."[53] As far as landlords were concerned, Lalor saw them as "aliens and enemies," never part of Ireland.[54]

Mitchel embraced Lalor's ideas of peasant ownership of the land completely. Critics have said that Mitchel stole Lalor's ideas and made them his own, a charge his defenders refuted by saying that, like other great men, Mitchel and Lalor shared the same ideas.[55] Mitchel and Lalor both admitted that they were identical in their thinking on the land question.[56]

Mitchel's increasing radicalism made the more cautious Gavan Duffy uncomfortable. Mitchel was now, like Lalor, a social revolutionary and drifting toward advocating rebellion, or at least open defiance of English law. Mitchel wrote: "I found that as I became more revolutionary, Duffy became more constitutional and safe, and insisted on preaching organization, education and so forth."[57] A rift between Mitchel and Duffy was inevitable. Duffy and others, such as Smith O'Brien, wanted to continue with the original goals of the *Nation* to build up the Irish nation. Most members of the confederation sided with Duffy while Mitchel found support from T.D. Reilly, M. Doheny, John Fisher Murray, and Father Kenyon. In February 1848 Mitchel left the staff of the *Nation* and pondered his next move. His mother suggested that he return home to Derry and resume his career.[58] Mitchel, however, had gone too far to step back now at this critical time. On February 12, 1848 Mitchel began publication of his own paper, the *United Irishman*. The short-lived paper became very popular and read by people eager to hear more about his ideas. Mitchel was the sole owner of the publication so had the freedom to write what he wished without any constraints placed on him by Gavan Duffy or others. Besides Mitchel himself, writers to the new, more radical paper included: "not only Reilly, but Father Kenyon, a good Tipperary priest and one of the most accomplished scholars in Ireland; John Martin, a Protestant and a landlord; and James Clarence Mangan— Catholics, Protestants, and Pagans, but all resolute revolutionaries."[59]

Mitchel's more radical position at the end of 1847 and early 1848 was caused by several reasons; foremost among them was that he detested the worsening desolation and suffering brought on by the famine, evictions, and the influence of Lalor. By this time, Mitchel's political philosophy was clear. For one, by 1848 Mitchel encouraged the people to resist English law, to stop paying rents, and to prevent the export of food from Ireland.[60] Second, he called the people to arm themselves, for what good was opinion, he said, if it was not "armed opinion."[61] By 1848 he saw parliamentary debate and all talk of an Irish parliament as futile. "For my part, I admit that I am weary of constitutional agitation and I will never lift a finger to help it more."[62] It was English law, in his opinion, that caused food to be shipped out of the country when the people were starving, caused them to lose their land and die. In a letter to Lord Russell published in the *United Irishman*, he wrote:

> What had the law done for their poor paupers throughout Ireland? It was the "law" that carried off all the crops they raised and shipped them to England; it was the "law" that took labour of their hands and gave them half food for it while they were able to work; and cast them off to perish like supernumerary kittens. The "law" told them they must not wear the cloth they wove nor eat the corn they raised, nor dwell in the houses they built or remonstrate against the hard usage, "law" scourged and bullied them, imprisoned them, gagged and coerced them; to bring them to a more submissive mind.[63]

Mitchel did not advocate that people take up arms immediately but that they be prepared. He disliked any type of secret organizations or conspiracy and in this regard differed from the men of the '98 Rebellion. "Theirs was a secret conspiracy, ours is a public one."[64] He openly challenged his opponents and English leaders without fear of arrest.

News of the Paris Revolution hastened the path to open revolt in Ireland. "The exciting news that came in every week from France, Germany, and Italy," Mitchel later wrote, "intoxicated our people like wine; and the enemy knew that men's minds were entirely turned away from what used to be called 'moral' agitation, which had, indeed, been discovered to be extremely immoral."[65] At the first meeting after learning of the Paris Revolution, the confederation drew up a resolution urging the clubs to arm themselves.[66] At a subsequent meeting on March 15 in the Music Hall on Abbey Street, Dublin, a proclamation of support for the Paris revolutionaries was composed and a delegation consisting of William Smith O'Brien and Thomas Franis Meagher appointed to deliver it.[67] The delegation's welcome in Paris, however, was lukewarm and disappointing.[68] Lamartine, poet and minister of foreign affairs for the provisional government in Paris, was warned by the British ambassador to avoid provoking the Irish

278

situation, otherwise the British embassy in Paris would be closed.[69] At this time, the English government also dispatched a mission to the Vatican that resulted in Pope Pius IX issuing a document forbidding priests from political activities. This decree had its intended effect and resulted in Mitchel's collaborator, Father Kenyon, being suspended by his bishop.[70]

The English took other preventive measures as well. Viceroy Lord Clarendon stationed 8,000 troops in Dublin and dispatched spies and informers throughout the country.[71] To further discourage insurgency the government passed the Treason Felony Act making revolution or inciting revolution a felony crime similar to stealing or murder. To be accused of treason in Ireland might be a badge of courage, but now those accused with sedition would be treated as common criminals and be punished by transportation.[72] Mitchel's plan was to make preparations but wait until the harvest and then take a stand and prevent food from being exported from the country.[73] Mitchel's writing at this time became more radical and extreme. He had his own style though showed influence of the Bible, Carlyle, and Swift. Some of his best writings were in the form of letters and many of these appeared in the *United Irishman*. His response to the Paris Revolution was found in his Letter to the Small farmers:

> The earth is awakening from sleep; a flash of electric fire is passing through the dumb millions. Democracy is girding himself once more like a strong man to run a race and slumbering nations are arising in their might, and shaking their locks. Oh! My countrymen, look up! Arise from the death-dust where you have long been lying, and let this light visit your eyes also, and touch your soul. Let your ears drink in the blessed words, "Liberty! Fraternity! Equality!" Which are soon to ring from pole to pole. Clear steel will ere long, drawn upon you in your desolate darkness; and the rolling thunder of the people's cannon will drive before it many a heavy cloud that has long hidden from you the face of heaven. Pray for that dad; and persevere life and health, that you may worthily meet it. Above all, let the man amongst you who has no gun, sell his garment and buy one.[74]

This type of rhetoric did not go unnoticed. The English government was alarmed over Mitchel's articles that contained instructions for street fighting and recipes for making homemade bombs. A certain amount of anti-government rhetoric and assembly was tolerated in Ireland. Mitchel could address Lord Clarendon, Lord Lieutenant of Ireland, as "Her Majesty Executioner General," "General Butcher of Ireland," or "High Commissioner of Spies," without reprisals.[75] England was the only country in Europe where people could hold rallies to protest grievances and verbally assault the leadership. In most other

European countries, one would be imprisoned immediately. Mitchel, however, was going too far. The times were too dangerous and the English feared that the Irish would be influenced by the English Chartists, who were planning a big rally.[76]

Mitchel fully expected to be arrested but this did not deter him from continuing his attacks. His last writings in the *United Irishman,* entitled: "Letter to Protestant Farmers," was the immediate cause for his arrest.

> And for the institutions of this country, I loathed and despise them; we are sickening and dying of these institutions, fast; they are consuming us like the plague, degrading us to paupers in mind and body, and estate—yes making our very souls beggarly and cowardly. They are a failure and a fraud, these institutions;—from the topmost crown-jewel to the meanest detective's notebook, there is no soundness in them. God and man are weary of them. Their last hour is at hand; and I thank God that I live in the days when I shall witness the utter down fall, and trample upon the grave of the most portentous, the grandest, meanest, falsest, and cruelest tyranny that ever deformed this world.[77]

In this letter, Mitchel called for the creation of an Irish Republic and openly advocated revolution to achieve this goal. "And how are we to meet that day? In arms, my countrymen, in arms. Thus, and not otherwise, have ever nations of men sprung to liberty and power."[78] This open call for revolution and appeal to the Protestants of the north did not go unanswered by the government.

O'Brien and Meagher were arrested first and put on trial. Expecting the worst, everyone was surprised when O'Brien was acquitted, thanks to two Catholics on the jury. In Meagher's case there was a packed jury with only one Catholic, but there was another unexpected victory when the one Quaker on the jury voted to acquit. Mitchel would not be so fortunate since the government was determined that these results would not be repeated. Mitchel was arrested for sedition on May 25, 1848. By the end of the second day he was convicted and on May 27 sentenced to fourteen years transportation.[79]

There was immediate talk in the streets of Dublin of revolution and possible rescue after hearing of Mitchel's conviction and sentencing. For his part, Mitchel refused to sign a paper in Newgate Prison discouraging a rescue.[80] Nothing was done, however, and in retrospect Mitchel thought this was a mistake. "Their decision was wrong and I firmly believe, fatal. But their motives were pure and their courage unquestionable, I am bound to admit."[81]

Although the threat from Mitchel was eliminated, the government still expected trouble. Semi-military rule was established and *habeas corpus* suspended. Young Irelanders moved about the country trying to organize some

280

resistance but without much success. In Mullinahone, Tipperary, 6,000 men, for example, armed with pikes assembled but then left when they found no food. All the efforts to start a mass resistance by the Irish peasantry failed. The Revolution of 1848 in Ireland ended ingloriously with the exchange of a few shots of gunfire in a cabbage patch in Ballingary.[82]

Following his conviction, Mitchel was placed on a boat and sent first to Bermuda and, from there, to Cape Town. His final destination was Van Dieman's Island near Australia, known today as Tasmania. The rest of Mitchel's life falls beyond the scope of this study but was not in any way uneventful. To summarize, Mitchel remained on Van Dieman's Island until his escape in 1853. He succeeded in making it to Australia and, from there, sailed to California and on to New York City, where he was greeted as a hero by the local Irish population.[83] In New York, he returned to journalism and began publishing the *Citizen*. At this time, his health problems, brought on by his years of exile, forced him to relocate to a warmer climate in Knoxville, Tennessee, where he launched another paper, the *Southern Citizen*. At this time, he began to write his history of the famine, the *Last Conquest of Ireland (Perhaps)*. During this period of his life, he made two trips to France, one in 1859 lasting four months and then again in 1860, remaining two years working as a correspondent for the *Charleston Standard*.[84]

In 1862 Mitchel returned to the United States and settled in Virginia. In a strange twist, Mitchel became an advocate for the southern cause in the American Civil War. His pro-Confederacy positions appeared in the *Richmond Inquirer*. It should be added that Mitchel lost two sons in the Civil War: John Mitchel Jr. was killed at Fort Sumter at the outbreak of hostilities in April 1861; and William Mitchel fell at Gettysburg on July 4, 1863.[85]

After the war, Mitchel received a prison sentence for his support of the Confederacy. After his release, he moved back to New York and began another journalistic venture, the *Irish Citizen*. At this time, he also wrote his *History of Ireland,* which covered Irish history from the Treaty of Limerick until 1852.[86]

In one final gesture of defiance, Mitchel returned to Ireland in 1874 and declared himself a parliamentary candidate to represent Tipperary. He was victorious but Disraeli debated whether a convicted felon should be permitted in the Parliament. By this time, however, Mitchel's health was failing and this question was irrelevant. John Mitchel died on March 20, 1875 at the home of his brother-in-law in Newry.[87]

Unlike many other Young Irelanders who died soon after 1848, Mitchel had many years to ponder the mistakes of 1848. He was under no illusion that it would be a difficult struggle but he felt it was worth the risk since it was, "better that men should perish by the bayonets of the enemy than by their laws."[88] There were several reasons that explain why a large scale uprising did not succeed in Ireland in 1848. For one, there was a lack of funds to buy weapons and, of the

80 confederation clubs, none or very few were in the rural districts where the revolution was expected to start.[89] It seemed that, with so many famine deaths and evictions, the Irish peasantry were ready for revolt, but they were too weak and demoralized from starvation to act. Mitchel did not consider Ballingary a failure, however. "If the people had been half-armed, half-clothed, and one quarter fed, they would have acted otherwise."[90] Finally, Mitchel and others in the Young Ireland movement were idealists and intellectuals with little grasp of the rural mentality.[91] Mitchel had never lived among the common people in the agricultural districts, but had only visited them. He believed that the people would simply rise up and destroy the enemy. His argument that there was enough food in Ireland during the famine years was probably correct and was supported by others. His contention, however, that England caused the famine deliberately as a form of genocide did not bear up to the facts.[92]

In the final analysis, Mitchel's legacy was in his influence on future Irish leaders, especially Michael Davitt of the Land League and the socialist John Connolly. Patrick Pearse, leader of the Easter Rebellion in 1916, called Mitchel a prophet: "Mitchel was of the stuff of which the great prophets and ecstatics have been made. He did really hold converse with God; he did really deliver God's word to man, delivered it fiery tongued."[93] Mitchel and Young Ireland are considered precursors of the Sinn Fein movement of the twentieth century. The founder of Sinn Fein, Arthur Griffith, compared Mitchel with the Hungarian hero of 1848, Louis Kossuth. Both were lawyers who became journalists to help their country. Here, however, the comparison ends, Griffith said. "Kossuth's country responded to the call, Mitchel's country shrank back . . . Kossuth was an enthusiastic republican; Mitchel was a nationalist, cared not two pence for republicanism in the abstract. Kossuth was a writer of ability—Mitchel, a man of the first literary genius. Finally, Kossuth's great virtues were clouded by his vanity; Mitchel, like all proud men, had no vanity . . . Fortune has confined the fame of John Mitchel to the country he served, while it has given the name Louis Kossuth a world significance."[94]

It seems that Mitchel was not unlike many of his contemporaries of 1848, an intellectual and idealist who had a romantic vision of revolution. He failed in 1848, but his words and courage inspired a nation for many generations.

Notes

1. William Dillon, *Life of John Mitchel* 1 (London: Kegan Paul, Trench & Co., 1888), x-xi.

2. *Ibid.*, 1-16.

3. *Ibid.*, 4.

4. T.F. O'Sullivan, *The Young Irelanders* (Tralee: The Kerryman Ltd, 1945), 134.

5. Gearoid O'Tuathaigh, *Ireland Before the Famine 1798-1848* (Dublin: Gill and Macmillan, 1979), 76-77.

6. *Ibid.*

7. *Ibid.*, 162.

8. *Ibid.*, 148.

9. *Ibid.*, 117.

10. *Ibid.*, 186-87.

11. P.A.S. (P.A. Sillard of the '48), *The Life of John Mitchel with an Historical Sketch of the '48 Movement in Ireland* (Dublin: James Duffy & Co., 1889), 4.

12. O'Tuathaigh, 188.

13. P.A.S., 7. See T.S. Rolleston, ed., *Prose Writings of Thomas Davis* (London: Walter Scott, 1889).

14. P.A.S., 35-37.

15. Dillon, 139.

16. *Ibid.*, 82-84.

17. *Ibid.*, 84.

18. P.A.S., 33.

19. *Ibid.*, 33-34.

20. *Ibid.*, 34.

21. O'Tuathaigh, 190.

22. Cecil Woodham-Smith, *The Great Hunger* (New York and Evanston: Harper & Row, 1962), 330.

23. O'Tuathaigh, 195.

24. Woodham-Smith, 330.

25. Dillon, 116.

26. *Ibid.*, 118.

27. *Ibid.*, 144-45.

28. John Mitchel, *Jail Journal*, Arthur Griffith, preface (Dublin: M.H. Gill & Son, [1940]), xxxv.

29. Dillon, 116.

30. Woodham-Smith, 35.

31. Redcliffe Salaman, *The History and Social Influence of the Potato* (Cambridge: Cambridge University Press, 1985), 300.

32. *Ibid.*, 304.

33. *Ibid.*, 317.

34. John Mitchel, *An Apology for the British Government in Ireland* (Dublin: O'Donoghue and Company, 1905), 50.

283

35. *Ibid.*, 49.

36. *Ibid.*, 12-13.

37. John Mitchel, *The Last Conquest of Ireland (Perhaps)* (Glasgow: Cameron, Ferguson & Co., n.d.), 68.

38. Mitchel, *An Apology*, 11.

39. *Ibid.*

40. *Ibid.*, 16.

41. Dillon, 216.

42. *Ibid.*, 104.

43. *Ibid.*, 146-47.

44. Mitchel, *An Apology*, 39.

45. *Ibid.*, 26.

46. *Ibid.*, 40.

47. *Ibid.*, 30.

48. *Ibid.*, p52-53.

49. Dillon, 184.

50. *Ibid.*, 189.

51. *Ibid.*, 189.

52. *Ibid.*

53. Letter of James Lalor to John Mitchel, July 21, 1847, in L. Fogarty, *James Finton Lalor: Patriot and Political Essayist (1807-1849)* (Dublin: The Talbot Press, 1921), 44.

54. *Ibid.*, 43.

55. Dillon, 151.

56. Fogarty, xxix.

57. Letter of John Mitchel to James Lalor, January 4, 1848, in Fogarty, 121.

58. Dillon, 180.

59. *Ibid.*, 204.

60. *Ibid.*, 192.

61. *Ibid.*, 195.

62. *Ibid.*, 194.

63. *Ibid.*, 225.

64. *Ibid.*, 197.

65. Mitchel, *The Last Conquest*, 164.

66. Dillon, 214.

67. *Ibid.*, 218.

68. *Ibid.*, 219-20.

69. Woodham-Smith, 341.

70. *Ibid.*, 342.

71. Mitchel, *Jail Journal*, xli.

72. Woodham-Smith, 340.

73. Dillon, 220.

74. *Ibid.*, 218.

75. Woodham-Smith, 339.

76. *Ibid.*, 337-38.

77. Mitchel, *The Last Conquest*, 179.

78. *Ibid.*, 180.
79. Dillon, 242-43.
80. Mitchel, *Jail Journal*, xlvi.
81. *Ibid.*
82. Woodham-Smith, 357-58.
83. P.A.S., 245.
84. *Ibid.*, 250-51.
85. *Ibid.*, 252.
86. *Ibid.*, 248.
87. *Ibid.*, 279.
88. Mitchel, *Jail Journal*, xli.
89. Woodham-Smith, 345.
90. Mitchel, *Jail Journal*, 146.
91. Woodham-Smith, 337.
92. O'Tuathaigh, 218.
93. O'Sullivan, 131.
94. Arthur Griffith, in John Mitchel, *Jail Journal*, xv.

285

Tocqueville and the
French Revolution of 1848

Seymour Drescher
University of Pittsburgh

Alexis de Tocqueville experienced the Revolution of 1848 with a deep sense of *déjà vu*. His entire life had been spent as an heir and witness to what now seemed like an endless cycle of upheavals and reactions. He was born into a noble family deeply traumatized by the French Revolution of 1789. His mother was the granddaughter of Malesherbes, who defended Louis XVI at his trial before the Revolutionary Convention in 1793, and was himself executed early the next year. Tocqueville's own parents were arrested during the Revolutionary Terror of 1793-94 and remained in prison until three months after Thermidor and Robiespierre's fall from power.

The Great Revolution, as it subsequently came to be called, left a lasting imprint on Tocqueville's family. Alexis's father, Hervé de Tocqueville, awoke one morning in prison to find that his hair had turned completely white. His mother's emotional stability and health never completely recovered from the experience. By the time Alexis was born to the couple, on 11 Thermidor of the Revolutionary year XIII (July 29, 1805), the family had withdrawn completely from discussions of public life, but the young Alexis remembered the sad solemnity that marked the annual commemorations of the king's execution.[1]

Tocqueville's own life was to be marked by reverberations of that revolution. When he was nine years old Napoleon Bonaparte abdicated, recovered power for a brief hundred days, and was finally recaptured and exiled. A brother of Louis XVI retrieved the Bourbon legacy as Louis XVIII in 1814. He fled before Napoleon in 1815, and returned after the battle of Waterloo to reign for another nine years. In 1824 Louis's younger brother inherited the French throne. He managed to reign for only six more years as Charles X before fleeing into exile in the wake of another revolution in 1830. That July Revolution resulted in the enthronement of Louis Philippe, the head of the Orleans branch of the royal family. Louis Philippe's overthrow, in 1848, marked only another step in a series of upheavals. After three years of a second republic, its president, Louis-Napoleon Bonaparte, repeated his uncle's *coup d'état* against the Republic.

Even excluding Napoleon's hundred days, the average duration of these regimes was less than nine years. Tocqueville never spent two decades of his life under a single regime. Born at the height of the autocratic rule of the first imperial Bonaparte, he was destined to die under Napoleon III, in 1859. It is no wonder that Tocqueville felt that his life coincided with the repeated failure of constitutional liberty in France. His entire career as a writer and legislator was an unrelenting effort to free his country from a vicious cycle of revolution and despotism with no end in sight.

Tocqueville's early experiences and reflections convinced him that ordered liberty in his country could never be achieved by an attempt to reincorporate the principle of aristocracy into French politics. His father had been returned to a position of administrative authority under the restored Bourban monarchy in 1814. Alexis was himself being groomed for a position in the French magistracy when the Revolution of 1830 intervened. He maintained his official position under a cloud of suspicion because of his family background. Convinced that democracy was the wave of the world's future, Tocqueville decided to visit the United States.

In contrast to France, the American polity in 1831 was a stable federated republic. Its constitution had endured for nearly half a century. Together with his traveling companion, Gustave de Beaumont, Tocqueville journeyed through America in 1831-32.[2] In 1835 he published the first part of his *Democracy in America*, in which he attempted to convey two major messages to his French compatriots: The history of Europe had demonstrated a long historical development from inequality to equality; and democracy was the wave of the future. The most critical choice for any society was whether that transformation to equality would lead to orderly political liberty or to revolution and despotism. *Democracy in America* surveyed a society that had made a successful choice in favor of freedom.

In *Democracy,* his one passing reference to the American revolutionary experience emphasized a sharp difference between the United States and France. The upheaval that accompanied America's war for independence from England was portrayed as relatively minor when compared to the French Revolution's blood-drenched struggle for survival, and its subsequent expansion over much of Europe. What was most significant for Tocqueville was the American Founding Fathers' ability to bring their revolutionary upheaval to an end with the ratification of an enduring constitution. Entirely new in the history of great nations was America's creation of a set of organic laws "without costing humanity a single tear or drop of blood."[3] In a comparative perspective, the United States had become democratic without ever having had to experience a democratic revolution.

While Tocqueville was writing his first *Democracy* in the early 1830s, many Frenchmen were still attempting to instigate fresh revolutionary outbreaks. Significantly, even in that first *Democracy*, Tocqueville focused his reader's attention not on the potential for further and more popular revolution but on the more durable malady of authoritarian despotism. In France, despotism had become part and parcel of the revolutionary cycle. "If we do not succeed in founding the peaceful rule of the majority," he warned his readers, "we will sooner or later find ourselves subject to the *unlimited* power of a single individual."[4] By the time Tocqueville finished his second *Democracy* in 1840, he concluded that, for France and Europe, a new kind of democratic despotism might emerge from the new egalitarian society. "A mild despotism" might come to power France, not by revolutionary violence but by bureaucratic stealth.

In this respect, the very fear of revolution in France could be more corrosive of political liberty than a real danger of revolutionary violence. The *Democracy* of 1840 contained a chapter pointedly entitled, "Why Great Revolutions Will Become Rare."[5] Tocqueville had that single chapter published separately as an article in the Parisian *Revue des Deux Mondes*. Three years later he anonymously reiterated the same message in a series of newspaper articles on the political situation of France. One key article was entitled, "Why the Majority do not Want Revolution"; and another, "The Parties Outside the Majority can Make no Revolution."[6] Tocqueville's argument was straightforward. The great majority of Frenchmen, especially the peasantry, had benefited enormously from the revolution by strengthening their ownership of the land. The Great Revolution of 1789 had therefore made them averse to any further upheaval that might threaten those gains. The upper and middle classes were even more fearful of upheavals that might call into question the sanctity of property, a major achievement of the French Revolution. Since landed property was the principal qualification for the right to vote or hold office in the constitutional monarchy between 1815 and 1848, France's real political risk for the foreseeable future was that these wealthy proprietors might attempt to stifle the process of political reform from an exaggerated fear of igniting another revolution. Fear of revolution might lead to tolerating despotism.

In 1839, just as he was completing the second part of the *Democracy*, Tocqueville was elected to the Chamber of Deputies, the lower house of the French legislature. Under the electoral system of the constitutional monarchy, Tocqueville was necessarily elected by a very small percentage of the people. Nevertheless, as a legislator he continued to insist that France pursue policies in accord with its status as the most democratic society in Europe. He actively participated in a movement for ending French colonial slavery as an action demanded by France's emerging democracy. For Tocqueville, slave emancipation would fulfill the ideas of universal freedom and equality that had challenged

288

servitude throughout the world in 1789. A democratic France could not allow herself to be shamed by an "aristocratic" Britain, whose own government had emancipated Britain's colonial slaves. The British had also shown that a truly revolutionary undertaking, like slave emancipation, could be made to conform to a non-violent process. Echoing his *Democracy's* encomium to the American founding fathers, Tocqueville urged his fellow countrymen to note the example of the British Slave Emancipation Act of 1833. "Let us look at the facts," he wrote in 1843: "The claims of 800,000 slaves were broken at a single stroke . . . In ten years the abolition of slavery in the English colonies has not produced a *single* insurrection; it has not cost the life of a *single* man; and yet the Negroes are twelve times as numerous as the whites in the English colonies." Echoing his praise of American constitution-making in *Democracy*, Tocqueville again noted: "There was not a drop of blood shed, nor one estate destroyed throughout the vast extent of the English colonies."[7] Just as the English had produced a bloodless revolution, so too could the French, legally, peacefully, and without economic dislocation.

Despite his prognoses of the early 1840s, however, revolution again returned to France in 1848, complete with riots, barricades, and bloodshed. What had happened? Tocqueville had recognized, but underestimated, the fragility of a regime based on a narrow electoral franchise. French legislators of the July Monarchy were elected by a quarter of a million voters out of an adult population of twenty millions. As early as his journey to America, Tocqueville recognized that suffrage eventually would have to extend to almost all male citizens. Nevertheless, in the Chamber of Deputies he showed very little enthusiasm for the rapid expansion of the French electorate. He was more immediately concerned with reducing corruption in the existing system. He was disturbed by the political apathy of the enfranchised, but seemed equally fearful of any agitation by the un-enfranchised.

About a year before the Revolution of 1848, Tocqueville was invited to join a group of parliamentary reformers, including Beaumont, his American traveling companion. They were launching an extra-parliamentary agitation in favor of a very moderate extension of the suffrage. Tocqueville declined to join. He raised the objection that renewed agitation among the disenfranchised after a very long period of quiescence might awaken popular passions far beyond the campaigners' desires.[8]

Even before the outbreak of revolution in February 1848, Tocqueville became convinced that an assault on property would be the newest twist in the history of French revolutionary ideas. These ideas, under the aegis of socialism and communism, were challenging the principle of private property. Tocqueville thought that property, like marriage and family, were so rooted in human nature as to be essential to civilization itself. His *Democracy* of 1840 assumed that property rights had been enormously strengthened by the Great Revolution. Tocqueville now became more acutely aware of how property, as the most prominent remaining symbol of inequality in France, might itself be subverted in the course of an egalitarian revolution. "Does anyone think," he had asked the readers of his *Democracy of 1835*, "that democracy, having destroyed feudalism and vanquished kings, will be daunted by the bourgeois and the rich?"[9] Socialism, he noted in 1848, became the distinctive and most arresting characteristic of the February Revolution. Although the Great Revolution of 1789 had embodied the egalitarian revolution in attacking a host of privileges as remnants of inequality, the distribution of property remained the principal post-revolutionary obstacle to equality among men. "Was it not necessary," wrote Tocqueville in retrospect, that "at least the thought of abolishing it [property] should occur in the minds of those who did not enjoy it?"[10]

Just a month before the February Revolution, Tocqueville had become so impressed by the signs of an impending confrontation with socialist ideas that he predicted the coming conflict in an impassioned speech to the Chamber of Deputies. He noted that, at the end of January 1848, although there was still no physical violence in the land, "disorder has entered deeply into men's minds." "Social ideas" had become "passions of the working classes;" these ideas were directed not just against this or that law but against the very foundations of society. The combination of demoralization among the voting elite and rising discontent among the disfranchised lower class had produced an explosive situation. "Do you know what may happen in France in a year from now," he asked, "in a month, perhaps in a day? . . . You do not know; but you are aware that there is a storm on the horizon and that it is moving in your direction."[11] Less than a month later the storm broke.

Tocqueville viewed the Revolution of February 24, 1848 with deeply mixed feelings. His own cry of alarm to the Chamber of Deputies turned out to be far more prophetic than he himself had imagined or wished. He experienced the fall of the July Monarchy, however, with a sense of relief as well as deep anxiety; anxiety, because any end to the French revolutionary cycles seemed to be more distant than ever. The demise of the monarchy during the final meeting of the Chamber of Deputies on February 24 struck him as a poor theatrical reenactment of the *journées* of the first revolution, "like a bad tragedy performed by provincial actors."[12] It concealed the real originality of the working class revolutionaries, whose revolutionary demands appeared only when a republic was declared at the Paris Hotel de Ville a few hours later.

Nevertheless, Tocqueville was also relieved that the petty and stifled political life of the monarchy was at an end. He felt a kind of liberation at the breakup of that parliamentary world. Its old elite legislators, like himself, were now like river oarsmen suddenly finding themselves called to navigate in mid-ocean. The

Parisian worker's challenge to traditional society opened up by socialism offered him the opportunity to participate in the great politics of a revolution.

On March 2, 1848 the new republic's provisional government decreed a National Constituent Assembly based on universal male suffrage. This challenged Tocqueville to move from a constituency of a few hundred landholders to a departmental electorate of well over a hundred thousand voters from all classes. Tocqueville's successful adjustment to the new electoral order was one of the major feats of his political career. He returned to his department of La Manche on the Atlantic coast, uncertain as to how his new constituency would react to the candidacy of a former deputy who was at once both the descendant of the pre-revolutionary nobility and also the descendant of privileged notables of the July Monarchy.

In his favor was the long association of his name with the great republic on the other side of the Atlantic. Tocqueville lost no time in arranging for a reprinting of *Democracy in America*, with a new preface that emphasized his early choice of a democratic republic as the model for France. With its stable political system, its law abiding citizenry, and its respect for property rights, the United States was at once republican and conservative.

Tocqueville had not misjudged his constituency, which was both politically egalitarian and socially conservative. In a series of public appearances, he managed to win the support of provincial proprietors, increasingly frightened by Parisian working class demands for large-scale public projects in favor of urban labor. More surprising, even to Tocqueville, was his immense success at a mass meeting in the city of Cherbourg before a large working class population. His accurate estimate of the desires of his constituents was confirmed by his election to the National Constituent Assembly on Easter Sunday, March 19, 1848.[13]

The election victory was one of the most emotional moments of his political life. The next day, he wrote to his wife:

> I felt an extraordinary tug at my heart, and (something I dare say only to you), I cried like a child . . . In the time in which we are now living, such outbursts of emotion are not good . . . I need all my strength. I am at once dismayed and moved to see the confidence that this whole population places in me, even though I have no power over their fate . . . It seems as though I hold their whole future in my pocket; and yet who can do anything for the future of anyone in this great game of chance that France is playing today.[14]

Tocqueville's own electoral popularity was not just a matter of a passing moment. The following year, after the dissolution of the Constituent Assembly, he emerged as the top vote-getter in his department. For the rest of the Second Republic, he remained a firm supporter of universal male suffrage.

At the beginning of the revolution, Tocqueville's priority was to prevent the Republic from moving in the direction of socialism. As a member of the large conservative republican majority in the Constituent Assembly, he was anxious to confront the revolutionary Parisian leaders, who were bitterly disappointed by the outcome of the election. When some of the "reds" invaded the Constituent Assembly, on May 15, 1848, Tocqueville was among the majority of representatives who passively resisted the incursion until the sounds of approaching National Guardsmen caused the revolutionary cohort to flee the building. Tocqueville described the day's events to his constituents as the Assembly's successful resistance to a mob trying to impose a dictatorship of the minority over the representatives of the entire nation.[15] Tocqueville's description of his only direct encounter with revolutionaries was laden with contempt:

> It was a rabble, not a troop. I did see some drunks among them, but most of them seemed to be prey to a feverish excitement due to the shouting outside and the stifling, crushing discomfort and heat inside; they were dripping with sweat, although the nature and state of their clothing should have made the heat not particularly disagreeable, for sometimes a good deal of naked skin was showing.[16]

His portrait of one of the revolutionary leaders was even more scathing:

> It was at that moment that I saw a man go up onto the rostrum, and although I have never seen him again, the memory of him has filled me with disgust and horror ever since. He had sunken, withered cheeks, white lips, and a sickly, malign, dirty look like a pallid, moldy corpse; he was wearing no visible linen; an old black frockcoat covered his lean emancipated limbs tightly; he looked as if he lived in a sewer and only just come out. I was told that this was [August] Blanqui.[17]

If Tocqueville was accurate, the pathological description of Blanqui was as much a commentary on Paris's prisons as it was on its sewers.[18] Describing a hostile porter in his own apartment house during the June Days, a month later, Tocqueville characterized the man as a mentally disturbed café-crawler and wife beater, "in short a Socialist by birth, or rather by temperament."[19]

In the wake of the May 15 incursion, the Constituent Assembly undertook a series of acts designed to demobilize the working class. It began with the outlawing of Parisian clubs as centers of revolutionary activity and subversion. The next step was the closure of the national workshops, the products of a great state employment project created after the February Revolution. Tocqueville wholeheartedly supported the Assembly's policy. Resistance to the closureaquickly expanded into a major Parisian insurrection. Tocqueville fully expected a major confrontation and welcomed the general opposition to Parisian demands by the nationally elected representatives. He foresaw that the National Guard and the military would crush the insurgency. Tocqueville regarded the battle as a fundamental class struggle, analogous to the slave uprisings of antiquity. He viewed that struggle as a decisive battle for the basic principles of civilization. For Tocqueville, the June Days were both necessary and fateful. If they did not "quench the fire of revolution," he wrote in retrospect, "they delivered the nation from oppression by the Paris workmen and restored it to control of its own fate."[20]

The single most important tendency that Tocqueville perceived in the various socialist theories and practical demands was the state-centralist element that he had identified as the most pernicious and persistent element in French political culture. As he had written in the *Democracy* of 1840, the "unity, ubiquity, and omnipotence of the social power and the uniformity of its rules constitute the most striking feature of all political systems invented in our days. They recur in the most fantastic utopias. The human mind still pursues them in its dreams."

In 1848 Tocqueville felt that France directly faced a supreme political threat from this centralizing impulse. He was no longer engaged in theoretical analysis, but was a deeply partisan actor. His principal aim was to prevent the Revolution of 1848 from being identified with a "social" revolution, demanding a vast and indeterminate expansion of state power. The June Days found him at the barricades, acting as a volunteer liaison of the National Assembly to the army regulars and national guardsmen engaged in combat with the insurgents.[21]

In contrast to his descriptions of the Parisian workers on May 15, he sympathetically welcomed the thousands of men hastening to the aid of the National Assembly from every part of France. Thanks to the newly developing railway system, they converged on Paris from up to 200 leagues away in a few days. They were representatives of provincial France, farmers, shopkeepers, landlords, lawyers, doctors and nobles, "all mingled together in the same struggle."[22]

His final assessment was that the bid for a violent socialist, even a social, revolution had been buried, if only for the time being. He tried to seal that burial in a speech to the assembly on a "Right to Work" clause in the new constitution a few months later. In that speech, Tocqueville triumphantly invoked the mandate of universal suffrage against both the working class violence of May and June and the socialist implications of the right to work. He confidently proclaimed that France's ten million proprietors could "allow your doctrines to be elaborated without danger."[23]

Even as he spoke, however, he was aware of unmistakable signs that the violent crushing of the potential dictatorship of the radical left had opened the gates to the undermining of republican institutions by an anti-liberal reaction among the frightened conservatives. The classic means of political action—public meetings, associations, and newspapers—were being restricted and shut down, one by one. As Tocqueville later acknowledged in his *Recollections*, the violence of the June Days was followed by a "dread of, and perhaps a distaste for, free institutions," growing ever more irresistible. By 1850 he clearly anticipated that "all of *us*, Socialists, Montagnards and Liberal Republicans, will fall into common discredit."[24]

Because of his reputation as an outstanding expert on the American republic, Tocqueville was elected to the committee that drafted the constitution of the second French Republic. In the tense month between the May invasion of the assembly and the June Days, working on the first draft of the constitution was difficult. The nation clamored for quick results. Despite his position on the committee as an expert on the United States, Tocqueville was unsuccessful in getting his colleagues to break with some French precedents in preparing the new constitution. Foreign examples were held in relatively low esteem by the overwhelming majority of the constitutional drafting committee. Tocqueville was unable to get his fellow colleagues to begin by building the local foundations of politics before turning to the national government. At the national level, Tocqueville was fearful that a unicameral legislature would increase the potential for a repetition of the radical convention of 1793-94. He feared concentrating too much power in the hands of a single legislature, acting without check in the name of the majority. Vigorously advocating a bicameral legislature, Tocqueville evoked not only the dual legislature of the U.S. federal government but the bicameral legislative structure of all thirty state republics in the United States. As always, Tocqueville emphasized the necessity for brakes on legislative power, whether in the hands of temporary majorities or of unicameral legislatures.[25]

Tocqueville also wanted the French executive to be a strong institutional counterweight to a unicameral legislature. Here again, Tocqueville unsuccessfully advocated the creation of an American-style Electoral College as a layer of protection against an unwise decision by the new mass electorate. Tocqueville was most satisfied with that part of the constitution dealing with the judiciary.[26] His companion, Gustave de Beaumont, drafted much of the constitutional provisions for that branch.

From the tenor of Tocqueville's actions from February until well after the June Days, he was more concerned with volatile swings in mass moods and legislative haste than with the bureaucratic state apparatus that loomed so large in his *Democracy* of 1840. His voting pattern indicates that he was most concerned with crushing agitation from the left. He consistently voted in accord with the conservative republican wing of the Constituent Assembly on several critical issues. In July 1848 the assembly discussed proposals for restricting public assembly and voluntary associations. The legislators aimed at making the earlier restrictions on working class clubs permanent. Secret societies were banned. Political meetings had to be open to the public and had to document their activities. Tocqueville voted with the overwhelming majority (629 to 100) in favor of police surveillance of associations. He also voted with the much smaller majority (370 to 362) to exempt violators from a jury trial. In this respect, Tocqueville's vote contrasted with *Democracy's* emphasis on the jury as a foundational embodiment of political liberty in the United States.[27]

In general, Tocqueville remained committed to the anti-"rouge" majority through the end of his brief term as foreign minister in November 1849. The six months after his departure from the ministry were followed by a marked shift in his political position. As his health deteriorated, he increasingly had to absent himself from legislative sessions. He finally was forced to take almost a year's leave of absence from France during the winter and spring of 1850-51. His political allies found themselves increasingly at odds with the monarchical majority that had won the legislative elections of 1849. Tocqueville now saw the chief threat to both the republic and liberal institutions as coming at least as much from the monarchist, clerical, and Bonapartist right as from the radical republican left.

Tocqueville was dismayed by the assembly's passage of ever more restrictive French press and association laws in his absence. By 1850-51 a counter-revolutionary current was undermining the fundamental institutional liberties that Tocqueville thought he had rescued from the radical "rouges." The critical turning point was the assembly's subversion of universal manhood suffrage, guaranteed by the constitution he had helped to draft and ratify. By inserting a three year continuous residency requirement for eligibility to vote, the assembly effectively disenfranchised 30 percent of the poorest and most mobile sector of the electorate.[28]

Tocqueville estimated that the disenfranchisement in his own local area amounted to almost half of those who had voted in the elections of 1848 and 1849. He had come in at the top of his departmental list in the 1849 legislative election. His name was astonishingly inscribed on nearly every ballot cast in his department. He was now convinced that universal suffrage was, and would be, the fundamental source of political legitimacy in France. In *Democracy in America* his assessment of popular sovereignty at all levels of government had been balanced by the consideration that inexperienced voters might increase the instability of democratic politics and enhance the potential for a "tyranny of the majority."[29] By 1851, this fear was subordinated to the advantages of universal suffrage in legitimating political authority. If no part of the people were left out, revolutionary minorities could lay no claim to speak for the masses. France had obviously not been made immune from revolutions as he had forecast in the early 1840's, but universal male suffrage itself constituted a barrier against the unfolding of another "great revolution." Because the [Great] Revolution peopled France with ten million proprietors, he reminded the radicals in the National Assembly, the left's doctrines could trouble society, "but thanks to the French Revolution they will not prevail against it or destroy it."[30]

Tocqueville felt that the conservative-dominated Legislative Assembly later committed a huge blunder in restricting the suffrage right in the spring of 1850. The biggest loser was the legitimacy of the republic itself: "The absence of universal suffrage deprived us of the only moral force society possesses today, *the moral power of the universal vote*, without ridding us of the danger of the damages linked to that vote."[31] President Louis Napoleon Bonaparte began criticizing the disenfranchising Law of 1850 to present himself as the defender of popular suffrage. Tocqueville's final political act under the republic was to initiate a resolution in the *Conseil Générale* of his department calling for the abrogation of the law of 1850. By blatantly abandoning that principle, the legislature had subverted its own legitimacy. It opened the door to an executive overthrow of the republic by Louis Napoleon Bonaparte, elected president by universal suffrage in 1848 but prohibited by the constitution from running again at the expiration of his term in 1852.

The president finally moved to repeat his uncle's *coup d 'etat* against the republic on December 2, 1851. Tocqueville and more than two hundred legislators met to protest the seizure of power. They were quickly arrested by military forces acting under presidential orders. Almost fifty-eight years to the month that his parents were carried off to prison in Paris under orders from the revolutionary Committee of Public Security, their son was transported to Vincennes military barracks in a convict wagon. One can only imagine the reaction of the aged Hervé de Tocqueville on hearing news of his son's incarceration.

Alexis's experience was, of course, far less traumatic than that of his parents six decades earlier. The defiant legislators confined their protest to the legal forms prescribed by the constitution. They made no attempt to rally popular protest or to call for violent resistance to the military takeover. They were, "in the last analysis, more fearful of revolutionary action than of anything they believed the president might do."[32] Louis Napoleon reciprocated by releasing them after a few days. Tocqueville's delicate health and his prior civil relations with the president stood him in good stead. During the first night of his incarceration, a colonel of their acquaintance invited a few deputies, including Tocqueville, to sleep in the officer's quarters. Most other conservative and moderate legislators were also released from confinement within two days.[33]

Nevertheless, Tocqueville underestimated neither the seriousness of the coup nor the extent of its violent suppression of the Second Republic. One of his first acts after being released was to smuggle an account of the proceedings to England.

It quickly appeared in the *Times* of London. In the report, Tocqueville linked the fate of the people's representatives to the more violent repression of the street resistance in Paris. Indeed, he pointedly claimed that the overall suppression of resistance in France had been as deadly as that of the June Days in Paris. To an English friend, Tocqueville, with some exaggeration, compared the president's actions to those of the Committee of Public Safety under the Terror. He now drew attention to the thousands of "rouges" being exiled to the deadly colony of French Guiana. Sadly, Tocqueville acknowledged some responsibility for Napoleon's success to the law of May 31, 1850: It had given the president an incomparable weapon against the legislature.[34]

The ascendancy of Louis Napoleon Bonaparte offered Tocqueville final evidence that the French cycle of violent alterations between revolution and despotism continued unabated. In one sense, his predictions in the1840's that the odds were against another "great revolution" in French society had been clearly demonstrated in June 1848. The same demonstration would later be repeated in the provincial response to the Paris Commune of 1871. Nevertheless, even short of a great revolution, France seemed to be mired in a historical pattern that favored reliance on a centralized authoritarian state far more than institutions supporting self-government and political liberty. Despite his insistence on the illegitimacy of the Bonapartist coup, he privately conceded that the majority of the population had acceded to the oppression of a minority of fellow citizens at the end of the Second French Republic. In Spring 1852 he resigned from his last remaining political position—departmental *conseil générale*. He refused to take the oath of loyalty to the new regime. He told his constituents that he could not participate in an un-free institution, even one that momentarily represented "the will of France," ratified by a referendum.[35]

Tocqueville spent the last seven years of his life analyzing the roots of France's political pathology. In *The Old Regime and the Revolution* he dissected every organ of France's past in an effort to discover the historical roots of the laws and customs that governed its political life. His preface linked his history firmly to the present. "I never entirely lost sight of our modern society. I wanted to discover not only what illness killed the patient [pre-revolutionary France], but how the patient could have been cured . . . how [Frenchmen] were changed and transformed in the course of [the Revolution] yet never changed their nature, always reappearing with slightly different faces, but always recognizable."[36]

In that last work, Tocqueville again turned the reader's attention to respect for the majority. Obviously thinking of the revolutionaries of both the first and second French republics he wrote:

> Real and respectful submission to the will of the majority was as foreign to them as submission to the divine will. Almost all

revolutionaries since then have shown this double character. They are very far in this from the respect shown by the English and the Americans for the feelings of the majority of their fellow citizens. Among the English and Americans reason is proud and self-confident but never insolent; thus it has led to freedom, while our kind of reason has only invented new forms of slavery.[37]

By understanding both the old regime and the revolution, he hoped to demystify the debilitating passions that had ever since made his countrymen "tremble at the very idea of a revolution." In the end, he decided, revolutions were short and despotism was long. Only political liberty could effectively prevent his fellow citizens from being forever imprisoned in the institutions and customs that perpetuated the cycles of upheaval and repression.

Notes

1. See André Jardin, *Tocqueville: A Biography*, Lydia Davis and Robert Hemenway, trans. (New York: Farrar Straus & Giroux, 1988), chap. 1, "An Aristocratic Family during the Revolution."

2. See George Wilson Pierson, *Tocqueville and Beaumont in America* (New York: Oxford University Press, 1938).

3. Alexis de Tocqueville, *Democracy in America*, Arthur Goldhammer, trans. (New York: Literary Classics of the United States, 2004), 128.

4. *Ibid.*, 364.

5. *Ibid.*, 747-60.

6. See *Tocqueville and Beaumont on Social Reform,* Seymour Drescher, ed. and trans. (New York: Harper and Row, 1968), XI, "Letters on the Condition of France" (January 3 and 5, 1843), 192-200.

7. *Ibid.*, 129, 154.

8. Alexis de Tocqueville, *Recollections,* J. Mayer and A. Kerr, eds., George Lawrence, trans. (Garden City, NY: Doubleday, 1970), chap. 2.

9. Tocqueville, *Democracy in America*, 6.

10. Tocqueville, *Recollections*, 80.

11. *Moniteur*, 28 January 1848; and *Universel* (Paris, 1848).

12. Tocqueville, *Recollections*, 85.

13. The most thorough account of Tocqueville's electoral campaign is in Sharon B. Watkins, *Alexis de Tocqueville and the Second Republic, 1848-1852: A Study in Political Practice and Principles* (Lanham, MD: University Press of America, 2003), 31-39.

14. Jardin, 412.

15. Watkins, 64.

16. Tocqueville, *Recollections*, 117.

17. *Ibid.*, 128.

18. Seymour Drescher, *Dilemmas of Democracy* (Pittsburgh: University of Pittsburgh Press, 1968), 213.

19. Tocqueville, *Recollections*, 172.

20. *Ibid.*, 165.

21. See Watkins, chap. 4.

22. Tocqueville, *Recollections*, 170-71.

23. *Tocqueville and Beaumont on Social Reform*, 123.

24. Tocqueville, *Recollections*, 165-66.

25. Watkins, 89-96.

26. *Ibid.*, 99-123.

27. *Ibid.*, 177-78.

28. *Ibid.*, 442-47.

29. Tocqueville, *Democracy in America*, pt. I, chaps. 7 and 8, 301-18.

30. *Tocqueville and Beaumont on Social Reform*, 184.

31. Tocqueville, *Recollections*, 289. See also Watkins, 490-91, 523-25.

32. Watkins, 528.

33. *Ibid.*, 538-54.

34. *Ibid.*, 547.

35. Tocqueville, *Oeuvres* 10, *Correspondance et ecrits locaux* (Paris: Gallimard, 1995), Tocqueville to A.Z. Gallimand, 19 July 1852, 565.

36. Alexis de Tocqueville, *The Old Regime and the French Revolution,* Françoise Mélonio, ed., Alan S. Kahan, trans. (Chicago: University of Chicago Press, 1998), 85-86.

37. *Ibid.*, 300.

Hungary's Revolutionary Statesman, Louis Kossuth:
His Achievements and His Failures[1]

Steven Béla Várdy
McAnulty Distinguished Professor
Duquesne University

Kossuth's Place in History

Of all the prominent personalities in Hungarian history, no one is better known in the world than Louis (Lajos) Kossuth (1802-94), the celebrated leader of the Hungarian Revolution of 1848-49. The above statement holds true both for America and for Kossuth's native country, Hungary. While his name is fairly widespread in the United States, in Hungary there is hardly a city, town, or village without a Kossuth Street, a Kossuth Square, a Kossuth Club, or some other institution or organization named after this "governing president" of revolutionary Hungary.[2]

While Kossuth has been extremely popular among the common folk and the Hungarian political left—including the Marxists during the Soviet domination of Hungary (1945-90)—this does not always hold true for the tradition-bound conservative segment of Hungarian society. They all acknowledge Kossuth's fervent patriotism and his gift for oratory, but at the same time they question his political wisdom and his role in the history of his nation. These traditionalists repeatedly compare and contrast him—mostly unfavorably—with the great Hungarian reformer, Count Stephen (István) Széchenyi (1791-1860).[3]

Although less well known in Western Europe and in America than Kossuth, Count Széchenyi is generally viewed as the representative of a pragmatic and constructive national leader *par excellence*. In the early 1840s, when Kossuth's and Széchenyi's views concerning Hungary's future began to diverge, Kossuth still called Széchenyi "the greatest Hungarian." He acknowledged that, without Széchenyi's work and achievements, neither he (Kossuth), nor any of the other radical reformers could have emerged to prominence in the field of national politics. This view is held by most Hungarians, even by those who do not necessarily agree with all of Széchenyi's or Kossuth's policies and actions.

In contrast to Kossuth's radicalism, Széchenyi stood for gradualism, for measured and systematic economic, social, and political reforms within the confines of the Habsburg/Austrian Empire. He regarded Kossuth's ideas and actions as potentially dangerous for his nation's future. This was particularly true—so Széchenyi claimed—in connection with Kossuth's unreasonable effort to extricate the Kingdom of Hungary from the confines of the Austrian Empire. In light of mid-nineteenth-century Hungary's multinational character—in which the Magyars constituted less than half of the country's population—and in light of the rise of modern nationalism among the kingdom's half dozen or so distinct nationalities, Széchenyi regarded all such moves toward complete Hungarian independence as suicidal and self destructive. In his view, Kossuth's radicalism—his forced escalation of the political and military confrontation with the Habsburg dynasty, the consequent Russian military intervention, and the resulting inevitable Hungarian defeat—was responsible for ending the gradual and peaceful reform movement that he (Széchenyi) had initiated in the 1820s. It was also this total collapse of his reform movement—which he attributed mostly to Kossuth's policies—that drove Széchenyi to suicide.

Count Széchenyi died in despair in 1860.[4] It was, however, his systematic, progressive, and peaceful reform movement that reemerged in the 1860s, and then took shape in the form of the Austro-Hungarian Compromise of 1867. This agreement transformed the Austrian Empire into the dualistic state of Austria-Hungary, and gave the Hungarians a powerful role in running their own half of the monarchy.[5]

True, this dualistic arrangement had many shortcomings, the most important being the lack of attention paid to the aspirations of the other nationalities. The Compromise of 1867, however, made Hungary into a nearly equal partner with Austria, and the newly created Austro-Hungarian Empire served until the end of World War I as one of Europe's great powers.

However favorable for the Hungarians, the Austro-Hungarian Compromise was staunchly opposed and repeatedly condemned by the aging Kossuth from his exile in Italy. He appears to have been so blinded by his dislike of the Habsburgs that he was unable to accept any settlement that perpetuated the role of that dynasty in the life of his nation. Kossuth died a bitter exile, but his name and fame continued to outshine all other names within the galaxy of great Hungarians.[6]

Kossuth's Life and Political Career

Kossuth was born on September 19, 1802 into a minor Protestant Hungarian noble family, in the town of Monok in Hungary's Zemplén County. His ancestors had served for centuries as town and county administrators in such north Hungarian counties as Túrócz, Trencsén, Sáros and Zemplén.[7] True to his family traditions, Louis Kossuth studied law at the Law Academy of Sárospatak and, in 1823—when only twenty-one years old—he was admitted to the bar in Pest—a section of today's Budapest.

Following his admission to the legal profession, Kossuth became a practicing attorney in his native Zemplén County (1824-32). In 1832 he was named a deputy to the Hungarian feudal diet as a representative of one of the absentee aristocrats who held hereditary membership in the upper house. Kossuth immediately moved to the Hungarian royal capital of Pozsony (Pressburg, now Bratislava), where he followed the Diet's deliberations very carefully and soon began to publish his "Parliamentary Reports" (*Törvényhatósági Tudósítások* [1832-36]).[8] These reports gave a detailed description of the Diet's activities and deliberations. In addition to summarizing the debates, however, Kossuth also added his own commentary, in which he displayed an increasingly demanding and uncompromising tone toward the Habsburg dynasty. By doing so, he became very popular throughout Hungary, but his writings also placed him on a collision course with the political leadership in Vienna.

In consequence of his growing criticism of the Habsburg regime, in May 1837 Kossuth was arrested, accused of high treason, and sent to prison for four years. Given the atmosphere of those days, this event simply increased his popularity and assured his position as the upcoming leader of his nation. By the time that he was freed three years later by way of an amnesty, Kossuth had become a celebrated national hero among the Magyars in all of Hungary.

After his release from prison, Kossuth established and edited the daily *Pesti Hírlap* (Pest News [1841-44]), which immediately became the forum of the liberal and radical reformers. His radicalism and his increasingly demanding tone soon brought him into conflict once more, not only with the Habsburgs but also with the regime's aristocratic supporters. What was even more significant, however, was that his views and several of his political goals also clashed with the aspirations of the moderate reformers under Count Széchenyi's leadership. In 1841 an emotionally charged debate erupted between the two great reformers, which continued and intensified right up to the March Revolution of 1848.[9]

Kossuth agitated for radical social, political, and economic reforms, and at the same time he also worked for the creation of an independent industrial base for Hungary. He did so via the so-called "Trade Defense League" (*Védegylet*) that he helped to establish.[10] At this time, Kossuth—along with the more pragmatic Francis (Ferenc) Deák (1803-76)[11]—also became one of the primary authors of the so-called "Opposition Program" of June 1847. This political program was adopted by all of the opposition parties and became the cornerstone of the reform movement that led to the Revolution of 1848.[12]

By 1847-48—when he served as an elected representative of the Pest County nobility in the National Diet—Kossuth had become the acknowledged leader of the Hungarian national political revival movement. On March 3, 1848, in a parliamentary petition to Austrian Emperor Ferdinand I (King Ferdinand V of Hungary [r. 1832-48]), Kossuth proposed the introduction of universal and uniform taxation, elimination of all vestiges of feudalism, reformation of the system of national defense, and the appointment of a Hungarian government responsible to the elected legislature. He also demanded that the "hereditary lands"—mostly German-speaking provinces that make up modern Austria—be granted a constitution.[13] The content of Kossuth's petition soon became known far and wide, and it was undoubtedly a major contributing factor in the outbreak of the Viennese Revolution on March 13, 1848. This was followed two days later by a similar revolution in Hungary (Buda and Pest), and then in such other major centers of Habsburg power as Prague in Bohemia, Zagreb in Croatia, and Milan in northern Italy.

In consequence of this petition, on March 17, 1848, King Ferdinand consented to the establishment of a representative Hungarian government to be responsible to a broadly elected Hungarian parliament. Ferdinand also appointed Count Louis (Lajos) Batthyány (1806-49) as Hungary's first prime minister. In the new government, Kossuth became the minister for finances but, by virtue of his mass popularity, his actual role was much more significant.[14] As an example, he had a major role in formulating the so-called "April Laws" of 1848, which transformed Hungary from a largely dependent land into an autonomous parliamentary democracy within the confines of the Austrian Empire.[15]

While engaged in economic and financial reforms, Kossuth found time to start a new daily for the purposes of spreading his ideas and increasing his national prestige. *Kossuth Hírlapja* (Kossuth's Herald) was launched on July 1, 1848 and for over a year it continued to play a significant role in the formation of Hungarian public opinion. The two most important issues—which affected Hungary's very existence—included the country's relationship to Austria within the Habsburg Empire and the new government's handling of the national minority question, which pitted the Magyars against the non-Magyars in the Kingdom of Hungary. The latter included the Croats of Croatia-Slavonia, the Serbs of southern Hungary (now Vojvodina), the Slovaks of northern Hungary, and the Vlachs (later renamed Romanians) of eastern Hungary or Transylvania. Kossuth's answer was to establish a Hungarian National Honvéd Army consisting of 200,000 new recruits to take on the challenge to his nation. While asserting Hungary's military prowess, he never managed to formulate a pragmatic view about these two critical issues on which the country's future depended.

In light of the radicalization of the political situation in Hungary, in September 1848 the moderate Batthyány government resigned and authority over the country was assumed by the newly created National Defense Committee (*Országos Honvédelmi Bizottmány*) headed by Kossuth himself.[16] Being threatened by Prince Windischgrätz's imperial army, in January 1849 Kossuth transferred the seat of his government from Buda-Pest to the eastern city of Debrecen, from where he directed Hungary's national defenses.[17] Meanwhile, he also intervened in military strategy, appointed and relieved military commanders rather frequently, and formulated his plans for Hungary's separation from the Austrian Empire.

In retrospect, one of his greatest mistakes was his decision on April 14, 1849 to dethrone the Habsburg dynasty and to have himself elected the governor, or rather "governing president" (*kormányzó elnök*), of Hungary.[18] He did this against the wishes of many of his influential supporters and military commanders, among them the very able and influential General Arthur Görgey (1818-1916). It was this unfortunate decision that precipitated the massive Russian invasion, which ultimately resulted in the defeat of the revolution. Caught between the Austrian imperial army and the czarist Russian army, the Hungarians had no chance to save their revolution.

After a series of military defeats and the collapse of the Hungarian armed forces, on August 11, 1849 Kossuth transferred his powers to General Görgey, and six days later fled to the Balkan provinces of the Ottoman Turkish Empire.[19] He left behind a shattered country, a defeated and dejected nation, and the series of inevitable retributions that embroiled his nation for several years to come. Moreover, Kossuth accused General Görgey of betraying his country when, in the face of overwhelming odds, on August 13, 1849 Görgey capitulated to the Russian imperial army. He continued to perpetuate this accusation in the years to come, so as to transfer the blame for this defeat from himself to his most capable general.[20]

Kossuth spent the next forty-five years of his life in exile. After internal exile in Anatolia (Asia Minor) (1849-51), he toured the United States (1851-52), lived in England (1852-61), and then for over three decades settled in Italy (1861-94). During the 1850s and early 1860s he became involved in various anti-Habsburg schemes, which all turned out to be pipe dreams. The passing of years did not favor Kossuth, since he had to witness the birth of a peaceful resolution to the Hungarian Question in the form of the Austro-Hungarian Compromise of 1867. He protested against this dualistic arrangement in a strongly worded letter—the so-called "Cassandra Letter"—to Francis Deák (1803-76), the chief Hungarian architect of the compromise, but his protests had no impact on the outcome of this political solution.[21]

In 1865 Kossuth moved to the city of Turin (Torino) in northwestern Italy, where he lived out his life as a celebrated, but increasingly forgotten, exile. After the establishment of Austria-Hungary in 1867, the world paid progressively less attention to him. His political influence declined to the point of insignificance.

His popularity with the Hungarian masses, however—both at home and in the United States—remained constant. His prestige among the common folk even increased with the passing of years. Following his death in 1894, Kossuth was denied an official state funeral. His remains, however, were repatriated to Budapest, where he was interred in the Hungarian pantheon in the presence of many millions of his countrymen.

Kossuth's Visit to America and His Influence on American Society

One of Kossuth's great undertakings was his celebrated visit to the United States (December 4, 1851-July 14, 1852) with the intention of securing American help for the resumption of his struggle against the Habsburg dynasty. He came with great hopes but returned to Europe as a disillusioned and dejected man, knowing that his hopes for American involvement would never materialize.

Kossuth was already well known and highly respected by the American public long before his arrival in the United States. Most Americans viewed him as the embodiment of the most cherished principles of human freedom and equality. Following his arrival, his brilliant oratorical skills, his human magnetism, and his very presence in the United States were so overpowering that millions of Americans fell under his spell. His name resounded everywhere during the early 1850s, and his cult spread far and wide across the continent. Counties, cities, towns, streets, town squares, and even babies born during his American tour were named after him. At the same time, dozens of books, hundreds of pamphlets, thousands of articles and essays, as well as over two hundred poems were written to, for, or about him by some of America's most illustrious intellectuals. His powerful presence also influenced the Hungarian image in America. This image went from "the unknown" to that of a "truly noble nation" fighting for its freedom against the forces of evil.[22]

Kossuth even influenced American fashion during his days in the United States. The most visible manifestations of this Kossuth fashion-craze was the appearance of the so-called "Kossuth-hat" (a tall black hat decorated with feather plumes in the front), the "Kossuth-jacket" (braided Hungarian nobleman's jacket), the "Kossuth-trousers" (Hungarian cavalry or hussar trousers), and the "Kossuth-beard" (which surrounded the individual's face in a horseshoe fashion).[23] The combination of these items, particularly as worn by Kossuth with his elegant noble demeanor, presented an overpowering spectacle to mid-nineteenth-century, celebrity-hungry America. Some hucksters even named their wares after Kossuth. An example was the black fishmonger in New York who made an instant hit and lots of money with his "Kossuth oysters" that he sold during the Hungarian statesman's visit to that city.[24]

305

Kossuth's influence in America continued for many years following his visit to the United States. As an example, barely a decade after he had delivered a memorable speech to the Ohio Legislature on February 7, 1852, some of his words found their way into President Lincoln's famous "Gettysburg Address" of 1863. In 1852 Kossuth stated that "The spirit of our age is Democracy—All for the people, and all by the people. Nothing about the people, without the people. That is Democracy, and that is the ruling tendency of the spirit of our age."[25] This Kossuthian definition of democracy appeared in Abraham Lincoln's "Gettysburg Address" as follows: "We here highly resolve . . . that this nation, under God, shall have a new birth of freedom; and that, government of the people, by the people, for the people, shall not perish from the earth."[26] The similarity between these two statements by Kossuth and by Lincoln had undoubtedly been recognized by others before us, for these nearly identical expressions are inscribed on a commemorative plaque on the walls of Columbus City Hall, as well as on the walls of the Kossuth House in Washington, DC.[27]

Kossuth's influence persisted even a century after his visit, and fifty years after his death, when a World War II "liberty ship" was named after him. Politicians and statesmen continued to quote him routinely on many topics, for many decades, and in many different connections. Even as recently as June 1999, when President Árpád Göncz of Hungary made his first official state visit to the United States, President Bill Clinton began his welcome speech with a quotation from one of Kossuth's speeches delivered a century and a half ago.[28] Above and beyond this, however, Kossuth is the only Hungarian whose name is known to many Americans, and who is represented in the United States by three life-size standing statues, a life-size bust, and about half a dozen bronze plaques.[29]

Kossuth's Inability to Break America's Neutrality

Notwithstanding Kossuth's unusual mass popularity, he left the United States a bitter and disappointed man. He tried to find a solution to Hungary's problems through America's intervention into European affairs, but that turned out to be a vain dream. At the time of his arrival in the United States, he may have been vaguely conscious of America's noninterventionist sentiment inherited from the "Father of the Country" (George Washington), but he certainly was not aware of the depth of that sentiment. He was convinced that he would be able to change this isolationist sentiment in favor of a new policy of intervention; this was particularly true in light of his close relationship with the newly emerging Young America, which was "an amorphous movement . . . identified with aggressive nationalism, manifest destiny, and sympathy for the European revolutions of 1848."[30] The Young America Movement had reached its climax precisely at the time of Kossuth's visit to the United States. That was the moment when George

306

N. Sanders (1812-13) of Kentucky[31] "formulated a program of southward expansion, aid to the republican elements in foreign countries, and free trade."[32] This was precisely what Kossuth needed. Thus, he sought the support of Young America even before his departure to the United States. Then, on his arrival, he expanded his early contacts into a close working relationship with the leaders of the movement, among them Senator Lewis Cass (1782-1866) of Michigan, Senator Henry Foote (1804-80) of Mississippi, and the French-born Senator Pierre Soulé (1801-70) of Louisiana. The latter was an "advocate of American imperialism," but at the same time he was also "a strong protagonist of slavery."[33] This did not appeal to Kossuth, but he put his anti-slavery feelings aside for the sake of his political goals. He was hoping to stay out of this emotional controversy that ultimately worked against him and his hoped-for success in the New World.

There were a number of others who favored the policy of intervention, but they were generally more careful and less outspoken than the members of Young America. Moreover, they always viewed intervention from the vantage point of American foreign policy interests, and tended to disregard ethically and emotionally-based arguments, which generally characterized Kossuth's speeches. Among the latter were President Zachary Taylor (r.1849-50), who died unexpectedly on July 9, 1850, well over a year before Kossuth's arrival, and Senator Stephen Arnold Douglas (1813-61) from Illinois, known as the "little giant," who in 1860 was Abraham Lincoln's rival for the presidency of the United States.[34]

Kossuth received a tumultuous reception during the early period of his seven month tour of the United States.[35] Nevertheless, he was unable to nudge the American government in the direction of intervention. This became evident already in January 1852, when he paid a visit to President Millard Fillmore (r.1850-53), who left no doubt in Kossuth's mind that no cause of any sort could make him break with the Washingtonian policy of nonintervention. When speaking to Kossuth, Fillmore pointed to his recently delivered State of the Union Message, where he asserted that:

> no individuals have the right to hazard the peace of the country, or to violate its laws upon vague notions of altering or reforming governments in other states. . . . Friendly relations with all, but entangling alliances with none, has long been a maxim with us. Our true mission is not to propagate our opinions, or impose upon other countries our form of government by artifice or force; but to teach by example, and show by our success, moderation and justice, the blessings of self-government and the advantages of free institutions.[36]

This was a widely held view in mid-nineteenth-century America, which not even Kossuth's brilliant oratory was able to alter.

Although initially more flexible on the idea of intervention, by the end of 1851 Daniel Webster too was of the opinion that "the [Kossuth] fever is . . . abating . . . It has met cooling influences from sober minds, North and South."[37] While at that moment this was more wishful thinking than reality, in the long run, Webster's assessment proved to be correct. Moreover, even before Kossuth's arrival in the capital city, Webster gave up the idea of intervention altogether. He wrote to his friend Richard Milford Blatchford (1798-1875) that he would "treat him [Kossuth] with respect, but shall give him no encouragement that the established policy of the country will be from any degree departed from. . . . If he should speak to me of the policy of intervention, I shall have ears more deaf than adders."[38] This consideration was the reason behind Webster's decision to decline to participate in Kossuth's reception in New York City, even though he had been specifically invited by the New York reception committee.[39]

The situation was similar with the U.S. Congress, which was in the midst of the controversy over slavery, and which was in no mood to take up the cause of America's intervention into European affairs. Only with some reluctance and much maneuvering by Kossuth's supporters did the House and the Senate finally agree to receive Kossuth and to permit him to address the joint session of the congress.[40]

This view of nonintervention was generally shared by most Americans, and it gained even more currency when Kossuth began to question the policy of neutrality advanced by George Washington over a half a century earlier. When Kossuth undertook to criticize this policy as being outdated, and which the United States as a new great power had outgrown, it was interpreted as an uncalled-for personal attack by a foreigner against the "father" of the American nation. One of the typical examples of this new phenomenon was the attitude expressed by the Boston Unitarian clergyman, Rev. Francis Parkman, the father of the noted historian Francis Parkman (1823-93), who, in November 1852, made the following statement about Kossuth's efforts to undermine the Washingtonian principle of nonintervention: "No one respects the talents of Louis Kossuth more than I do. But if the Archangel Gabriel and his brother Michael were to quit their celestial homes and come to Boston, clothed in white robes and bearing palms in their hands, and should undertake to teach the doctrines of Washington's Farewell Address—so help me heaven, not meaning to be profane, I should pluck them by their robes and say to them, go back where you came from, praise God, and mind your own business."[41]

Kossuth returned to Europe shattered and disappointed by the lack of American willingness to intervene into the affairs of Hungary and the Austrian Empire.[42] Like many others before and after him, he too proved to be unable to crack America's attachment to the policy of nonintervention that had dominated American thinking and American foreign policy for over a century right up to

World War I and then also through much of the interwar years. His disappointment with American foreign policy, however, never altered his admiration for American democracy, nor for American society—with the exception of the institution of slavery. Slavery was an institution that he could never fathom, and which was the second of the two major issues that undercut his political goals in America. When interviewed four decades later, at the age of eighty-eight, by James Creelman (1859-1915) of the *New York Herald*, Kossuth still held on to his belief in the greatness of American democracy. He declared that "he had lived to see all his idols shattered, all but the great republic across the Atlantic Ocean."[43] Then he continued: "Your country is the one power that is steadily gaining strength. Your greatest danger is your wealth. When nations become rich they lose their energy and gradually drift away from their moral ideals. . . . Yet, God forbid that harm should come to the United States, the hope of mankind in the future!"[44]

Kossuth and the Slavery Question in America

In addition to Kossuth's inability to break America's attachment to the Washingtonian principle of neutrality and nonintervention, the other cause of Kossuth's failure during his American tour was his inability to deal effectively with the slavery question. The anti-slavery forces tried to enlist him into their ranks, but Kossuth fought desperately to avoid being dragged into the quagmire of American domestic politics, which—he feared—could only hurt his cause.[45] His admiration for American democracy was amply demonstrated by his constant praise of the American political system and the American way of life before, during, and after his stay in America.[46] His disdain for slavery, however, was crouched in obtuse sentences. He feared that his remarks during those emotional antebellum times would turn half of the nation against him and thus hurt his hope for American support.

Slavery was undoubtedly the most important issue in pre-Civil War America. The issue of slave emancipation was kept on the front burner by "a small but dedicated corps of idealists, concentrated in New England,"[47] who wanted to free the slaves immediately. These "abolitionists" and "Free-Soilers" were bent on eradicating this "Great National Sin" virtually immediately, and also wished to prevent the extension of this shameful institution into the new western territories. Most Northerners agreed with these abolitionists, although not to the point of necessarily endangering the territorial integrity of the United States at the expense of quick emancipation.

The champions of slave emancipation were opposed by the increasingly embittered Southerners (not all of them slave owners, and not all of them believers in slavery in the long run), who felt threatened by an ever more overbearing

"Yankee imperialism." Northern condemnation of their way of life prompted Southerners to close ranks and to reject demands for immediate emancipation, even at the expense of perhaps leaving the Union. This danger was temporarily avoided by the Compromise of 1850, which was the result of a major compromise between the moderates and the radicals on both sides of the fence.[48] The results, however, were not quite what they expected. While the Southerners viewed it as a "definitive adjustment and settlement," the abolitionists regarded it as a "shameful concession to evil" and continued to agitate for the elimination of all slavery everywhere.

Kossuth had learned about the slavery controversy even before he came to America. In his heart, he was naturally against human bondage. Given his problems and his political goals, however, he was not about to sacrifice his cause—the Hungarian national cause—on the altar of this smoldering social problem within the United States. Thus, even before his arrival in America, he was resolved to keep out of the slavery question and to "maintain a strict neutrality" in this deserving, but politically very destructive political question. It was this resolve that ultimately got him into trouble, and made certain that his political goals in the United States would never be achieved.

It is indicative of Kossuth's powerful influence that his presence in the United States had an impact on every aspect of American domestic politics. Following his arrival, both major political parties sought his favors and his support. These included the Democratic Party, which was saturated with the ideas of Jacksonian democracy, but at the same time supported the institution of slavery, and the Whig Party, which favored federalism, was less dedicated to mass democracy, yet opposed the institution of slavery. Kossuth's misfortune on arrival was that he found himself in the middle of the slavery controversy, and whichever direction he took, he faced this emotional issue that was tearing the country apart and taking it in the direction of a civil war.

The abolitionists viewed Kossuth as the "champion of human freedom" and rightfully expected him to support their cause. They had already proclaimed their sympathy for the defeated Hungarians while Kossuth was in exile in the Ottoman Empire. In their eyes, the former "governing-president" of Hungary symbolized humanity's unending struggle for freedom and equality against tyranny. Being totally dedicated to the cause of liberty and to the ethical values of their hard working Puritan/Calvinist ancestors, the irreconcilable abolitionists of New England believed that the defeated and exiled Kossuth was really "their own hero." They were convinced that, in the person of the Hungarian national leader, they finally found someone to fit their moral code; a man who could serve as "the martyr of their struggle for human freedom." They resented when Kossuth repeatedly referred to the United States as "this free, great and glorious country."[49] In their view, America was a land of human bondage, and reference to it as "the land of liberty" was wrong and hypocritical.

310

Their indignation was even greater when they saw the strange spectacle of the advocates of black slavery in America speaking up for political freedom in Hungary. Supporters of the Compromise of 1850 were now organizing and chairing committees dedicated to Hungary's political freedom. Or, as put by the anti-slavery forces, "while slaves rattled their chains outside the[ir] door[s],"[50] they shamelessly collected funds for the liberation of Hungary.

In response to this phenomenon, the abolitionists decided to draw a parallel between Hungary and the United States, between Kossuth's people and America's black slaves, and between the Habsburg dynasty and the slaveholding aristocracy of the South. They did not even want Kossuth to come to the United States for fear that he would be polluted by America's befouled society and would lose his moral purity and integrity. William Lloyd Garrison (1805-79) and his supporters were absolutely outraged at the prospect of Kossuth's visit to America and begged him not to come to "America's polluted soil."[51]

Similar views were voiced by many other Northern intellectuals, who were not necessarily Garrison's outright supporters, but who had high regard for the former Hungarian governor. These included John Greenleaf Whittier (1807-92), Gamaliel Bailey (1807-59), Horace Mann (1796-1859), Henry Ward Beecher (1813-87), as well as numerous other lesser known personalities.[52] They asked the question: How can Americans welcome Kossuth, the acknowledged "apostle of human freedom," when their own country supports the enslavement of millions?

Notwithstanding this skeptical and sometimes cynical attitude of the radical abolitionists toward Kossuth's imminent arrival in America, the majority of them were still thrilled at the prospect of welcoming him to the "land of unfreedom." Among them was the ex-slave Frederick Douglass (1817-95) who, on learning of Kossuth's decision to come, wrote as follows: "He will be Godsend. . . . He stands forth a liberator, and commands the cooperation of the Sons of Freedom everywhere to emancipate the serf and the slave."[53] His projection, however, turned out to be wrong. Kossuth declined to become an advocate of slave emancipation, for which decision he later had to suffer the consequences.

The radical abolitionists undertook a massive effort to inform Kossuth about American realities by sending him important documents on the slavery question. They also inundated him with hundreds of letters and asked him to cease praising American society. Garrison himself went so far as to write a poem about slavery in America, in which he called on Kossuth to put his moral weight on the side of human liberty:

> Say slavery is a stain upon our glory,
> Accursed in Heaven, and by the earth abhorred;
> Show that our soil with Negro blood is gory,

311

And certain are the judgments of the Lord;
So shall thy name immortal be in story,
And thy fidelity the world applaud.[54]

Kossuth, therefore, was fully informed about the seething emotions concerning slavery in the United States long before his arrival. Had he wanted to, he could have stood up immediately as an advocate of emancipation. He failed to do so, however, because he wished to concentrate solely on Hungary's national goals and did not want to be sidetracked by America's internal social problems. He thus decided to remain neutral. With this decision he severed his ties with the abolitionists and also elicited their wrath.

Kossuth's misguided decision to keep out of the slavery controversy propelled him into an uncomfortable situation just a few days after his arrival in New York City. Barely a week after his disembarkation, he was visited by a black delegation under the leadership of George Downing, the same fishmonger who, on Kossuth's arrival, was peddling "Kossuth-oysters" to the New York public. The delegation came to wish him well on his crusade for the liberation of Hungary, and "to pay homage to the great principle, which you [Kossuth] announce with so much distinctness and uphold with so much power: the principle that a man has a right to the full exercise of his faculties in the land which gave him birth."[55] Kossuth sidestepped the slavery question by responding with the noncommittal remark to the effect that "the time for addresses has passed, and the time for action has come"[56] but without specifying what this action was to be directed against. That he was not thinking about slavery is evident by his repeated disclaimers of having any interests in abolitionism. Several months later, in one of his speeches in New Orleans, for example, he posed the question: "What have I to do with abolitionism or anti-abolitionism?"[57] He responded immediately: "Nothing in the world. That is not my matter. I am no citizen of the United States; I have neither the right nor the will to interfere with your domestic concerns; I claim for my nation the right to regulate its own institutions; I therefore must respect, and indeed I do respect, the same rights in others."[58]

Kossuth under the Attack of the Abolitionists

When Kossuth, the alleged "champion of liberty," declined to be dragged into the slavery controversy under the pretext of "nonintervention"—even though at the same time he advocated intervention on behalf of Hungary—many anti-slavery crusaders began to lash out against him. The most prominent among them was William Lloyd Garrison, the founding president of the American Anti-Slavery Society (1833), who virtually overnight turned from an ardent Kossuth-admirer into a vitriolic Kossuth-hater. He lashed out in an angry editorial, in

312

which he proclaimed that "Kossuth is lost. All our hopes have faded. He says that the cause of abolition is not his concern, not even to the point of expressing his views about it. At the same time he claims that it is our religious duty to emancipate Hungary. This is what I call consistency!"[59]

According to this pioneer anti-slavery crusader, Kossuth had "placed his selfish mission above the transcendent interest of the human race—subordinating American slavery to European political oppression."[60] In consequence of this decision—so Garrison claimed—Kossuth "means to be deaf, dumb, blind, in regard to it [slavery]!" Moreover, "to subserve his own purpose, and to secure the favor of a slaveholding and slave-breeding people, he skulks, he dodges, he plays fast and loose, he refuses to see a stain on the American character, any inconsistency in pretending to adore liberty and at the same time, multiplying human beings for the auction block and the slave shambles."[61]

Edmund Quincy (1808-77), one of Garrison's major sympathizers, also switched his views on Kossuth. He concluded that Kossuth had a one-track mind and his only goal in life was the liberation of Hungary.[62] They undoubtedly knew that he was sympathetic to the plight of the slaves, but they were also convinced that he was willing to sacrifice all basic human goals for the only goal that prompted him to visit the New World. Having come to this conclusion, Garrison and his supporters took every chance to condemn Kossuth. They compared Kossuth himself to an escaped slave, and called Emperor Francis Joseph (r. 1848-1916) his former slave-master.[63]

Garrison's anti-Kossuth efforts intensified with the passage of time. Within a few weeks after the latter's arrival to the United States, these efforts became a virtual crusade that degenerated into a series of vitriolic personal attacks. One of Garrison's associates, for example, declared that "I had rather have a great man, than the political liberation of twenty Hungaries."[64] Garrison himself went far beyond this point, launching attack after attack against the Hungarian statesman, referring to him by all sorts of derogatory adjectives. He called the former Hungarian governor-president "cowardly," "slippery," "selfish," "deaf, dumb and blind," "a criminal," and he also claimed that Kossuth was "as demented as the renowned Don Quixote."[65] He asserted that, similar to his Spanish predecessor, Kossuth was unable to differentiate between giant warriors and windmills. Moreover, Kossuth's persistent praising of American society was similar to one going "into a notorious house of ill-fame, and praise its polluted inhabitants as the most virtuous of all flesh."[66] Garrison incorporated all of his accusations into a book-size "Letter to Louis Kossuth," in which he systematically refuted all of Kossuth's arguments concerning America as the land of liberty. He also characterized the former governor-president of Hungary as a double-faced hypocrite, who was willing to say and do virtually anything to curry favor with Americans, so as to gain their financial, political, and military support for the Hungarian cause.[67] Thereafter, Kossuth remained a perpetual target of Garrison's venomous attacks; Garrison seized every opportunity to discredit the exiled Hungarian statesman and thus undercut his effort to gain American support for his national cause. That attack, however, was not even essential, as mid-nineteenth-century America was simply not ready to break with the Washingtonian tradition of neutrality and nonintervention in European affairs.

Conclusions

Louis Kossuth was undoubtedly a major nineteenth-century statesman and national leader, as well as an impressive public speaker in an age when oratory was among the most important assets of a public figure. Even today, he is by far the most widely known Hungarian in much of the Western World, including the United States.

Kossuth was a Magyar patriot in an age of national rebirth, when intense nationalism often led people and their leaders astray. Through most of his life he fought for what he believed to be the best interests of his nation, and many of his social and political reform goals were indeed commendable. His ability to carry people with him emotionally toward these goals, however, was not matched by a sense of realism and pragmatism. For this reason, he also fought for goals that were not only unrealistic under the given conditions (*e.g.*, Hungary's extreme multinational composition), but also self-defeating. The most significant of these unrealistic aspirations was his demand for Hungary's total independence from the Habsburg Empire. Had that goal been achieved and implemented in 1848-49, it would undoubtedly have led to Hungary's dismemberment along ethnic-linguistic lines in a period when the Magyars constituted less than half of the country's inhabitants.

In retrospect, it would have been much wiser for Kossuth to work for Hungary's federalization within the confines of the Habsburg Empire. That would have placed the Magyars in a much more auspicious and fortunate position than what befell them after World War I, when their country was dismembered under the most unfavorable circumstances. The Treaty of Trianon (June 4, 1920) left one-third of the nation on the "other side" of the new frontiers. Moreover, such a federalization in 1848-49 would still have made Hungary into an influential component of a European great power. By virtue of this fact, Hungary's influence on European politics would have been much greater than after World War I, when it was forced to join the ranks of half a dozen minor Central European states of little significance.

Ultimately, Kossuth failed because he was unable to operate within the limits of political realism. This applies equally to his goal for Hungary's political independence, as well as to his mistaken belief that he would be able to sway

American political leaders to support him in a renewed war against the Habsburgs. As a result of these misconceptions, he led the Hungarian Revolution of 1848-49 in a direction toward national catastrophe; and he toured the United States with the unattainable goal in mind of gaining American military support, even though such an involvement would have gone against the country's traditions and national interests. In consequence of these mistaken presumptions, the glories of the Hungarian Revolution went down in defeat, and his American visit turned into a hollow "triumphal tour."[68] He returned to Europe as a bitterly disappointed man under the pseudonym of Mr. Alexander Smith. "For this reason"—as concluded by István Deák in one of his recent assessments of Kossuth's achievements in America—"it is no more than patriotic self-delusion to take pride in the great success of the speeches Kossuth gave in America, in his illustrious admirers, or in American towns named after him."[69]

In this respect, Kossuth's American tour and "achievements" were very similar to Emperor Francis Joseph's visit and "achievements" at the 1863 *Fürstentag* (Congress of Princes) in Frankfurt, where he hoped to be offered the German imperial crown. That, however, was not to be. In light of Prussia's and King William's absence from Frankfurt, the Congress of German Princes degenerated into a meaningless farce, and Emperor Francis Joseph was forced to return to Vienna empty-handed.[70] His return was presented and portrayed to his people as a "triumphal tour." The citizens of Vienna, however, saw through the camouflage and immediately came up with a new meaning to the many earlier ones of the five vowels of the motto "AEIOU," already popularized by the Habsburgs in the fifteenth century. The glorious Latin expression, *Austria Est Imperare Orbi Universo* (Austria rules the whole world), was now transformed into the sarcastic German pronouncement, *Auch Eine Illumination Ohne Ursache* (This too is a festivity without substance).[71]

In Kossuth's case, it is noteworthy that, even though he returned to Europe completely empty-handed, the memory of his American visit still survived in popular consciousness as a "triumphal tour." This is much more than was given to Francis Joseph and the Habsburgs on the eve of the formation of the German Empire under the Hohenzollern dynasty.

Notes

1. Since during the last few years I have published over a dozen articles about Kossuth and his relationship to the United States, it is unavoidable that the current study should contain some duplications. Some of my most important relevant studies include: "Kossuth amerikai 'diadalútja' 1851-1852-ben" [Kossuth's 'Triumphant Tour' of America in 1851-1852], *Debreceni Szemle* [Debrecen Review], New Series, 6/3 (1998): 331-39; "Louis Kossuth's Words in Abraham Lincoln's Gettysburg Address," *Eurasian Studies Yearbook* 71 (1999): 27-32; "Kossuth Lajos hatása az amerikai társadalomra és közgondolkodásra" [Louis Kossuth's Impact upon American Society and Mentality], *Valóság* [*Reality*] 42, no. 9 (September 1999): 36-43; "Kossuth és az amerikai demokrácia" [Kossuth and American Democracy], in *Emlékkönyv L. Nagy Zsuzsa 70. születésnapjára* [Memorial Volume on the Occasion of Zsuzsa L. Nagy's 70th Birthday], János Angi and János Barta, eds. (Debrecen: Multiplex Media—Debrecen University Press, 2000), 173-82; "Epilogue. Kossuth and Mid-Nineteenth-Century America," in *The Life of Governor Louis Kossuth, with his Public Speeches in the United States, and with a Brief History of the Hungarian War of Independence. Illustrated by Handsome Engravings. By An Officer of the Hungarian Army* (New York: Published at 128 Nassau Street, 1852. [Reprinted in Budapest: Osiris Kiadó, 2001]), 181-99; "A magyar szabadságharc, Kossuth, és Amerika" [The Hungarian War of Liberation, Kossuth, and America], *Nyelvünk és Kultúránk* [Our Language and Culture], no. 116 (2002/1): 49-56; "Kossuth Lajos Amerikában 1851-1852-ben" [Louis Kossuth in American in 1851-1852], *Amerikai Magyar Népszava / Szabadság* [American Hungarian People's Voice / Liberty] 111, no. 17 (May 11, 2001): 14-16; "Kossuth és az amerikai rabszolgakérdés" [Kossuth and the American Slavery Question], *Valóság* 45., no. 9 (September 2002): 20-32; "Kossuth's Efforts to Enlist America into the Hungarian National Cause," *Hungarian Studies* (Bloomington-Budapest) 16, no. 2 (2002): 237-52; "Kossuth Lajos viszonya gróf Dembinszkyné Hogl Emíliához" [Louis Kossuth's Relationship to Countess Dembinszky, Emília Hogl], *Amerikai Magyar Népszava / Szabadság* [American Hungarian People's Voice / Liberty] 113, no. 3 (January 17, 2003): 12-13; "Az amerikai rabszolgakérdés hatása Kossuth Lajos amerikai körútjára 1851-1852-ben" [The Impact of the American Slavery Question on Louis Kossuth's Tour of America in 1851-1852], in *A Magyar Találkozó Krónikája* [Proceedings of the Hungarian Congress] 42, Lél F. Somogyi, ed. (2003), 137-50; "Kossuth Lajos állítólagos amerikai leszármazottai" [Kossuth's Alleged American Descendants], *Valóság* 46, no. 11 (November 2003): 39-46; and "Kossuth and the Slavery Question in America," *East European Quarterly* 39 (December 2005), in press. Five of the above studies have been republished in Béla Várdy and Agnes Huszár Várdy, *Újvilági küzdelmek. Az amerikai magyarság élete és az óhaza* [Struggles in the New World. Life of Hungarian Americans and Their Relationship to the Old Country] (Budapest: Mundus Magyar Egyetemi Kiadó, 2005), 41-89. In Hungarian, the first author of this study publishes under the name "Várdy, Béla."

2. For a balanced account of Louis (Lajos) Kossuth's life and achievements, see especially István Deák, *The Lawful Revolution. Louis Kossuth and the Hungarians, 1848-1849* (New York: Columbia University Press, 1979). See also Domokos Kosáry, *Kossuth Lajos a reformkorban* [Louis Kossuth in the Age of Reform] (Budapest: Antiqua, 1946);

Várdy: LOUIS KOSSUTH

István Barta, *A fiatal Kossuth* [Young Kossuth] (Budapest: Akadémiai Kiadó, 1966); and György Szabad, *Kossuth politikai pályája* [Kossuth's Political Path] (Budapest: Kossuth Könyvkiadó, 1977).

3. On Count Széchenyi's life and achievements, see George Bárány, *Stephen Széchenyi and the Awakening of Hungarian Nationalism, 1791-1841* (Princeton: Princeton University Press, 1968). See also: Gyula Szekfü, ed., *A mai Széchenyi* [Today's Széchenyi] (Budapest: Révai Kiadó, 1935); György Spira, *A Hungarian Count in the Revolution of 1848* (Budapest: Akadémiai Kiadó, 1981); and Domokos Kosáry, *Széchenyi István és kora* [Stephen Széchenyi and his Age] (Budapest: Akadémiai Kiadó, 1992).

4. Domokos Kosáry, *Széchenyi Döblingben* [Széchenyi in the Döbling Asylum] (Budapest: Akadémiai Kiadó, 1981).

5. György Szabad, *Hungarian Political Trends between the Revolution and the Compromise, 1849-1867* (Budapest: Akadémiai Kiadó, 1972).

6. See Gyula Szekfü, "Az öreg Kossuth, 1867-1894" [Old Kossuth, 1867-1894], in *Emlékkönyv Kossuth Lajos születésének* 150 évfordulójára [Memorial Volume on the Occasion of the 150th Anniversary of Louis Kossuth's Birth] 2, Zoltán Tóth, ed., (Budapest: Akadémiai Kiadó, 1952), 341-433.

7. On the genealogy of the Kossuth family, see József Berkes, "A Kossuth család rövid története" [The Short History of the Kossuth Family], Bácsország. *Vajdasági Honismereti Szemle* [Bács-Land. The Voivodina Patriotic Review] 99, nos. 7-9 (July-September 2002): 46-51.

8. Lajos Kossuth, *Országgyülési tudósítások* [Parliamentary Reports], vols. 1-3, ed., *A Keleteurópai Tudományos Intézet Történettudomány Intézetének Munkaközössége* (Budapest: Magyar Történelmi Társulat, 1948-49); vols. 4-5, ed. István Barta (Budapest: Akadémiai Kiadó, 1959-61).

9. *Gróf Széchenyi István írói és hírlapi vitája Kossuth Lajossal* [Count Stephen Széchenyi's Literary and Publicistic Debate with Louis Kossuth], 2 vols., Gyula Viszota, ed. (Budapest: Magyar Történelmi Társulat, 1927-30).

10. Domokos Kosáry, *Kossuth és a Védegylet. A magyar nacionalizmus történetéhez* [Kossuth and the Trade Defense League. Study of the History of Hungarian Nationalism] (Budapest: Athenaeum, 1942).

11. On Deák, see Béla K. Király, *Ferenc Deák* (Boston: Twayne Publishers, 1975).

12. *Kossuth Lajos az utolsó rendi országgyülésen, 1847-48* [Louis Kossuth at the Last Feudal Diet, 1847-48], István Barta, ed. (Budapest: Akadémiai Kiadó, 1951). The text of the Opposition Program is printed on pp. 152-57 of this work.

13. *Ibid.*, 156.

14. *Kossuth Lajos az elsœ magyar felelœs minisztériumban, 1848 április-szeptember* [Louis Kossuth in the First Hungarian Responsible Ministry, April-September 1848], István Sinkovics, ed. (Budapest: Akadémiai Kiadó, 1957).

15. On the "April Laws," see: Deák, *The Lawful Revolution*, 91-99; and Steven Béla Várdy, *Historical Dictionary of Hungary* (Lanham & London: The Scarecrow Press, 1997), 106.

16. *Kossuth Lajos az Országos Honvédelmi Bizottmány élén. Part I. 1848 szeptember-december* [Louis Kossuth at the Head of the National Defense Committee. Part I. September-December 1848], István Barta, ed. (Budapest: Akadémiai Kiadó, 1952); and *Kossuth Lajos az Országos Honvédelmi Bizottmány élén. Part II. 1849 január*

317

PROFILES OF REVOLUTIONARIES

1-április 14. [Louis Kossuth at the Head of the National Defense Committee. Part II. January 1-April 14, 1849], István Barta, ed. (Budapest: Akadémiai Kiadó, 1953).

17. *A szabadságharc fŒvárosa Debrecen, 1849 január–május* [Debrecen, the Capital of the Hungarian War of Independence, January-May 1849], István Szabó, ed. (Debrecen: Debrecen Város és Tiszántúli Református Egyházkerület Könyvnyomda Vállalata, 1948).

18. *Kossuth Lajos kormányzóelnöki iratai, 1849 április 15-augusztus 15* [Governing President Louis Kossuth's Papers, April 15-August 15, 1849], István Barta, ed. (Budapest: Akadémiai Kiadó, 1955).

19. The text of Kossuth's abdication of August 11, 1849 is reprinted in *Ibid.*, 845-46.

20. The surrender at Világos on August 13, 1849, and the subsequent Kossuth-Görgey controversy, is discussed by Deák, *Lawful Revolution*, 321-29; and by Domokos Kosáry, *A Görgey-kérdés története* [History of the Görgey Question] (Budapest: Athenaeum, 1936).

21. See the already cited work by Gyula Szekfü, "Az öreg Kossuth," 341-433.

22. On the changing image of Hungary and the Hungarian nation in the United States, see Steven Béla Várdy, "Image and Self-Image among Hungarian-Americans since the Mid-Nineteenth Century," *East European Quarterly* 35, no. 3 (September 2001): 309-42; and Várdy-Várdy, *Újvilági küzdelmek*, 325-48.

23. See Donald S. Spencer, *Louis Kossuth and Young America. A Study in Sectionalism and Foreign Policy, 1848-1852* (Columbia and London: University of Missouri Press, 1977), 60-63. Kossuth's unusual popularity is demonstrated, among others, by Reverend Edmund [Ödön] Vasváry's (1888-1977) archival collection of Hungarica-Americana, which after his death ended up in his native city of Szeged, Hungary. About 10 percent of the collection—34 out of 436 boxes—deal with Kossuth and his relationship to America. Cf.: András Csillag, "The Edmund Vasváry Collection," *Hungarian Studies* 1, no. 1 (1985): 123-30; Steven Béla Várdy, "Reverend Edmund Vasváry: Personal Reminiscences about a Chronicler of the Hungarian-American Past," *Eurasian Studies Yearbook* 71 (1999): 207-12.

24. Concerning this Kossuth cult, see: Kende Géza, *Magyarok Amerikában. Az amerikai magyarság története* [Hungarians in America. The History of Hungarian Americans] 1 (Cleveland: A Szabadság Kiadása, 1927),77-115; István Gál, "Az amerikai Kossuth-kultusz" [American Kossuth-Cult], in István Gál, *Magyarország, Anglia és Amerika* [Hungary, England, and Amerika] (Budapest: Officina, 1944), 187-94; Endre Sebestyén, *Kossuth: A Magyar Apostle of World Democracy* (Pittsburgh: Expert Printing Company, 1950), 205-18; Joseph Széplaki, *Louis Kossuth. The Nation's Guest. A Bibliography of his Trip to the United States, December 4, 1851-July 14, 1852* (Ligonier, PA: Bethlen Press, 1976), 9-24; Spencer, 29-81; and John H. Komlós, *Kossuth in America, 1851-1852* (Buffalo: East European Institute, State University of New York College at Buffalo, 1973), 75-94.

25. See Steven Béla Várdy, "Louis Kossuth's Words in Abraham Lincoln's Gettysburg Address,"27-32. See also the article, "Ohio Legislature," in *Ohio State Journal*, February 7, 1952. I would like to thank Mr. Béla Kovách of Columbus, Ohio, for sending me photocopies of the *Journal's* relevant pages. See also Széplaki, 10; Sebestyén, 130; and Komlós, 119.

318

26. Abraham Lincoln's "Gettysburg Address," *Encyclopedia of American History* (Guilford, CT: The Dushkin Publishing Group, Inc., 1973), 142.

27. Széplaki, 11.

28. The author and his wife, Dr. Agnes Huszár Várdy, were invited guests at this White House reception for President Göncz on June 8, 1999.

29. These include the full standing Kossuth-statues of Cleveland (1902), New York City (1929), Algona, Kossuth County, Iowa (2001), and the Kossuth bust in the U.S. Capitol (1990). Bronze plaques can be found in Washington, D.C., Pittsburgh, Columbus, St.Louis, Los Angeles, New Orleans, and perhaps in a few other cities. Unfortunately, a recently published handbook that contains a list of Kossuth statues in America, fails to mention the original one in Cleveland. See *Magyar Amerika. A tengerentúli magyarok mai élete történetekben és képekben* [Hungarian America. The Current Life of Overseas Hungarians in Stories and in Pictures], László Tanka, ed. (Budapest: Médiamix Kiadó, 2002), 211.

30. Richard B. Morris, ed., *Encyclopedia of American History* (New York: Harper & Brothers, 1953), 217.

31. George Nicholas Sanders of Kentucky was the editor-in-chief of the influential *Democratic Review*, which became a fanatical herald of the policy of American expansionism and interventionism. See Spencer, 116-20.

32. *Ibid.*, 217-18.

33. *Dictionary of American Biography* 17, 406.

34. *Ibid.*, 18-27, 37-47, 112-16, 137-40.

35. Concerning the main stops on Kossuth's tour of the United States, see Széplaki, 22-24.

36. *Congressional Globe*, 31st Congress, 1st Session, 15; quoted by Komlós, 103.

37. Webster to Abbott Lawrence, December 29, 1851, in *The Letters of Daniel Webster*, C.H. Van Tyne, ed. (New York, 1902), 508; and Spencer, 107.

38. Webster to Blatchford, December 30, 1851, in *The Writings and Speeches of Daniel Webster* 18 (Boston: Little, Brown and Co., 1903), 501-2; also quoted by Komlós, 100.

39. For a summary of the congressional debate on this issue, see Dénes Jánossy, *A Kossuth-emigráció Angliában és Amerikában, 1851-1852* [The Kossuth-Emigration in England and America, 1851-1852] 1 (Budapest: Magyar Történelmi Társulat, 1940), 219.

40. *Ibid.*, 217-22; Spencer, 83-120; Komlós, 97-113.

41. Quoted in Richard Henry Dana, Jr., *The Journal of Richard Henry Dana* 2, Robert F. Lucid, ed. (Cambridge: Cambridge University Press, 1968), 52; and Spencer, 172.

42. Kossuth's lack of success in gaining American military and political support for the Hungarian cause is discussed by this author in his "Kossuth amerikai 'diadalútja'," 331-39.

43. James Creelman, *On the Great Highway. The Wanderings and Adventures of a Special Correspondent* (Boston: Lothrop, Lee & Sheppard Co., 1901), 243.

44. *Ibid.*, 253.

45. On Kossuth and the slavery question, see, especially, my: "Kossuth's Efforts to Enlist America": 237-52; and "Kossuth and the Slavery Question in America," in press.

46. See Szekfü, "Az öreg Kossuth," 341-433.

47. Spencer, 65.

48. The main points of the Compromise of 1850 were as follows: 1) California to be admitted as a free state; 2) Utah and New Mexico Territories to enter the Union with or without slavery; 3) slave trade (but not slavery) to be abolished in Washington, DC; 4) ending the abolitionist practice of aiding runaway slaves, as demanded by the Fugitive Slave Law of 1793. Cf., *The Encyclopedia of American History* (Guilford, CT: The Dushkin Publishing Group, Inc., 1973), 71.

49. This expression appears in many of Kossuth's speeches, some of the most important of which can be found in *Selected Speeches of Kossuth* (condensed and abridged with Kossuth's express sanction), Francis W. Newman, ed. (London: Trübner & Co., 1853). Several of his early speeches, delivered between New York City and Pittsburgh, can be also be found in *The Life of Governor Louis Kossuth,* cited in note #1, above. Also quoted in Spencer, 72.

50. Spencer, 67.

51. *The Liberator* 21, November 7, 1851; quoted in: *Ibid.*, 68; and Jánossy, 229.

52. *The National Era*, September 11, 1851; and Charles L. Brace, *Hungary in 1851*, with an *Experience of the Austrian Police* (New York, 1852). Cf., Spencer, 69.

53. *Frederick Douglass's Papers*, November 27, 1851; quoted in Spencer, 70.

54. Wendell Phillips Garrison, *William Lloyd Garrison, 1805-1879* 3 (Boston, 1889), 346. See also Spencer, 71.

55. *The New York Herald*, December 13, 1851; *The New York Times*, December 13, 1851; *The Liberator*, December 18, 1851. Cf. Spencer, 76-77.

56. *Ibid.*

57. Quoted by William Warren Rogers, "The 'Nation's Guest' in Louisiana: Kossuth visits in New Orleans," *Louisiana History* 9 (Fall 1968): 355-64 (quotation on p. 362). See also, *The New York Times*, April 12, 1852.

58. *Ibid.*

59. *The Liberator* 21 (1851), 203. Cf., Jánossy, 229. The quoted text has been retranslated from Hungarian to English.

60. *The Liberator* 22 (1852), 138; quoted in *William Lloyd Garrison, The Story of His Life as Told by His Children* 3 (Boston: Houghton Mifflin Co., 1894), 340, 345. See also, Komlós, 143.

61. *The Liberator* 22 (1852), 203; quoted in John L. Thomas, *The Liberator: William Lloyd Garrison* (Boston: Little, Brown and Co. 1963), 371. See also, Komlós, 141.

62. Edmund Quincy's article in the December 18, 1851 issue of *The National Anti-Slavery Standard*. Cf., Spencer, 80.

63. Spencer, 71-72, 103-4.

64. *Ibid.*, 78; William H. Furness to William Lloyd Garrison, December 30, 1851; reprinted in *Garrison, The Story of His Life* 3, 347.

65. *Ibid.*

66. *The Liberator* 21, December 18, 1851. Cf., Spencer, 78.

67. William Lloyd Garrison, "Letter to Louis Kossuth concerning Freedom and Slavery in the U.S.," in *The Liberator* 22, January 9 and February 20, 1852. See also, Spencer, 76-81.

68. See Várdy, "Kossuth amerikai 'diadalútja'."

69. István Deák, "Kossuth: The Vain Hopes of a Much Celebrated Exile," *The Hungarian Quarterly* 43, no. 166 (Summer 2002), available online at:<www. hungary/hungq/no166/10.html>, p.3. For some additional recent assessments of Kossuth on the occasion of the 200th anniversary of his birth and the 150th anniversary of his visit to the United States, see: Tibor Frank, "To Fix the Attention of the Whole World Upon Hungary," in *ibid.*; Domokos Kosáry, "Az eszközök egyike valék. Mit ért el Kossuth?" [I Was Only One of the Instruments. What did Kossuth Achieve?], in *História* 24, nos. 9-10 (September-October, 2002): 51-53; and László Csorba, "Egy politikus 'remete' Turinból" [A Political 'Hermit' from Turin], in *ibid.*, 54-64.

70. C.A. Macartney, *The Habsburg Empire, 1790-1918* (New York: The Macmillan Co., 1969), 535; Hajo Holborn, *A History of Modern Germany* 2 (NewYork: Alfred A. Knopf, 1963-1971), 168.

71. Várdy, *Historical Dictionary of Hungary*, 86; Béla Tóth, *Szájról szájra. A magyarság szálló igéi* [From Mouth to Mouth. Hungarian Proverbs] (Budapest: Athenaeum, 1901), 175-76.

Index of Proper Terms

Catalonia, Army of, 164
Catherine II (Russian empress), 239, 258
Cawley, John, 45
Celaya, 149-51, 155
Cercle social, 13, 194-95
Cervato de la Cueza, 163
Chacabuco, battle of (1817), 11, 169-70
Chadds Ford, 178
Chandos, Duke of, 33, 36, 45
Charles III (Spanish king), 138, 140, 144
Charles/Carlos IV (Spanish king), 121, 138, 144
Charles X (French king), 286
Charles XII (Swedish king), 64
Charlottesville, 72
Chartists, 280
Chartres, 12, 187
Cherbourg, 291
Chernaya River, 249
Chesapeake Bay, 5, 97
Chesterfield, Lord, 36
Chiapas, 158
Chile, 10, 162, 167, 168, 170-72, 175, 182
Chileans, 11, 170, 172, 174
China, 241
Chinese (the), 275
Chłopicki, Józef, 261, 262
Christianity/Christians, 58, 66, 117, 233
Christophe, Henry, 131
Church of England (Anglican/Episcopalian), 30, 76, 79, 88, 181, 233, 269, 276
Church Slavic, 246
Cibber, Colley, 33
Cintra Convention, 217
Clare, Martin, 36
Clarendon, Lord, 279
Clavière, Étienne, 189, 192, 194, 198, 199
Clavigero, Francisco Javier, 140
Clontarf, 272
Coahuila, 157
Cobbett, William, 178
Cochrane, Thomas, 172-74
Coercive/Intolerable Acts (1774), 93, 94
Colbentz, 196
Colima, 141

Colombia, 77, 174, 182
Columbus, 306
Committee of Twelve, 206
Compromise of 1850, 310, 311
Concord, battle of (1775), 94
Condarco, José Antonio Álvarez, 168
Confederacy (CSA), 281
Congregationalists, 233
Connolly, John, 282
Constantine (Russian grand duke), 260, 261
Constantinople, 203
Constitution, USS, 232
Constitutional Bases (1815), 260
Continental Association, 94
Continental System, 144
Coolidge, Joseph, 232
Corbin, Margaret, 113
Córdoba, 167, 169
Cornwallis, Charles, 5, 97
Corrientes, 163
Cossacks, 230
Covenanters, 268
Cracow, 16, 260, 263, 264:
    Committee (1848), 17, 264
Creelman, James, 309
Crimean War (1853-56), 264
Croatia (-Slavonia), 303
Croats, 21, 303
Crockett, Davy, 180
Cruz, Tomás Godoy, 168
Cuba, 181
Cumberland, 112
Currency Act (1764), 92
Custis, Daniel Parke, 91
Custis, George Washington Parke, 113
Custis, John (Jack), 91
Custis, Martha (Patsy), 91
Cuyo, 11, 167-69
Czartoryska, Izabela, 15, 256
Czartoryski, Adam Jerzy, 15-17, 256-65
Czartoryski, Adam Kazimierz, 15, 256, 260
Dahomey, 116
Dalkeith, Earl of, 36
Dancing School/Assembly (the), 62, 63
Danton, Georges Jacques, 201, 206
Darby, Abraham, 42-43